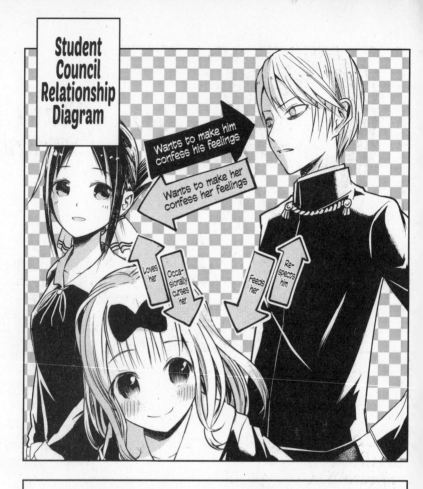

Student Council Relationship Diagram

Wants to make him confess his feelings
Wants to make her confess her feelings
Re-spects him
Feeds her
Occa-sionally curses her
Loves her

The battle campaigns thus far...

The two main characters hail from eminent families and are of good character. Shuchiin Academy is home to the most promising and brilliant students. It is there that, as members of the student council, Vice President Kaguya Shinomiya and President Miyuki Shirogane meet. An attraction is immediately apparent between them... But six months have passed and still nothing! The two are too proud to be honest with themselves—let alone each other. Instead, they are caught in an unending campaign to induce the other to confess their feelings first. In love, it's all about the journey! This is a comedy about young love and a game of wits... Let the battles begin!

KAGUYA-SAMA LOVE IS WAR

BATTLE CAMPAIGNS

3

◆ Battle 21 ◆
Kaguya Wants to Be Covered ·················· 5

◆ Battle 22 ◆
Chika Fujiwara Wants to Be Eaten ·················· 27

◆ Battle 23 ◆
Miyuki Shirogane Wants to Show Off ·················· 47

◆ Battle 24 ◆
Yu Ishigami Wants to Live ·················· 67

◆ Battle 25 ◆
Kaguya Wants to Be Noticed ·················· 87

◆ Battle 26 ◆
Miyuki Shirogane Wants to Work ·················· 107

◆ Battle 27 ◆
Kaguya Wants to Control It ·················· 126

◆ Battle 28 ◆
Kaguya Wants Him to Join In ·················· 147

◆ Battle 29 ◆
Ai Hayasaka Wants to Stave Them Off ·················· 167

◆ Battle 30 ◆
Miyuki Shirogane Can't Lose ·················· 187

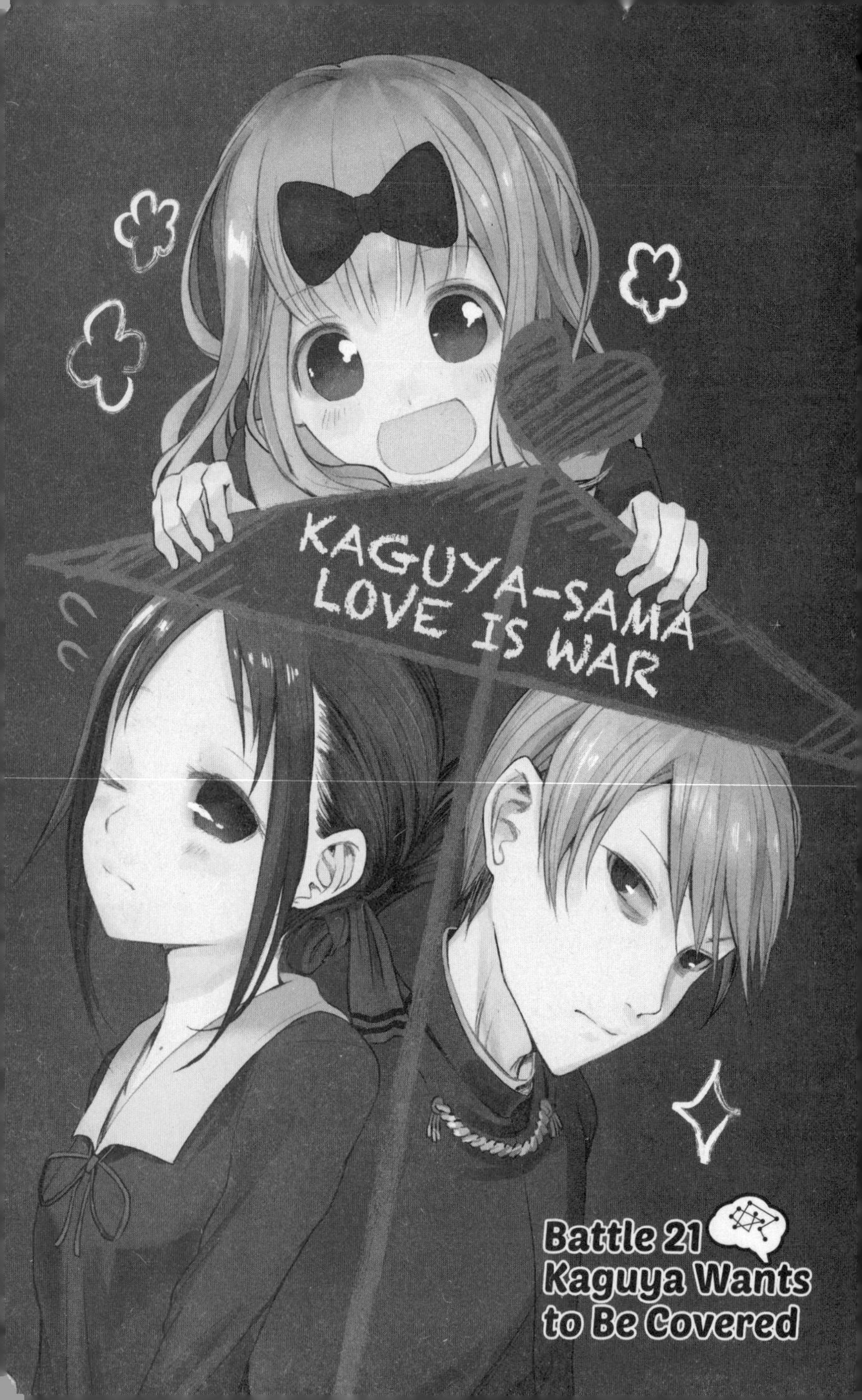
KAGUYA-SAMA
LOVE IS WAR
Battle 21
Kaguya Wants
to Be Covered

KAGUYA-SAMA

LOVE IS WAR

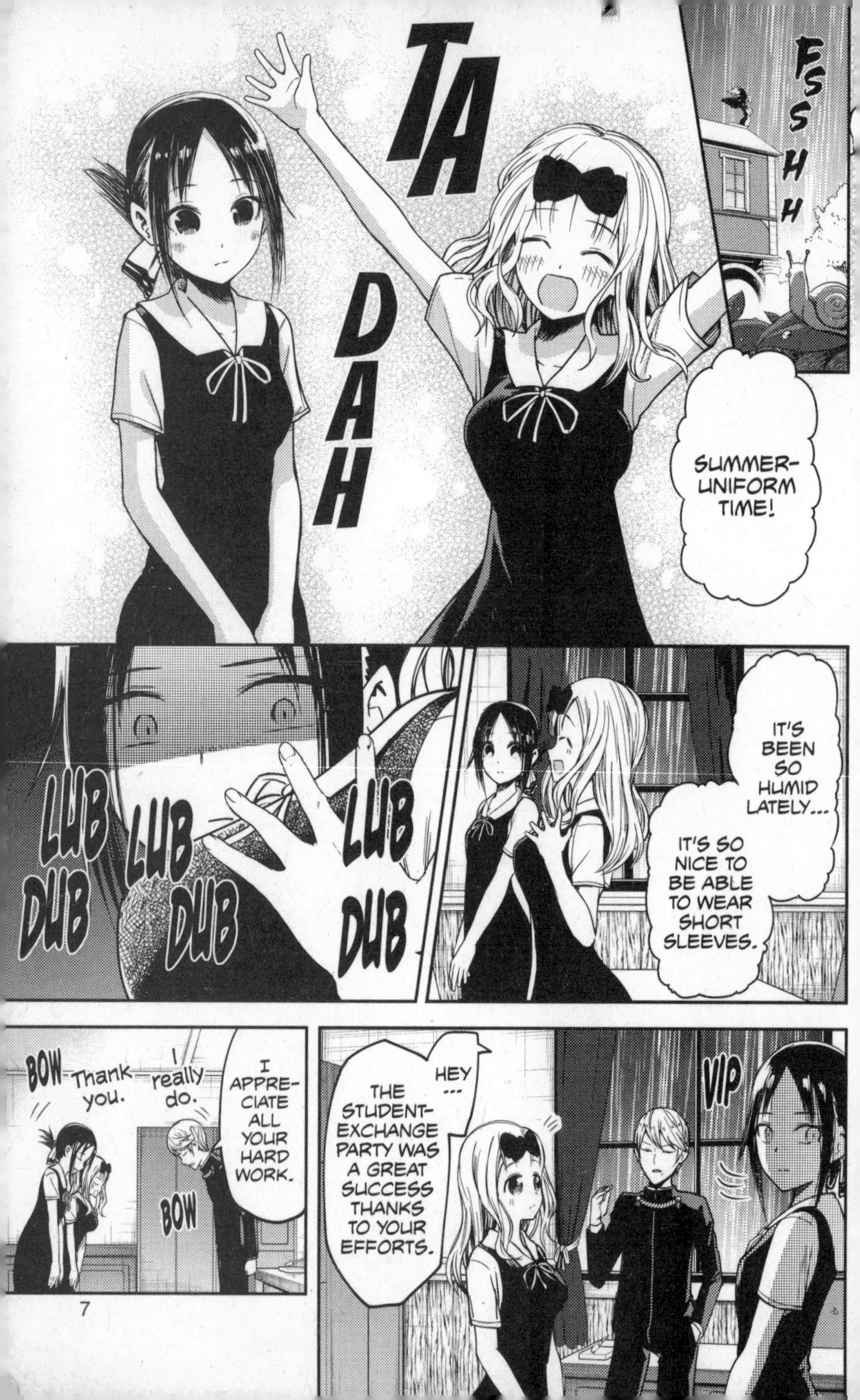
FSSHH
TA DAH
SUMMER-UNIFORM TIME!
IT'S BEEN SO HUMID LATELY...
IT'S SO NICE TO BE ABLE TO WEAR SHORT SLEEVES.
LUB DUB
LUB DUB
LUB DUB
VIP
HEY...
THE STUDENT-EXCHANGE PARTY WAS A GREAT SUCCESS THANKS TO YOUR EFFORTS.
I APPRECIATE ALL YOUR HARD WORK.
I really do.
BOW
Thank you.
BOW

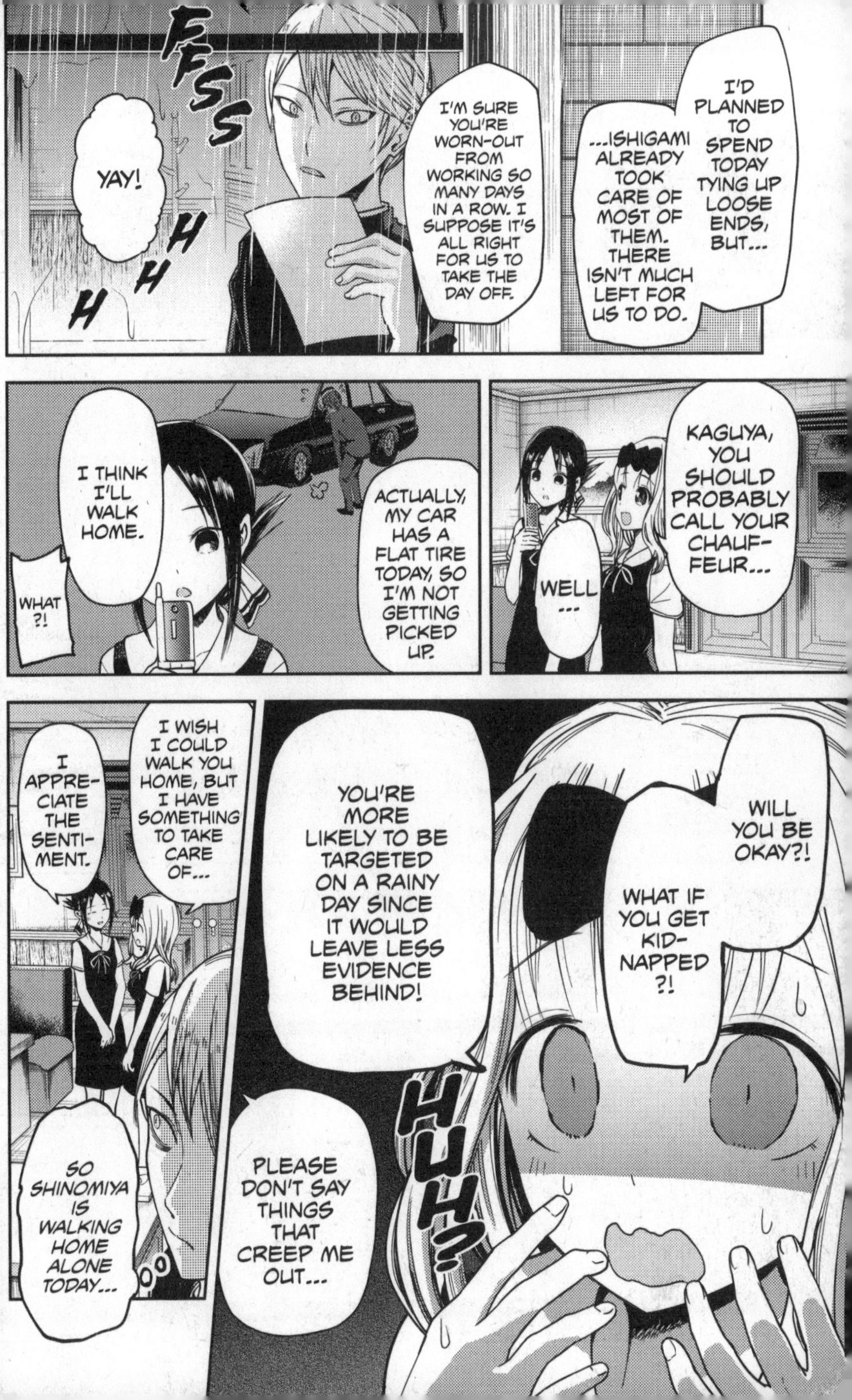
I'D PLANNED TO SPEND TODAY TYING UP LOOSE ENDS, BUT...
...ISHIGAMI ALREADY TOOK CARE OF MOST OF THEM. THERE ISN'T MUCH LEFT FOR US TO DO.
I'M SURE YOU'RE WORN-OUT FROM WORKING SO MANY DAYS IN A ROW. I SUPPOSE IT'S ALL RIGHT FOR US TO TAKE THE DAY OFF.
FFSSHHH
YAY!
KAGUYA, YOU SHOULD PROBABLY CALL YOUR CHAUFFEUR...
WELL...
ACTUALLY, MY CAR HAS A FLAT TIRE TODAY, SO I'M NOT GETTING PICKED UP.
I THINK I'LL WALK HOME.
WHAT?!
WILL YOU BE OKAY?!
WHAT IF YOU GET KIDNAPPED?!
YOU'RE MORE LIKELY TO BE TARGETED ON A RAINY DAY SINCE IT WOULD LEAVE LESS EVIDENCE BEHIND!
HUH?!
PLEASE DON'T SAY THINGS THAT CREEP ME OUT...
I WISH I COULD WALK YOU HOME, BUT I HAVE SOMETHING TO TAKE CARE OF...
I APPRECIATE THE SENTIMENT.
SO SHINOMIYA IS WALKING HOME ALONE TODAY...

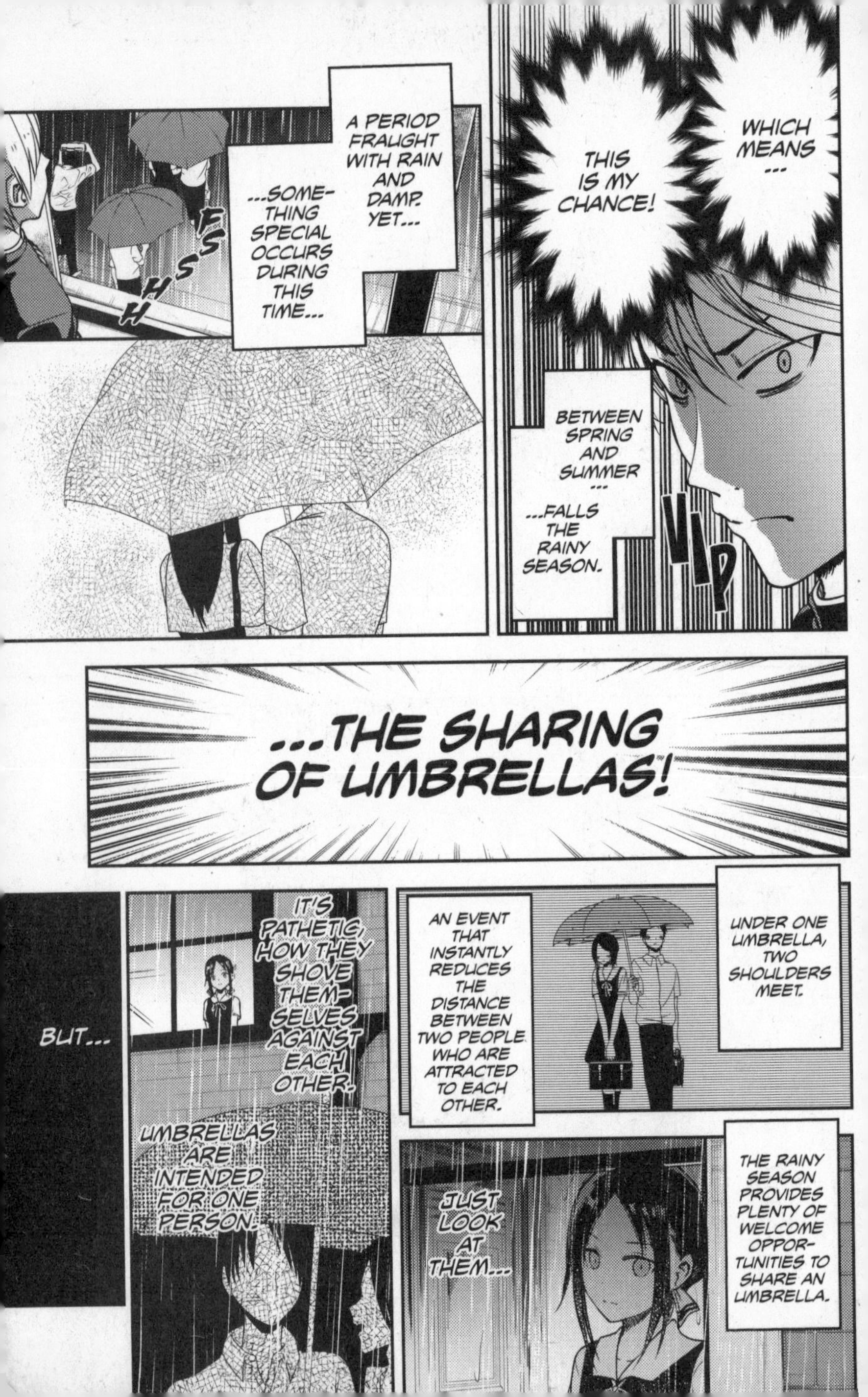
BETWEEN SPRING AND SUMMER ...
...FALLS THE RAINY SEASON.
A PERIOD FRAUGHT WITH RAIN AND DAMP. YET...
...SOMETHING SPECIAL OCCURS DURING THIS TIME...
FSSHH
WHICH MEANS ...
THIS IS MY CHANCE!
VIP
...THE SHARING OF UMBRELLAS!
UNDER ONE UMBRELLA, TWO SHOULDERS MEET.
AN EVENT THAT INSTANTLY REDUCES THE DISTANCE BETWEEN TWO PEOPLE WHO ARE ATTRACTED TO EACH OTHER.
THE RAINY SEASON PROVIDES PLENTY OF WELCOME OPPORTUNITIES TO SHARE AN UMBRELLA.
JUST LOOK AT THEM...
IT'S PATHETIC, HOW THEY SHOVE THEMSELVES AGAINST EACH OTHER.
UMBRELLAS ARE INTENDED FOR ONE PERSON.
BUT...

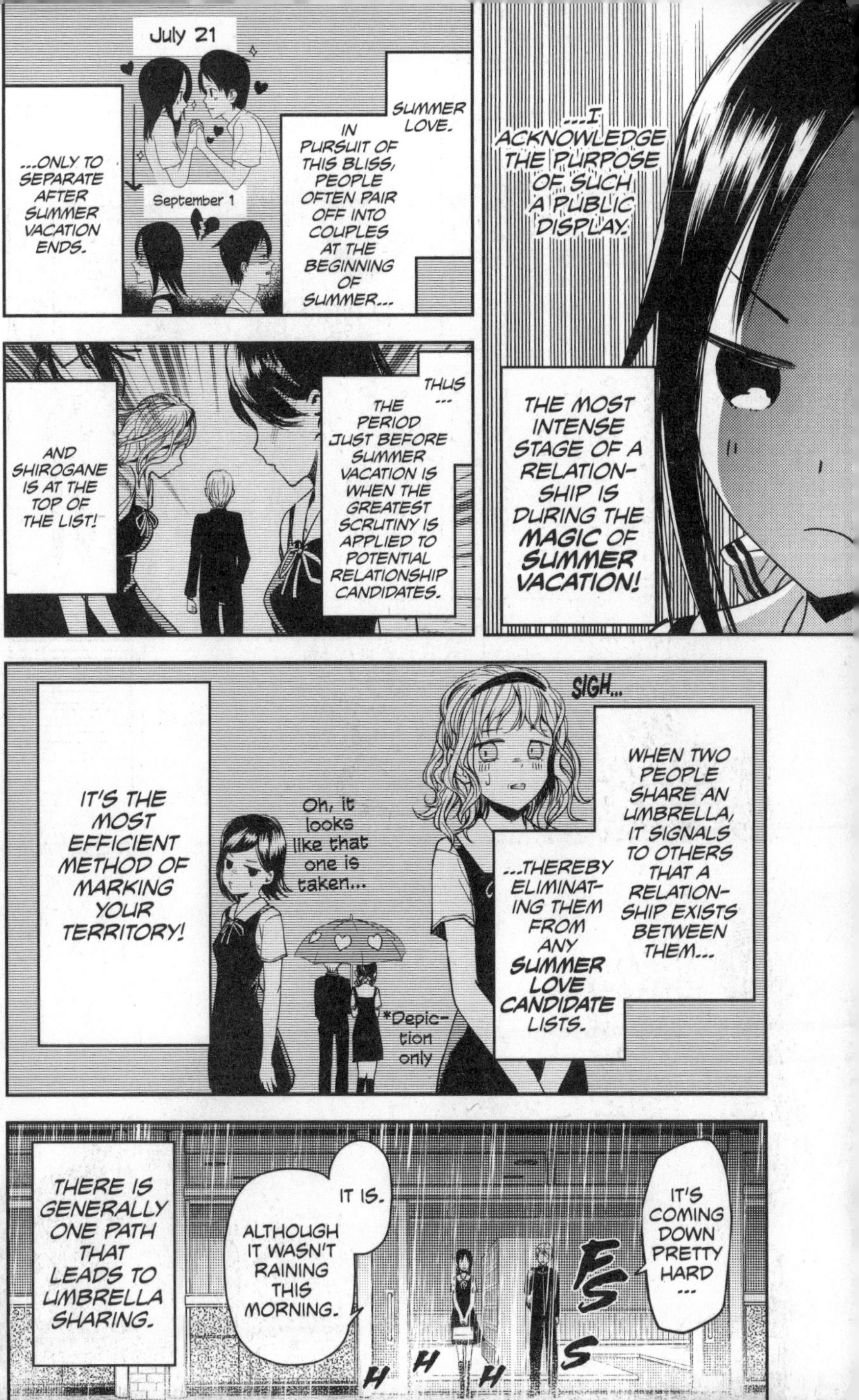
...I ACKNOWLEDGE THE PURPOSE OF SUCH A PUBLIC DISPLAY.
THE MOST INTENSE STAGE OF A RELATIONSHIP IS DURING THE MAGIC OF SUMMER VACATION!
SUMMER LOVE.
IN PURSUIT OF THIS BLISS, PEOPLE OFTEN PAIR OFF INTO COUPLES AT THE BEGINNING OF SUMMER...
July 21
September 1
...ONLY TO SEPARATE AFTER SUMMER VACATION ENDS.
THUS...
THE PERIOD JUST BEFORE SUMMER VACATION IS WHEN THE GREATEST SCRUTINY IS APPLIED TO POTENTIAL RELATIONSHIP CANDIDATES.
AND SHIROGANE IS AT THE TOP OF THE LIST!
SIGH...
WHEN TWO PEOPLE SHARE AN UMBRELLA, IT SIGNALS TO OTHERS THAT A RELATIONSHIP EXISTS BETWEEN THEM...
...THEREBY ELIMINATING THEM FROM ANY SUMMER LOVE CANDIDATE LISTS.
Oh, it looks like that one is taken...
*Depiction only
IT'S THE MOST EFFICIENT METHOD OF MARKING YOUR TERRITORY!
IT'S COMING DOWN PRETTY HARD...
FSS
IT IS.
ALTHOUGH IT WASN'T RAINING THIS MORNING.
THERE IS GENERALLY ONE PATH THAT LEADS TO UMBRELLA SHARING.
HHH

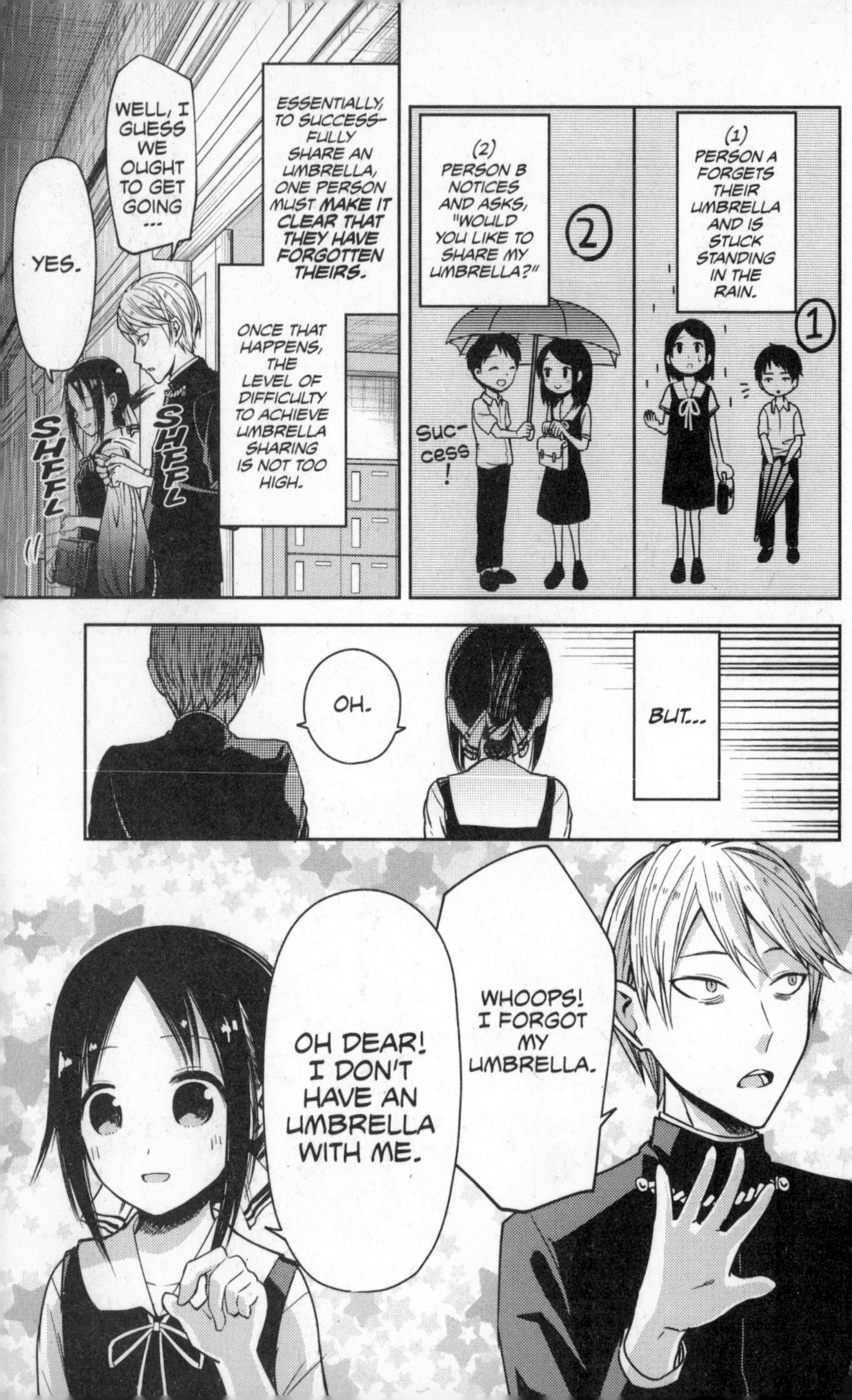
(1) PERSON A FORGETS THEIR UMBRELLA AND IS STUCK STANDING IN THE RAIN.
1
(2) PERSON B NOTICES AND ASKS, "WOULD YOU LIKE TO SHARE MY UMBRELLA?"
2
Suc-cess!
ESSENTIALLY, TO SUCCESSFULLY SHARE AN UMBRELLA, ONE PERSON MUST MAKE IT CLEAR THAT THEY HAVE FORGOTTEN THEIRS.
ONCE THAT HAPPENS, THE LEVEL OF DIFFICULTY TO ACHIEVE UMBRELLA SHARING IS NOT TOO HIGH.
WELL, I GUESS WE OUGHT TO GET GOING...
YES.
SHFFL
SHFFL
BUT...
OH.
WHOOPS! I FORGOT MY UMBRELLA.
OH DEAR! I DON'T HAVE AN UMBRELLA WITH ME.

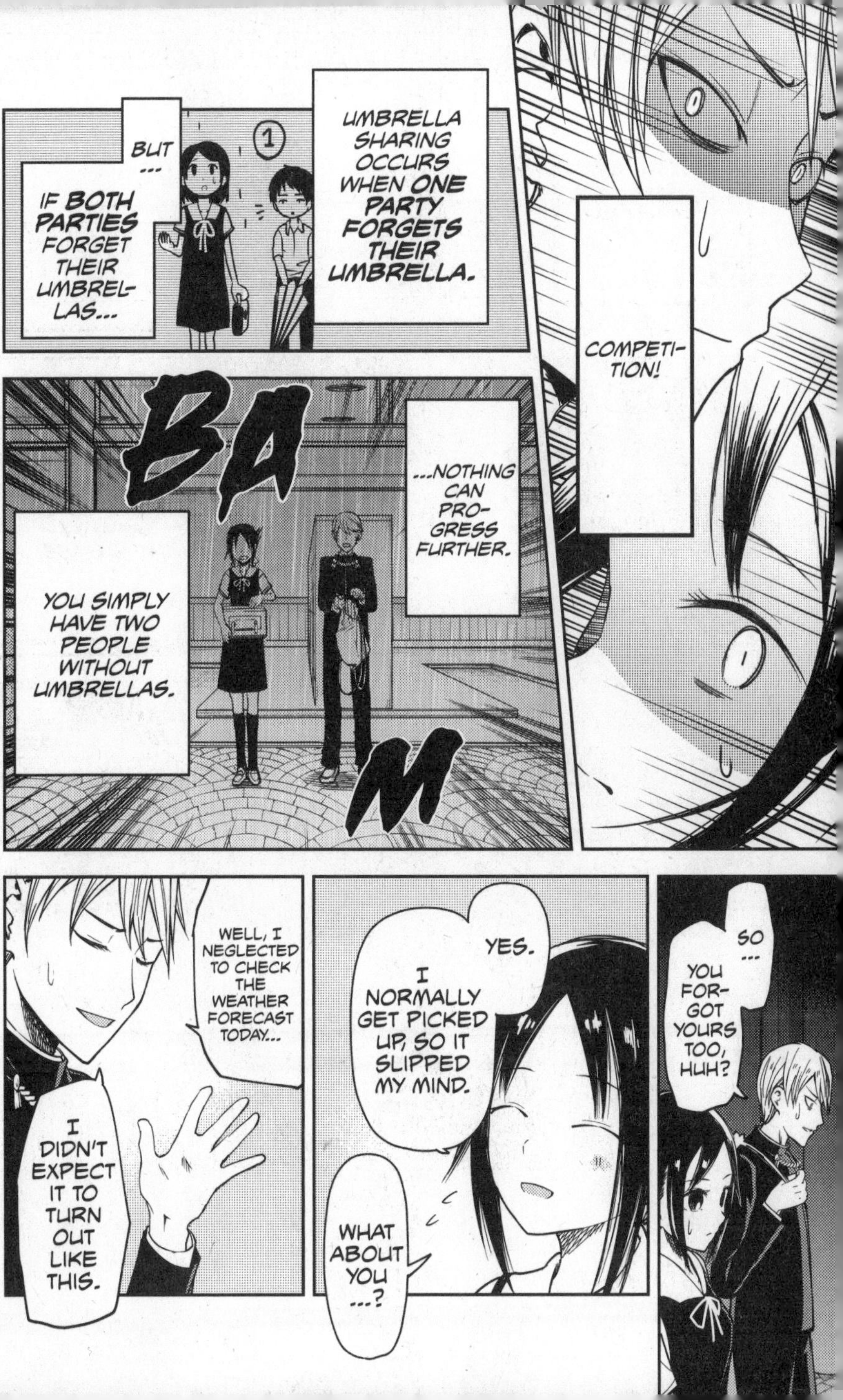
COMPETITION!
UMBRELLA SHARING OCCURS WHEN ONE PARTY FORGETS THEIR UMBRELLA.
BUT...
IF BOTH PARTIES FORGET THEIR UMBREL-LAS...
1
...NOTHING CAN PRO-GRESS FURTHER.
BAM
YOU SIMPLY HAVE TWO PEOPLE WITHOUT UMBRELLAS.
SO...
YOU FOR-GOT YOURS TOO, HUH?
YES.
I NORMALLY GET PICKED UP, SO IT SLIPPED MY MIND.
WHAT ABOUT YOU ...?
WELL, I NEGLECTED TO CHECK THE WEATHER FORECAST TODAY...
I DIDN'T EXPECT IT TO TURN OUT LIKE THIS.

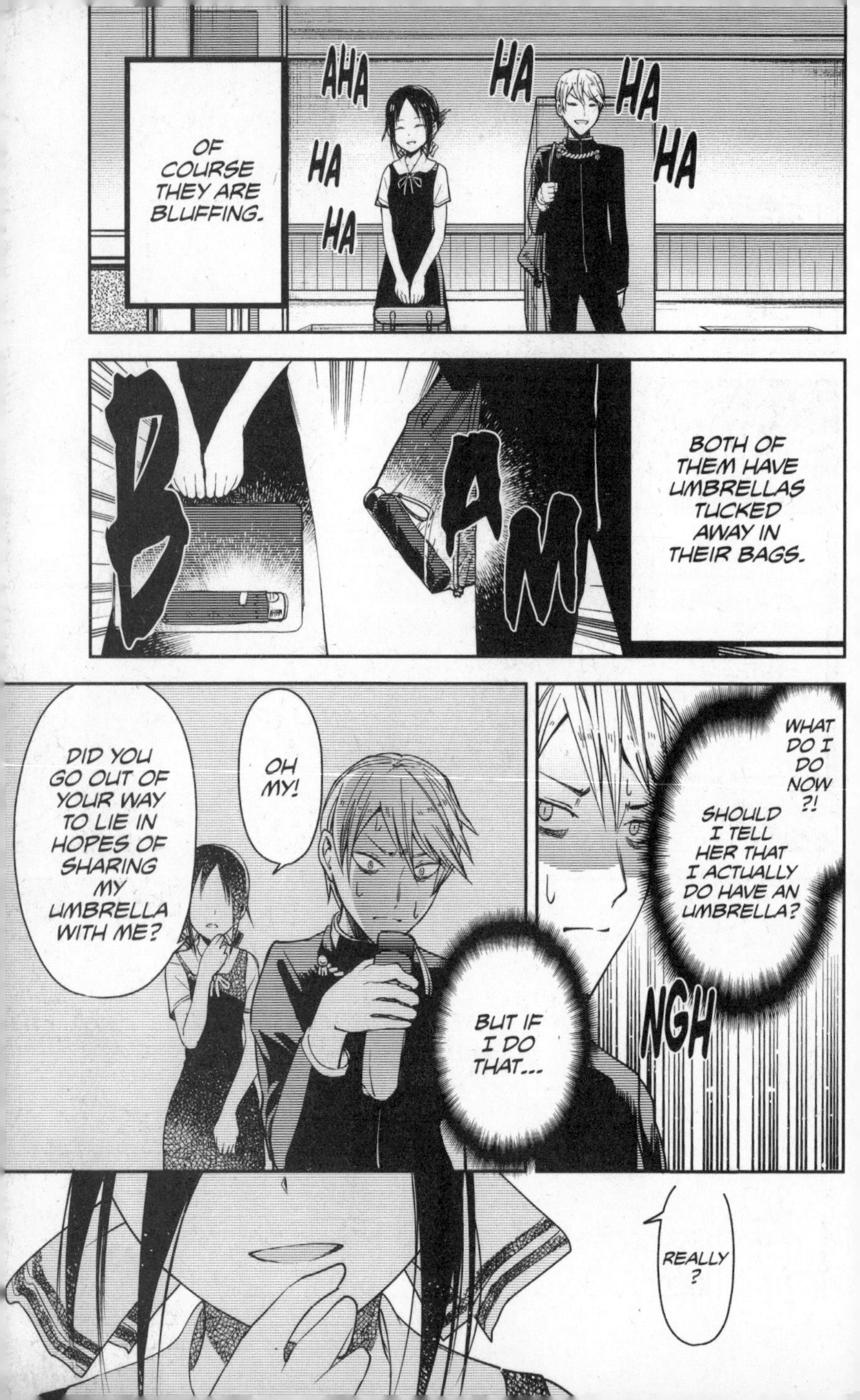
HA HA HA
AHA HA HA
OF COURSE THEY ARE BLUFFING.
BOTH OF THEM HAVE UMBRELLAS TUCKED AWAY IN THEIR BAGS.
BAM
WHAT DO I DO NOW?!
SHOULD I TELL HER THAT I ACTUALLY DO HAVE AN UMBRELLA?
NGH
BUT IF I DO THAT...
OH MY!
DID YOU GO OUT OF YOUR WAY TO LIE IN HOPES OF SHARING MY UMBRELLA WITH ME?
REALLY?

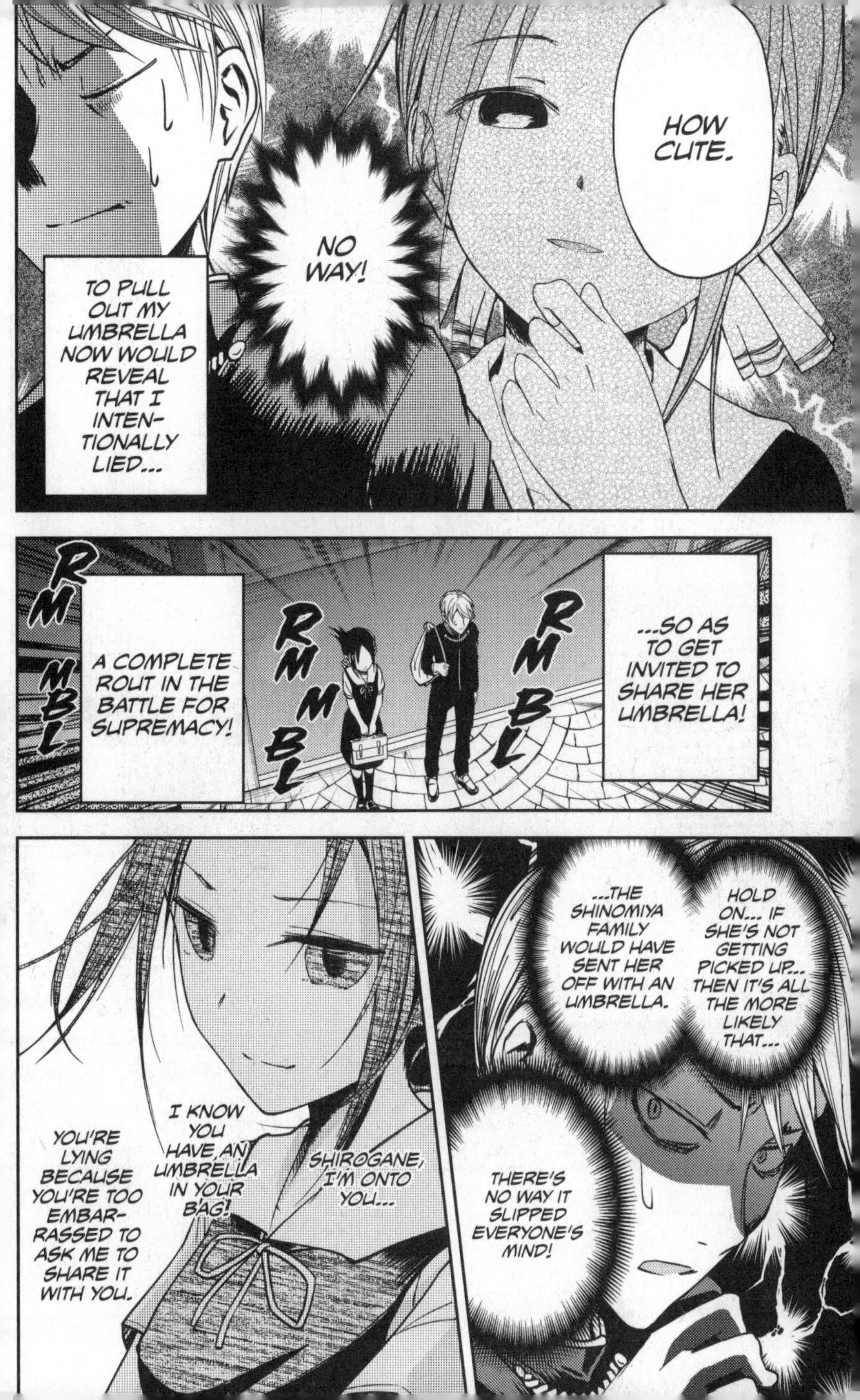
HOW CUTE.
NO WAY!
TO PULL OUT MY UMBRELLA NOW WOULD REVEAL THAT I INTENTIONALLY LIED...
...SO AS TO GET INVITED TO SHARE HER UMBRELLA!
RMBL
RMMBL
A COMPLETE ROUT IN THE BATTLE FOR SUPREMACY!
RMMBL
HOLD ON... IF SHE'S NOT GETTING PICKED UP... THEN IT'S ALL THE MORE LIKELY THAT...
...THE SHINOMIYA FAMILY WOULD HAVE SENT HER OFF WITH AN UMBRELLA.
THERE'S NO WAY IT SLIPPED EVERYONE'S MIND!
SHIROGANE, I'M ONTO YOU...
I KNOW YOU HAVE AN UMBRELLA IN YOUR BAG!
YOU'RE LYING BECAUSE YOU'RE TOO EMBARRASSED TO ASK ME TO SHARE IT WITH YOU.

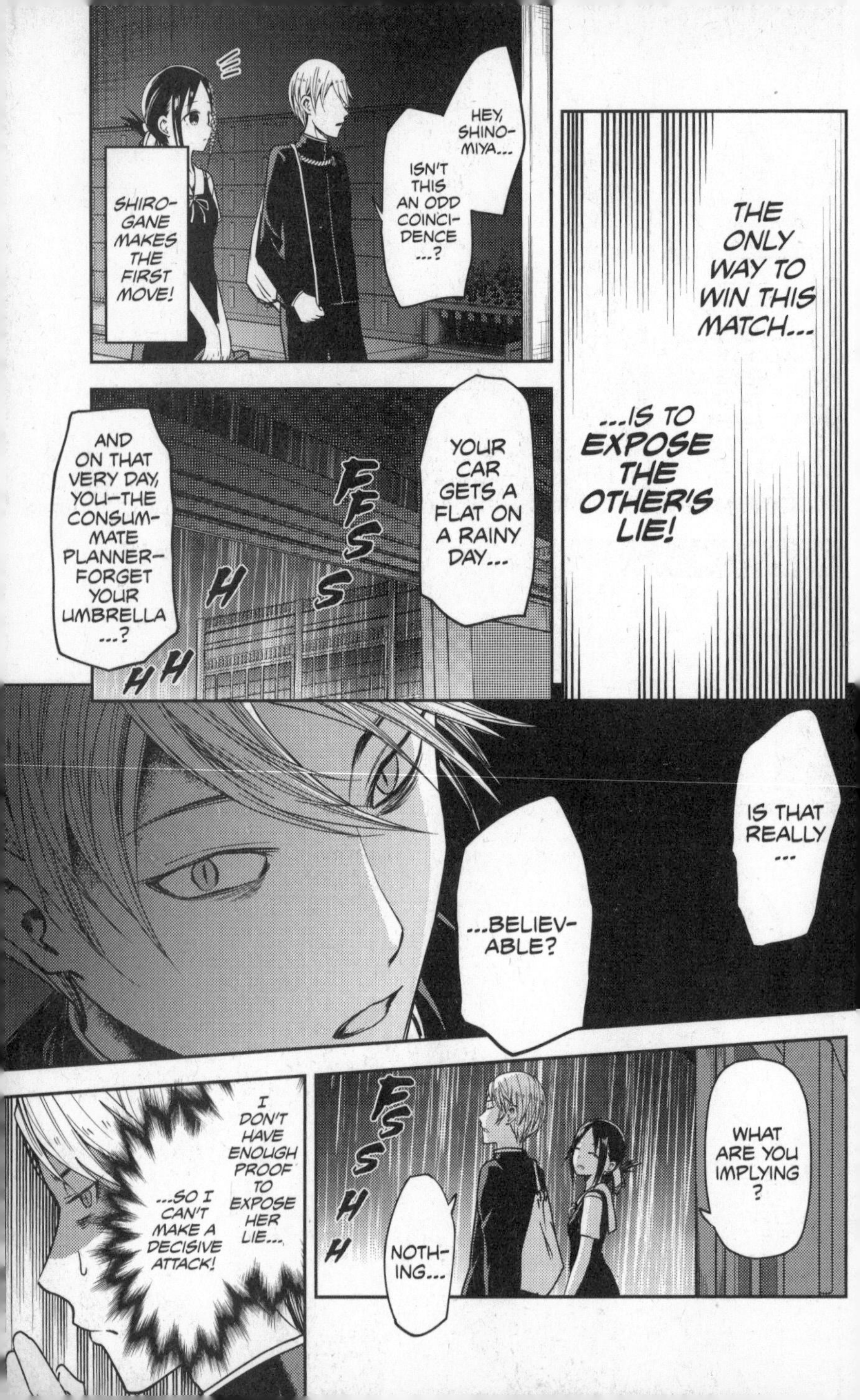
THE ONLY WAY TO WIN THIS MATCH...
...IS TO EXPOSE THE OTHER'S LIE!
HEY, SHINOMIYA...
ISN'T THIS AN ODD COINCIDENCE...?
SHIROGANE MAKES THE FIRST MOVE!
YOUR CAR GETS A FLAT ON A RAINY DAY...
FSSHHH
AND ON THAT VERY DAY, YOU—THE CONSUMMATE PLANNER—FORGET YOUR UMBRELLA...?
IS THAT REALLY...
...BELIEVABLE?
WHAT ARE YOU IMPLYING?
FSSHH
NOTHING...
I DON'T HAVE ENOUGH PROOF TO EXPOSE HER LIE...
...SO I CAN'T MAKE A DECISIVE ATTACK!

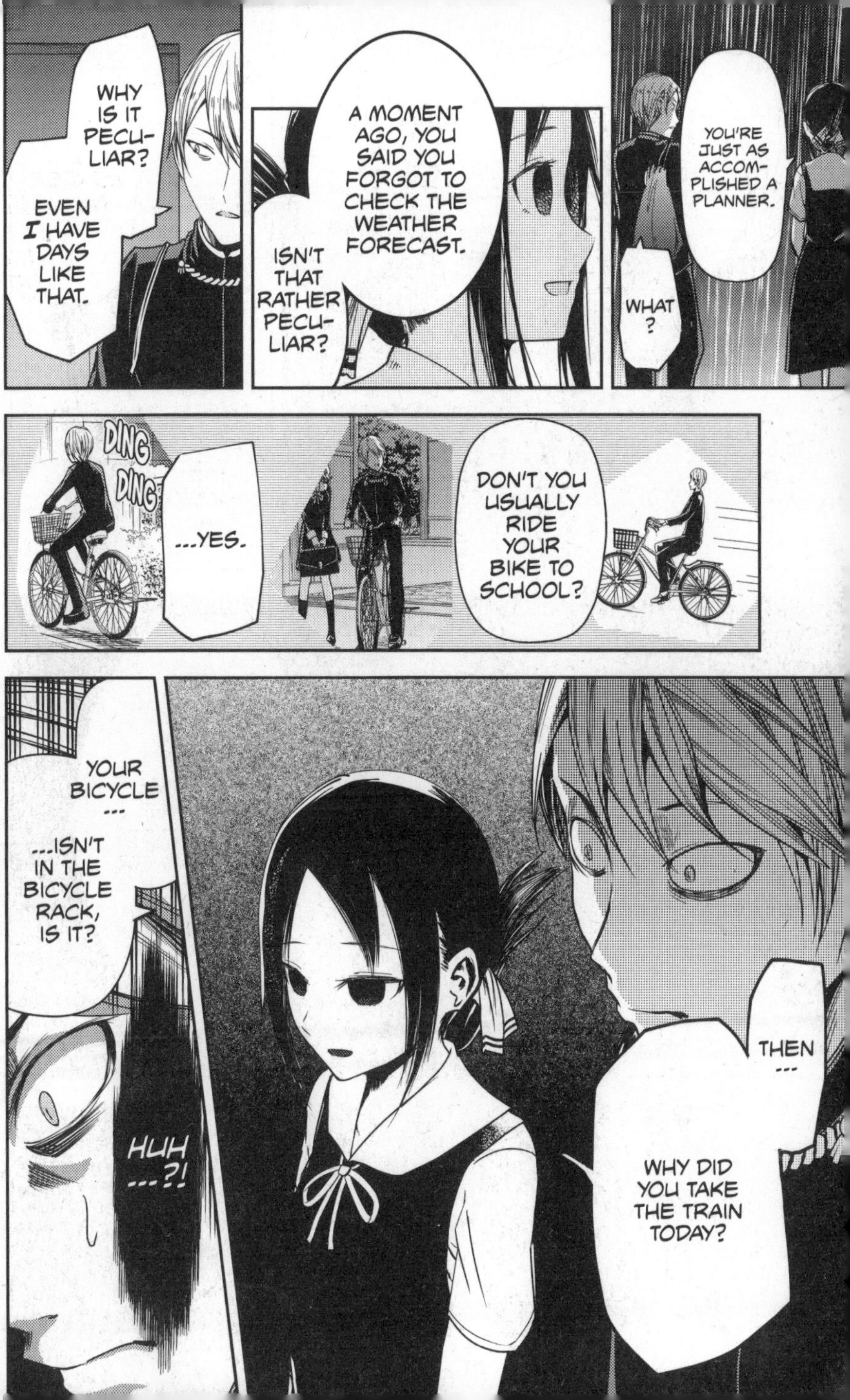
YOU'RE JUST AS ACCOM-PLISHED A PLANNER.
WHAT?
A MOMENT AGO, YOU SAID YOU FORGOT TO CHECK THE WEATHER FORECAST.
ISN'T THAT RATHER PECU-LIAR?
WHY IS IT PECU-LIAR?
EVEN I HAVE DAYS LIKE THAT.
DON'T YOU USUALLY RIDE YOUR BIKE TO SCHOOL?
...YES.
DING DING
YOUR BICYCLE...
...ISN'T IN THE BICYCLE RACK, IS IT?
HUH...?!
THEN...
WHY DID YOU TAKE THE TRAIN TODAY?

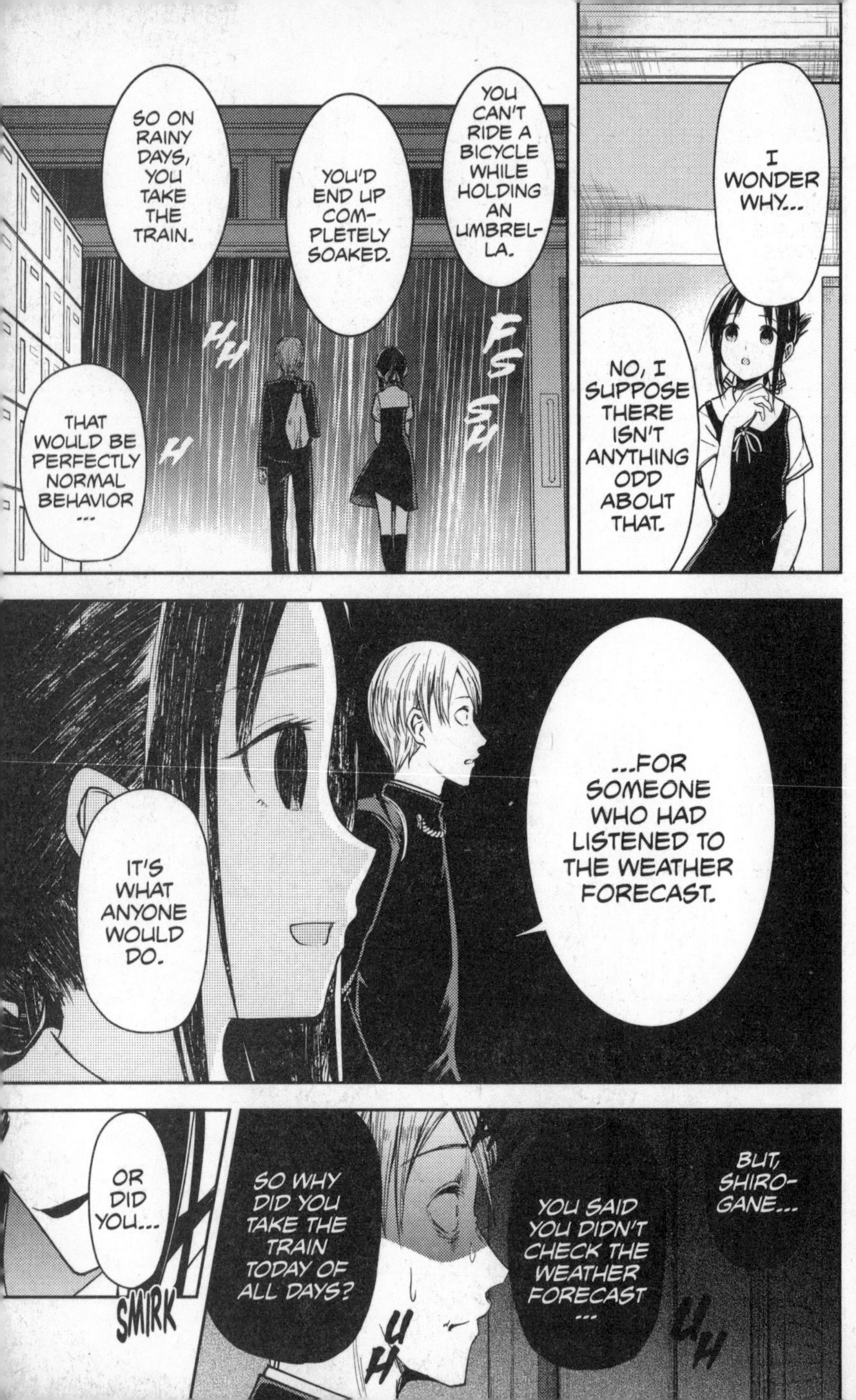
I WONDER WHY...
NO, I SUPPOSE THERE ISN'T ANYTHING ODD ABOUT THAT.
YOU CAN'T RIDE A BICYCLE WHILE HOLDING AN UMBREL-LA.
YOU'D END UP COM-PLETELY SOAKED.
SO ON RAINY DAYS, YOU TAKE THE TRAIN.
FSSH
HH
H
THAT WOULD BE PERFECTLY NORMAL BEHAVIOR ...
...FOR SOMEONE WHO HAD LISTENED TO THE WEATHER FORECAST.
IT'S WHAT ANYONE WOULD DO.
BUT, SHIRO-GANE...
YOU SAID YOU DIDN'T CHECK THE WEATHER FORECAST ...
UH
SO WHY DID YOU TAKE THE TRAIN TODAY OF ALL DAYS?
UH
OR DID YOU...
SMIRK

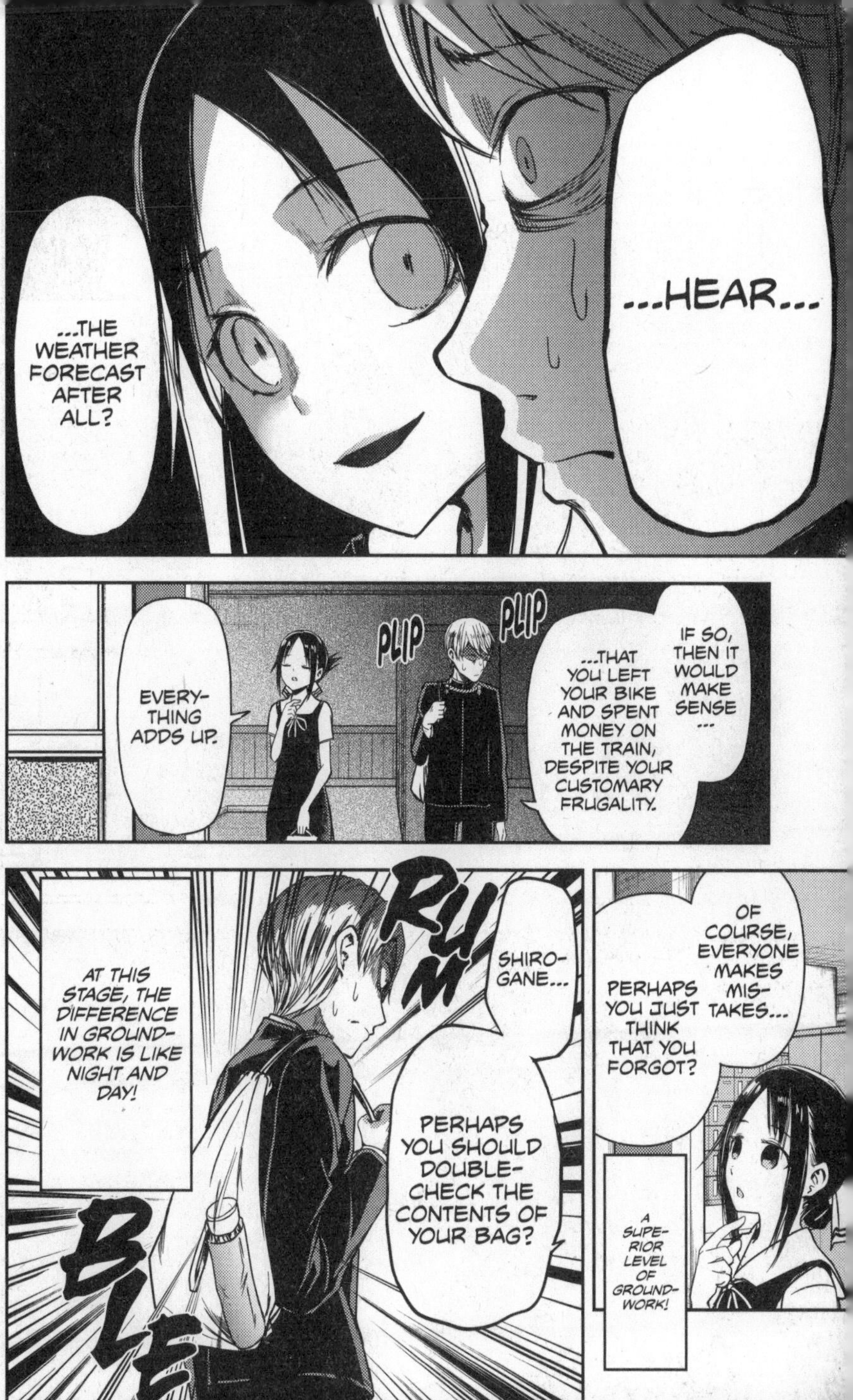
...HEAR...
...THE WEATHER FORECAST AFTER ALL?
IF SO, THEN IT WOULD MAKE SENSE ...
...THAT YOU LEFT YOUR BIKE AND SPENT MONEY ON THE TRAIN, DESPITE YOUR CUSTOMARY FRUGALITY.
PLIP
PLIP
EVERY-THING ADDS UP.
OF COURSE, EVERYONE MAKES MIS-TAKES...
PERHAPS YOU JUST THINK THAT YOU FORGOT?
A SUPE-RIOR LEVEL OF GROUND-WORK!
RUM
SHIRO-GANE...
PERHAPS YOU SHOULD DOUBLE-CHECK THE CONTENTS OF YOUR BAG?
AT THIS STAGE, THE DIFFERENCE IN GROUND-WORK IS LIKE NIGHT AND DAY!
BLE

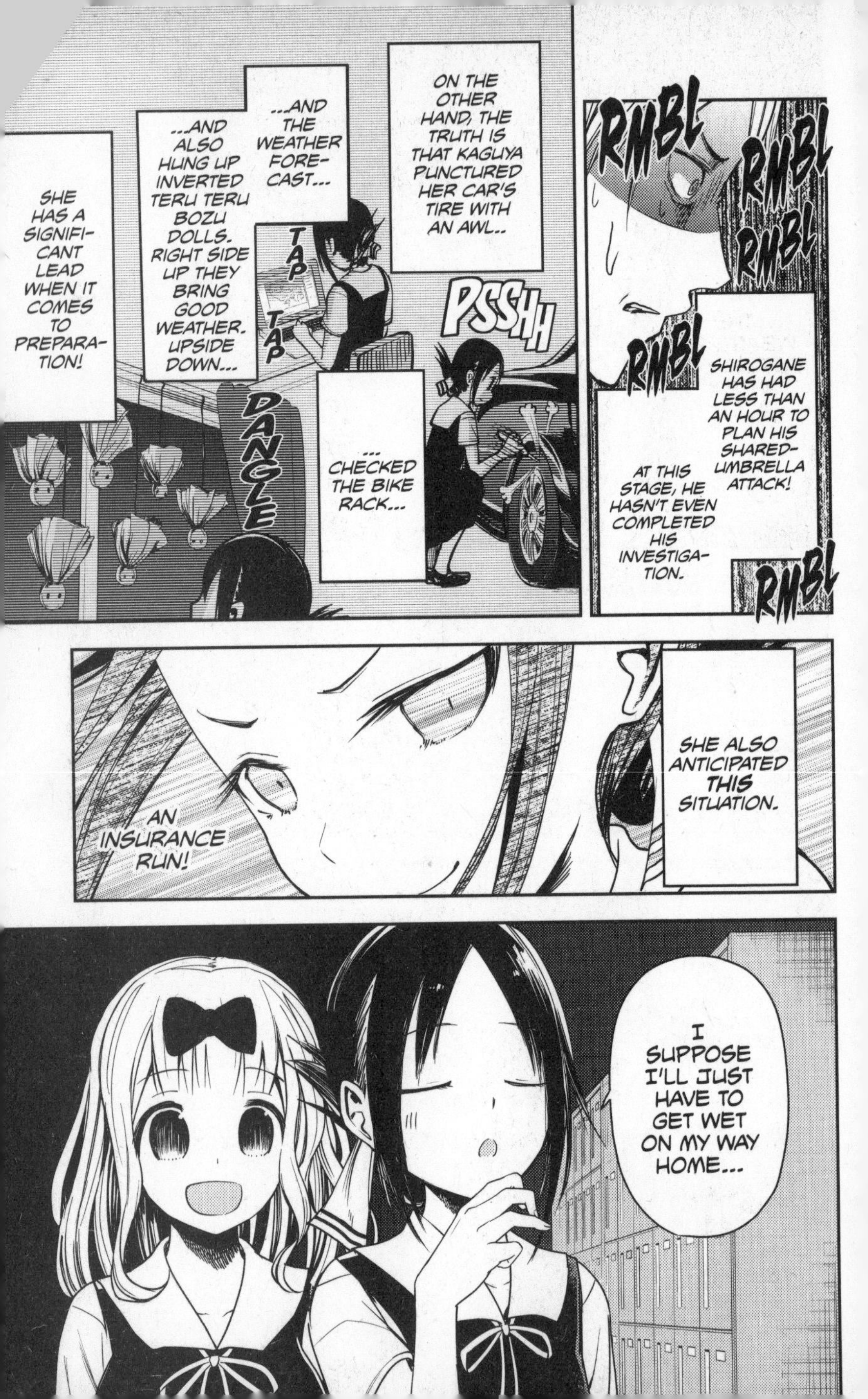
RMBL
RMBL
RMBL RMBL
RMBL
SHIROGANE HAS HAD LESS THAN AN HOUR TO PLAN HIS SHARED-UMBRELLA ATTACK!
AT THIS STAGE, HE HASN'T EVEN COMPLETED HIS INVESTIGATION.
RMBL
ON THE OTHER HAND, THE TRUTH IS THAT KAGUYA PUNCTURED HER CAR'S TIRE WITH AN AWL..
PSSHH
...CHECKED THE BIKE RACK...
...AND THE WEATHER FORECAST...
TAP
TAP
TAP
...AND ALSO HUNG UP INVERTED TERU TERU BOZU DOLLS. RIGHT SIDE UP THEY BRING GOOD WEATHER. UPSIDE DOWN...
DANGLE
SHE HAS A SIGNIFICANT LEAD WHEN IT COMES TO PREPARATION!
SHE ALSO ANTICIPATED THIS SITUATION.
AN INSURANCE RUN!
I SUPPOSE I'LL JUST HAVE TO GET WET ON MY WAY HOME...

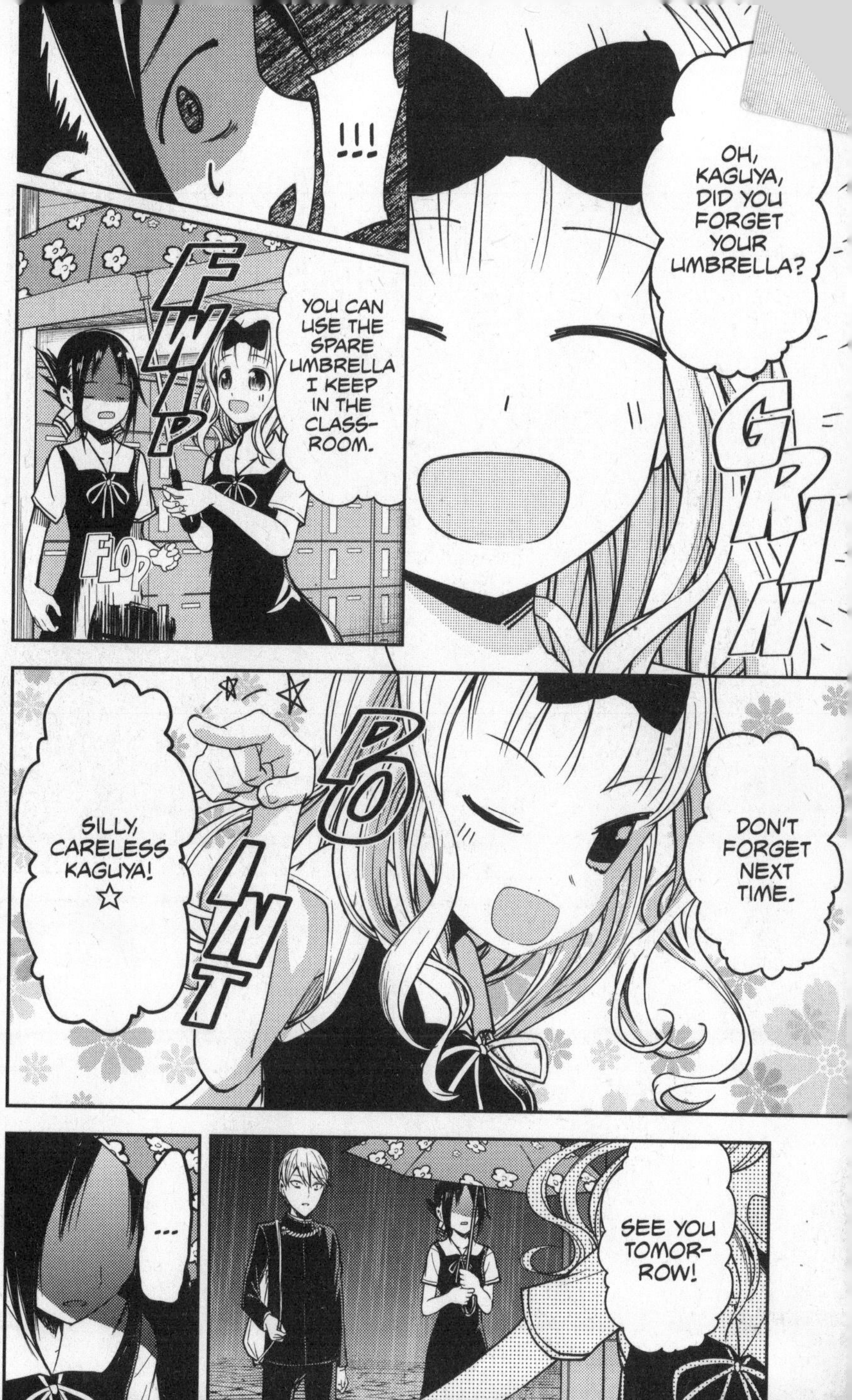
OH, KAGUYA, DID YOU FORGET YOUR UMBRELLA?
GRIN
!!!
YOU CAN USE THE SPARE UMBRELLA I KEEP IN THE CLASSROOM.
FWIP
FLOP
DON'T FORGET NEXT TIME.
POINT
SILLY, CARELESS KAGUYA! ☆
SEE YOU TOMORROW!
...

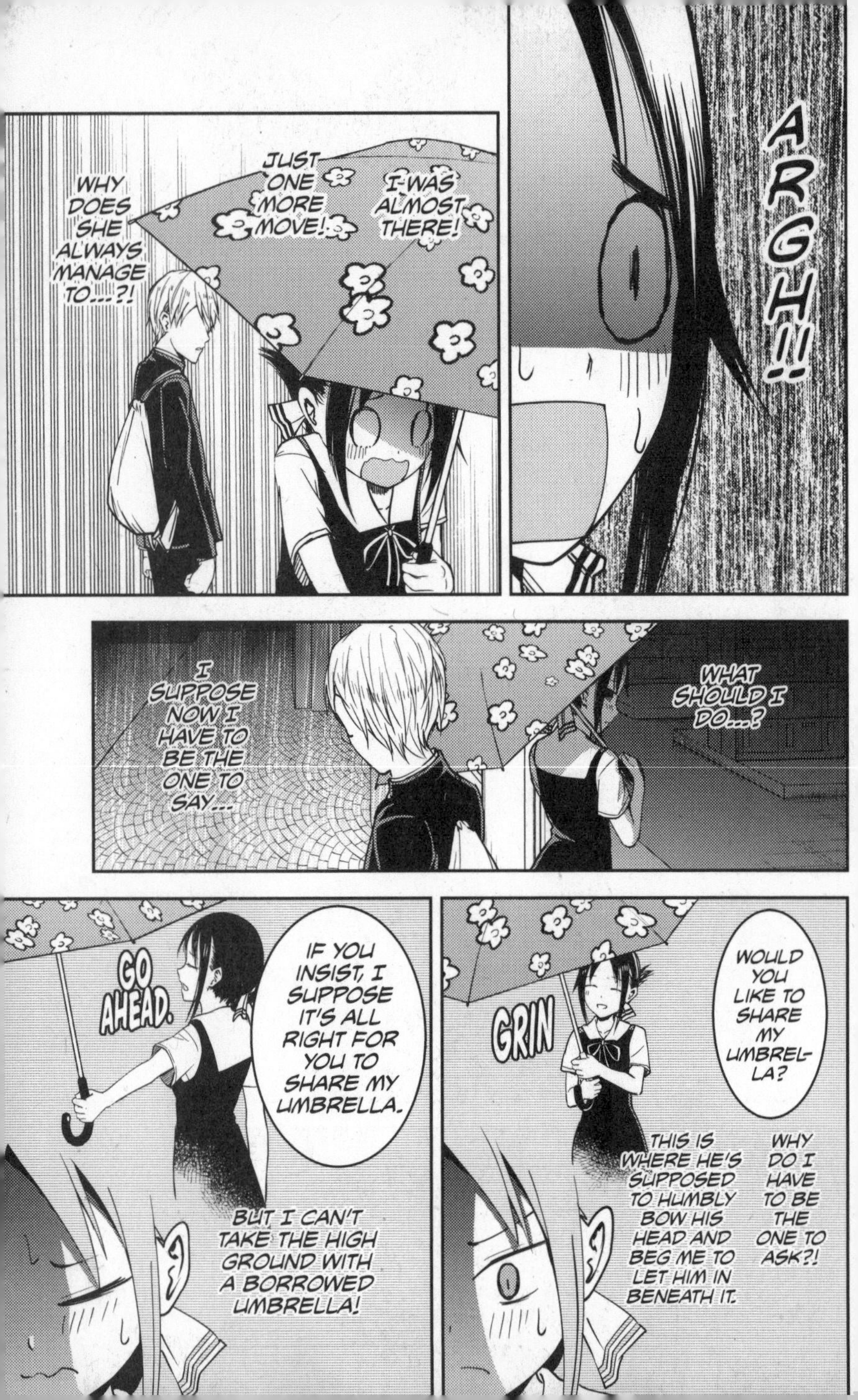
ARGH!!
I WAS ALMOST THERE!
JUST ONE MORE MOVE!
WHY DOES SHE ALWAYS MANAGE TO...?!
WHAT SHOULD I DO...?
I SUPPOSE NOW I HAVE TO BE THE ONE TO SAY...
WOULD YOU LIKE TO SHARE MY UMBREL-LA?
GRIN
WHY DO I HAVE TO BE THE ONE TO ASK?!
THIS IS WHERE HE'S SUPPOSED TO HUMBLY BOW HIS HEAD AND BEG ME TO LET HIM IN BENEATH IT.
IF YOU INSIST, I SUPPOSE IT'S ALL RIGHT FOR YOU TO SHARE MY UMBRELLA.
GO AHEAD.
BUT I CAN'T TAKE THE HIGH GROUND WITH A BORROWED UMBRELLA!

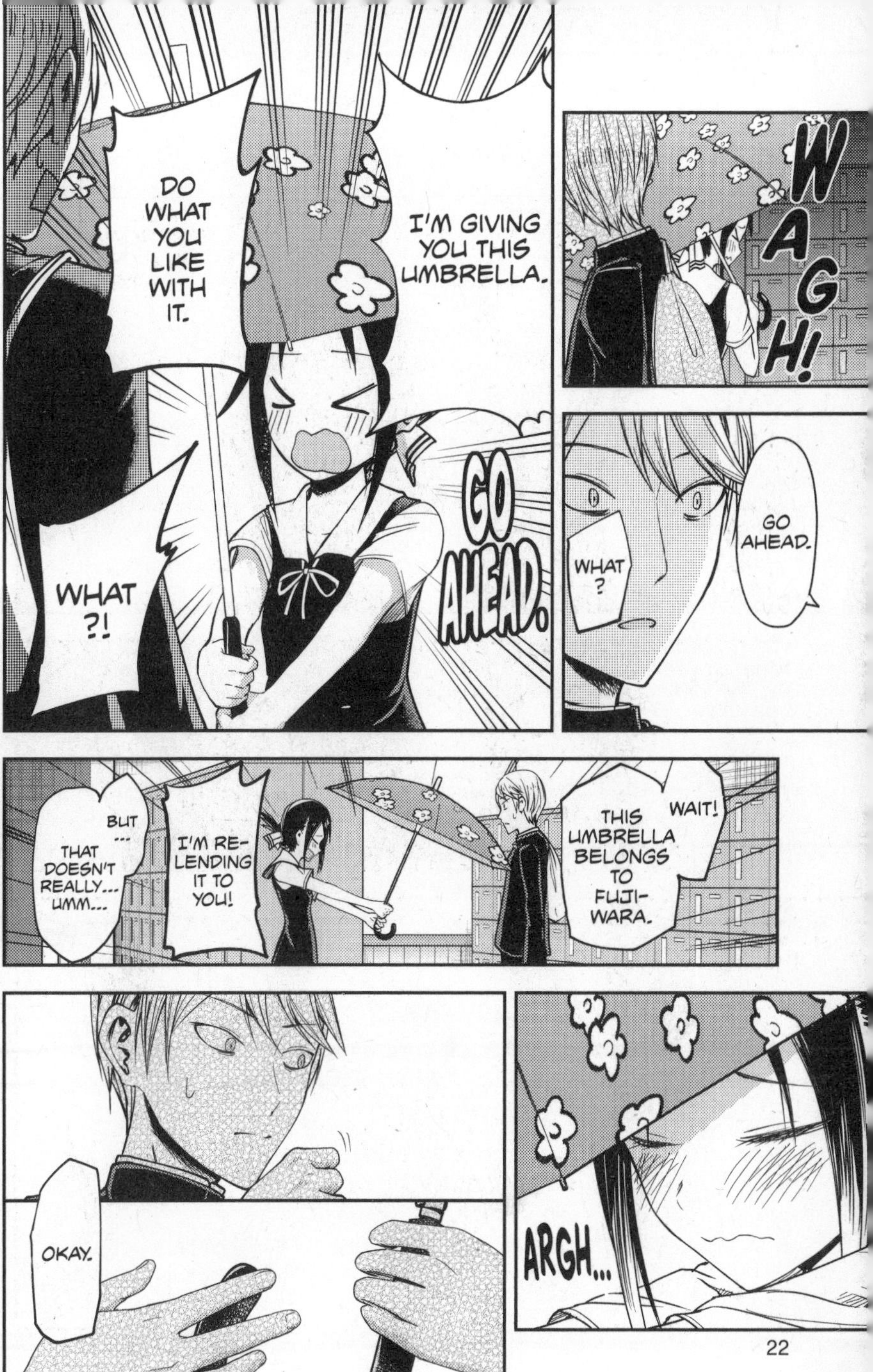
WAGH!
GO AHEAD.
WHAT?
I'M GIVING YOU THIS UMBRELLA.
DO WHAT YOU LIKE WITH IT.
GO AHEAD.
WHAT?!
WAIT! THIS UMBRELLA BELONGS TO FUJI-WARA.
I'M RE-LENDING IT TO YOU!
BUT... THAT DOESN'T REALLY... UMM...
ARGH...
OKAY.

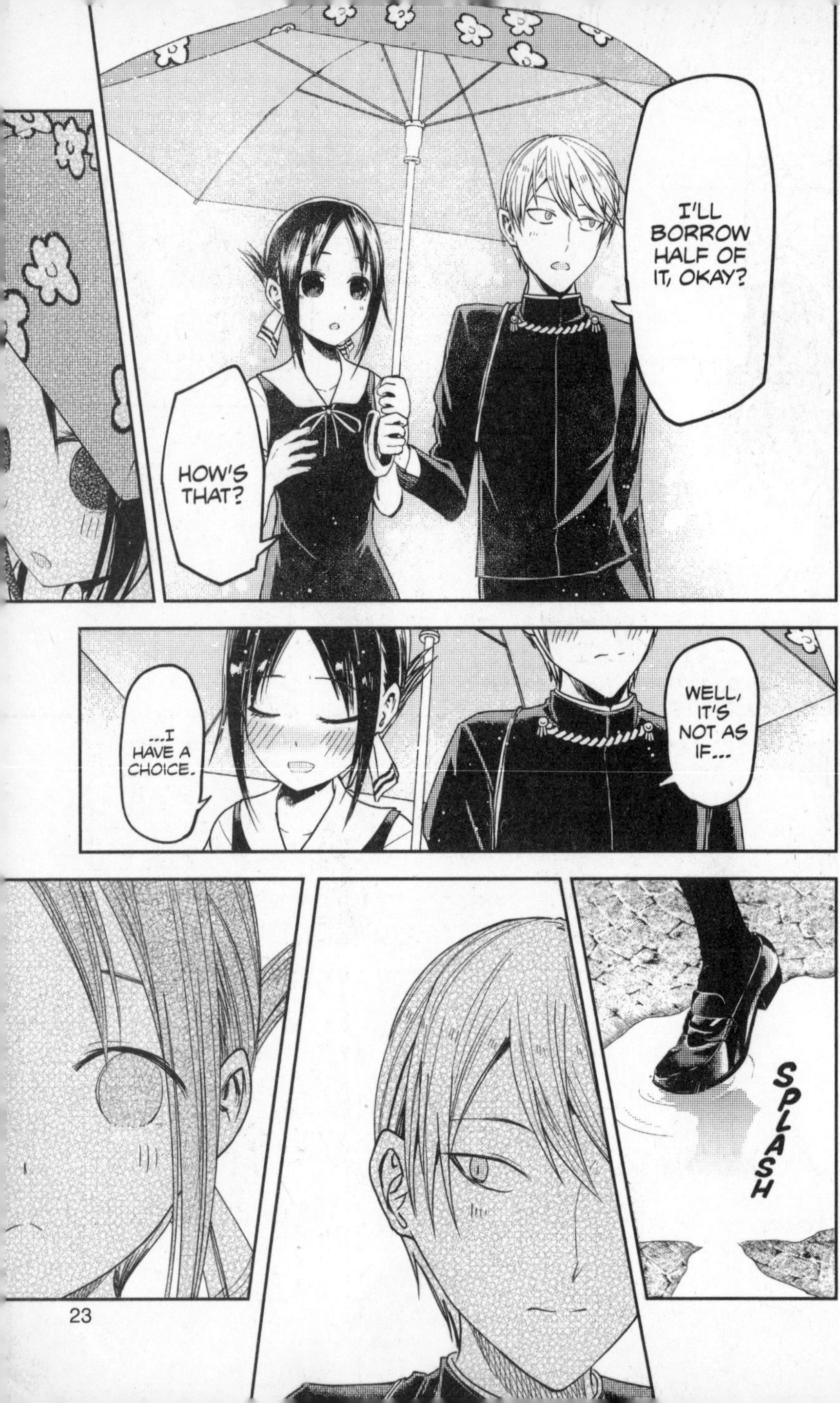
I'LL BORROW HALF OF IT, OKAY?
HOW'S THAT?
WELL, IT'S NOT AS IF...
...I HAVE A CHOICE.
SPLASH

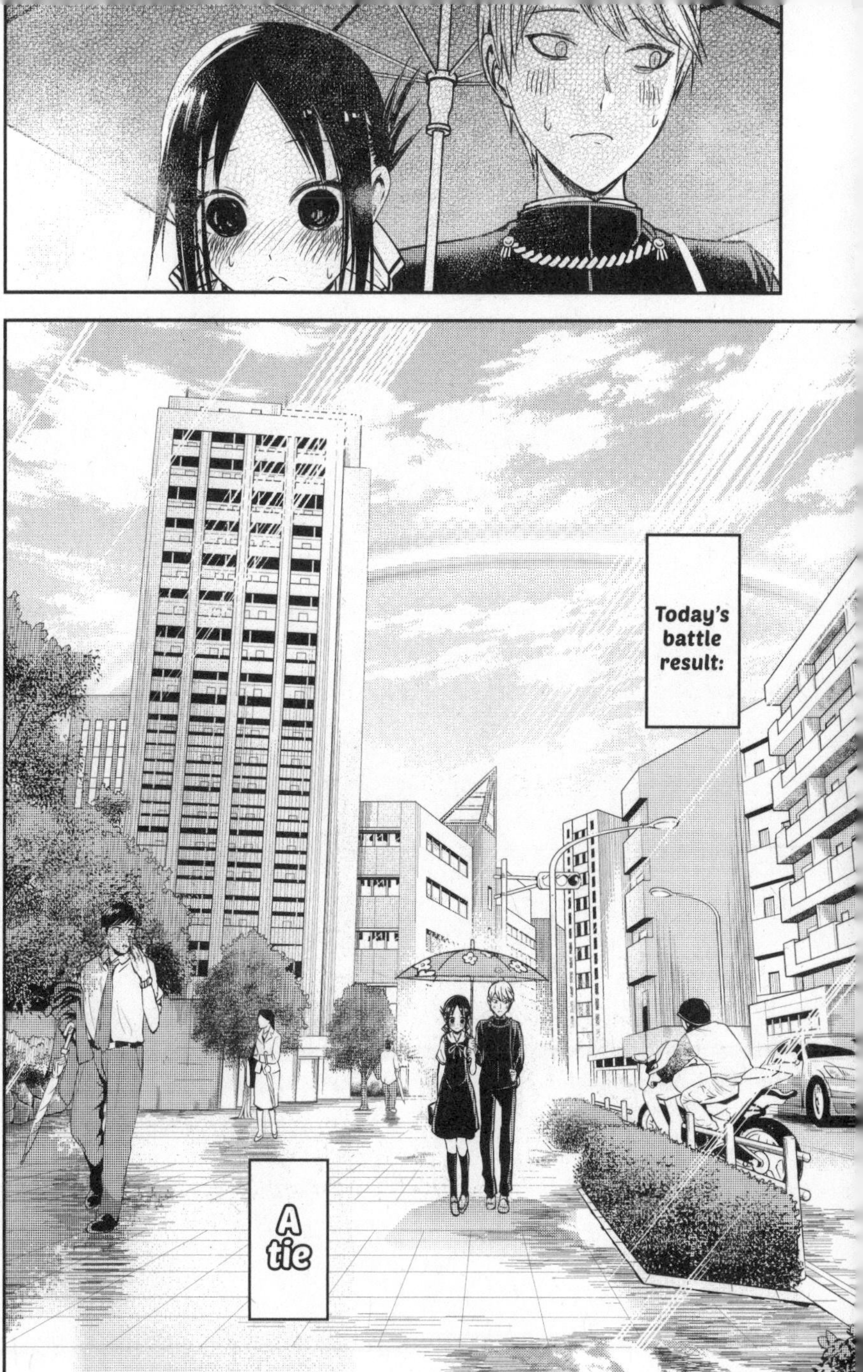
Today's battle result:
A tie

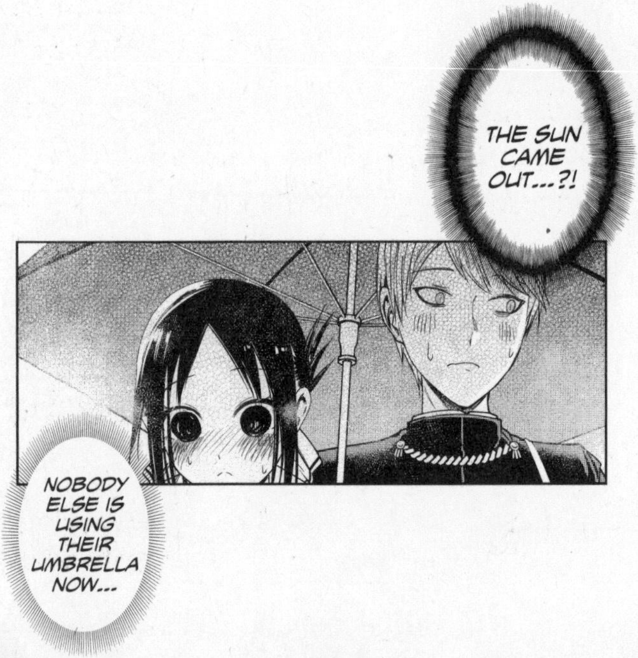
THE SUN CAME OUT...?!
NOBODY ELSE IS USING THEIR UMBRELLA NOW...

KAGUYA-SAMA
LOVE IS WAR

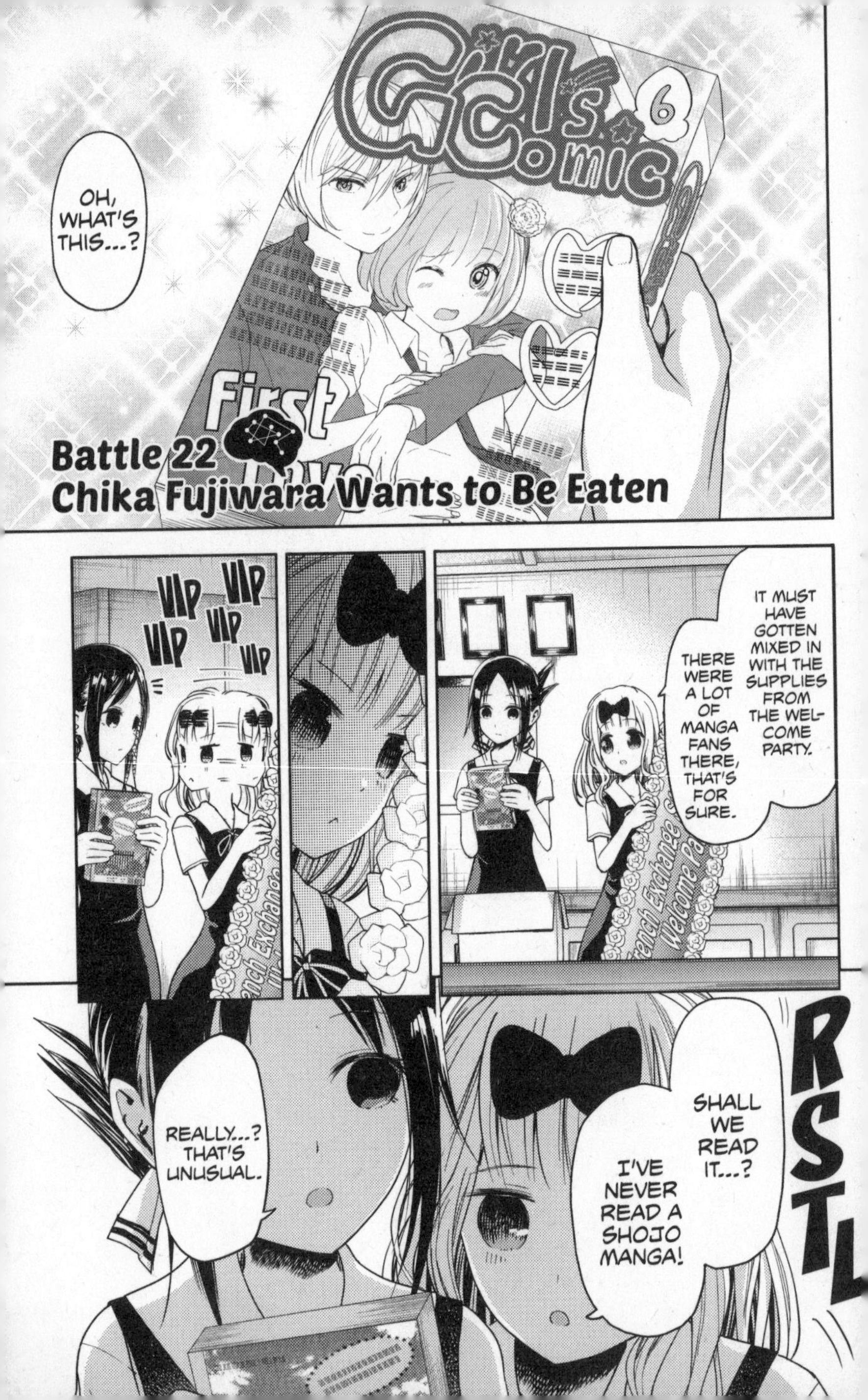

OH, WHAT'S THIS...?
Battle 22
Chika Fujiwara Wants to Be Eaten
IT MUST HAVE GOTTEN MIXED IN WITH THE SUPPLIES FROM THE WEL-COME PARTY.
THERE WERE A LOT OF MANGA FANS THERE, THAT'S FOR SURE.
VIP VIP VIP VIP VIP
RSTL
SHALL WE READ IT...?
I'VE NEVER READ A SHOJO MANGA!
REALLY...? THAT'S UNUSUAL.

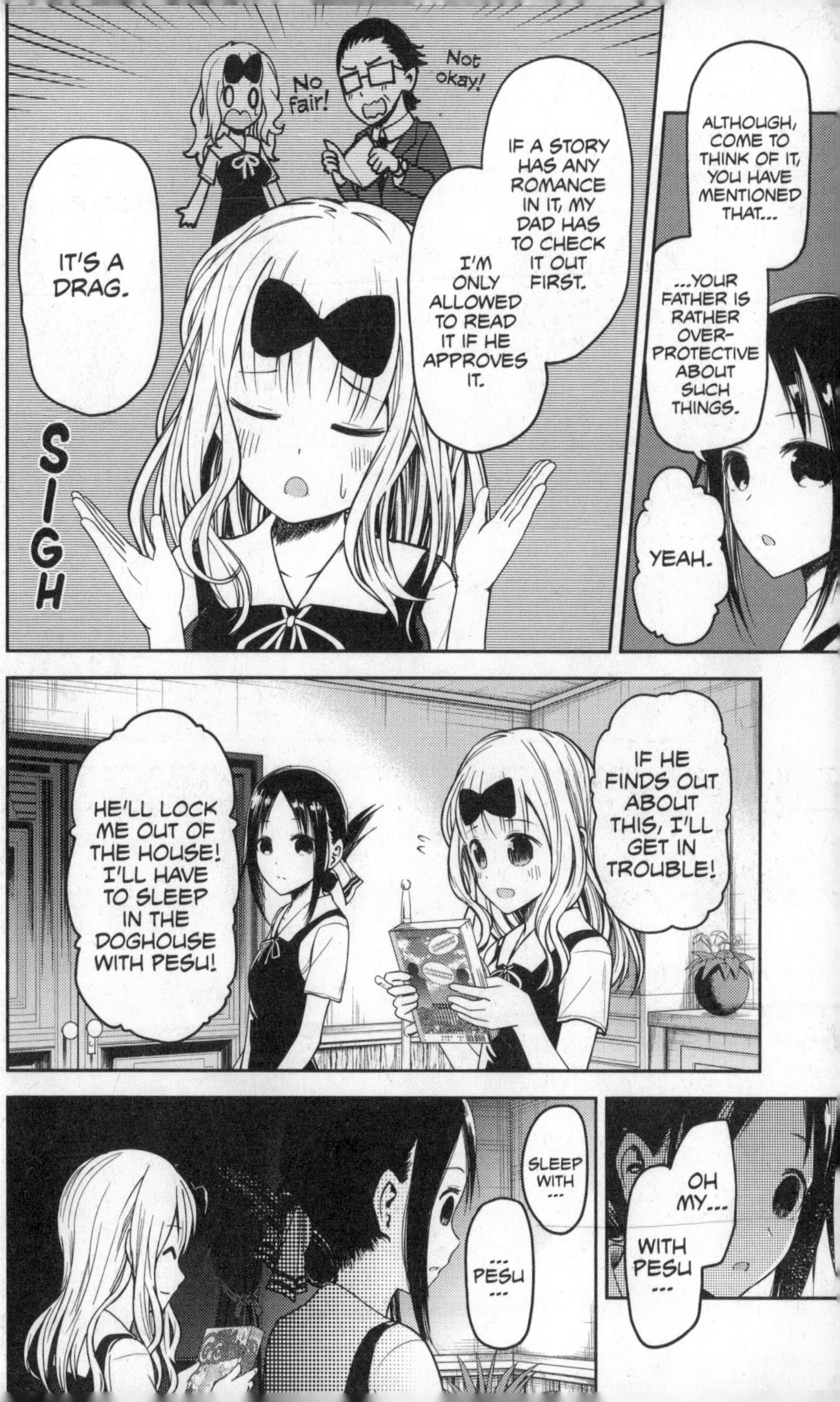
ALTHOUGH, COME TO THINK OF IT, YOU HAVE MENTIONED THAT...
...YOUR FATHER IS RATHER OVER-PROTECTIVE ABOUT SUCH THINGS.
YEAH.
IF A STORY HAS ANY ROMANCE IN IT, MY DAD HAS TO CHECK IT OUT FIRST.
I'M ONLY ALLOWED TO READ IT IF HE APPROVES IT.
Not okay!
No fair!
IT'S A DRAG.
SIGH
IF HE FINDS OUT ABOUT THIS, I'LL GET IN TROUBLE!
HE'LL LOCK ME OUT OF THE HOUSE! I'LL HAVE TO SLEEP IN THE DOGHOUSE WITH PESU!
OH MY...
WITH PESU...
SLEEP WITH...
...PESU...

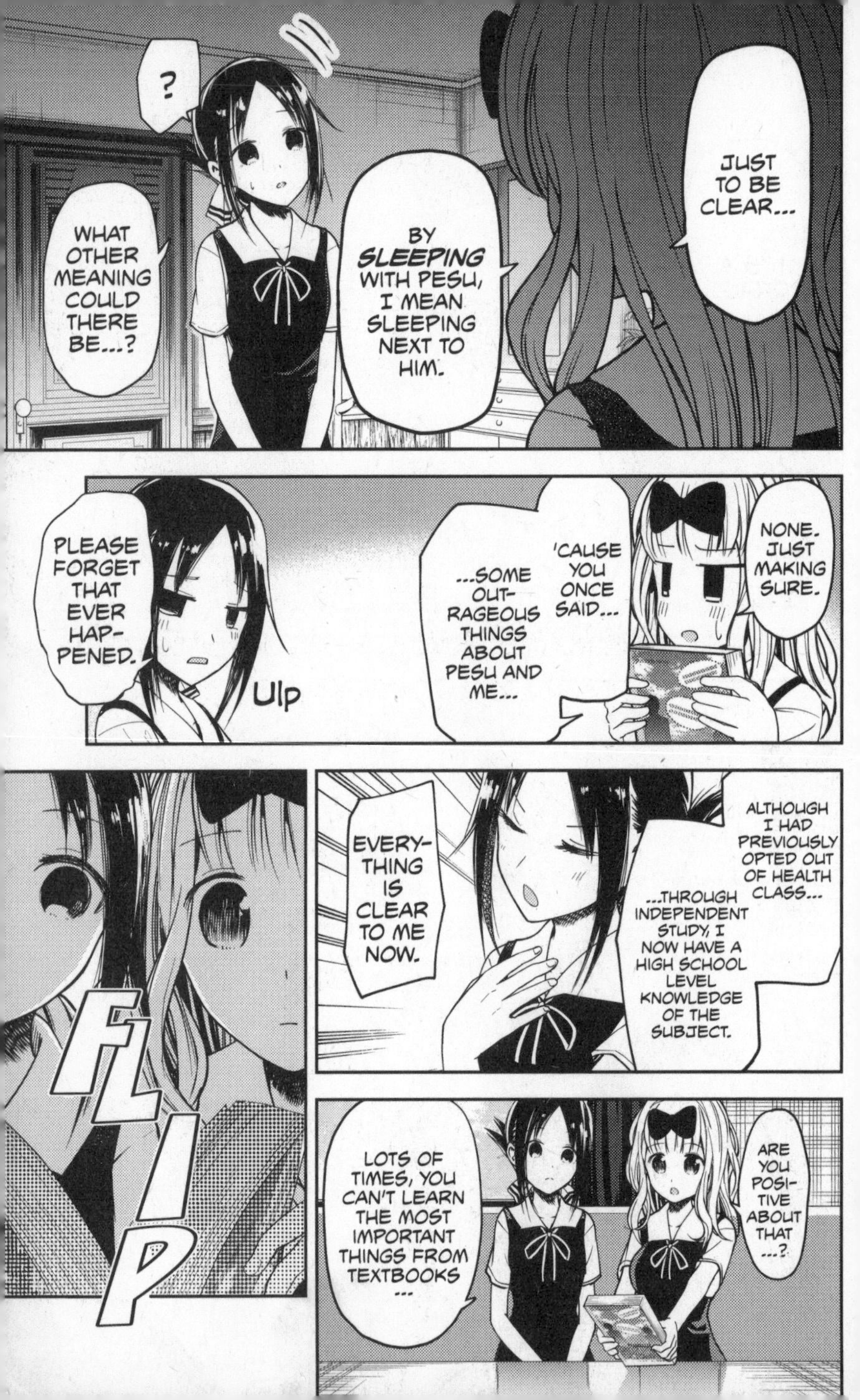
JUST TO BE CLEAR...
BY *SLEEPING* WITH PESU, I MEAN SLEEPING NEXT TO HIM.
?
WHAT OTHER MEANING COULD THERE BE...?
NONE. JUST MAKING SURE.
'CAUSE YOU ONCE SAID...
...SOME OUT-RAGEOUS THINGS ABOUT PESU AND ME...
PLEASE FORGET THAT EVER HAP-PENED.
Ulp
ALTHOUGH I HAD PREVIOUSLY OPTED OUT OF HEALTH CLASS...
...THROUGH INDEPENDENT STUDY, I NOW HAVE A HIGH SCHOOL LEVEL KNOWLEDGE OF THE SUBJECT.
EVERY-THING IS CLEAR TO ME NOW.
ARE YOU POSI-TIVE ABOUT THAT...?
LOTS OF TIMES, YOU CAN'T LEARN THE MOST IMPORTANT THINGS FROM TEXTBOOKS...
FLIP

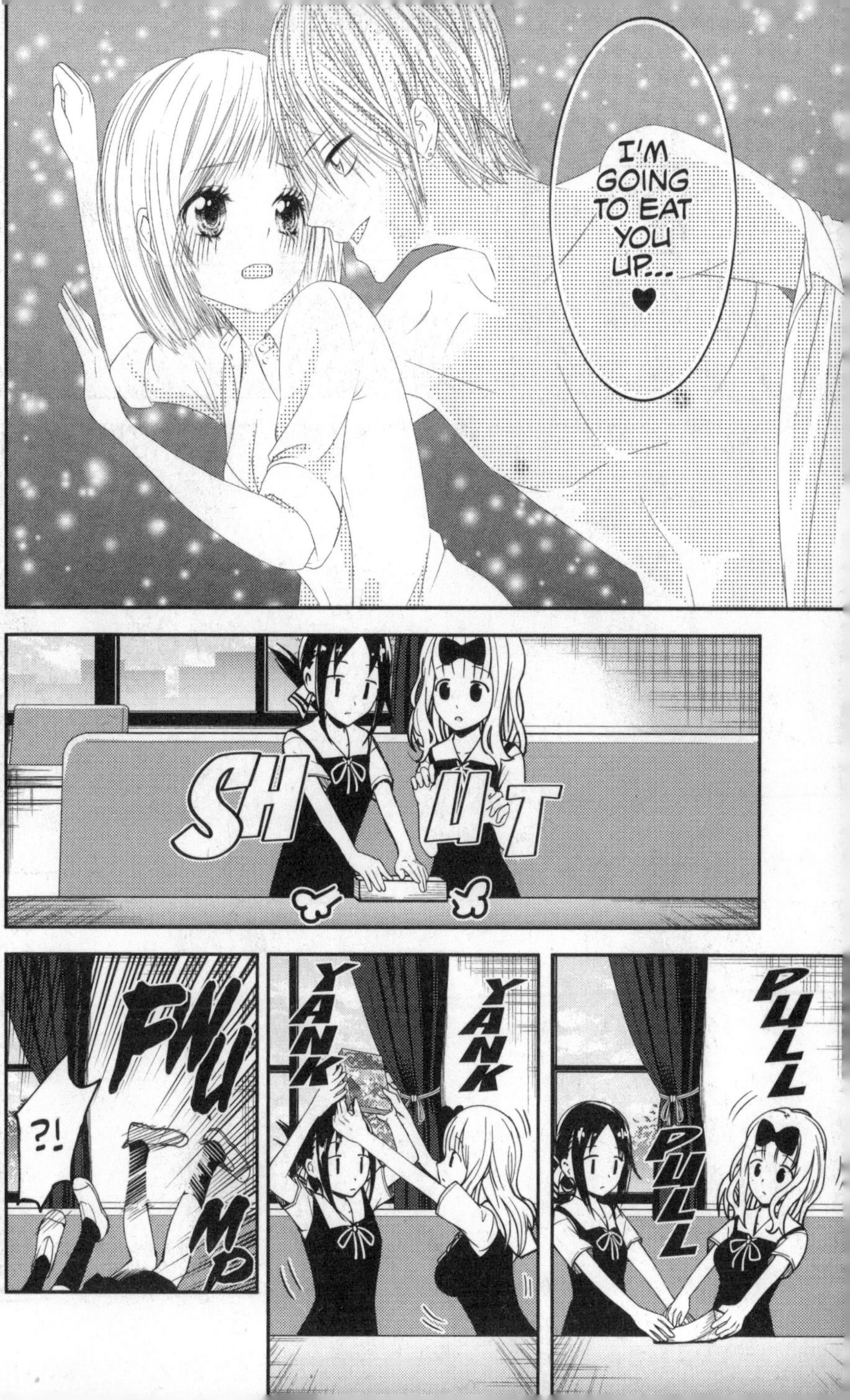
I'M GOING TO EAT YOU UP... ♥
SHUT
PULL
PULL
YANK
YANK
FWUMP
?!

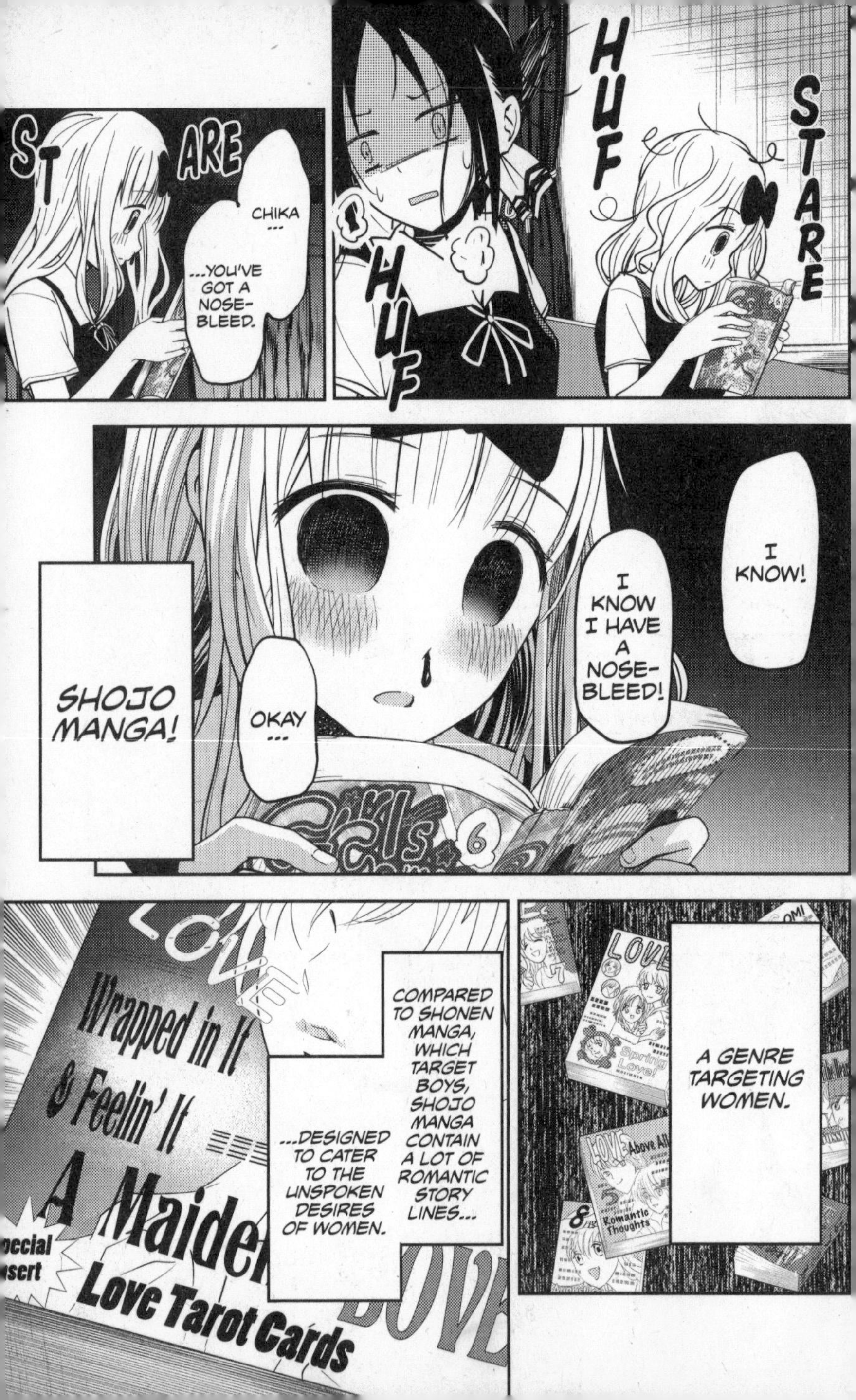
STARE
HUF HUF
ST ARE
CHIKA...
...YOU'VE GOT A NOSE-BLEED.
I KNOW!
I KNOW I HAVE A NOSE-BLEED!
OKAY...
SHOJO MANGA!
A GENRE TARGETING WOMEN.
LOVE
Spring Love!
Above All
Romantic Thoughts
COMPARED TO SHONEN MANGA, WHICH TARGET BOYS, SHOJO MANGA CONTAIN A LOT OF ROMANTIC STORY LINES...
...DESIGNED TO CATER TO THE UNSPOKEN DESIRES OF WOMEN.
LOVE
Wrapped in It & Feelin' It
A Maiden
Love Tarot Cards

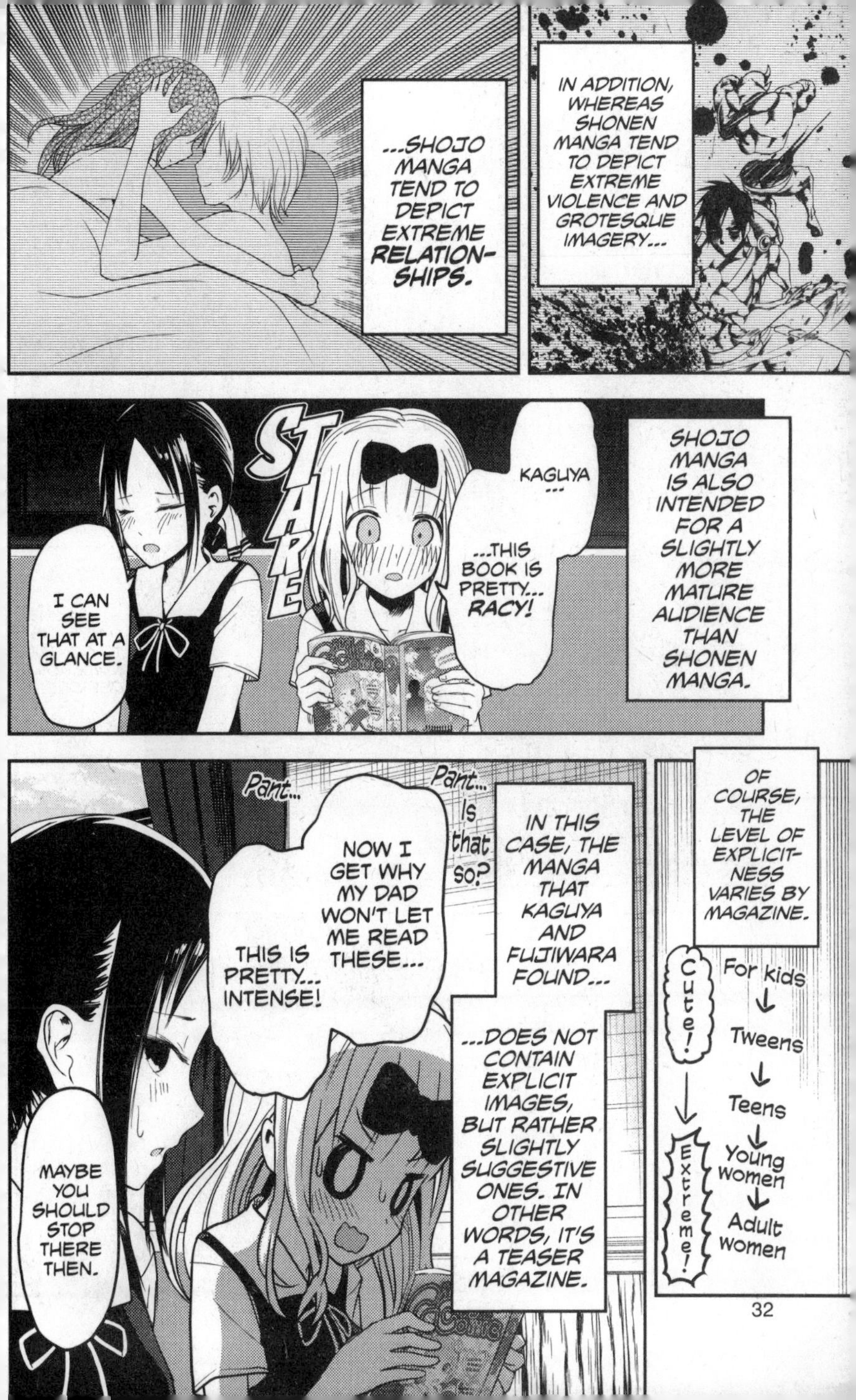
IN ADDITION, WHEREAS SHONEN MANGA TEND TO DEPICT EXTREME VIOLENCE AND GROTESQUE IMAGERY...
...SHOJO MANGA TEND TO DEPICT EXTREME RELATION-SHIPS.
SHOJO MANGA IS ALSO INTENDED FOR A SLIGHTLY MORE MATURE AUDIENCE THAN SHONEN MANGA.
KAGUYA...
...THIS BOOK IS PRETTY... RACY!
STARE
I CAN SEE THAT AT A GLANCE.
OF COURSE, THE LEVEL OF EXPLICIT-NESS VARIES BY MAGAZINE.
For kids
Tweens
Teens
Young women
Adult women
Cute!
Extreme!
IN THIS CASE, THE MANGA THAT KAGUYA AND FUJIWARA FOUND...
Pant... Is that so?
NOW I GET WHY MY DAD WON'T LET ME READ THESE...
Pant...
THIS IS PRETTY... INTENSE!
...DOES NOT CONTAIN EXPLICIT IMAGES, BUT RATHER SLIGHTLY SUGGESTIVE ONES. IN OTHER WORDS, IT'S A TEASER MAGAZINE.
MAYBE YOU SHOULD STOP THERE THEN.

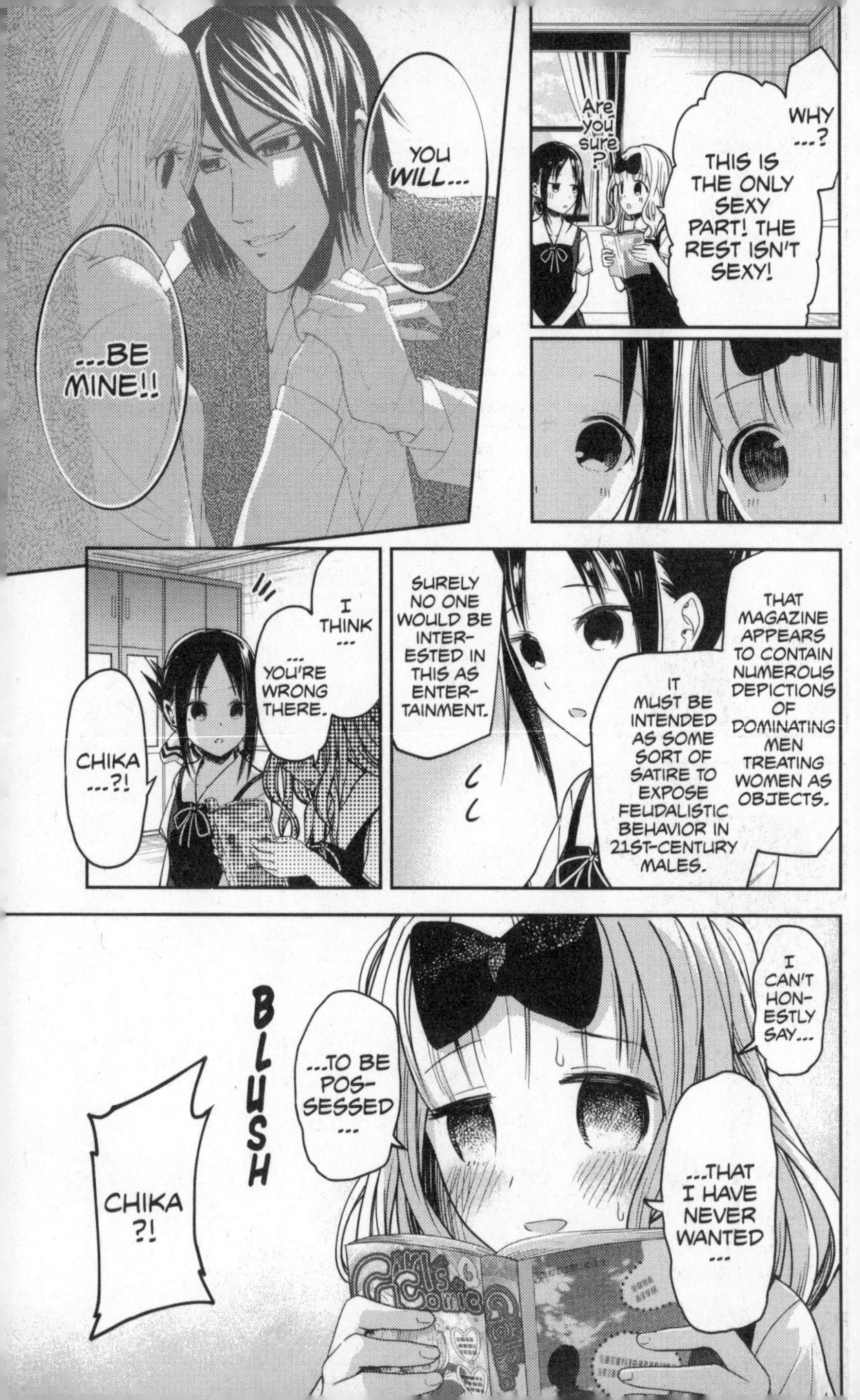
WHY ...? THIS IS THE ONLY SEXY PART! THE REST ISN'T SEXY!
Are you sure?
YOU WILL...
...BE MINE!!
THAT MAGAZINE APPEARS TO CONTAIN NUMEROUS DEPICTIONS OF DOMINATING MEN TREATING WOMEN AS OBJECTS.
IT MUST BE INTENDED AS SOME SORT OF SATIRE TO EXPOSE FEUDALISTIC BEHAVIOR IN 21ST-CENTURY MALES.
SURELY NO ONE WOULD BE INTER-ESTED IN THIS AS ENTER-TAINMENT.
I THINK ... ...YOU'RE WRONG THERE.
CHIKA ...?!
I CAN'T HON-ESTLY SAY...
...THAT I HAVE NEVER WANTED ...
...TO BE POS-SESSED ...
BLUSH
CHIKA ?!

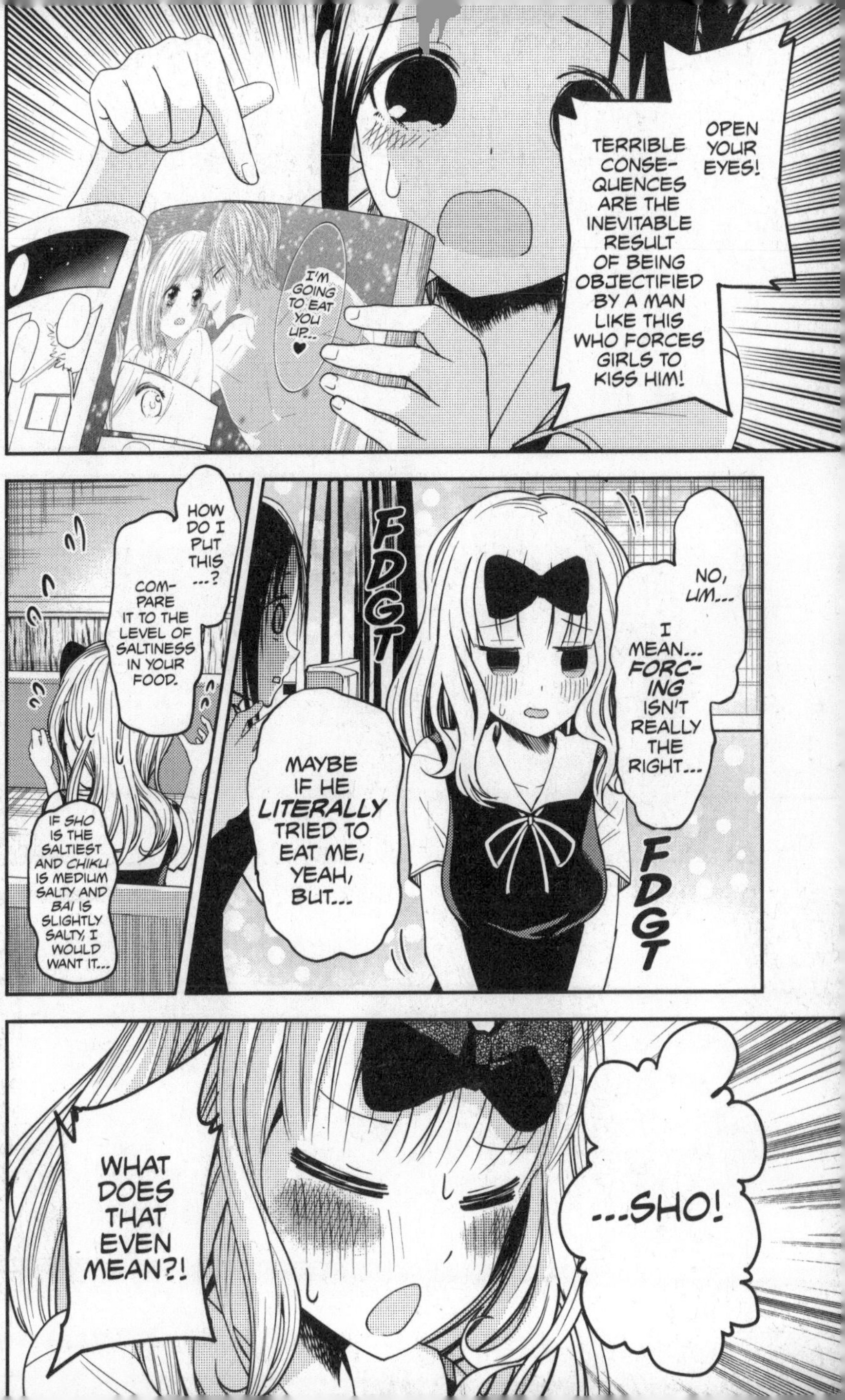
OPEN YOUR EYES!
TERRIBLE CONSEQUENCES ARE THE INEVITABLE RESULT OF BEING OBJECTIFIED BY A MAN LIKE THIS WHO FORCES GIRLS TO KISS HIM!
I'M GOING TO EAT YOU UP... ♥
NO, UM...
I MEAN... FORCING ISN'T REALLY THE RIGHT...
FDGT
FDGT
MAYBE IF HE LITERALLY TRIED TO EAT ME, YEAH, BUT...
HOW DO I PUT THIS...?
COMPARE IT TO THE LEVEL OF SALTINESS IN YOUR FOOD.
IF SHO IS THE SALTIEST AND CHIKU IS MEDIUM SALTY AND BAI IS SLIGHTLY SALTY, I WOULD WANT IT...
...SHO!
WHAT DOES THAT EVEN MEAN?!

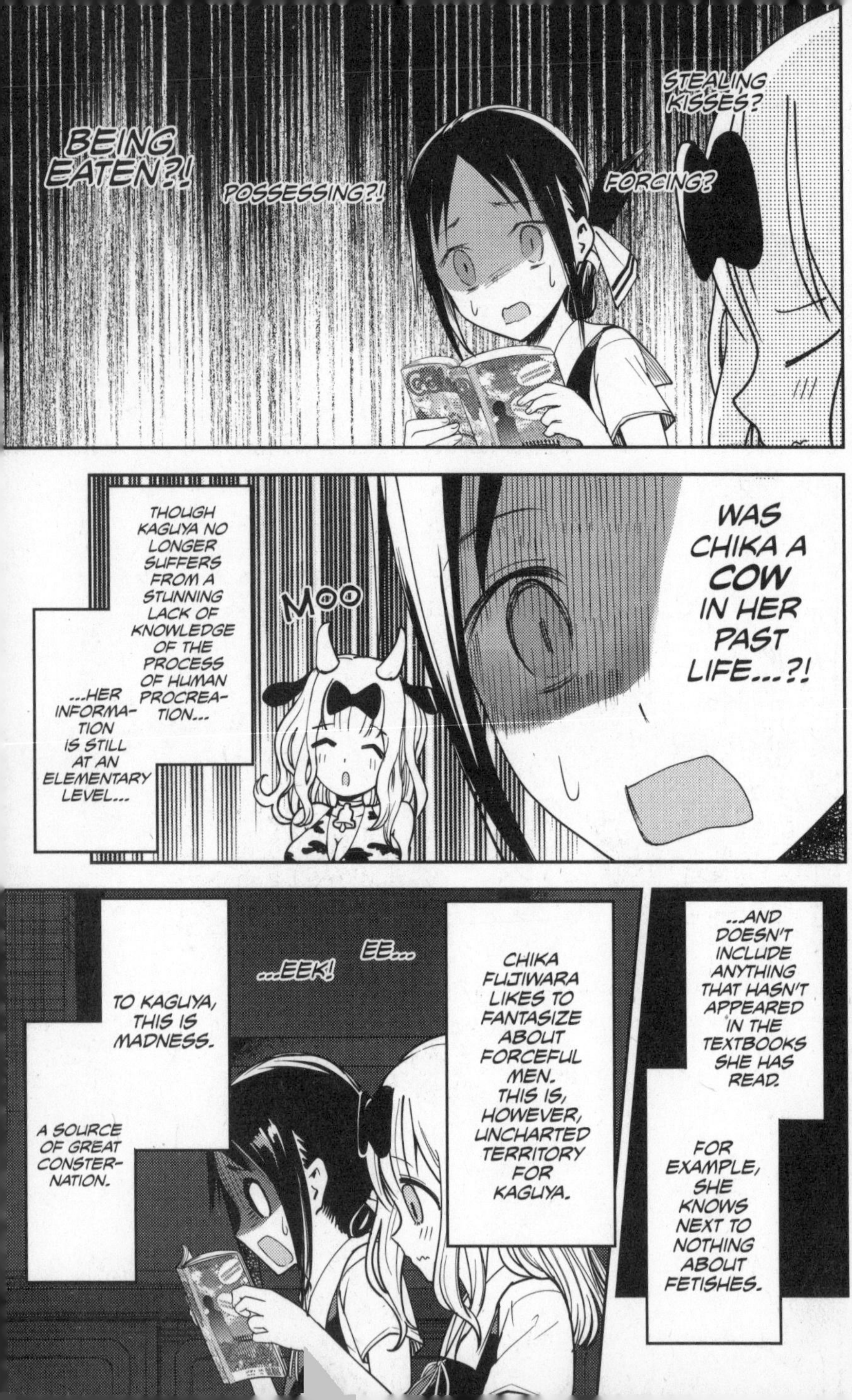
STEALING KISSES?
FORCING?
POSSESSING?!
BEING EATEN?!
WAS CHIKA A COW IN HER PAST LIFE...?!
MOO
THOUGH KAGUYA NO LONGER SUFFERS FROM A STUNNING LACK OF KNOWLEDGE OF THE PROCESS OF HUMAN PROCREATION...
...HER INFORMATION IS STILL AT AN ELEMENTARY LEVEL...
...AND DOESN'T INCLUDE ANYTHING THAT HASN'T APPEARED IN THE TEXTBOOKS SHE HAS READ.
FOR EXAMPLE, SHE KNOWS NEXT TO NOTHING ABOUT FETISHES.
CHIKA FUJIWARA LIKES TO FANTASIZE ABOUT FORCEFUL MEN. THIS IS, HOWEVER, UNCHARTED TERRITORY FOR KAGUYA.
EE...
...EEK!
TO KAGUYA, THIS IS MADNESS.
A SOURCE OF GREAT CONSTERNATION.

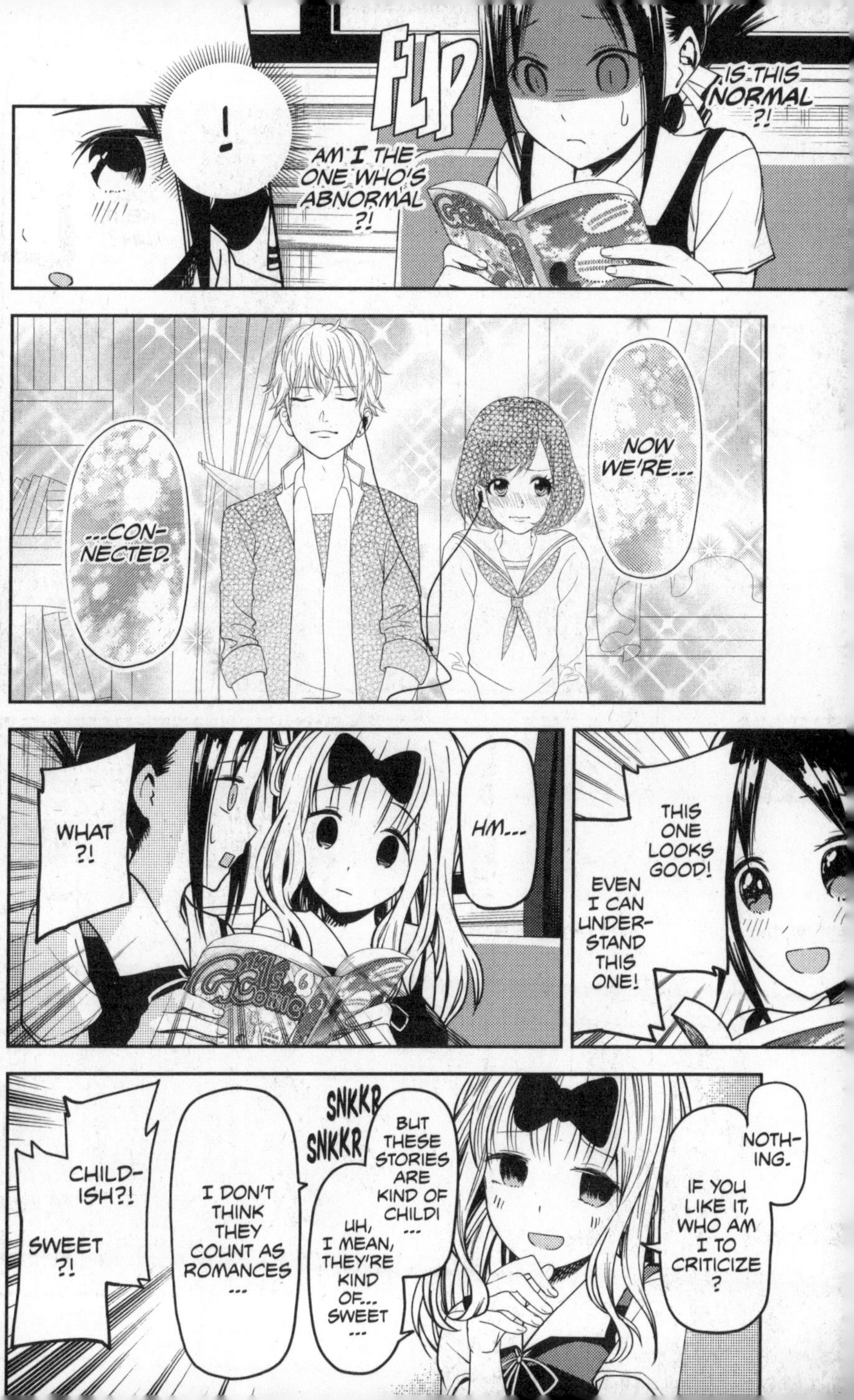
FLIP
IS THIS NORMAL ?!
AM I THE ONE WHO'S ABNORMAL ?!
!
NOW WE'RE...
...CON-NECTED.
THIS ONE LOOKS GOOD!
EVEN I CAN UNDER-STAND THIS ONE!
HM...
WHAT ?!
NOTH-ING.
IF YOU LIKE IT, WHO AM I TO CRITICIZE ?
BUT THESE STORIES ARE KIND OF CHILDI ...
UH, I MEAN, THEY'RE KIND OF... SWEET ...
SNKKR SNKKR
I DON'T THINK THEY COUNT AS ROMANCES ...
CHILD-ISH?!
SWEET ?!

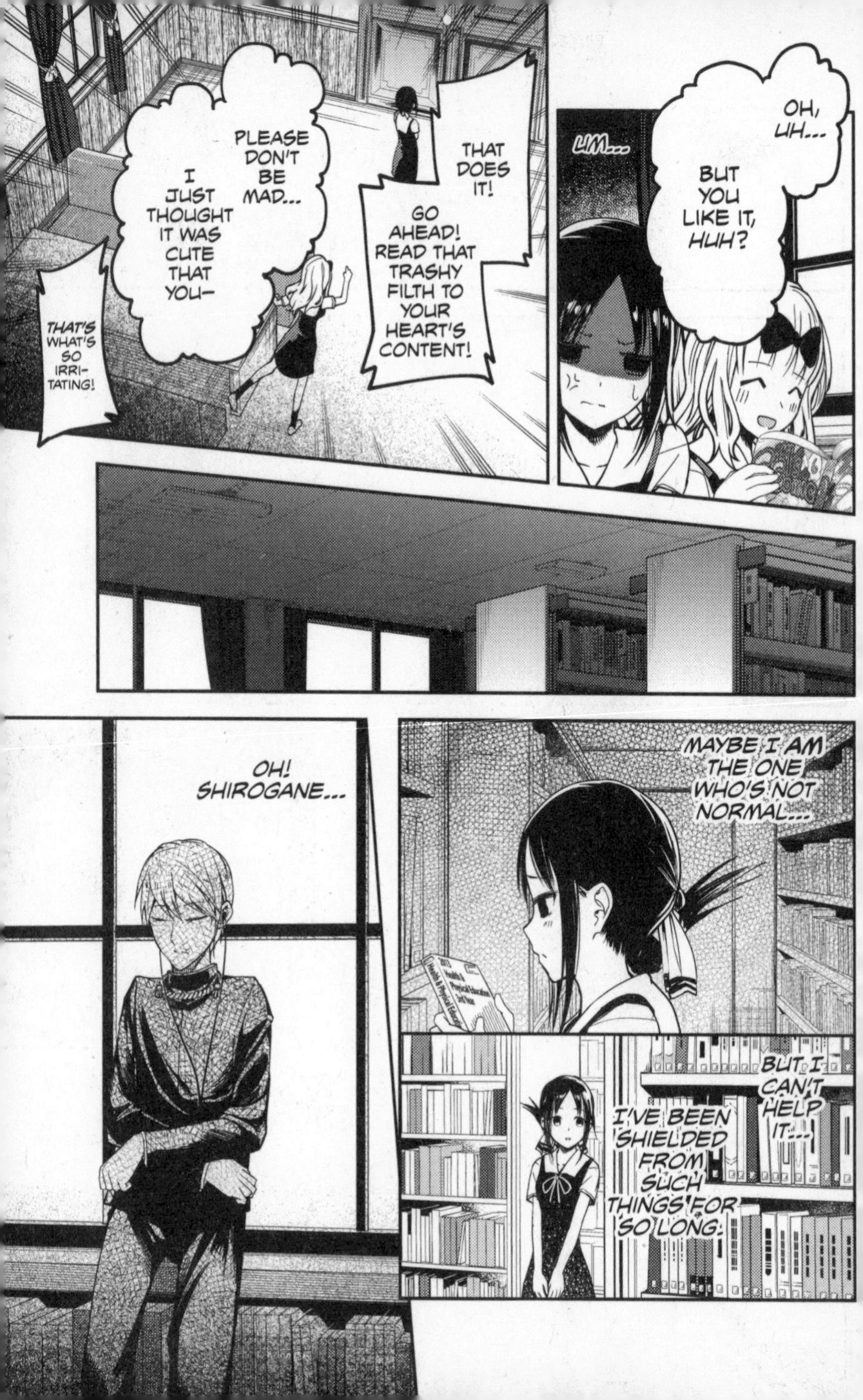
OH, UH...
BUT YOU LIKE IT, HUH?
UM...
THAT DOES IT!
GO AHEAD! READ THAT TRASHY FILTH TO YOUR HEART'S CONTENT!
PLEASE DON'T BE MAD...
I JUST THOUGHT IT WAS CUTE THAT YOU—
THAT'S WHAT'S SO IRRITATING!
MAYBE I AM THE ONE WHO'S NOT NORMAL...
BUT I CAN'T HELP IT...
I'VE BEEN SHIELDED FROM SUCH THINGS FOR SO LONG.
OH! SHIROGANE...

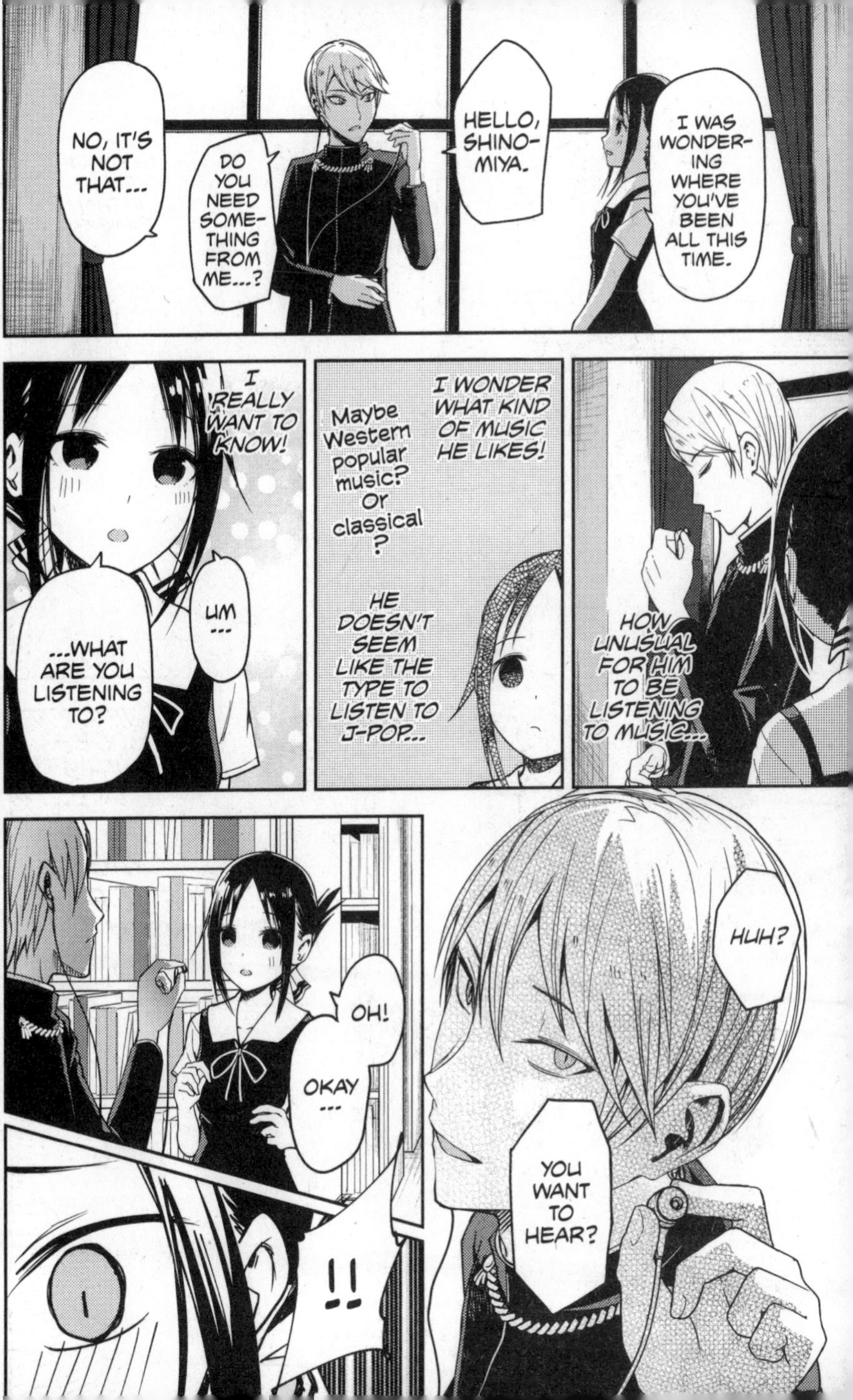

I WAS WONDERING WHERE YOU'VE BEEN ALL THIS TIME.
HELLO, SHINOMIYA.
DO YOU NEED SOMETHING FROM ME...?
NO, IT'S NOT THAT...
HOW UNUSUAL FOR HIM TO BE LISTENING TO MUSIC...
I WONDER WHAT KIND OF MUSIC HE LIKES!
Maybe Western popular music? Or classical?
HE DOESN'T SEEM LIKE THE TYPE TO LISTEN TO J-POP...
I REALLY WANT TO KNOW!
UM...
...WHAT ARE YOU LISTENING TO?
HUH?
YOU WANT TO HEAR?
OH!
OKAY...
!!

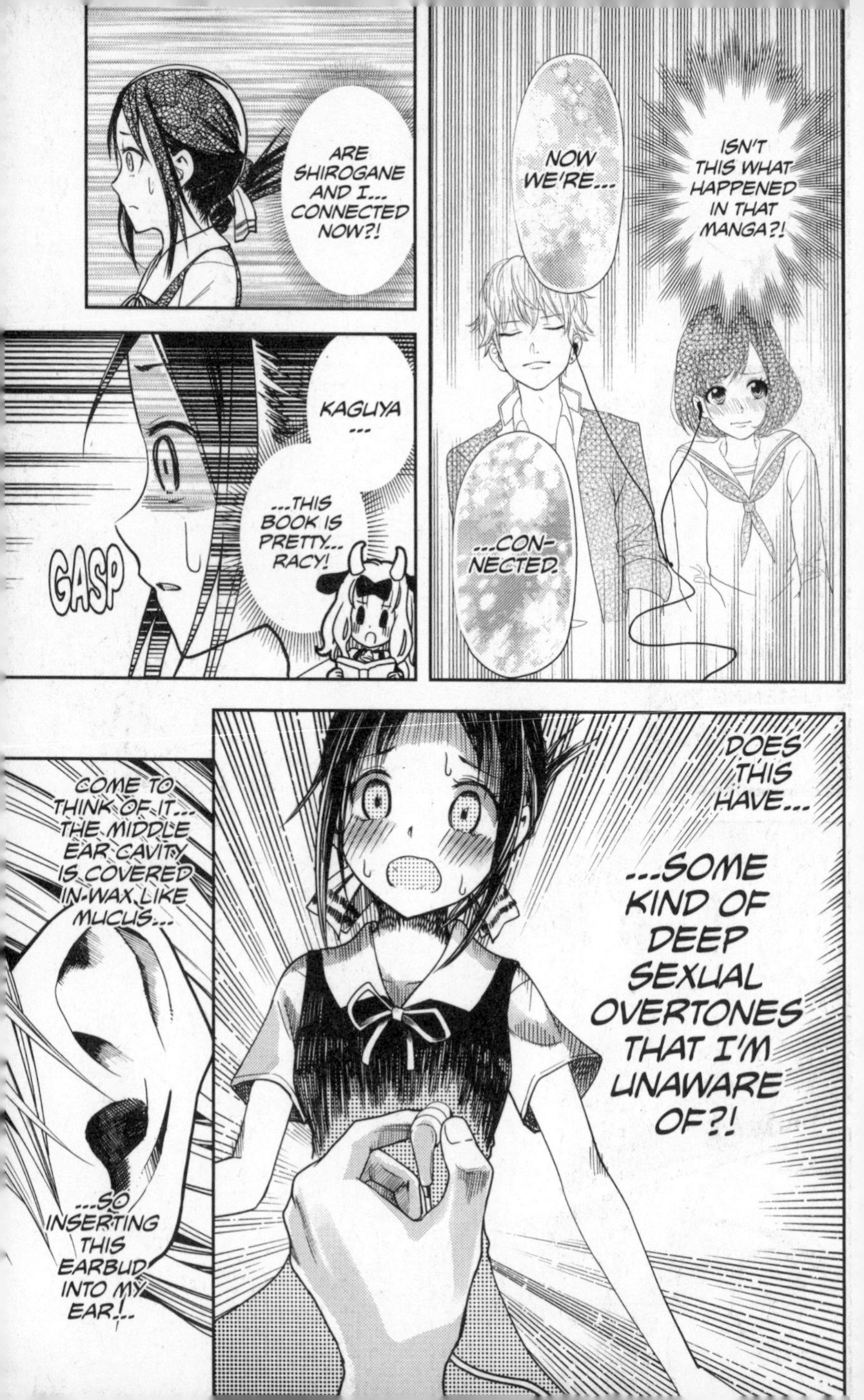
ISN'T THIS WHAT HAPPENED IN THAT MANGA?!
NOW WE'RE...
...CON-NECTED.
ARE SHIROGANE AND I... CONNECTED NOW?!
KAGUYA ...
...THIS BOOK IS PRETTY... RACY!
GASP
DOES THIS HAVE...
...SOME KIND OF DEEP SEXUAL OVERTONES THAT I'M UNAWARE OF?!
COME TO THINK OF IT... THE MIDDLE EAR CAVITY IS COVERED IN WAX-LIKE MUCUS...
...SO INSERTING THIS EARBUD INTO MY EAR!...

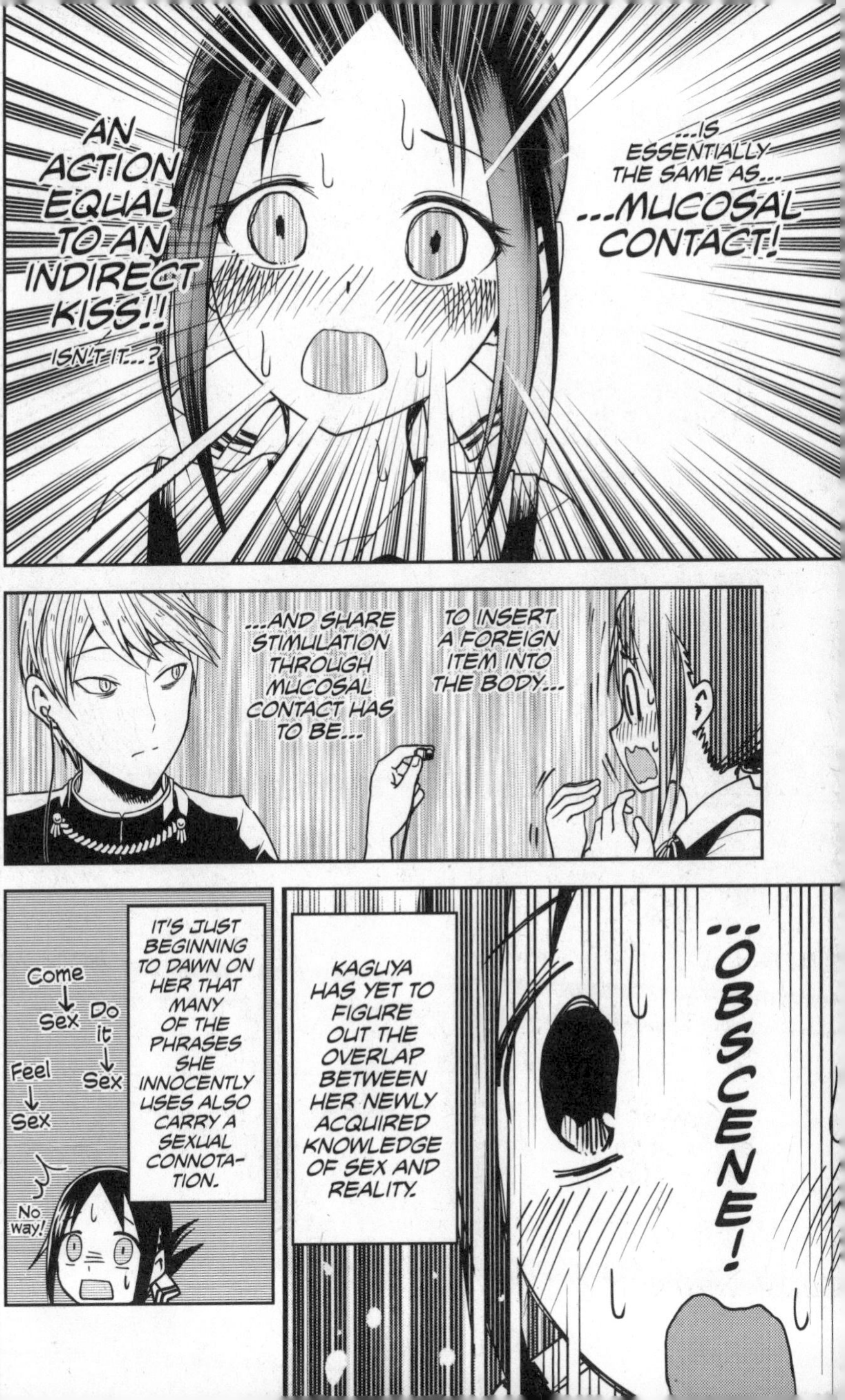
...IS ESSENTIALLY THE SAME AS...
...MUCOSAL CONTACT!
AN ACTION EQUAL TO AN INDIRECT KISS!!
ISN'T IT...?
TO INSERT A FOREIGN ITEM INTO THE BODY...
...AND SHARE STIMULATION THROUGH MUCOSAL CONTACT HAS TO BE...
...OBSCENE!
KAGUYA HAS YET TO FIGURE OUT THE OVERLAP BETWEEN HER NEWLY ACQUIRED KNOWLEDGE OF SEX AND REALITY.
IT'S JUST BEGINNING TO DAWN ON HER THAT MANY OF THE PHRASES SHE INNOCENTLY USES ALSO CARRY A SEXUAL CONNOTATION.
Do it → Sex
Come → Sex
Feel → Sex
No way!

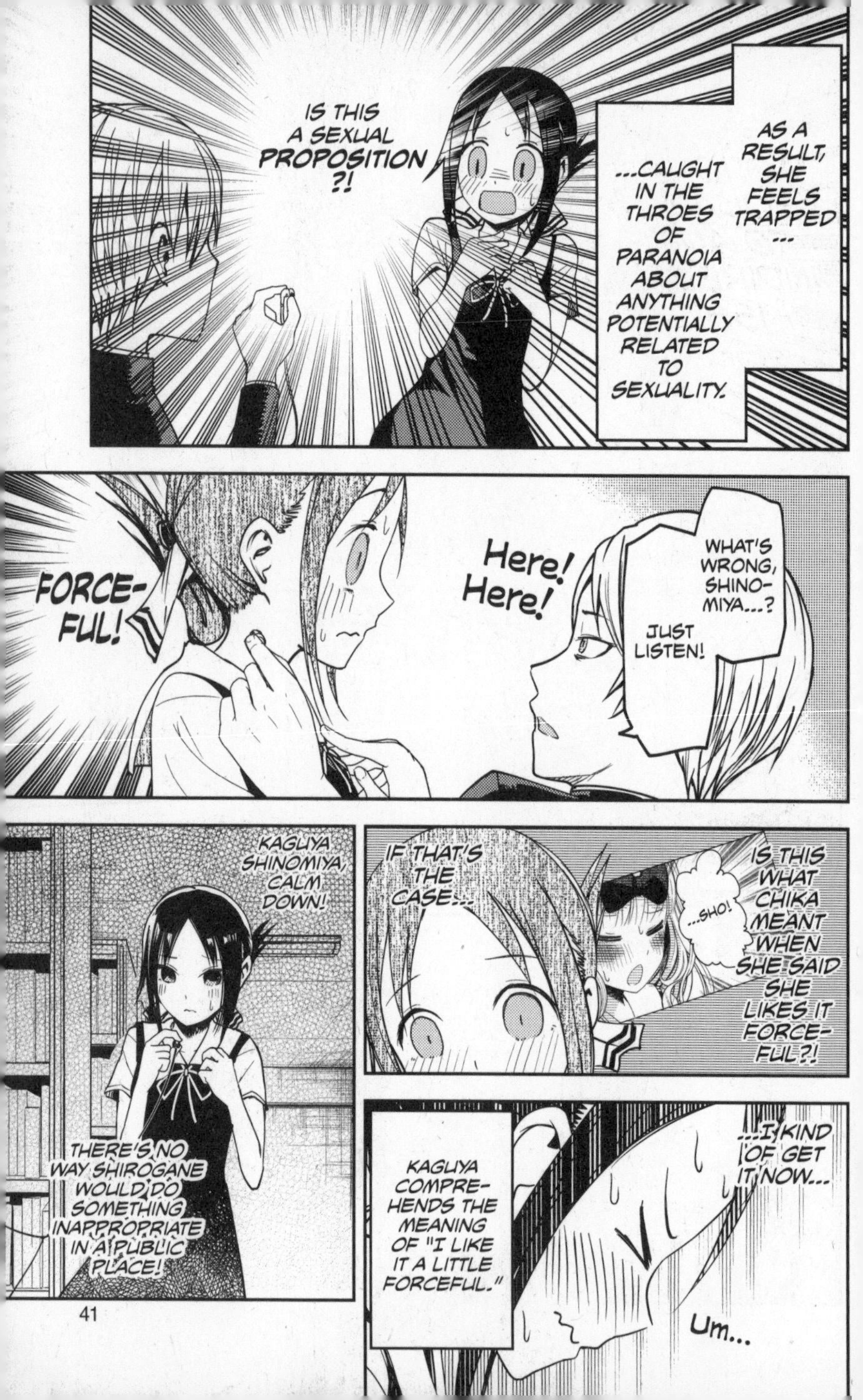
AS A RESULT, SHE FEELS TRAPPED...
...CAUGHT IN THE THROES OF PARANOIA ABOUT ANYTHING POTENTIALLY RELATED TO SEXUALITY.
IS THIS A SEXUAL PROPOSITION?!
WHAT'S WRONG, SHINOMIYA...?
JUST LISTEN!
Here! Here!
FORCE-FUL!
IS THIS WHAT CHIKA MEANT WHEN SHE SAID SHE LIKES IT FORCE-FUL?!
...SHO!
IF THAT'S THE CASE...
...I KIND OF GET IT NOW...
KAGUYA COMPRE-HENDS THE MEANING OF "I LIKE IT A LITTLE FORCEFUL."
Um...
KAGUYA SHINOMIYA, CALM DOWN!
THERE'S NO WAY SHIROGANE WOULD DO SOMETHING INAPPROPRIATE IN A PUBLIC PLACE!

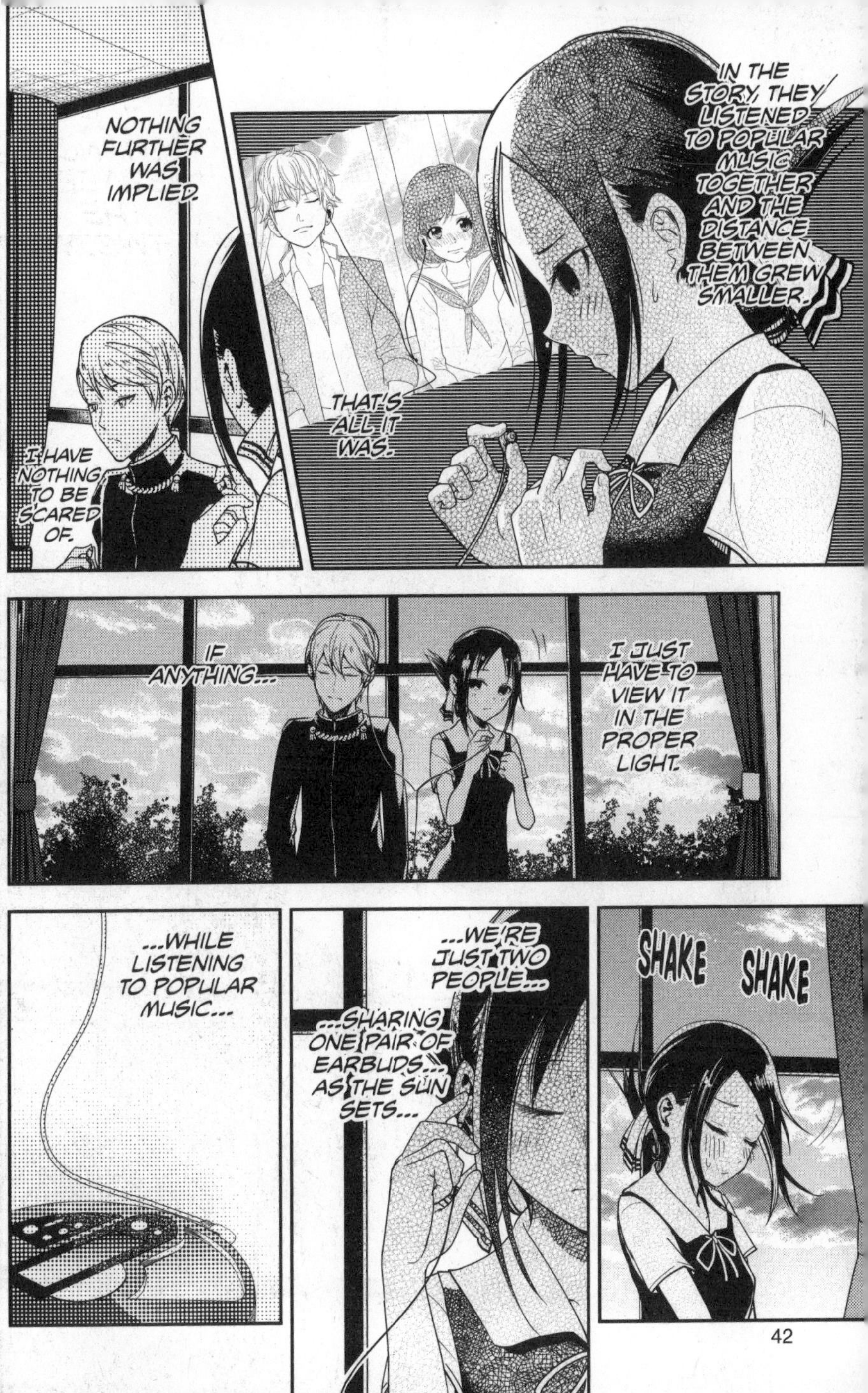
IN THE STORY, THEY LISTENED TO POPULAR MUSIC TOGETHER AND THE DISTANCE BETWEEN THEM GREW SMALLER.
THAT'S ALL IT WAS.
NOTHING FURTHER WAS IMPLIED.
I HAVE NOTHING TO BE SCARED OF.
I JUST HAVE TO VIEW IT IN THE PROPER LIGHT.
IF ANYTHING...
SHAKE
SHAKE
...WE'RE JUST TWO PEOPLE...
...SHARING ONE PAIR OF EARBUDS... AS THE SUN SETS...
...WHILE LISTENING TO POPULAR MUSIC...

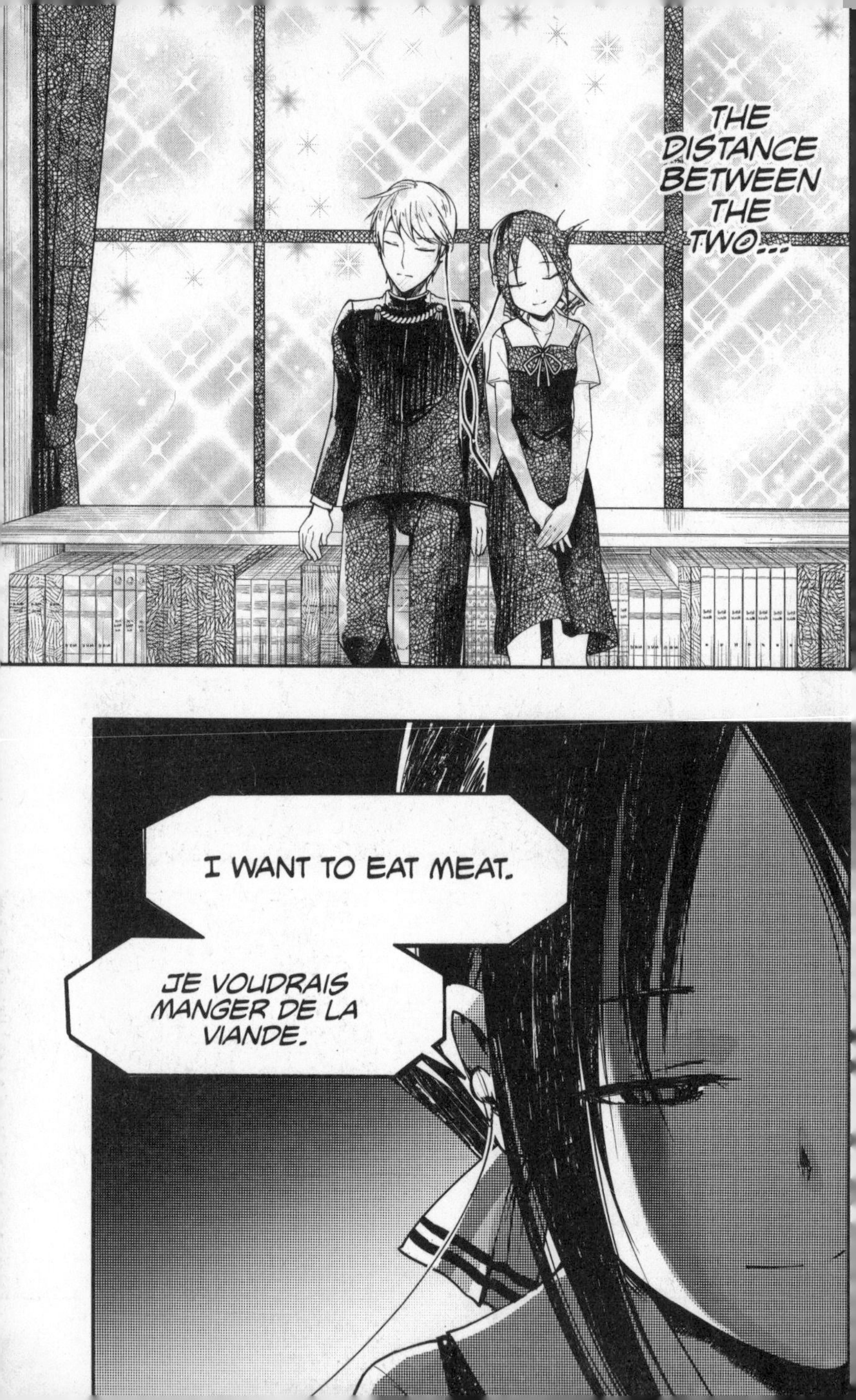
THE DISTANCE BETWEEN THE TWO...
I WANT TO EAT MEAT.
JE VOUDRAIS MANGER DE LA VIANDE.

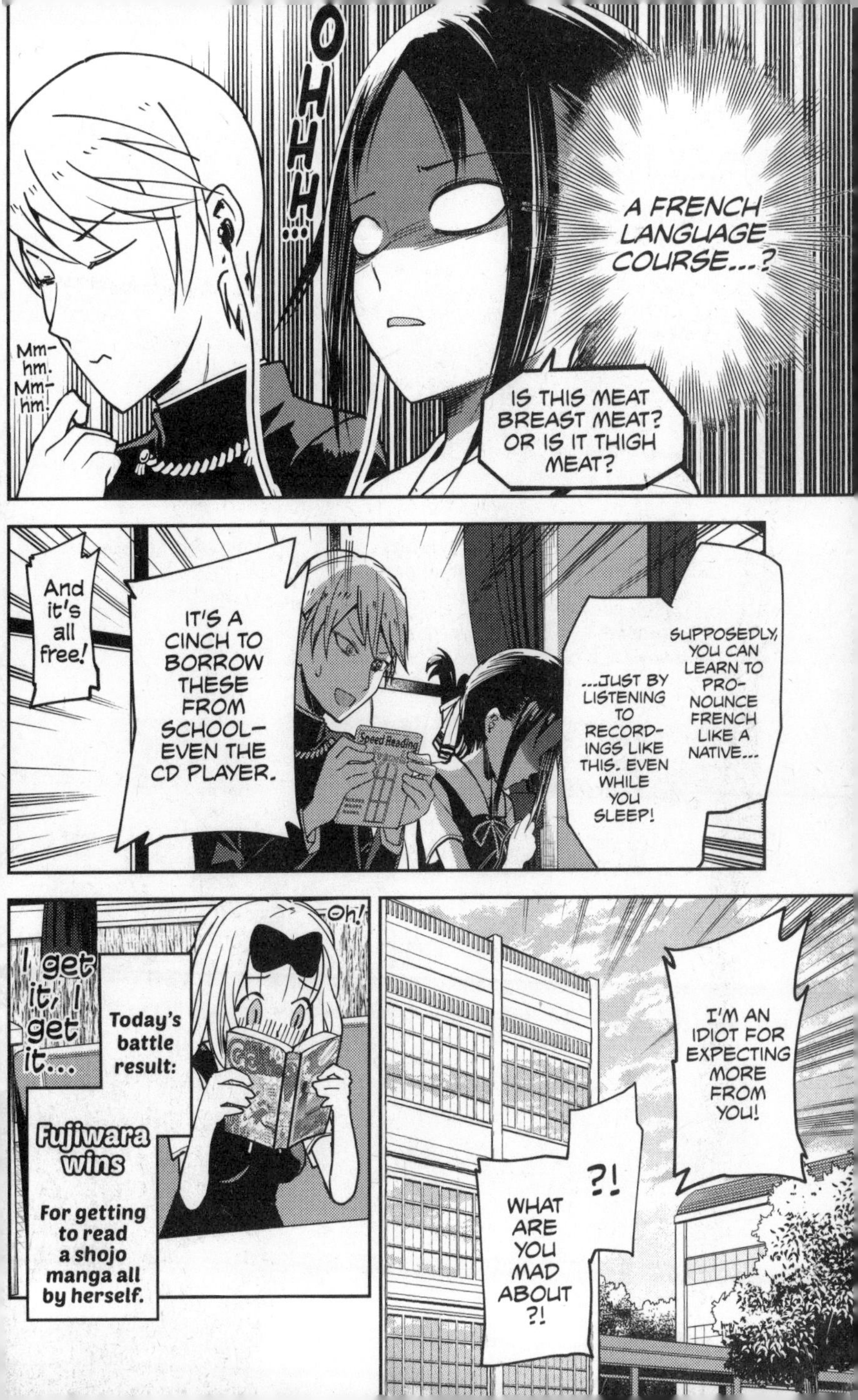
A FRENCH LANGUAGE COURSE...?
OHHHH...
IS THIS MEAT BREAST MEAT? OR IS IT THIGH MEAT?
Mm-hm. Mm-hm!
SUPPOSEDLY, YOU CAN LEARN TO PRO-NOUNCE FRENCH LIKE A NATIVE...
...JUST BY LISTENING TO RECORD-INGS LIKE THIS. EVEN WHILE YOU SLEEP!
IT'S A CINCH TO BORROW THESE FROM SCHOOL—EVEN THE CD PLAYER.
Speed Reading
And it's all free!
I'M AN IDIOT FOR EXPECTING MORE FROM YOU!
?!
WHAT ARE YOU MAD ABOUT?!
Oh!
I get it, I get it...
Today's battle result:
Fujiwara wins
For getting to read a shojo manga all by herself.

Translation of the French that appeared in Battle 20 "Miyuki Shirogane Wants to Talk"! (*See volume 2.)

Bonjour.
★Hello.

Merci beaucoup pour votre invitation d'aujourd'hui.
★Thank you very much for your invitation today.

C'est nous qui vous remercions d'être venus d'aussi loin.
★Thank you for coming from so far away.

Nous ferons tout notre possible pour que vous gardiez un souvenir impérissable durant votre séjour parmi nous.
★We will do our utmost to ensure that you have unforgettable memories during your stay with us.

Si vous avez besoin de quoi que ce soit, n'hésitez pas à nous le faire savoir.
★If you need anything, please do not hesitate to let us know.

Je vous remercie.
★Thank you.

La pluparts des contenus japonais sont focalisés sur le marché domestique.
Le Japon n'a pas encore établi la façon de se promouvoir à l'étranger.
Les prix montent en flèche à l'exportation,
il y a aussi les problèmes des ventes au rabais des licences des images...
★Most Japanese entertainment is focused on the domestic market. Japan has yet to establish itself abroad. Prices go up when products are exported, and there is also the problem of discounts when licensing images.

Comme c'est mignon.
★How cute.

Enchantée.
★Nice to meet you.

Enchanté mademoiselle. Je m'appelle Miyuki Shirogane.
★Nice to meet you, young lady. My name is Miyuki Shirogane.

Je suis président du conseil des élèves dans ce lycée.
★I'm the president of the student council.

Oh!
★Oh my!

Je suis très intéressée par la culture japonaise
et je souhaite faire mes études au Japon un de ces jours.
★I am very interested in Japanese culture. And I want to study in Japan someday.

Oui, oui je vois...
★Yes, yes, I see.

Haha! Exactement!
★Ha ha! Exactly!

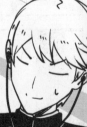

I've got this next time.

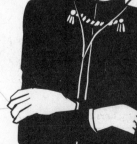

KAGUYA-SAMA
LOVE IS WAR

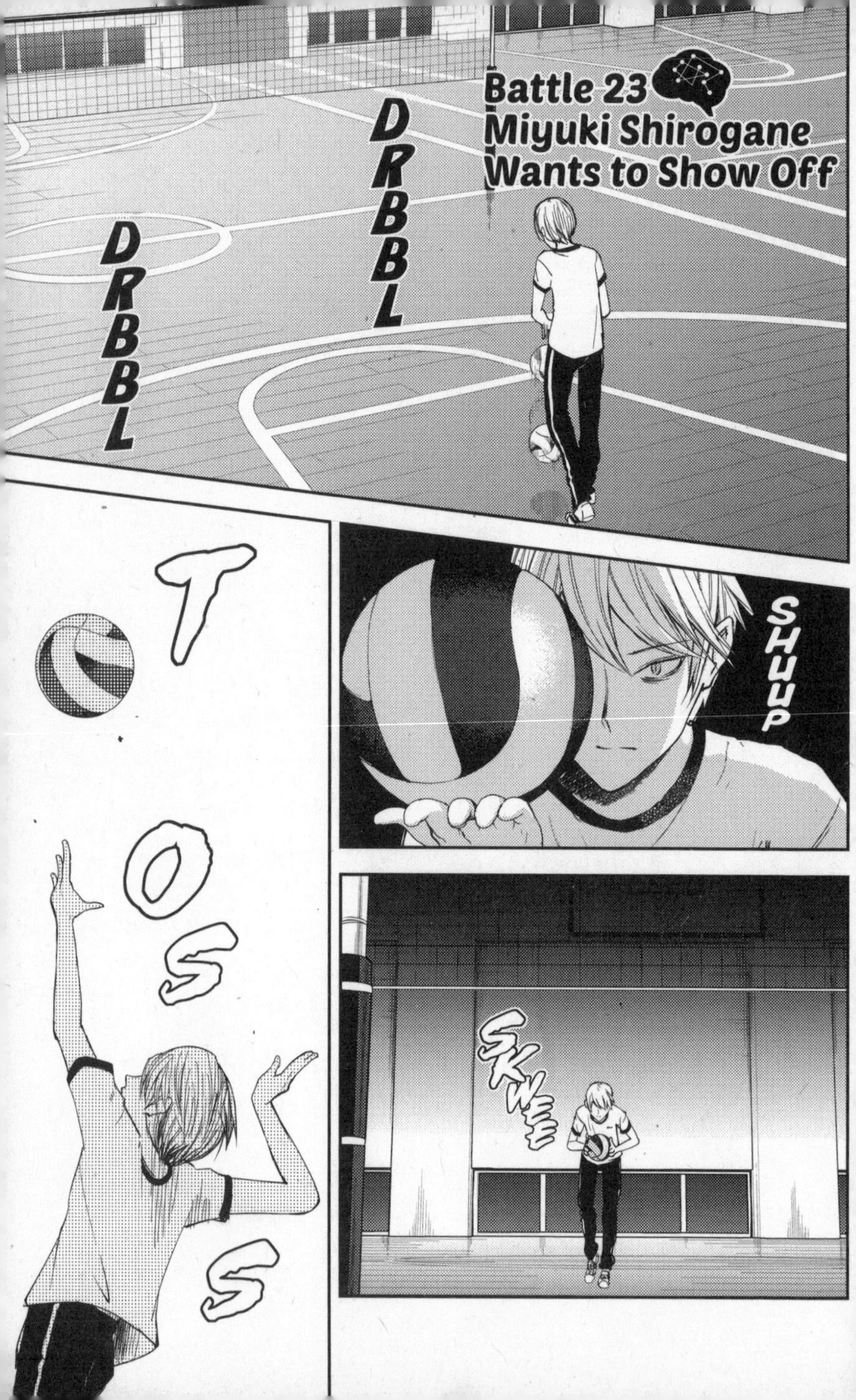
Battle 23
Miyuki Shirogane
Wants to Show Off
DRBBL
DRBBL
SHUUP
SKWEE
TOSS

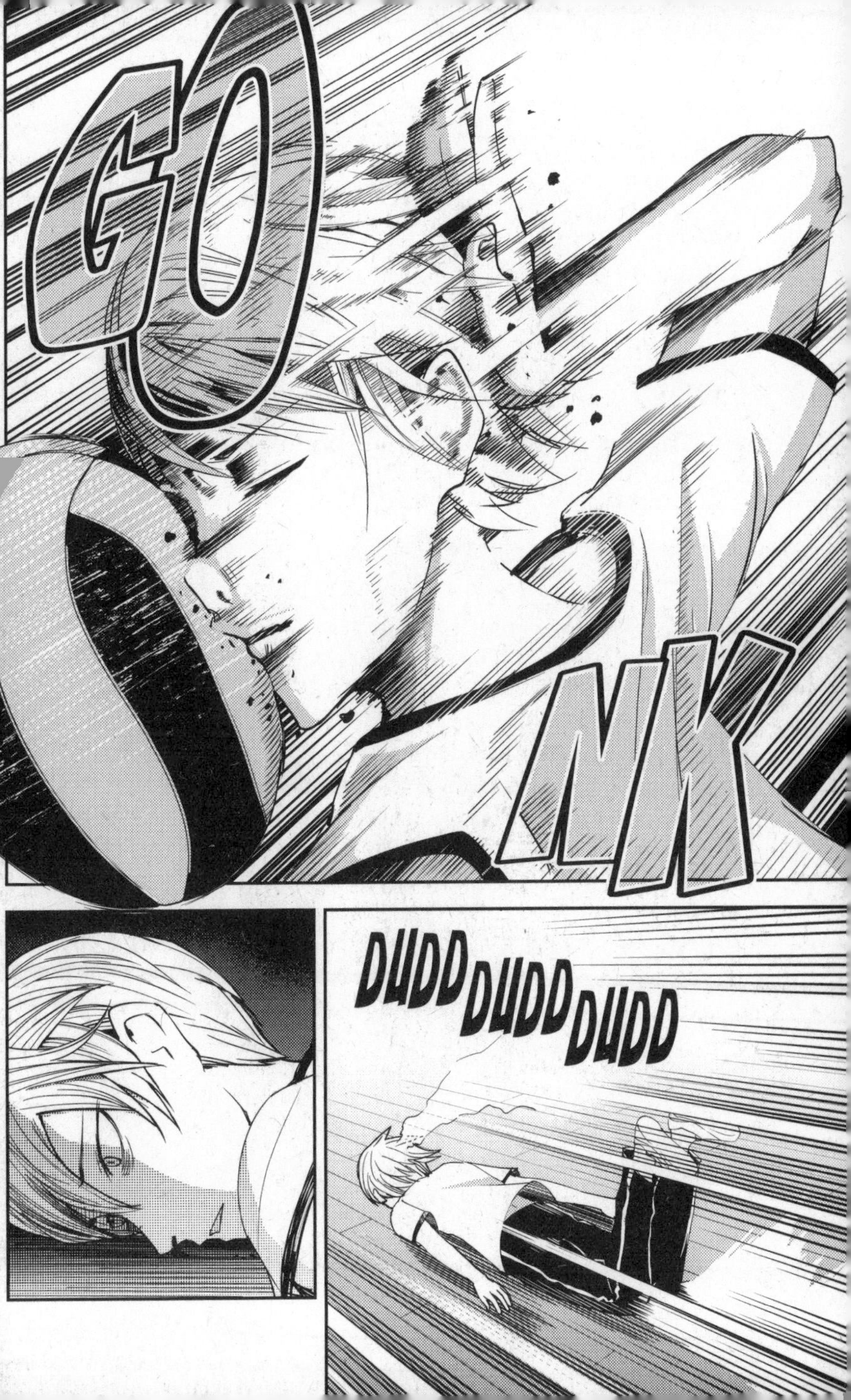
GO
NK
DUDD DUDD DUDD

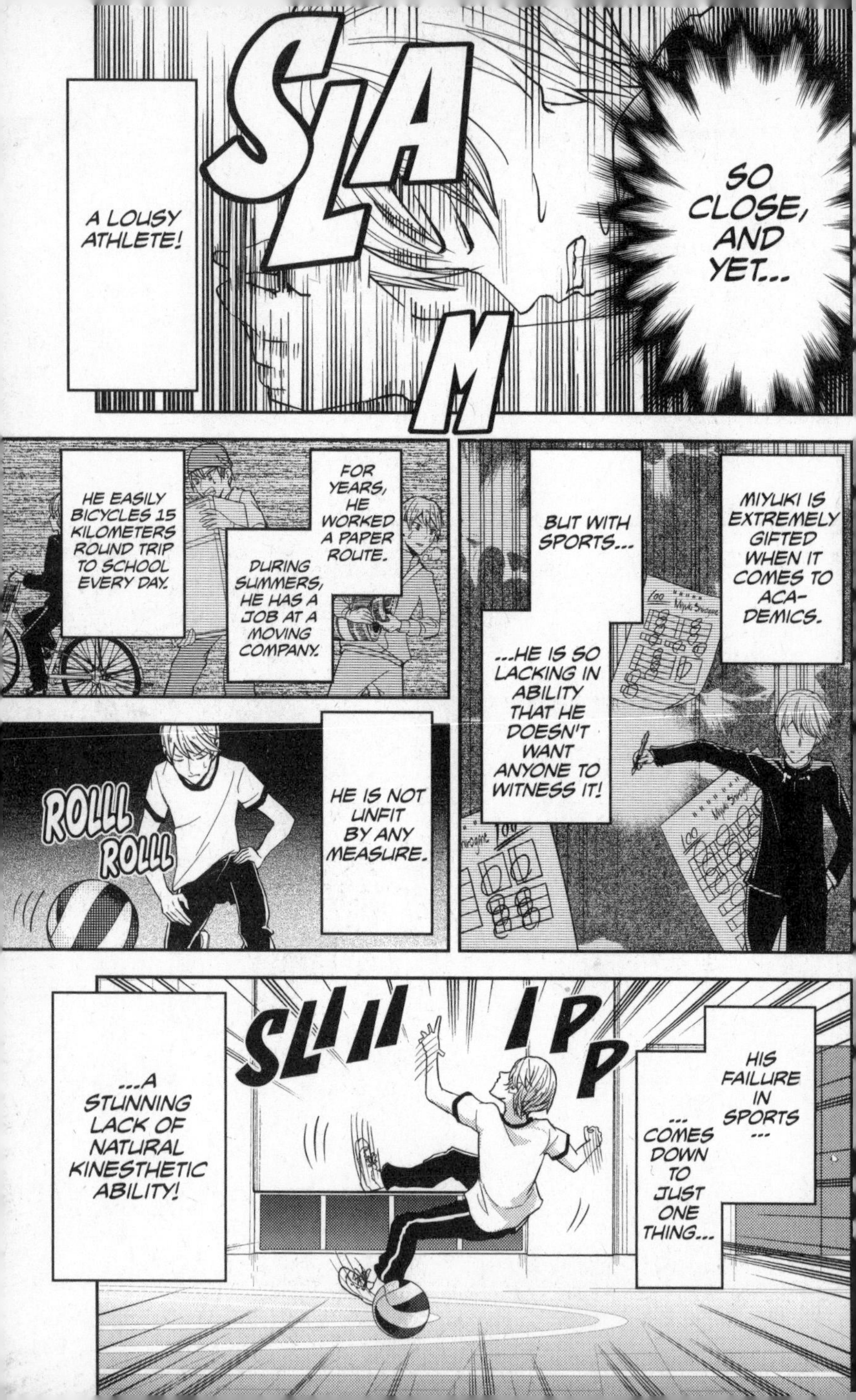
SO CLOSE, AND YET...
SLAM
A LOUSY ATHLETE!
MIYUKI IS EXTREMELY GIFTED WHEN IT COMES TO ACA-DEMICS.
BUT WITH SPORTS...
...HE IS SO LACKING IN ABILITY THAT HE DOESN'T WANT ANYONE TO WITNESS IT!
FOR YEARS, HE WORKED A PAPER ROUTE.
DURING SUMMERS, HE HAS A JOB AT A MOVING COMPANY.
HE EASILY BICYCLES 15 KILOMETERS ROUND TRIP TO SCHOOL EVERY DAY.
HE IS NOT UNFIT BY ANY MEASURE.
ROLLL ROLLL
HIS FAILURE IN SPORTS...
...COMES DOWN TO JUST ONE THING...
SLIIIPP
...A STUNNING LACK OF NATURAL KINESTHETIC ABILITY!

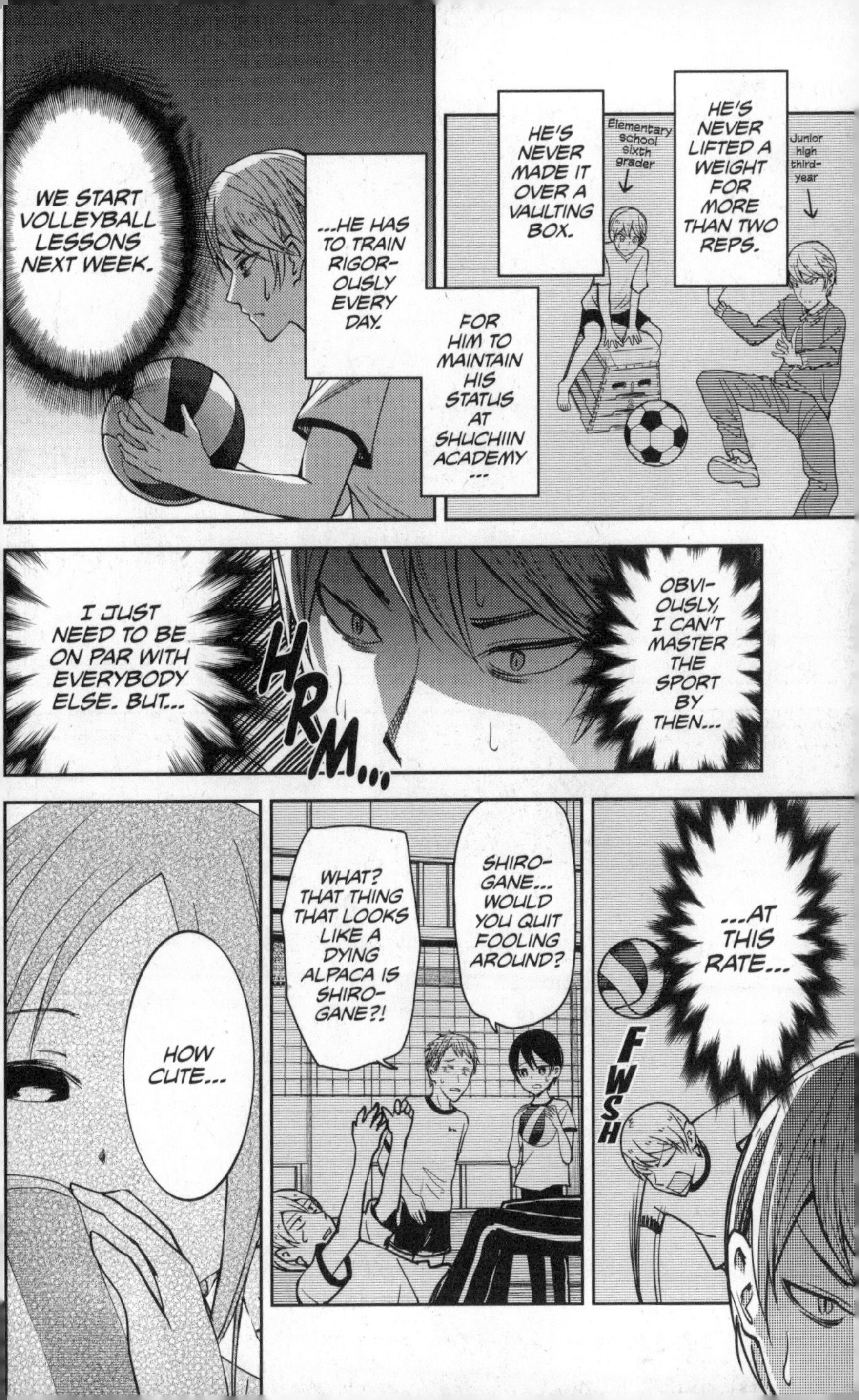
HE'S NEVER LIFTED A WEIGHT FOR MORE THAN TWO REPS.
Junior high third-year
HE'S NEVER MADE IT OVER A VAULTING BOX.
Elementary school sixth grader
FOR HIM TO MAINTAIN HIS STATUS AT SHUCHIIN ACADEMY...
...HE HAS TO TRAIN RIGOROUSLY EVERY DAY.
WE START VOLLEYBALL LESSONS NEXT WEEK.
OBVIOUSLY, I CAN'T MASTER THE SPORT BY THEN...
HRM...
I JUST NEED TO BE ON PAR WITH EVERYBODY ELSE. BUT...
...AT THIS RATE...
FWSH
SHIROGANE... WOULD YOU QUIT FOOLING AROUND?
WHAT? THAT THING THAT LOOKS LIKE A DYING ALPACA IS SHIROGANE?!
HOW CUTE...

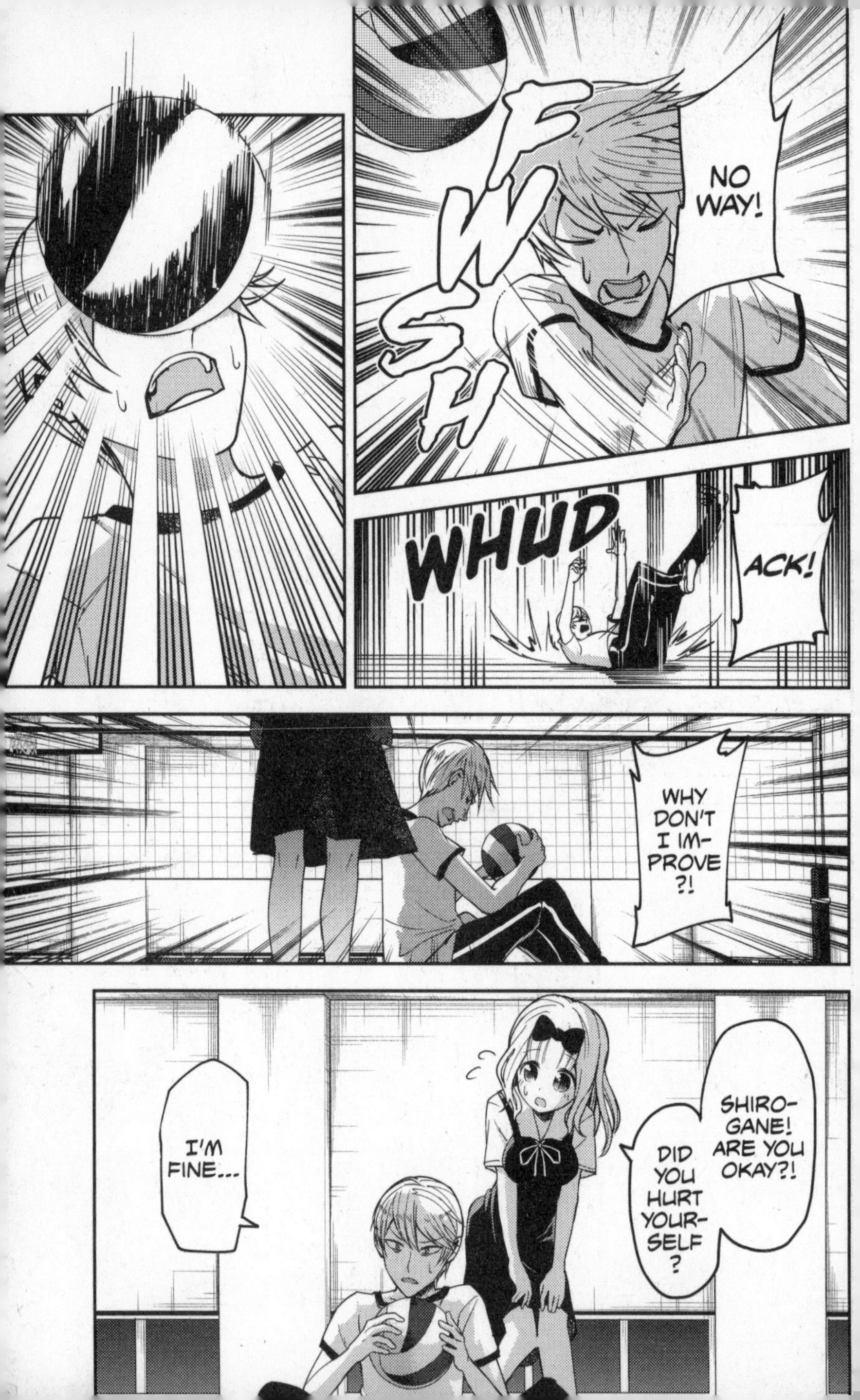
SWSH
NO WAY!
WHUD
ACK!
WHY DON'T I IM-PROVE?!
SHIRO-GANE! ARE YOU OKAY?!
DID YOU HURT YOUR-SELF?
I'M FINE...

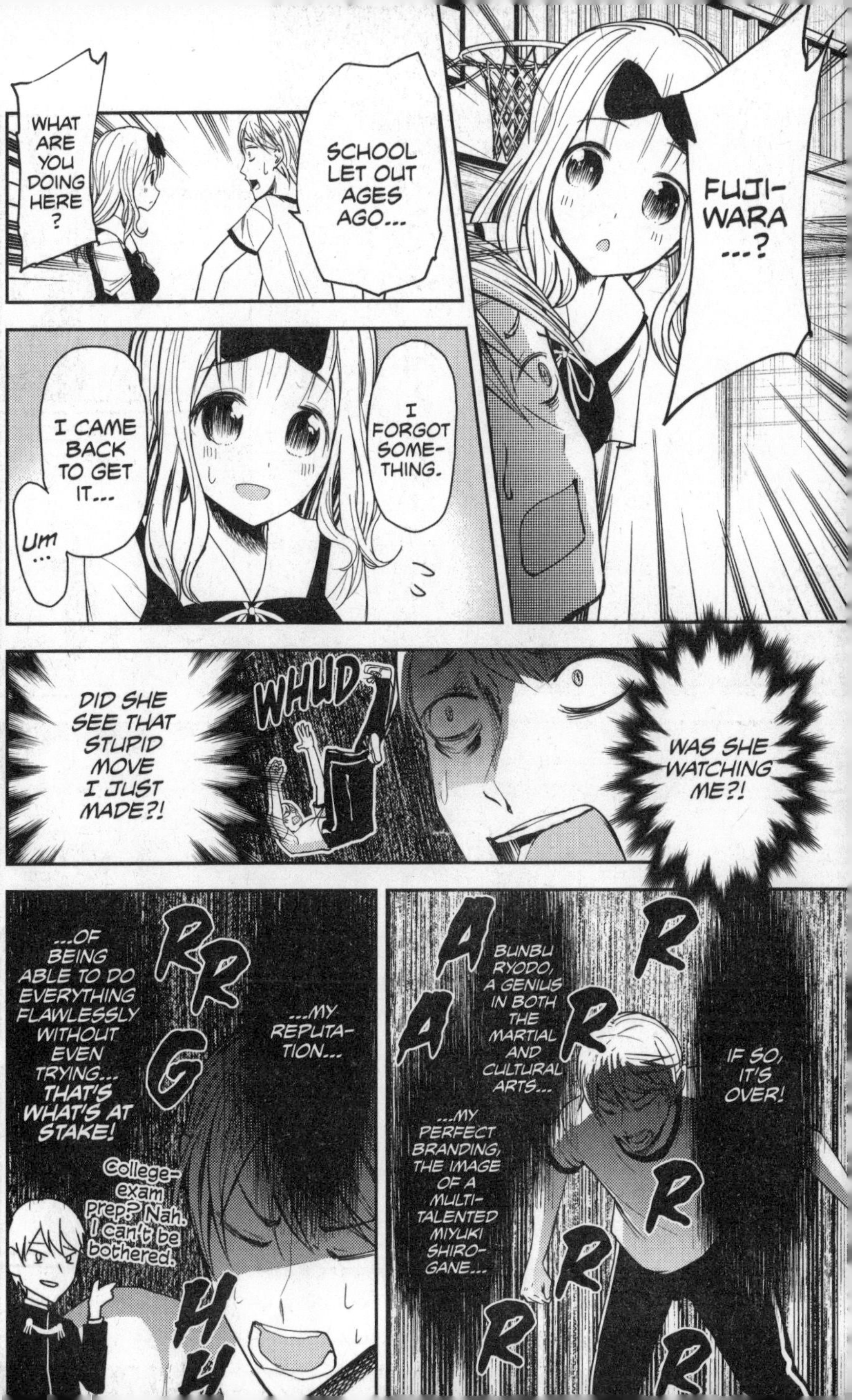
FUJI-WARA...?
SCHOOL LET OUT AGES AGO...
WHAT ARE YOU DOING HERE?
I FORGOT SOMETHING.
I CAME BACK TO GET IT...
Um...
WAS SHE WATCHING ME?!
WHUD
DID SHE SEE THAT STUPID MOVE I JUST MADE?!
IF SO, IT'S OVER!
BUNBU RYODO, A GENIUS IN BOTH THE MARTIAL AND CULTURAL ARTS...
...MY PERFECT BRANDING, THE IMAGE OF A MULTI-TALENTED MIYUKI SHIROGANE...
...MY REPUTATION...
...OF BEING ABLE TO DO EVERYTHING FLAWLESSLY WITHOUT EVEN TRYING... THAT'S WHAT'S AT STAKE!
College-exam prep? Nah. I can't be bothered.

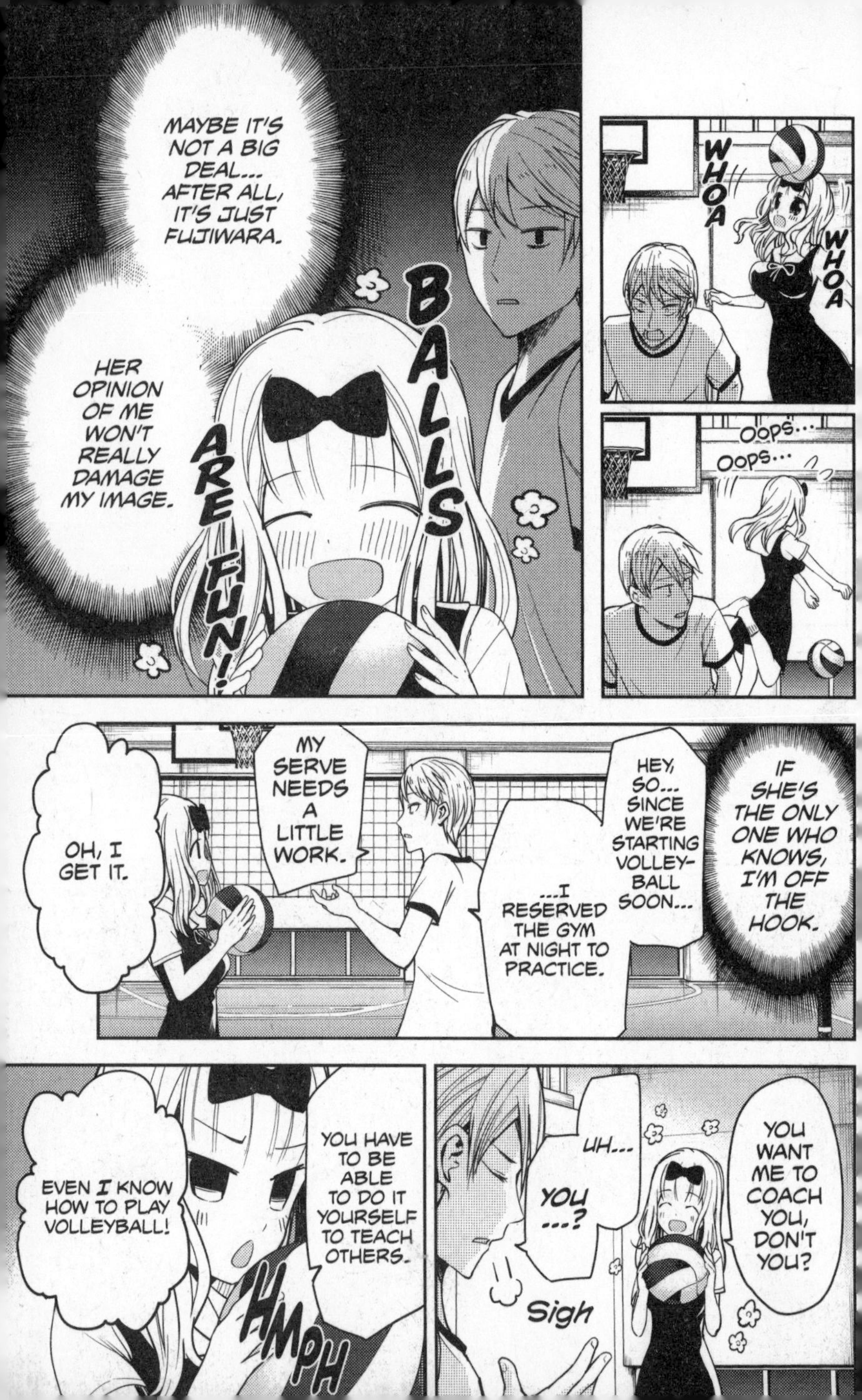
WHOA
WHOA
OOPS...
OOPS...
BALLS ARE FUN!
MAYBE IT'S NOT A BIG DEAL... AFTER ALL, IT'S JUST FUJIWARA.
HER OPINION OF ME WON'T REALLY DAMAGE MY IMAGE.
IF SHE'S THE ONLY ONE WHO KNOWS, I'M OFF THE HOOK.
HEY, SO... SINCE WE'RE STARTING VOLLEY-BALL SOON...
...I RESERVED THE GYM AT NIGHT TO PRACTICE.
MY SERVE NEEDS A LITTLE WORK.
OH, I GET IT.
YOU WANT ME TO COACH YOU, DON'T YOU?
UH...
YOU ...?
Sigh
YOU HAVE TO BE ABLE TO DO IT YOURSELF TO TEACH OTHERS.
EVEN I KNOW HOW TO PLAY VOLLEYBALL!
HMPH

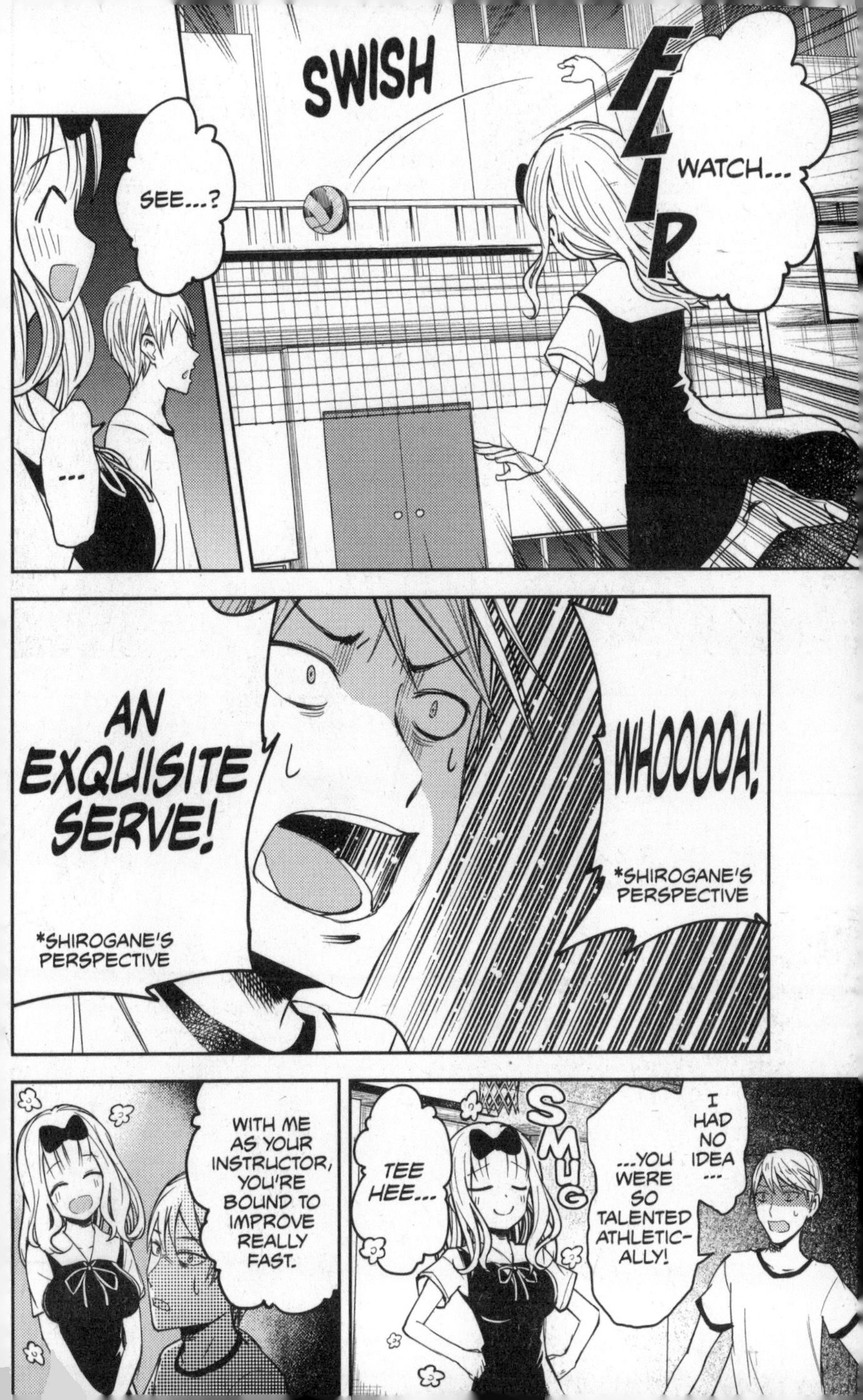
FLIP
WATCH...
SWISH
SEE...?
...
WHOOOOA!
*SHIROGANE'S PERSPECTIVE
AN EXQUISITE SERVE!
*SHIROGANE'S PERSPECTIVE
I HAD NO IDEA...
...YOU WERE SO TALENTED ATHLETIC-ALLY!
SMUG
TEE HEE...
WITH ME AS YOUR INSTRUCTOR, YOU'RE BOUND TO IMPROVE REALLY FAST.

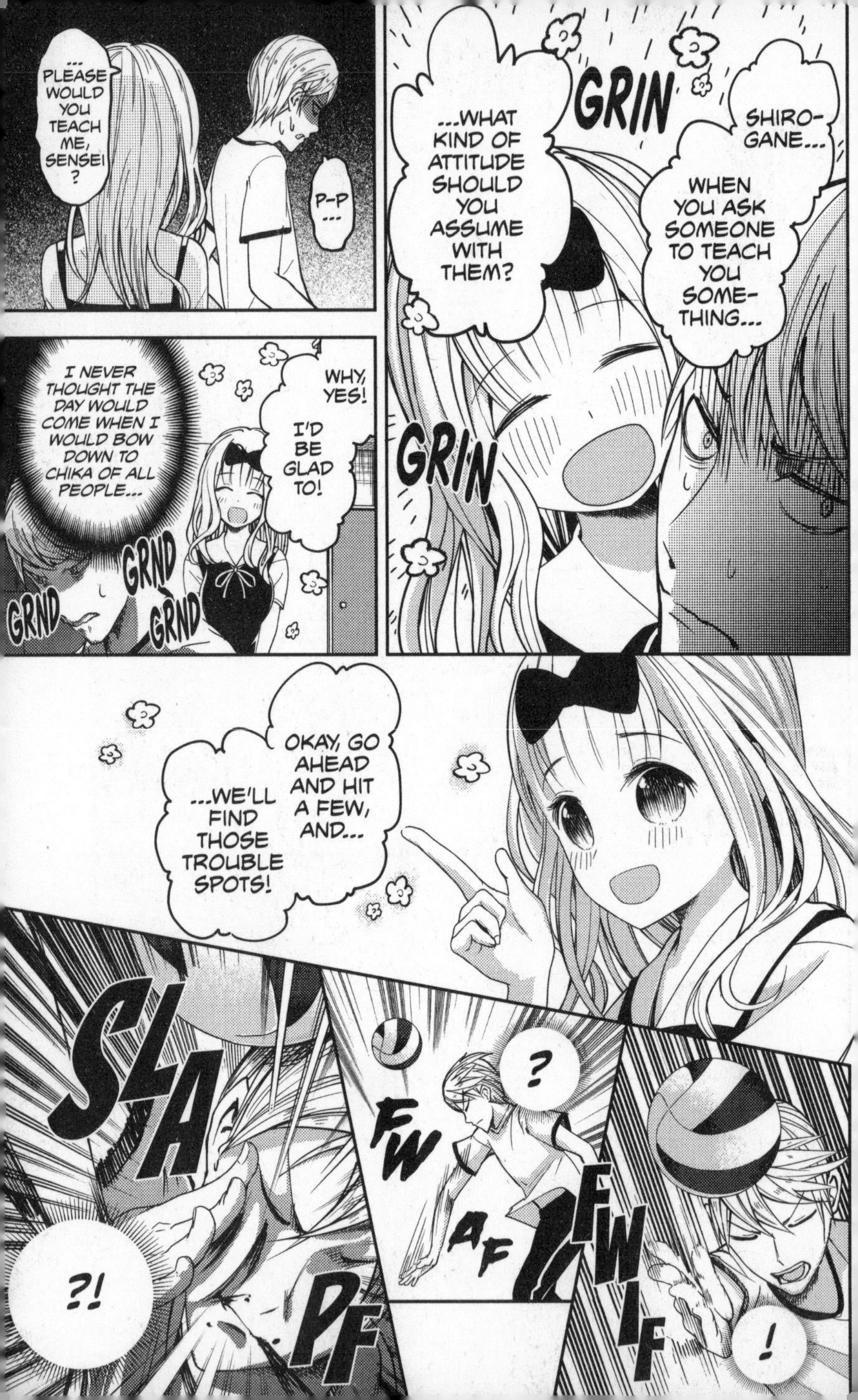
GRIN
SHIRO-GANE...
WHEN YOU ASK SOMEONE TO TEACH YOU SOME-THING...
...WHAT KIND OF ATTITUDE SHOULD YOU ASSUME WITH THEM?
GRIN
P-P...
...PLEASE WOULD YOU TEACH ME, SENSEI?
WHY, YES!
I'D BE GLAD TO!
I NEVER THOUGHT THE DAY WOULD COME WHEN I WOULD BOW DOWN TO CHIKA OF ALL PEOPLE...
GRND
GRND
GRND
OKAY, GO AHEAD AND HIT A FEW, AND...
...WE'LL FIND THOSE TROUBLE SPOTS!
FWIF
!
?
FW
AF
SLA
PF
?!

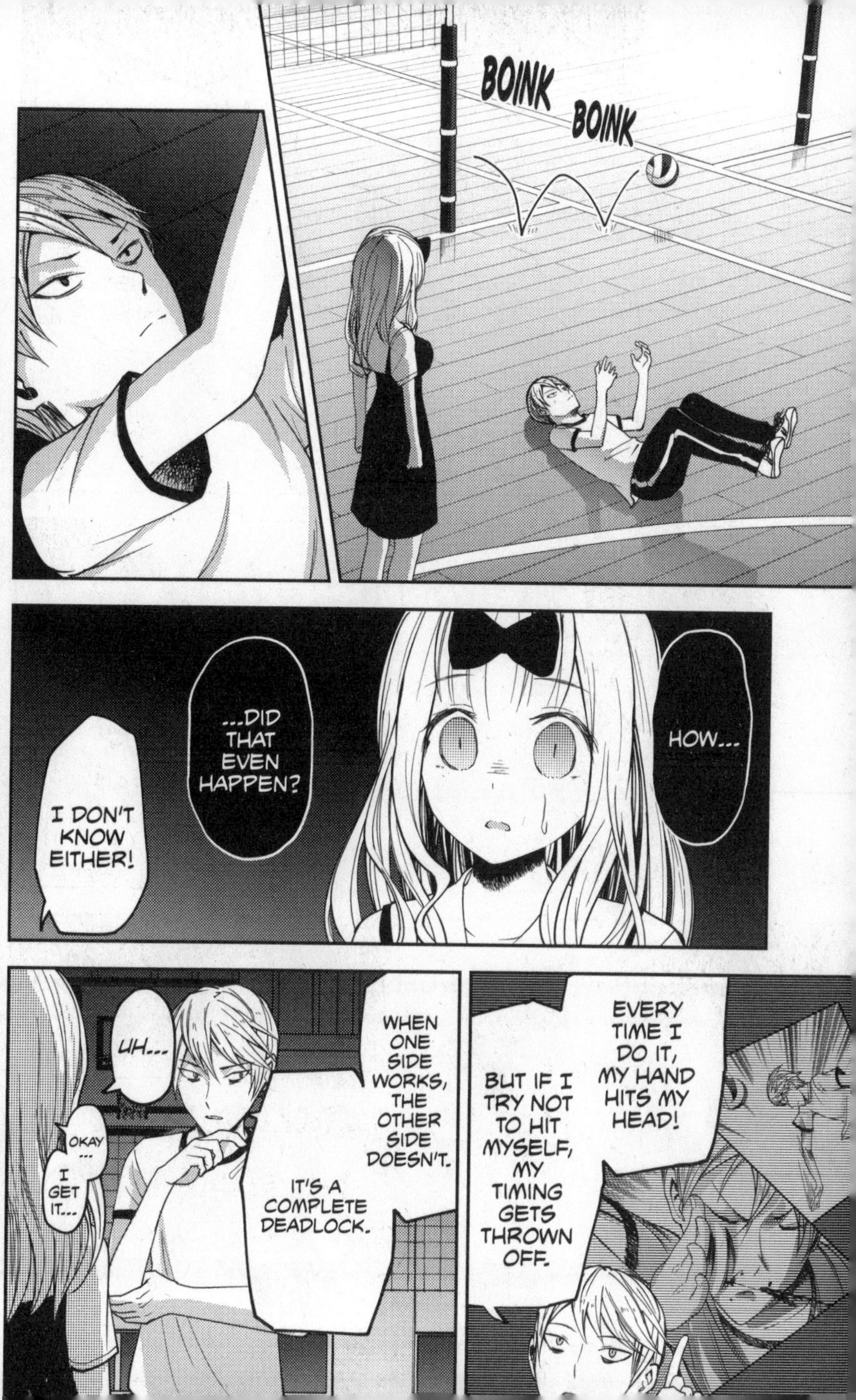
BOINK
BOINK
HOW...
...DID THAT EVEN HAPPEN?
I DON'T KNOW EITHER!
EVERY TIME I DO IT, MY HAND HITS MY HEAD!
BUT IF I TRY NOT TO HIT MYSELF, MY TIMING GETS THROWN OFF.
WHEN ONE SIDE WORKS, THE OTHER SIDE DOESN'T.
IT'S A COMPLETE DEADLOCK.
UH...
OKAY... I GET IT...

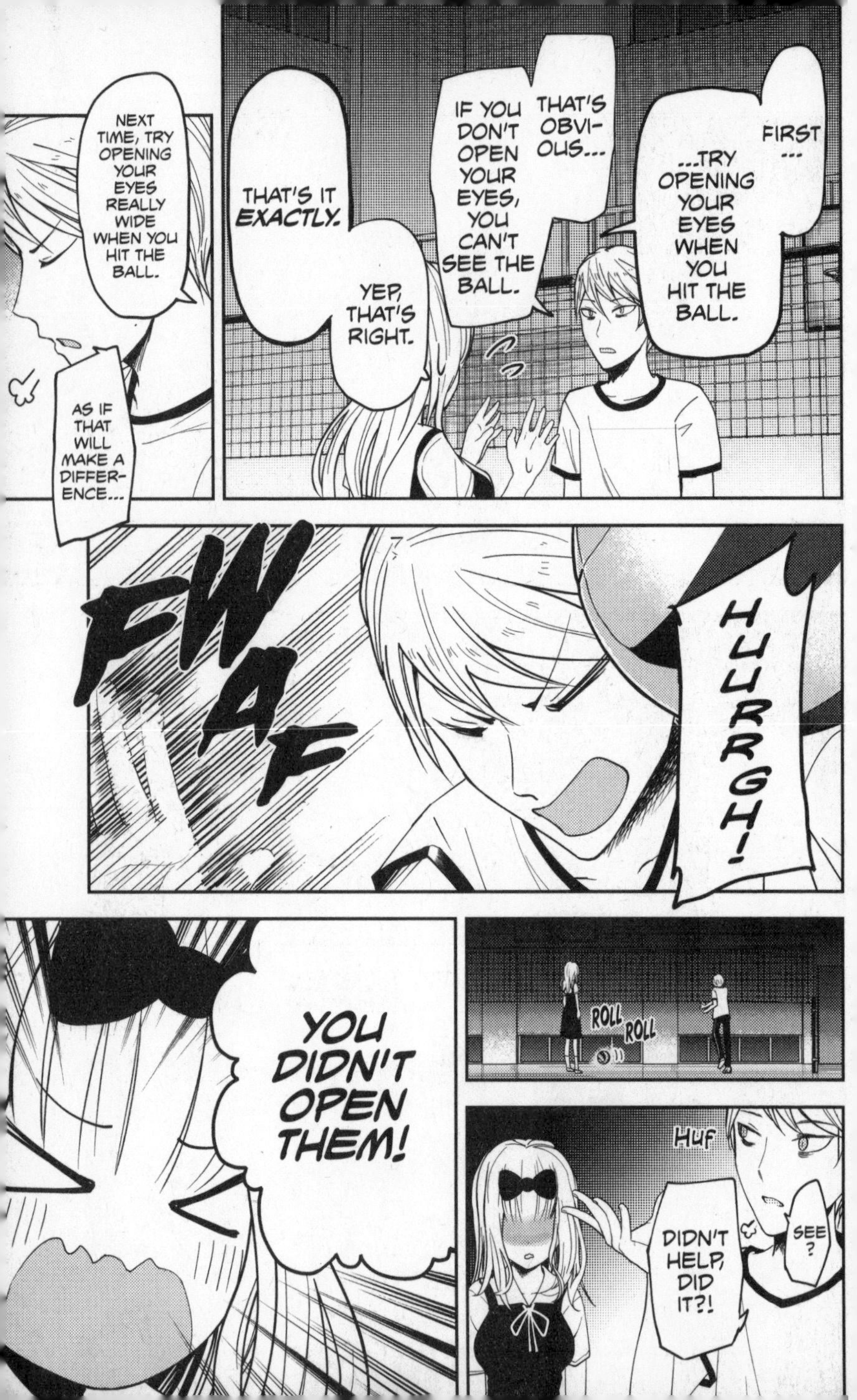
FIRST---
...TRY OPENING YOUR EYES WHEN YOU HIT THE BALL.
THAT'S OBVIOUS...
IF YOU DON'T OPEN YOUR EYES, YOU CAN'T SEE THE BALL.
THAT'S IT EXACTLY.
YEP, THAT'S RIGHT.
NEXT TIME, TRY OPENING YOUR EYES REALLY WIDE WHEN YOU HIT THE BALL.
AS IF THAT WILL MAKE A DIFFERENCE...
HUURRGH!
FWAF
ROLL
ROLL
Huf
SEE?
DIDN'T HELP, DID IT?!
YOU DIDN'T OPEN THEM!

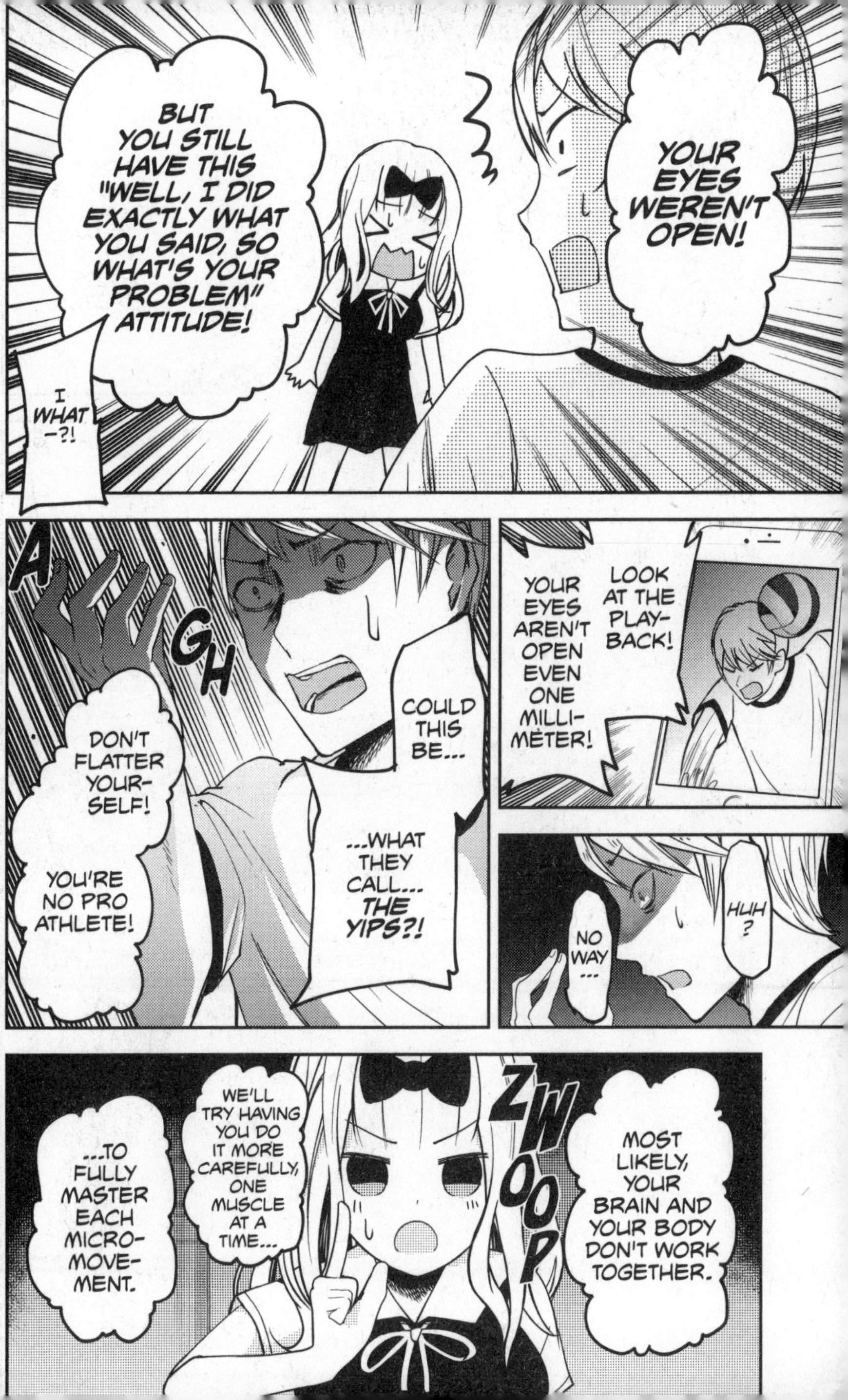
YOUR EYES WEREN'T OPEN!
BUT YOU STILL HAVE THIS "WELL, I DID EXACTLY WHAT YOU SAID, SO WHAT'S YOUR PROBLEM" ATTITUDE!
I WHAT—?!
LOOK AT THE PLAY-BACK!
YOUR EYES AREN'T OPEN EVEN ONE MILLI-METER!
HUH?
NO WAY...
AGH
COULD THIS BE...
...WHAT THEY CALL... THE YIPS?!
DON'T FLATTER YOUR-SELF!
YOU'RE NO PRO ATHLETE!
MOST LIKELY, YOUR BRAIN AND YOUR BODY DON'T WORK TOGETHER.
ZWOOP
WE'LL TRY HAVING YOU DO IT MORE CAREFULLY, ONE MUSCLE AT A TIME...
...TO FULLY MASTER EACH MICRO-MOVE-MENT.

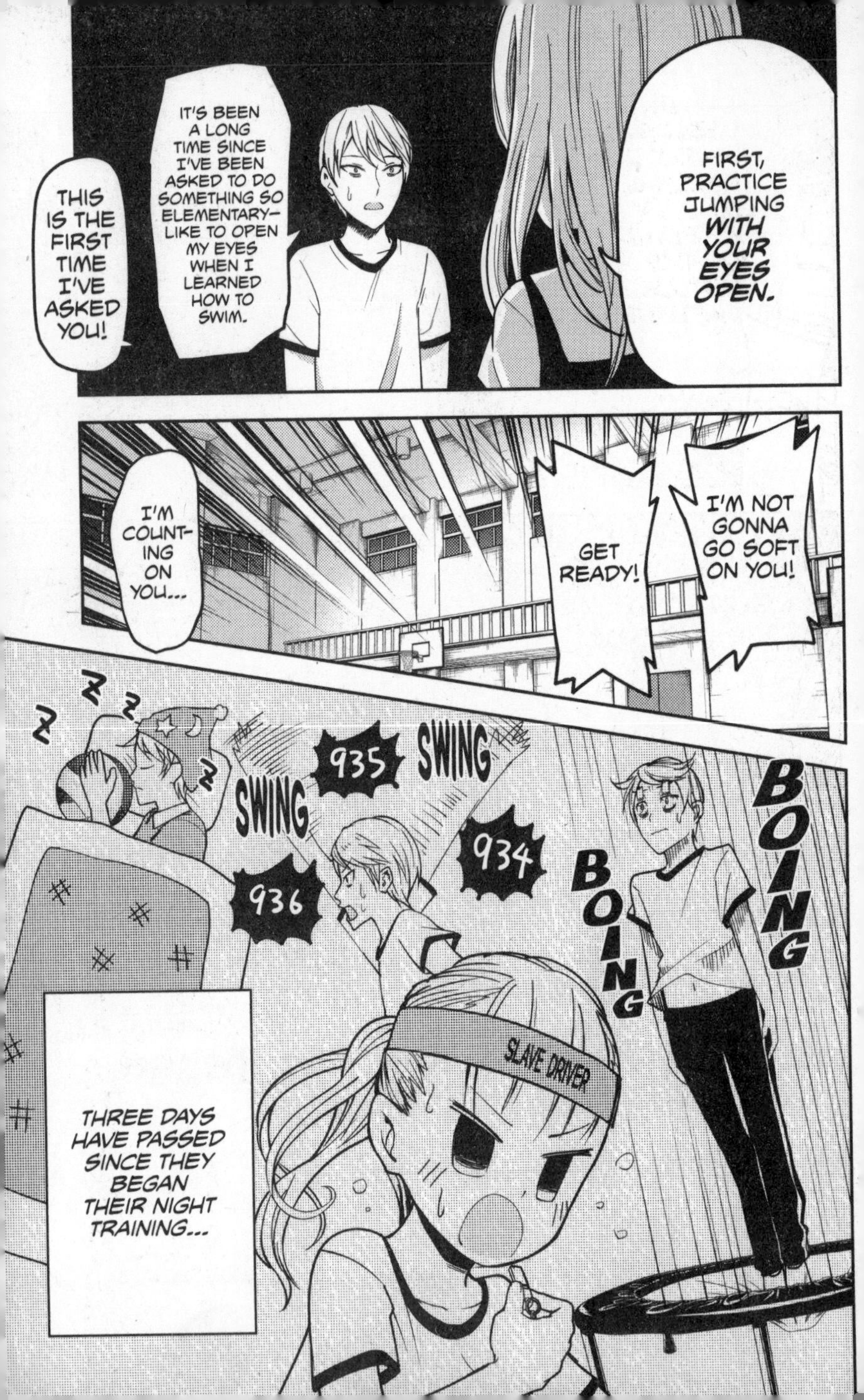
FIRST, PRACTICE JUMPING WITH YOUR EYES OPEN.
IT'S BEEN A LONG TIME SINCE I'VE BEEN ASKED TO DO SOMETHING SO ELEMENTARY—LIKE TO OPEN MY EYES WHEN I LEARNED HOW TO SWIM.
THIS IS THE FIRST TIME I'VE ASKED YOU!
I'M NOT GONNA GO SOFT ON YOU!
GET READY!
I'M COUNTING ON YOU...
BOING
BOING
934
SWING
935
SWING
936
Z Z Z Z
SLAVE DRIVER
THREE DAYS HAVE PASSED SINCE THEY BEGAN THEIR NIGHT TRAINING...

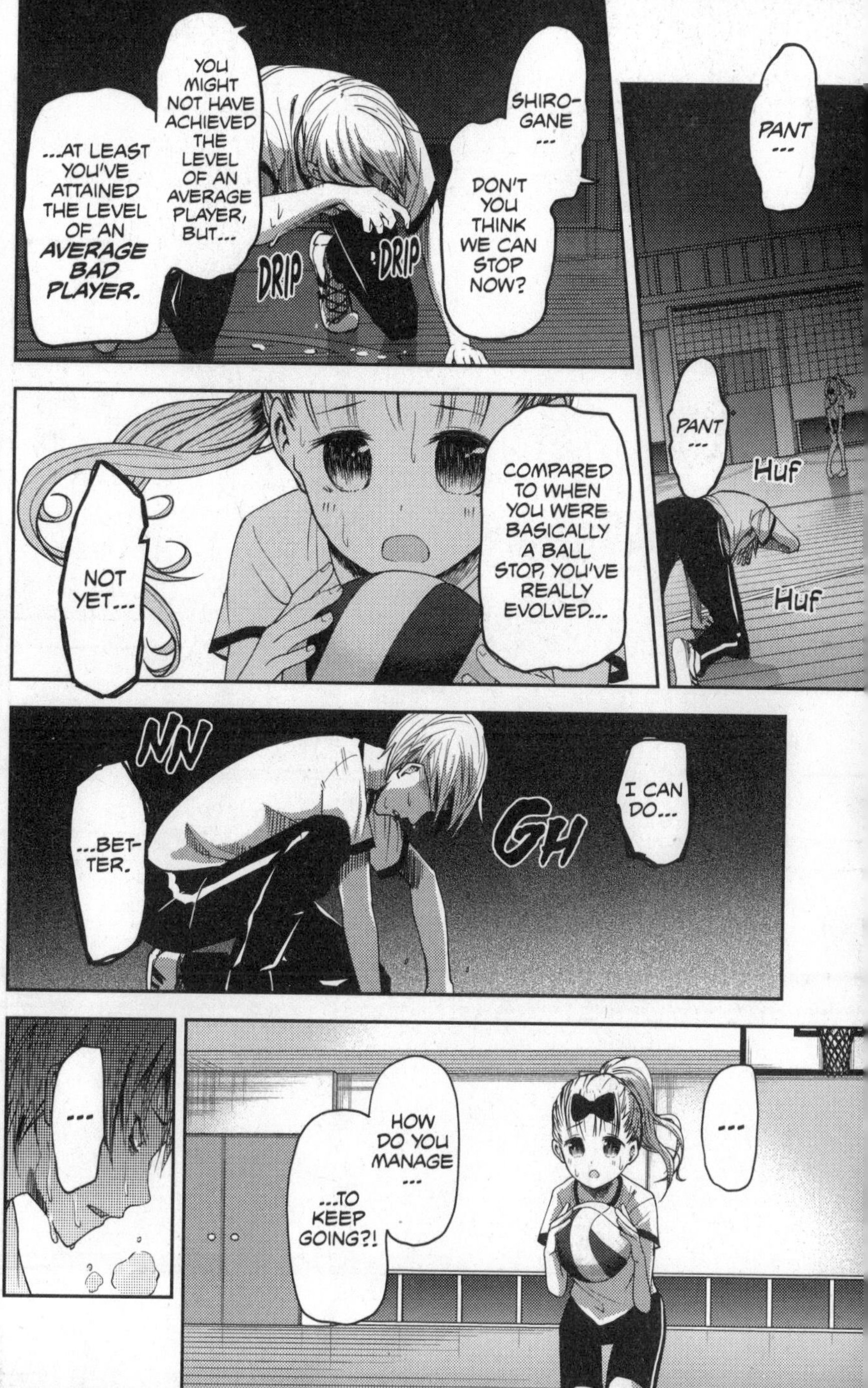
PANT...
PANT...
Huf
Huf
SHIRO-GANE...
DON'T YOU THINK WE CAN STOP NOW?
DRIP
DRIP
YOU MIGHT NOT HAVE ACHIEVED THE LEVEL OF AN AVERAGE PLAYER, BUT...
...AT LEAST YOU'VE ATTAINED THE LEVEL OF AN AVERAGE BAD PLAYER.
COMPARED TO WHEN YOU WERE BASICALLY A BALL STOP, YOU'VE REALLY EVOLVED...
NOT YET...
I CAN DO...
GH
NN
...BET-TER.
...
HOW DO YOU MANAGE...
...TO KEEP GOING?!
...

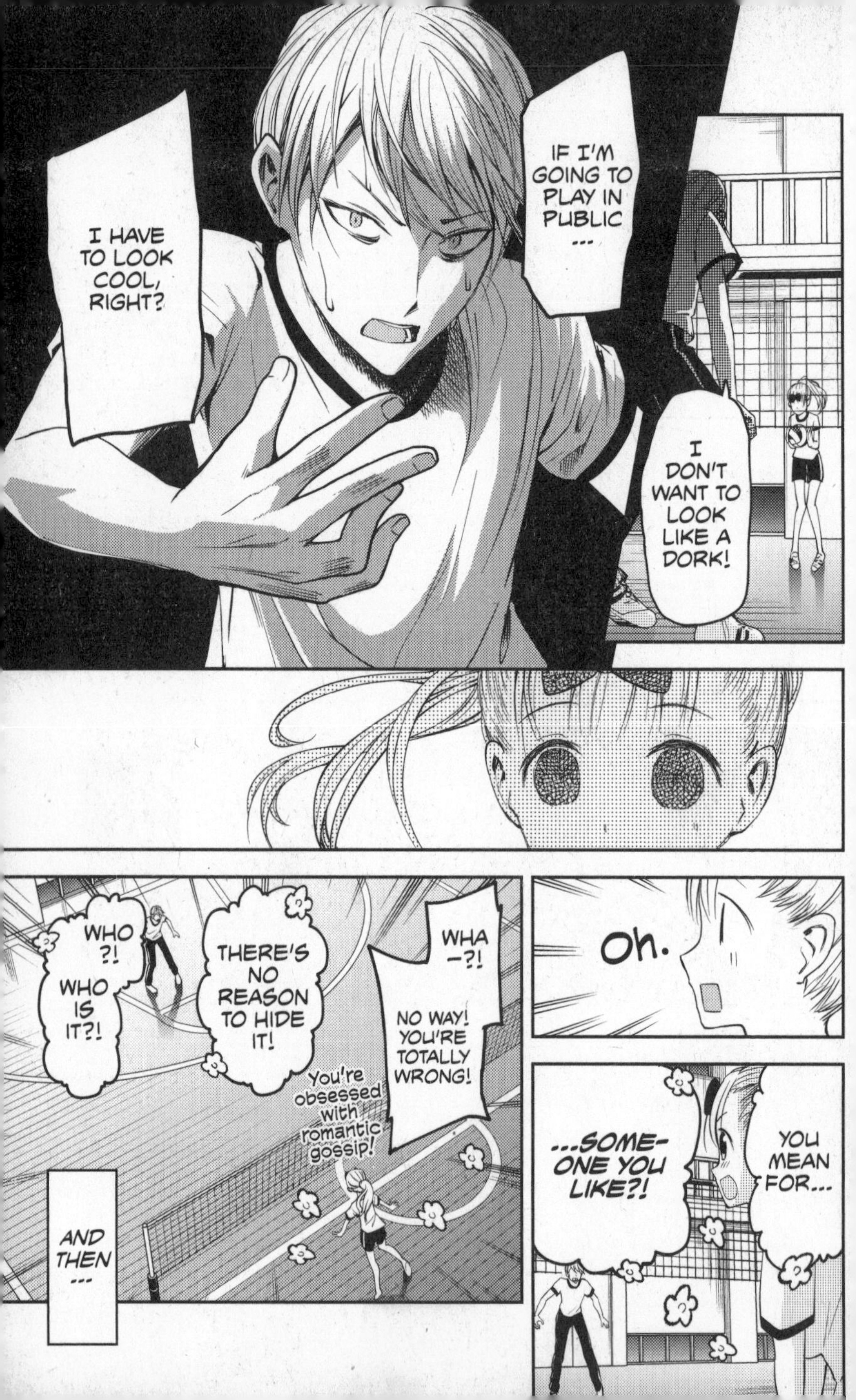

IF I'M GOING TO PLAY IN PUBLIC...
I HAVE TO LOOK COOL, RIGHT?
I DON'T WANT TO LOOK LIKE A DORK!
Oh.
YOU MEAN FOR...
...SOME-ONE YOU LIKE?!
WHA—?!
NO WAY! YOU'RE TOTALLY WRONG!
You're obsessed with romantic gossip!
THERE'S NO REASON TO HIDE IT!
WHO?! WHO IS IT?!
AND THEN...

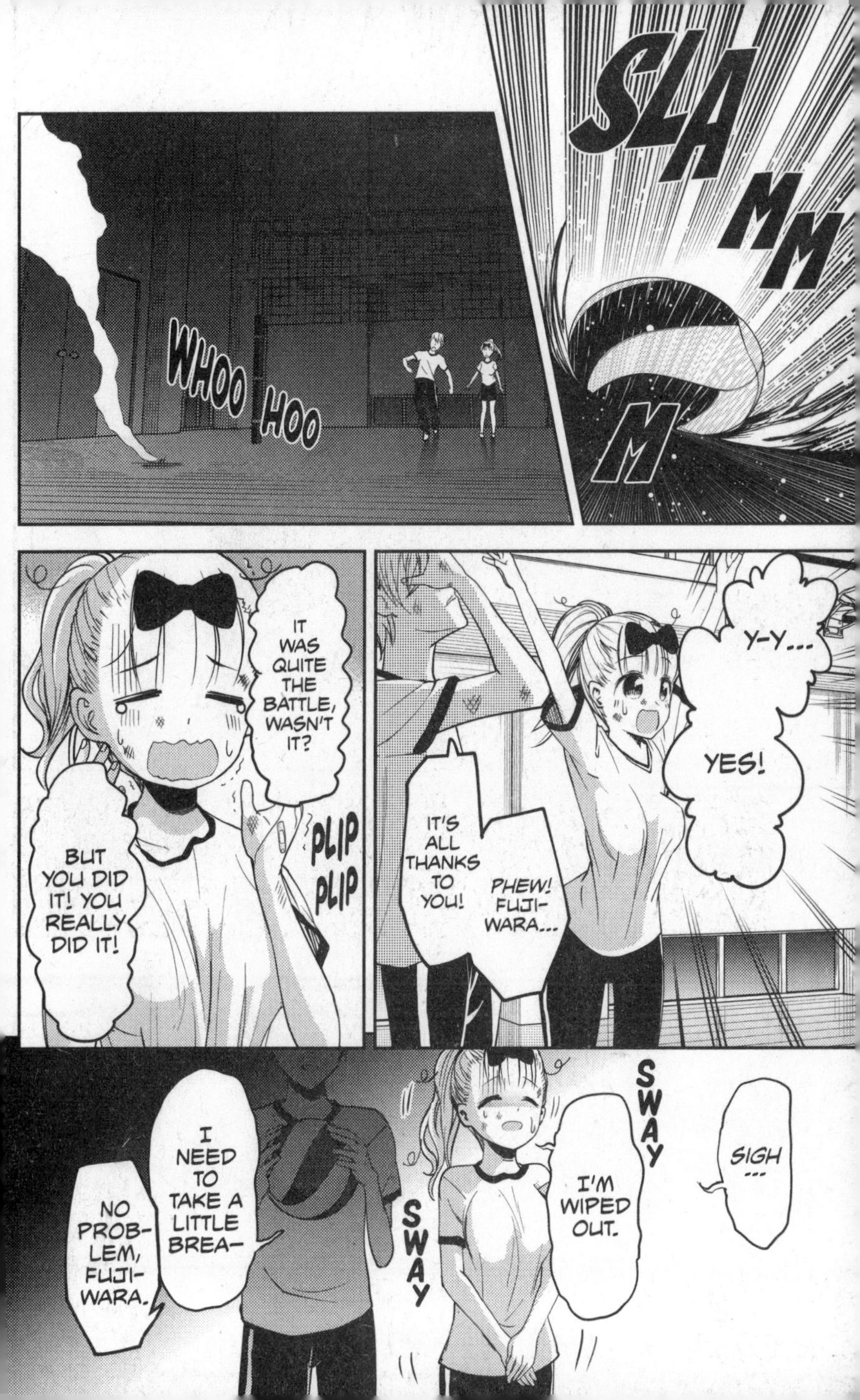
SLAMMM
WHOO HOO
Y-Y... YES!
PHEW! FUJI-WARA...
IT'S ALL THANKS TO YOU!
IT WAS QUITE THE BATTLE, WASN'T IT?
PLIP PLIP
BUT YOU DID IT! YOU REALLY DID IT!
SIGH...
SWAY SWAY
I'M WIPED OUT.
I NEED TO TAKE A LITTLE BREA—
NO PROB-LEM, FUJI-WARA.

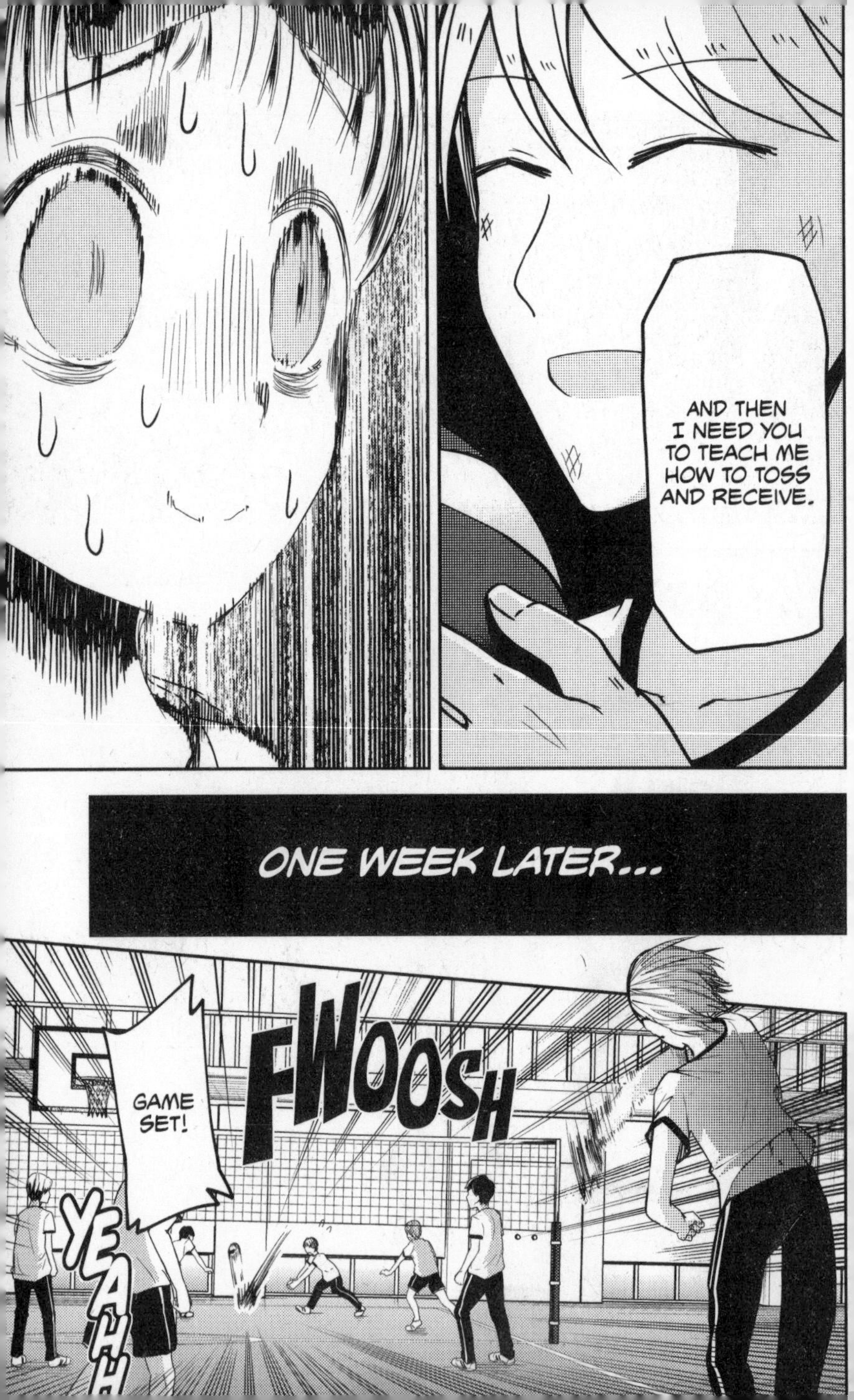
AND THEN I NEED YOU TO TEACH ME HOW TO TOSS AND RECEIVE.
ONE WEEK LATER...
FWOOSH
GAME SET!
YEAHHH

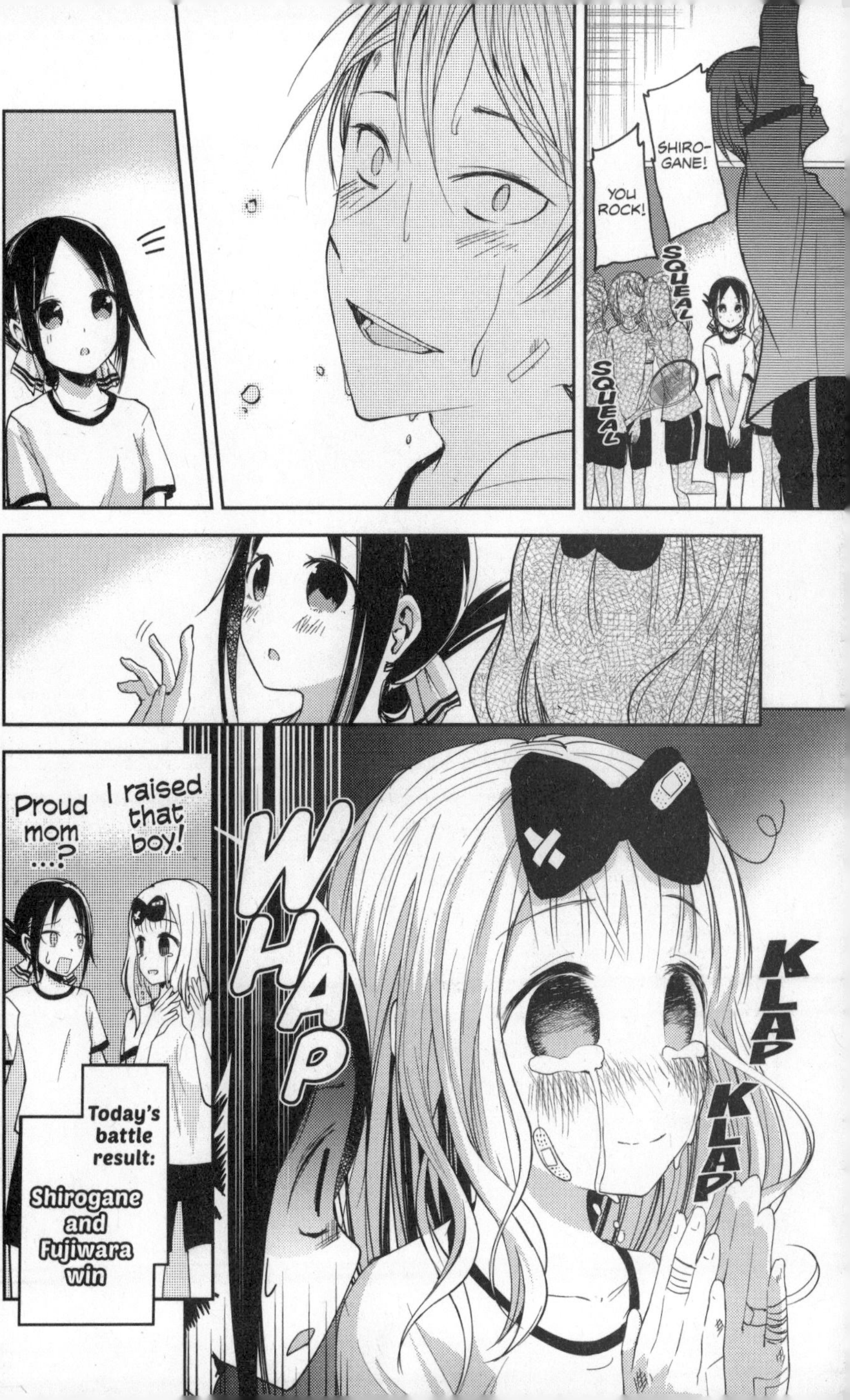
SHIRO-GANE!
YOU ROCK!
SQUEAL
SQUEAL
WHAP
KLAP KLAP
I raised that boy!
Proud mom ...?
Today's battle result:
Shirogane and Fujiwara win

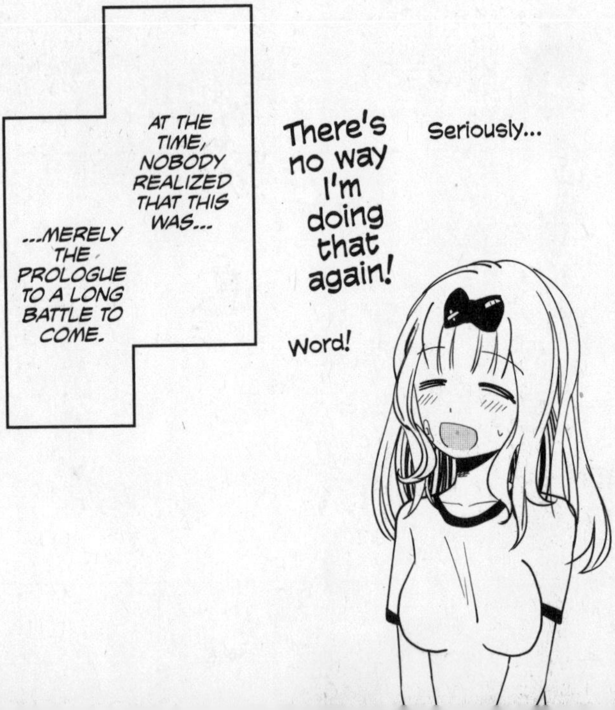

Seriously...
There's no way I'm doing that again!
Word!
AT THE TIME, NOBODY REALIZED THAT THIS WAS...
...MERELY THE PROLOGUE TO A LONG BATTLE TO COME.

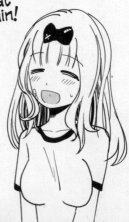

KAGUYA-SAMA

LOVE IS WAR

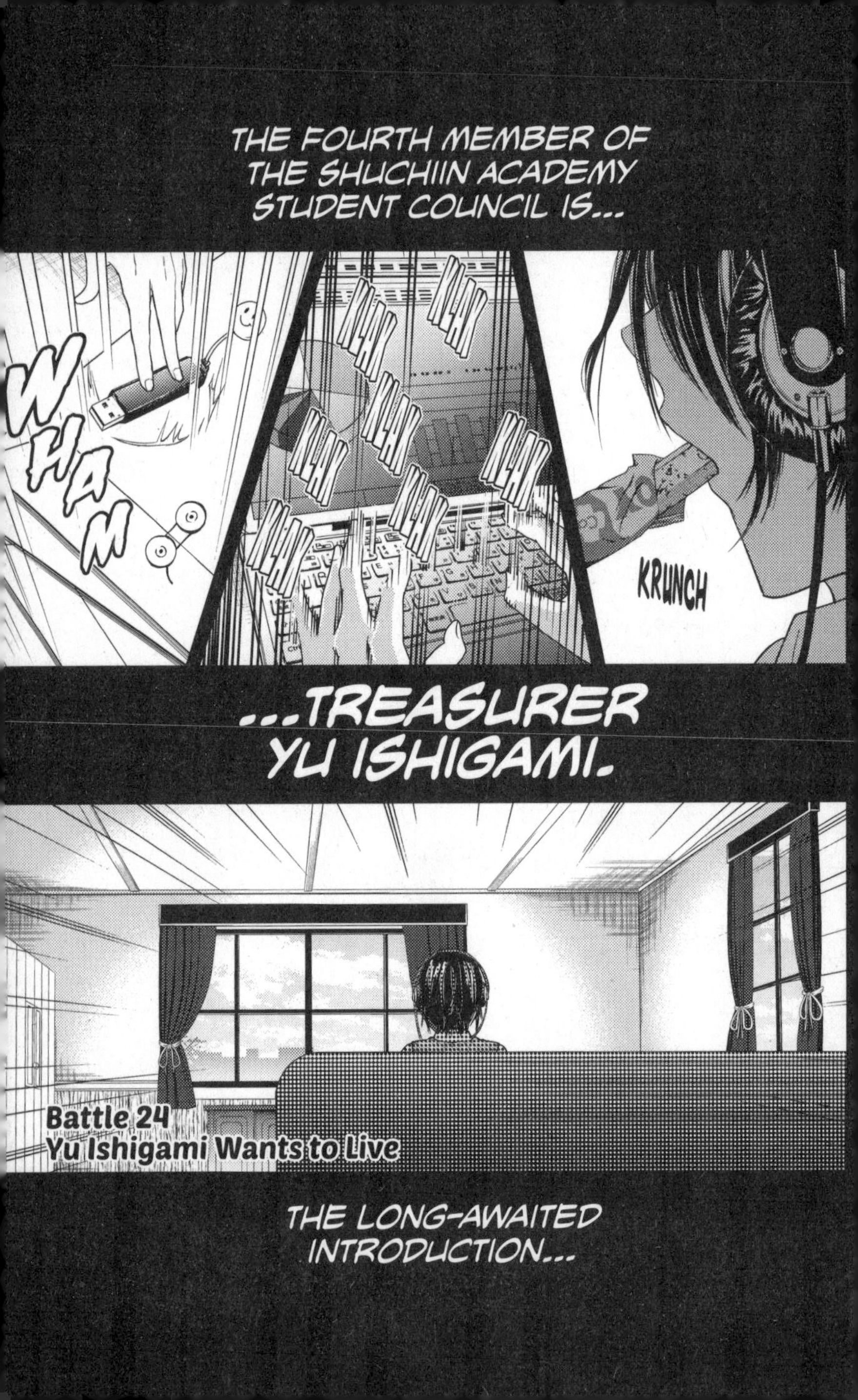
THE FOURTH MEMBER OF THE SHUCHIIN ACADEMY STUDENT COUNCIL IS...
KRUNCH
KLAK KLAK KLAK KLAK KLAK KLAK KLAK KLAK
WHAM
...TREASURER YU ISHIGAMI.
Battle 24
Yu Ishigami Wants to Live
THE LONG-AWAITED INTRODUCTION...

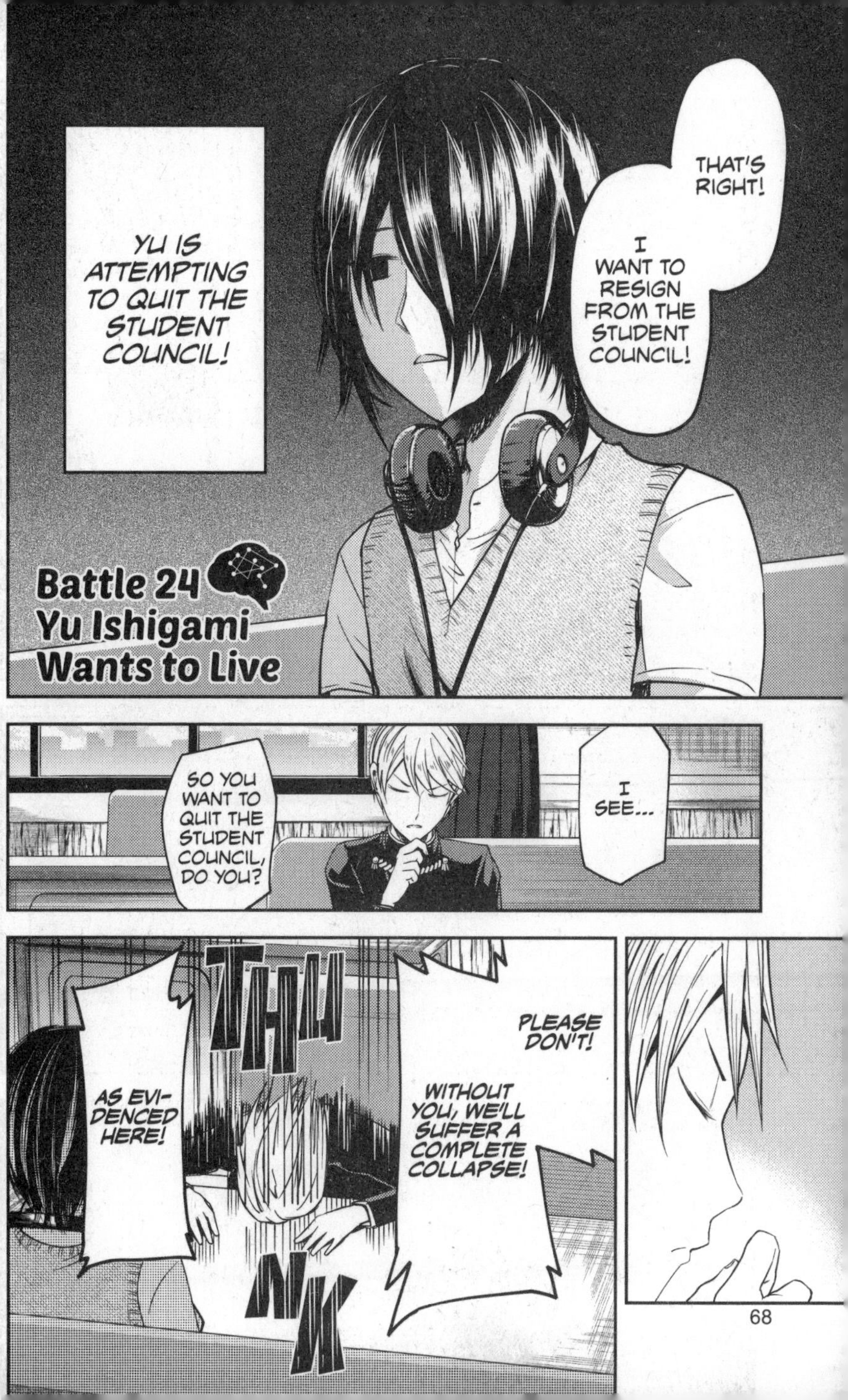
THAT'S RIGHT!
I WANT TO RESIGN FROM THE STUDENT COUNCIL!
YU IS ATTEMPTING TO QUIT THE STUDENT COUNCIL!
Battle 24
Yu Ishigami Wants to Live
I SEE...
SO YOU WANT TO QUIT THE STUDENT COUNCIL, DO YOU?
PLEASE DON'T!
WITHOUT YOU, WE'LL SUFFER A COMPLETE COLLAPSE!
THUNK
AS EVI-DENCED HERE!

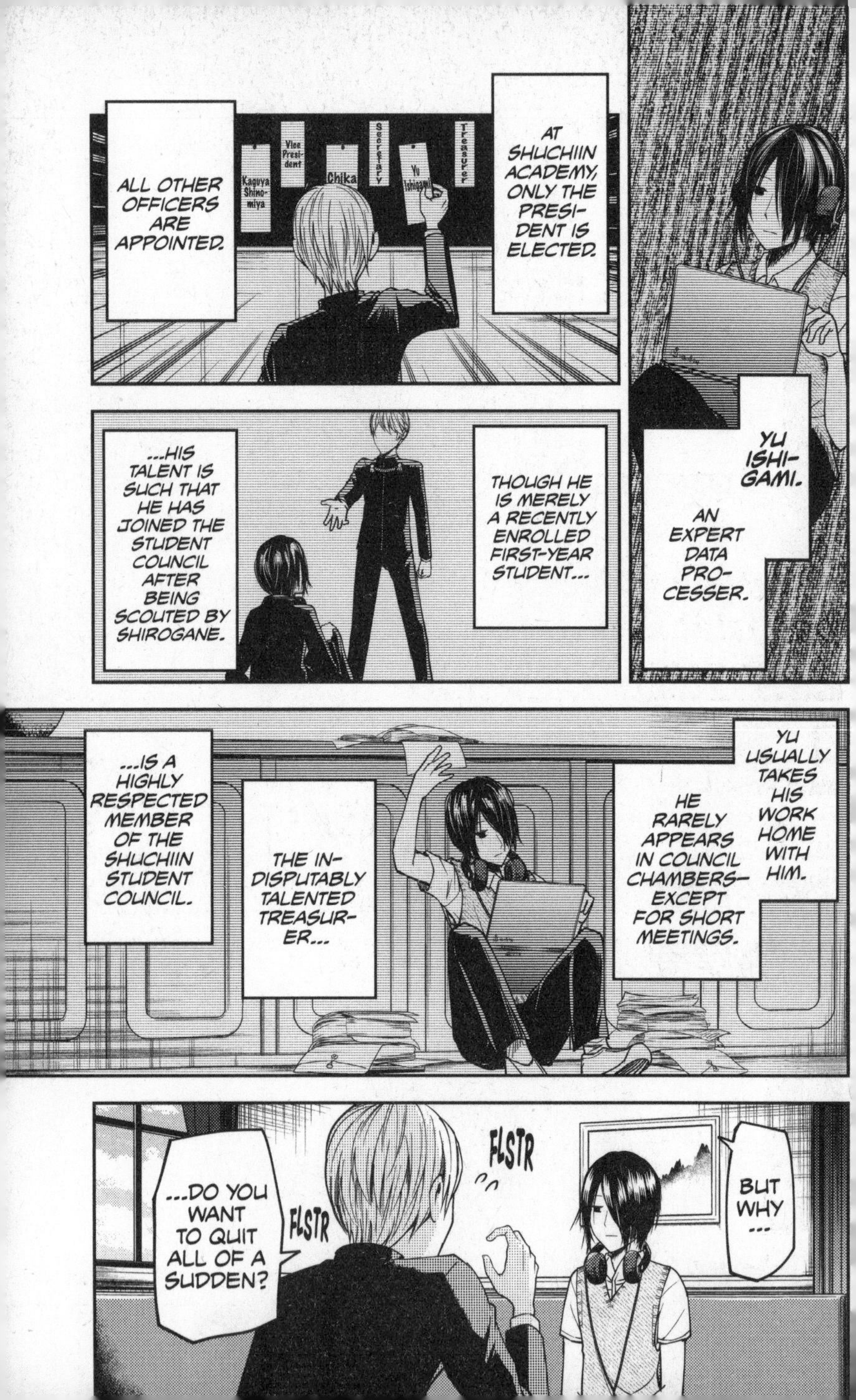
YU ISHIGAMI.
AN EXPERT DATA PROCESSER.
AT SHUCHIIN ACADEMY, ONLY THE PRESIDENT IS ELECTED.
Treasurer
Yu Ishigami
Secretary
Chika
Vice President
Kaguya Shinomiya
ALL OTHER OFFICERS ARE APPOINTED.
THOUGH HE IS MERELY A RECENTLY ENROLLED FIRST-YEAR STUDENT...
...HIS TALENT IS SUCH THAT HE HAS JOINED THE STUDENT COUNCIL AFTER BEING SCOUTED BY SHIROGANE.
YU USUALLY TAKES HIS WORK HOME WITH HIM.
HE RARELY APPEARS IN COUNCIL CHAMBERS—EXCEPT FOR SHORT MEETINGS.
THE INDISPUTABLY TALENTED TREASURER...
...IS A HIGHLY RESPECTED MEMBER OF THE SHUCHIIN STUDENT COUNCIL.
BUT WHY...
FLSTR
FLSTR
...DO YOU WANT TO QUIT ALL OF A SUDDEN?

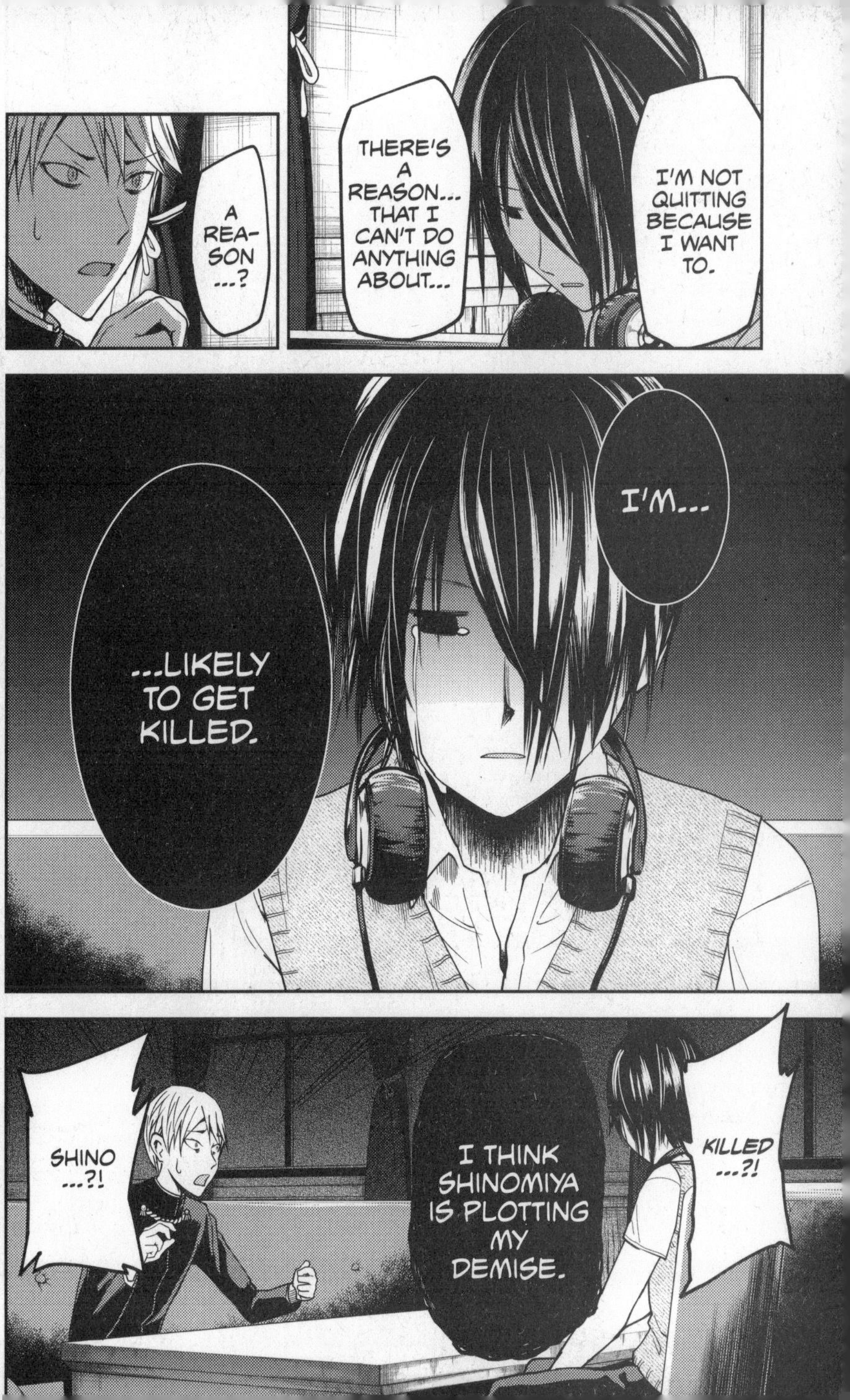
I'M NOT QUITTING BECAUSE I WANT TO.
THERE'S A REASON... THAT I CAN'T DO ANYTHING ABOUT...
A REA-SON ...?
I'M...
...LIKELY TO GET KILLED.
KILLED ...?!
I THINK SHINOMIYA IS PLOTTING MY DEMISE.
SHINO ...?!

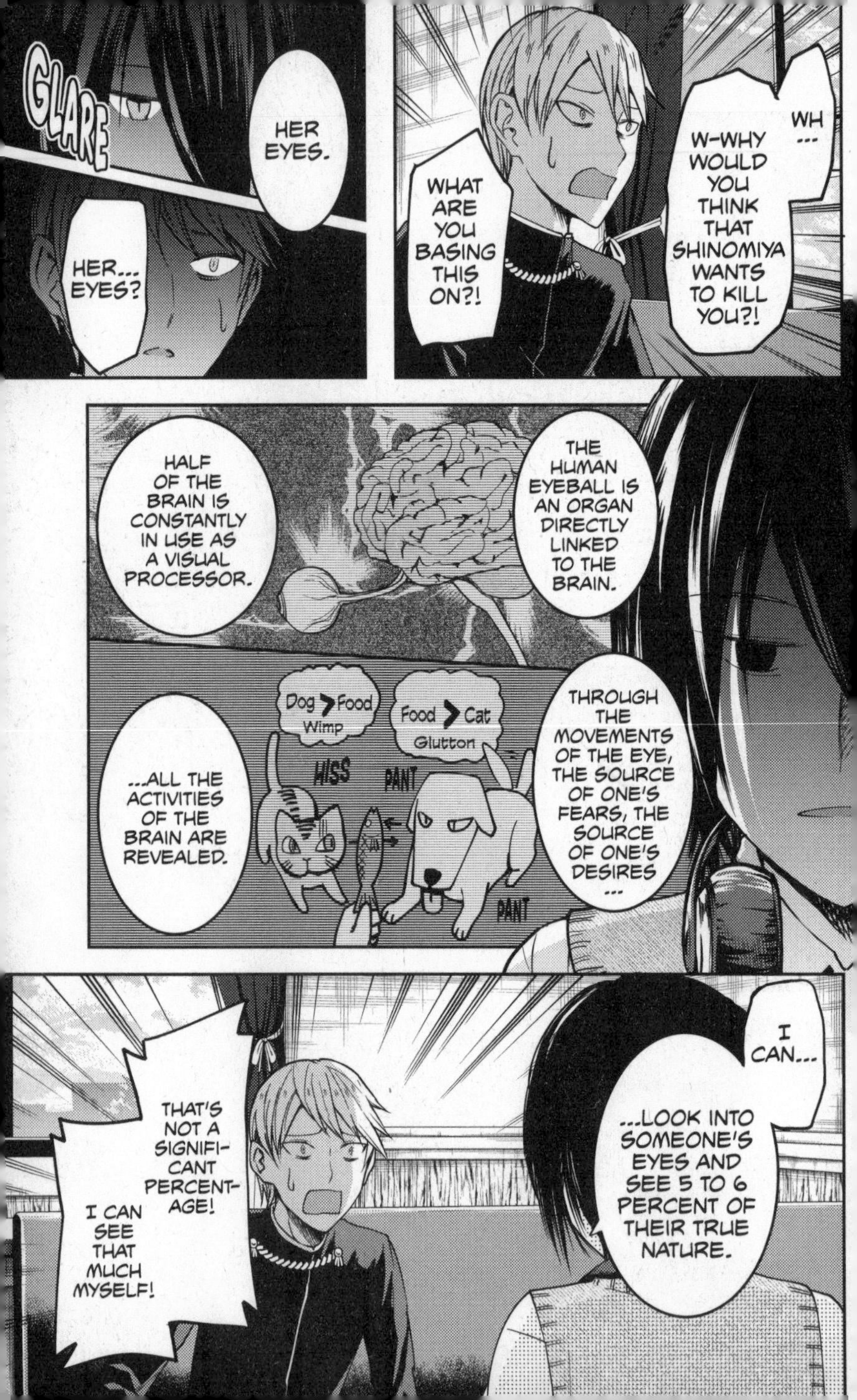
WH...
W-WHY WOULD YOU THINK THAT SHINOMIYA WANTS TO KILL YOU?!
WHAT ARE YOU BASING THIS ON?!
GLARE
HER EYES.
HER... EYES?
THE HUMAN EYEBALL IS AN ORGAN DIRECTLY LINKED TO THE BRAIN.
HALF OF THE BRAIN IS CONSTANTLY IN USE AS A VISUAL PROCESSOR.
THROUGH THE MOVEMENTS OF THE EYE, THE SOURCE OF ONE'S FEARS, THE SOURCE OF ONE'S DESIRES...
Food > Cat
Glutton
Dog > Food
Wimp
PANT
PANT
HISS
...ALL THE ACTIVITIES OF THE BRAIN ARE REVEALED.
I CAN...
...LOOK INTO SOMEONE'S EYES AND SEE 5 TO 6 PERCENT OF THEIR TRUE NATURE.
THAT'S NOT A SIGNIFI-CANT PERCENT-AGE!
I CAN SEE THAT MUCH MYSELF!

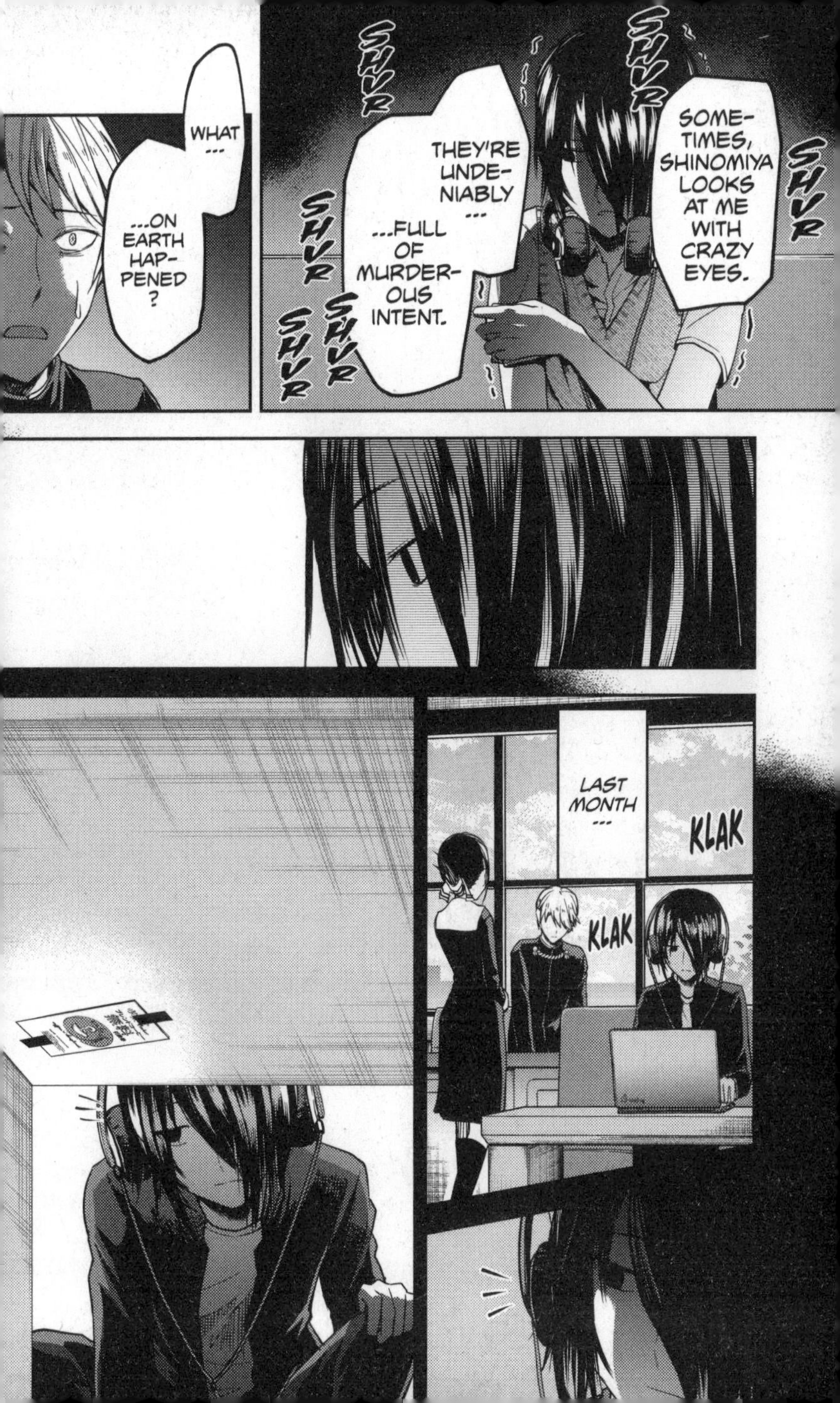
SHUR
SHUR
SOME-TIMES, SHINOMIYA LOOKS AT ME WITH CRAZY EYES.
SHUR
THEY'RE UNDE-NIABLY...
...FULL OF MURDER-OUS INTENT.
SHUR
SHUR
SHUR
WHAT...
...ON EARTH HAP-PENED?
LAST MONTH...
KLAK
KLAK

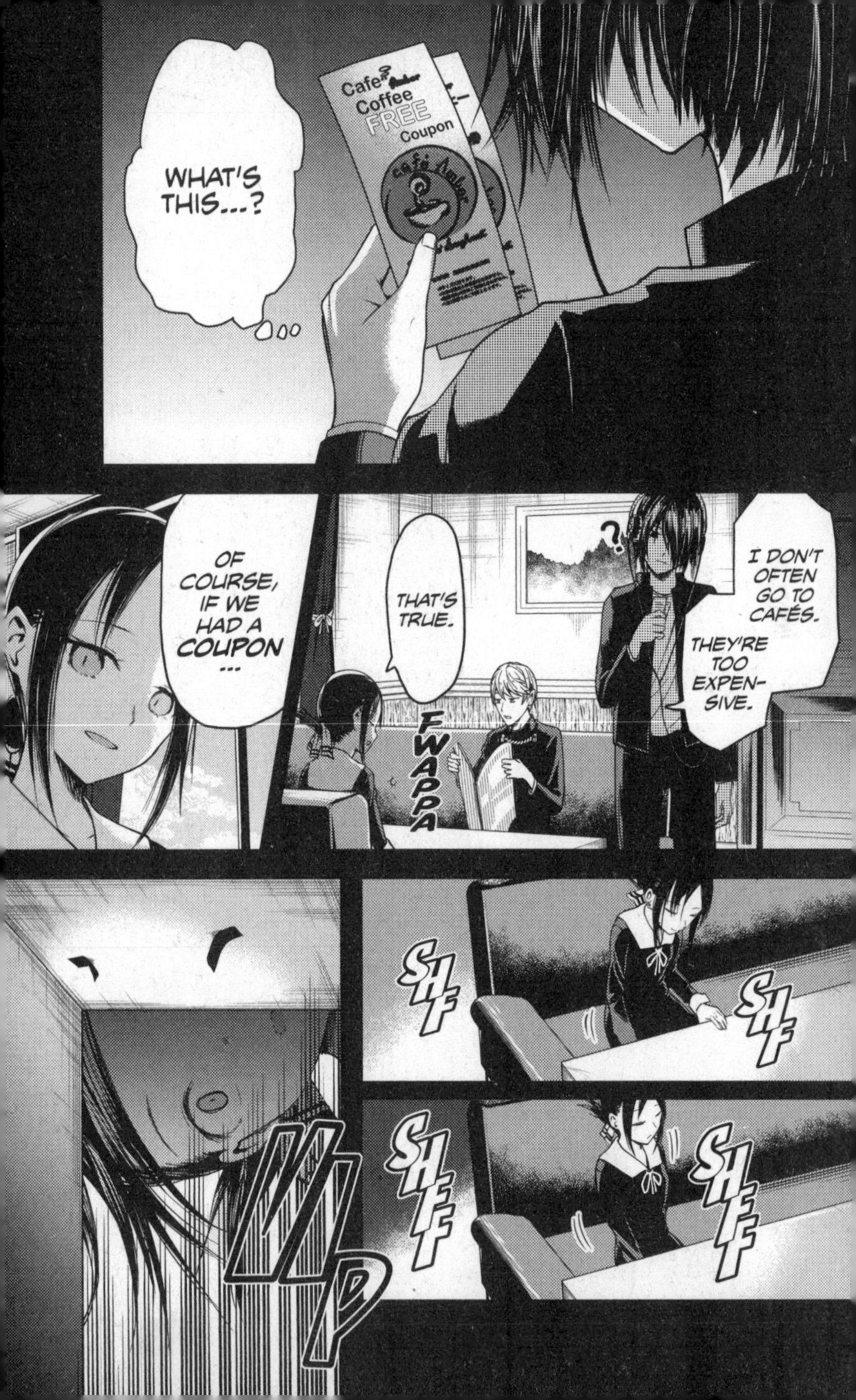
Coffee
FREE
Coupon
WHAT'S THIS...?
?
I DON'T OFTEN GO TO CAFÉS.
THEY'RE TOO EXPENSIVE.
THAT'S TRUE.
FWAPPA
OF COURSE, IF WE HAD A COUPON...
SHF
SHF
SHFF
SHFF

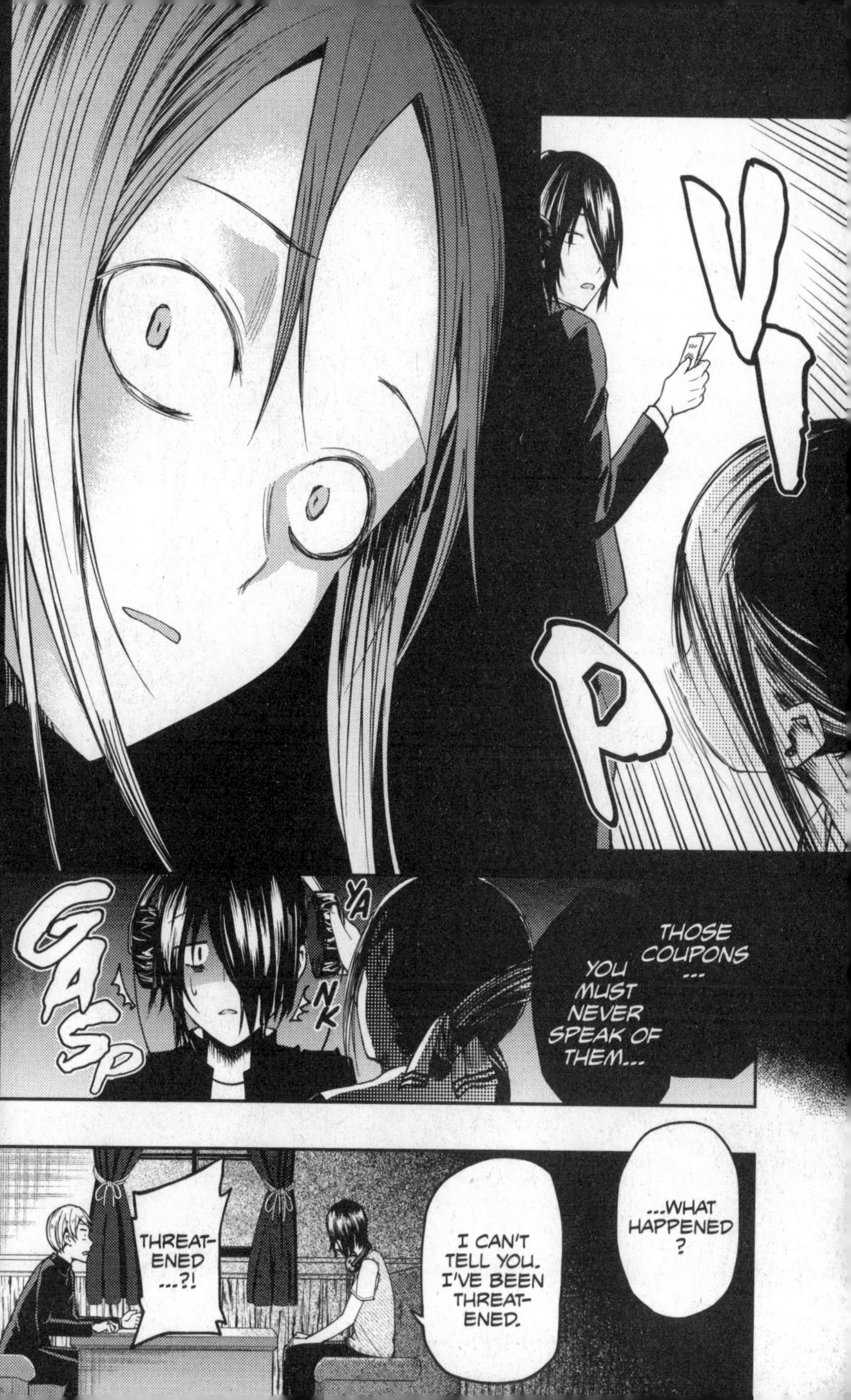
V
P
THOSE COUPONS... YOU MUST NEVER SPEAK OF THEM...
YANK
GASP
...WHAT HAPPENED?
I CAN'T TELL YOU. I'VE BEEN THREAT-ENED.
THREAT-ENED...?!

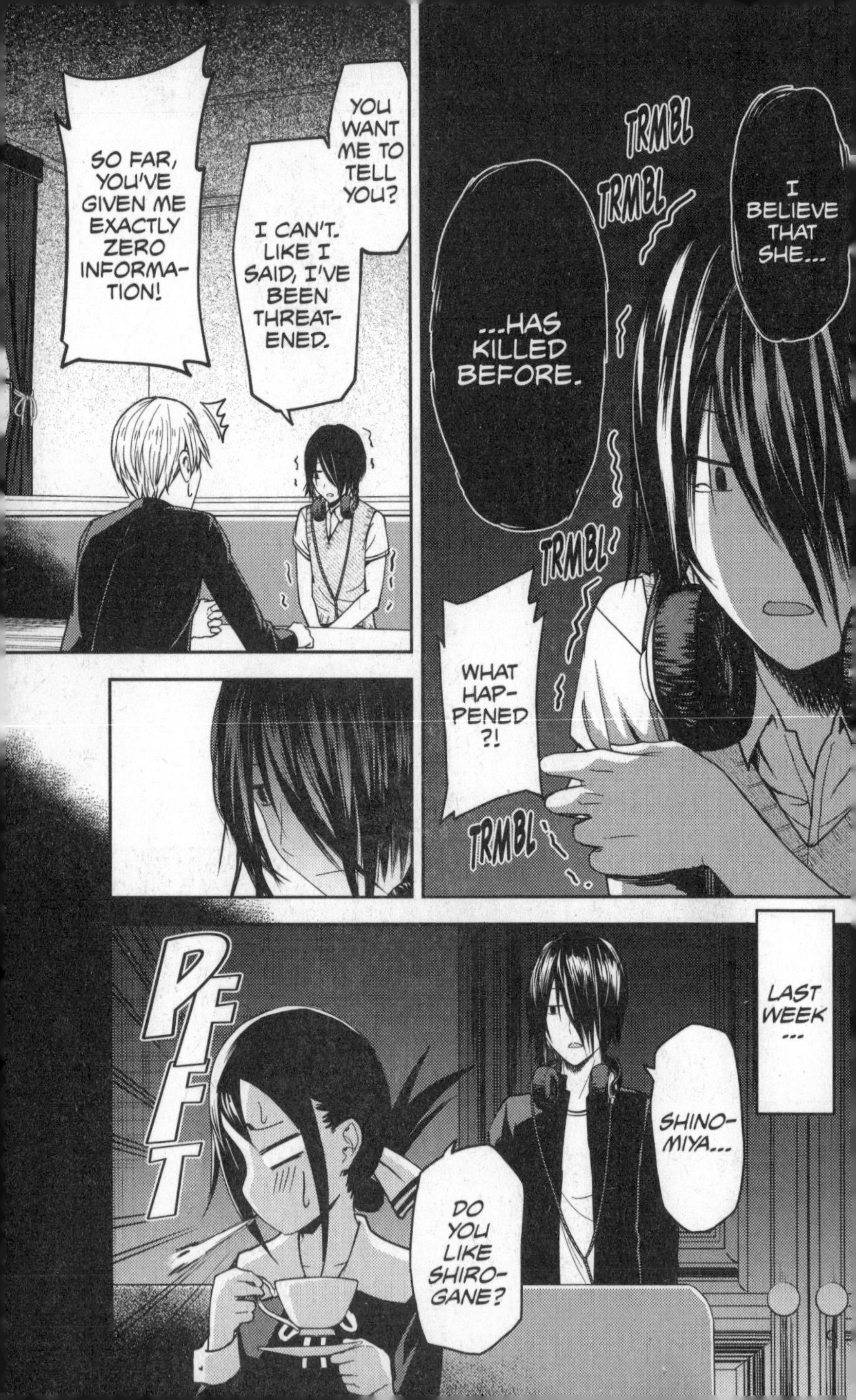

TRMBL
TRMBL
I BELIEVE THAT SHE...
...HAS KILLED BEFORE.
TRMBL
WHAT HAPPENED?!
TRMBL
YOU WANT ME TO TELL YOU?
I CAN'T. LIKE I SAID, I'VE BEEN THREATENED.
SO FAR, YOU'VE GIVEN ME EXACTLY ZERO INFORMATION!
LAST WEEK...
SHINOMIYA...
DO YOU LIKE SHIROGANE?
PFFT

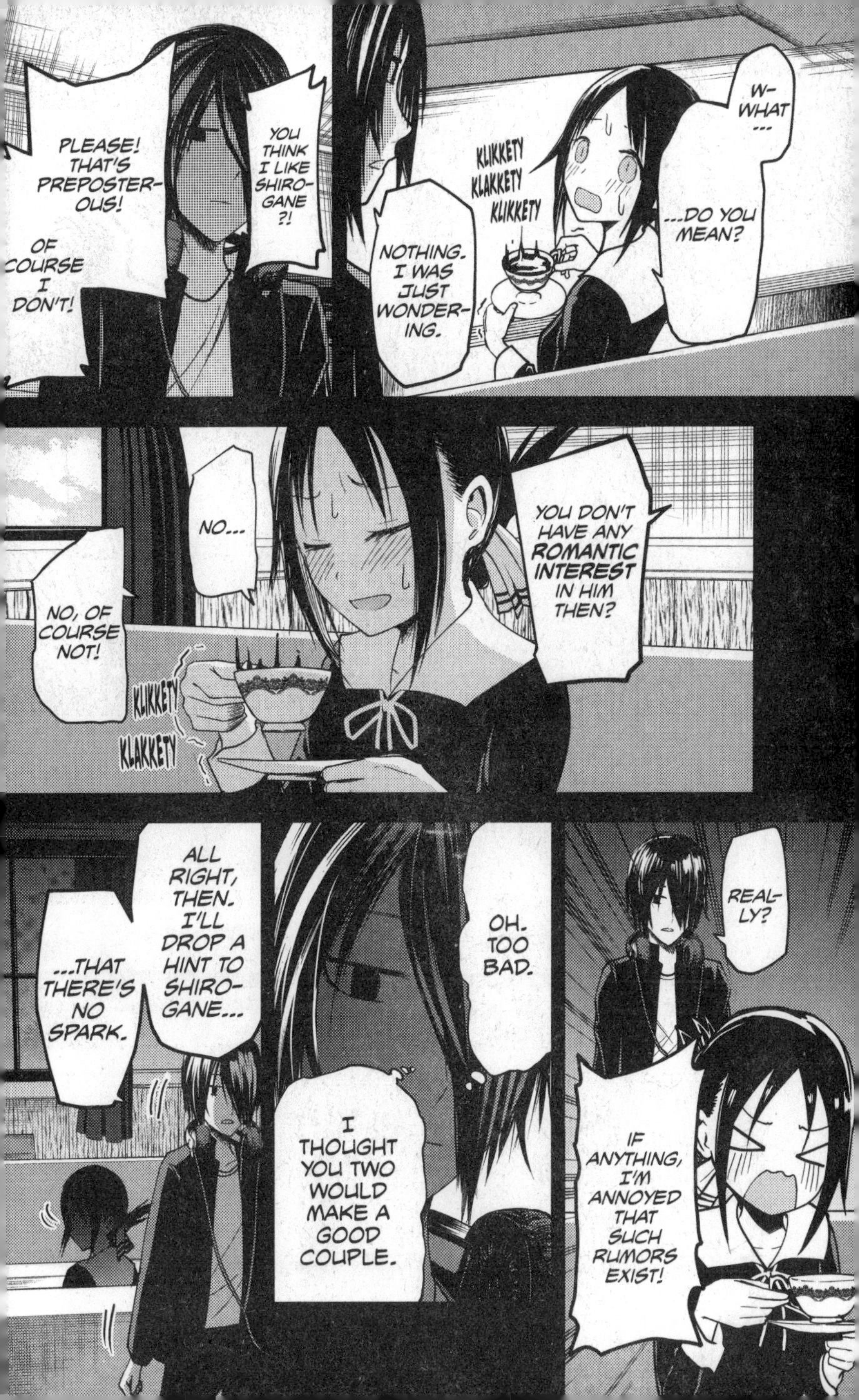
W-WHAT...
...DO YOU MEAN?
KLIKKETY KLAKKETY KLIKKETY
NOTHING. I WAS JUST WONDERING.
YOU THINK I LIKE SHIROGANE?!
PLEASE! THAT'S PREPOSTEROUS!
OF COURSE I DON'T!
YOU DON'T HAVE ANY ROMANTIC INTEREST IN HIM THEN?
NO...
NO, OF COURSE NOT!
KLIKKETY KLAKKETY
REALLY?
IF ANYTHING, I'M ANNOYED THAT SUCH RUMORS EXIST!
OH. TOO BAD.
I THOUGHT YOU TWO WOULD MAKE A GOOD COUPLE.
ALL RIGHT, THEN. I'LL DROP A HINT TO SHIROGANE...
...THAT THERE'S NO SPARK.

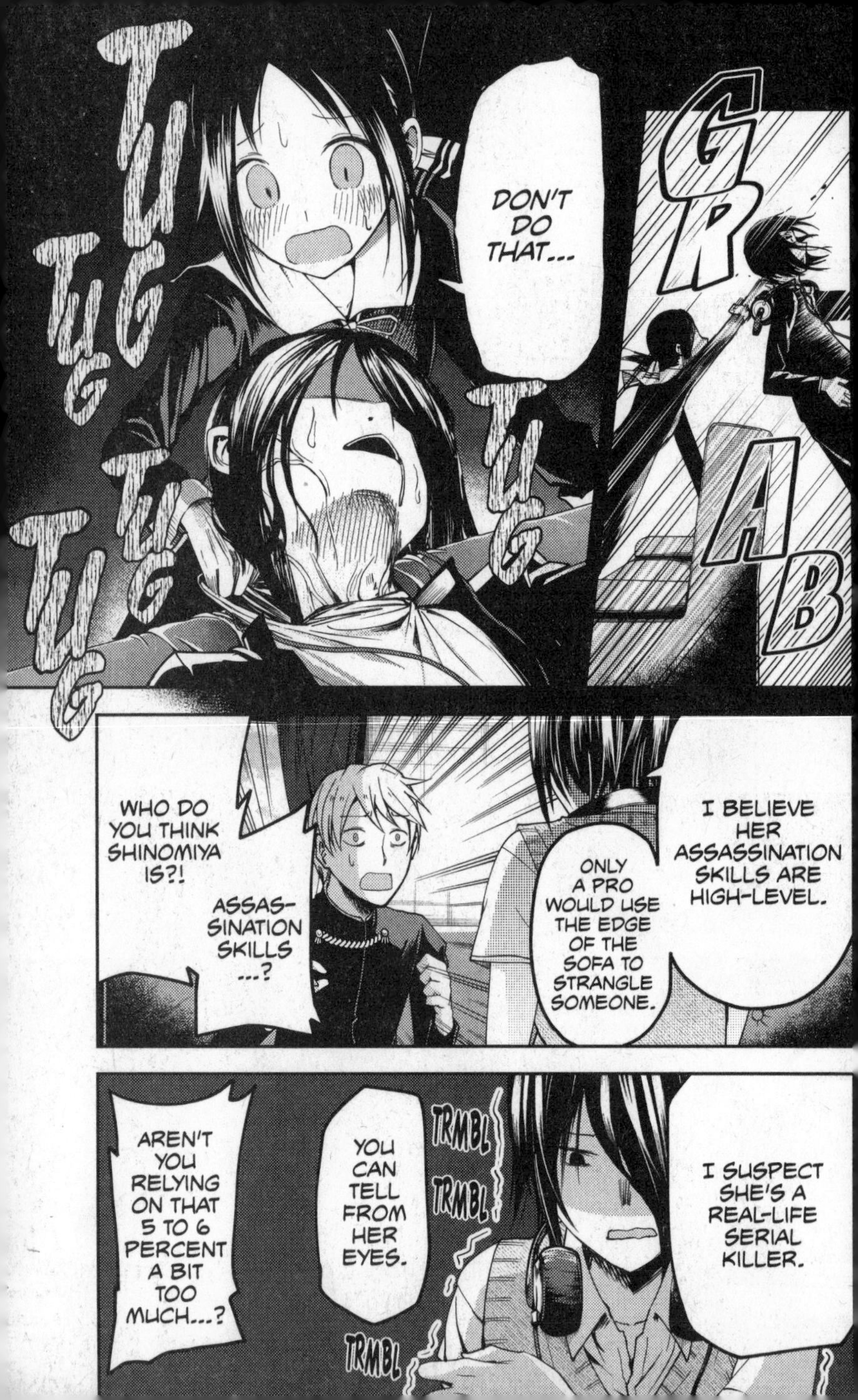
GRAB
DON'T DO THAT...
TUG TUG
TUG TUG
TUG TUG
I BELIEVE HER ASSASSINATION SKILLS ARE HIGH-LEVEL.
ASSAS-SINATION SKILLS ...?
ONLY A PRO WOULD USE THE EDGE OF THE SOFA TO STRANGLE SOMEONE.
WHO DO YOU THINK SHINOMIYA IS?!
I SUSPECT SHE'S A REAL-LIFE SERIAL KILLER.
TRMBL
TRMBL
YOU CAN TELL FROM HER EYES.
TRMBL
AREN'T YOU RELYING ON THAT 5 TO 6 PERCENT A BIT TOO MUCH...?

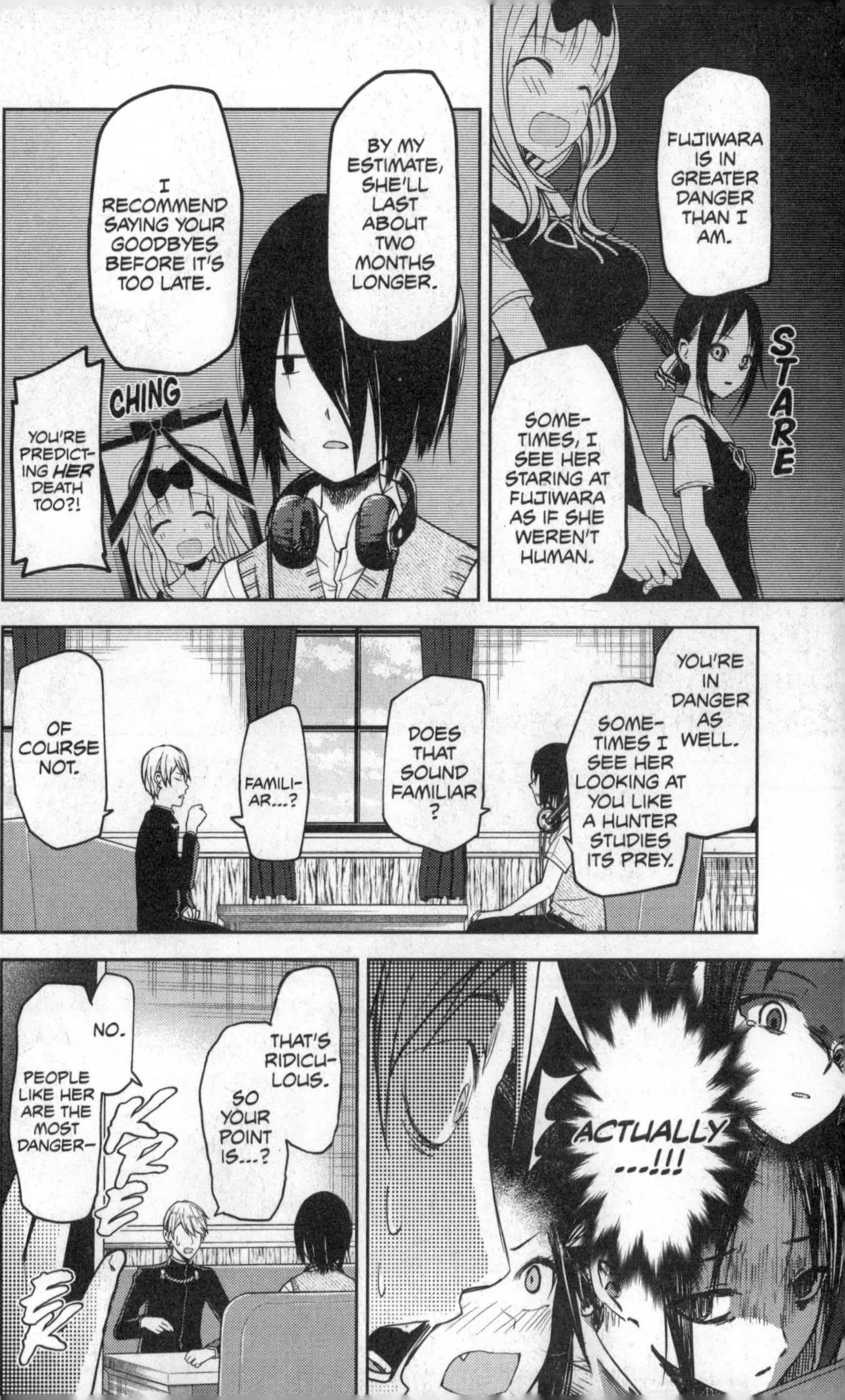
FUJIWARA IS IN GREATER DANGER THAN I AM.
SOMETIMES, I SEE HER STARING AT FUJIWARA AS IF SHE WEREN'T HUMAN.
STARE
BY MY ESTIMATE, SHE'LL LAST ABOUT TWO MONTHS LONGER.
I RECOMMEND SAYING YOUR GOODBYES BEFORE IT'S TOO LATE.
CHING
YOU'RE PREDICTING ***HER*** DEATH TOO?!
YOU'RE IN DANGER AS WELL.
SOMETIMES I SEE HER LOOKING AT YOU LIKE A HUNTER STUDIES ITS PREY.
DOES THAT SOUND FAMILIAR?
FAMILIAR...?
OF COURSE NOT.
ACTUALLY...!!!
THAT'S RIDICULOUS.
SO YOUR POINT IS...?
NO.
PEOPLE LIKE HER ARE THE MOST DANGER-

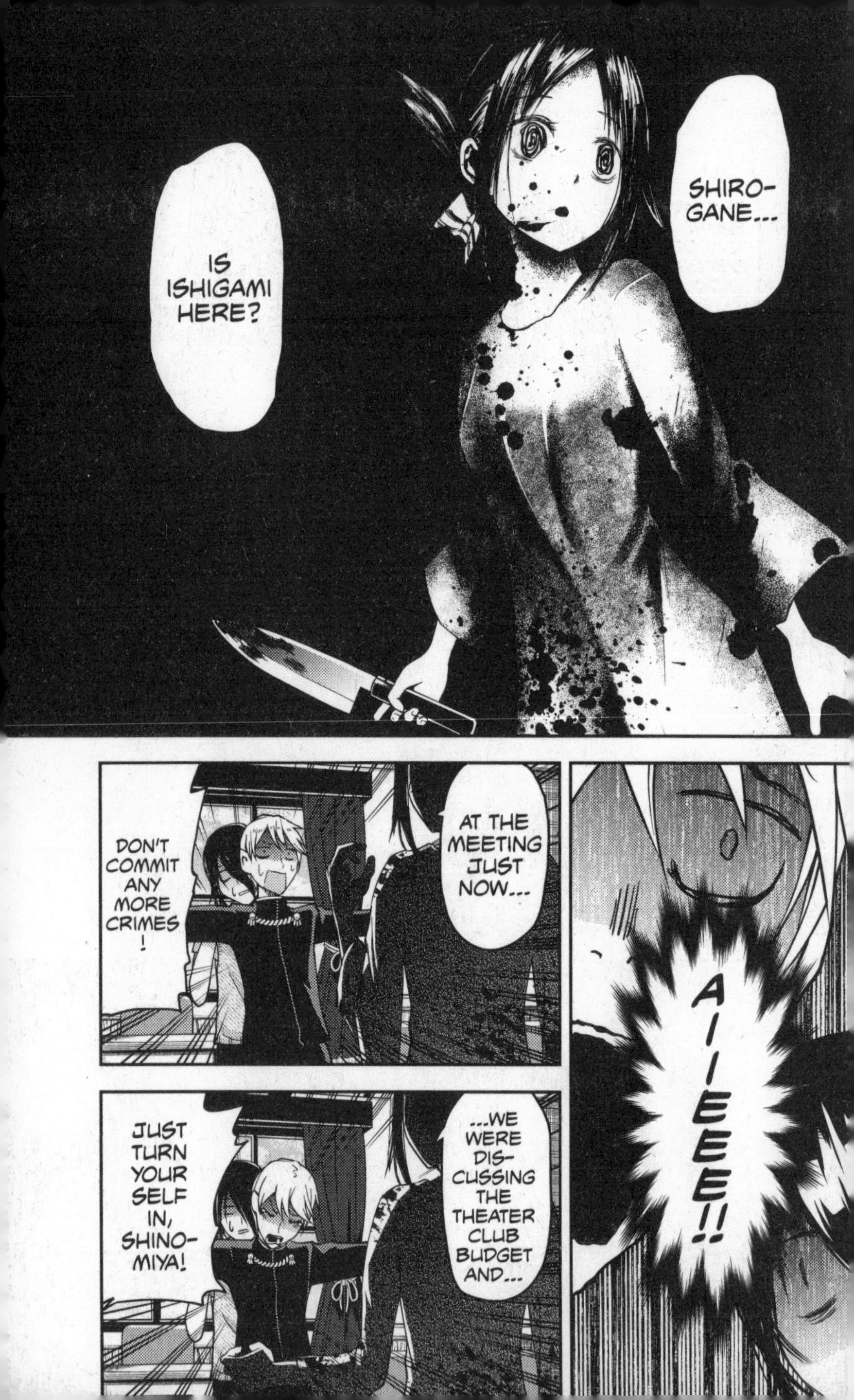
SHIRO-GANE...
IS ISHIGAMI HERE?
AIIEEE!!
AT THE MEETING JUST NOW...
DON'T COMMIT ANY MORE CRIMES!
...WE WERE DIS-CUSSING THE THEATER CLUB BUDGET AND...
JUST TURN YOUR SELF IN, SHINO-MIYA!

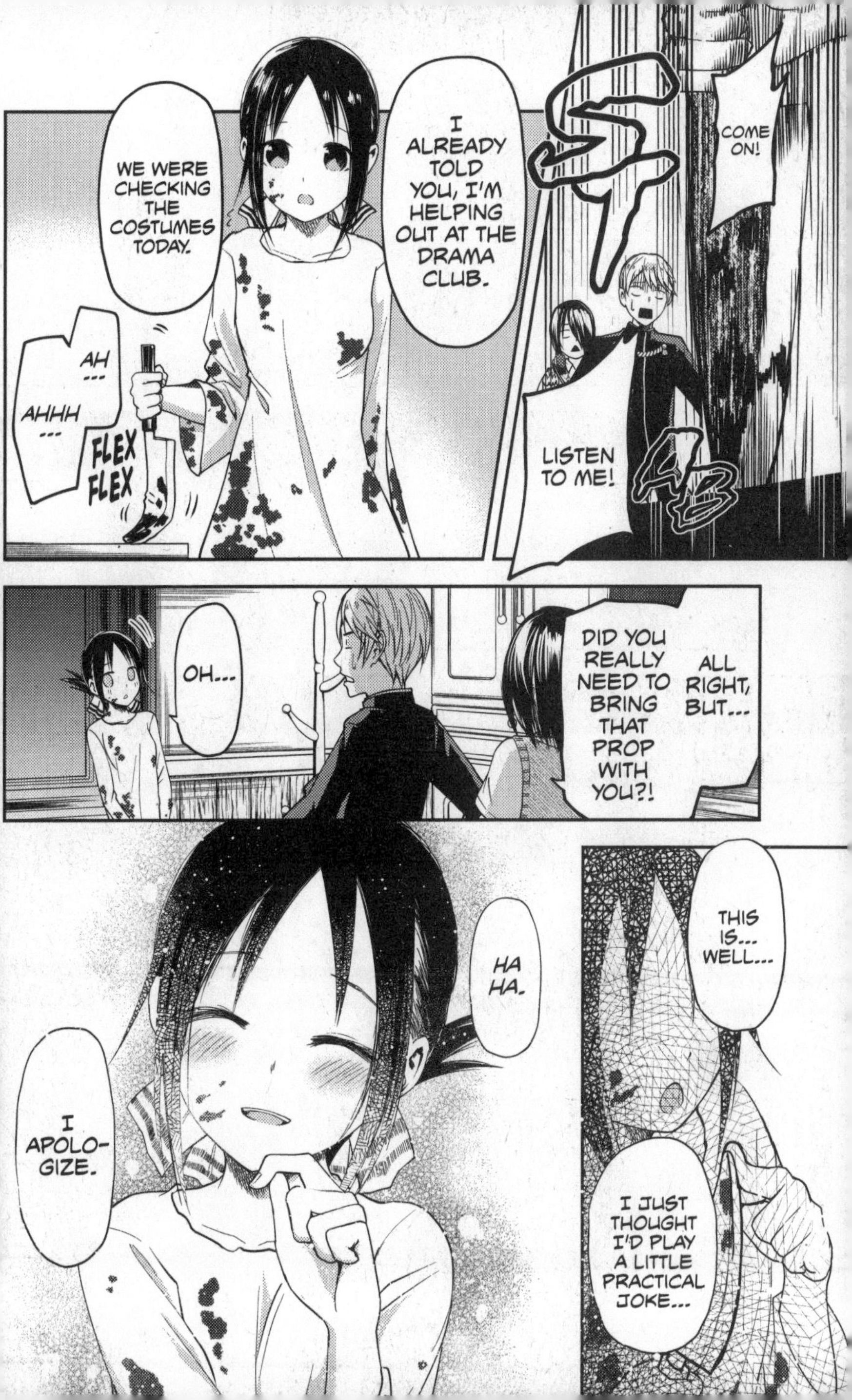
COME ON!
LISTEN TO ME!
I ALREADY TOLD YOU, I'M HELPING OUT AT THE DRAMA CLUB.
WE WERE CHECKING THE COSTUMES TODAY.
AH--- AHHH---
FLEX FLEX
ALL RIGHT, BUT...
DID YOU REALLY NEED TO BRING THAT PROP WITH YOU?!
OH...
THIS IS... WELL...
I JUST THOUGHT I'D PLAY A LITTLE PRACTICAL JOKE...
HA HA.
I APOLOGIZE.

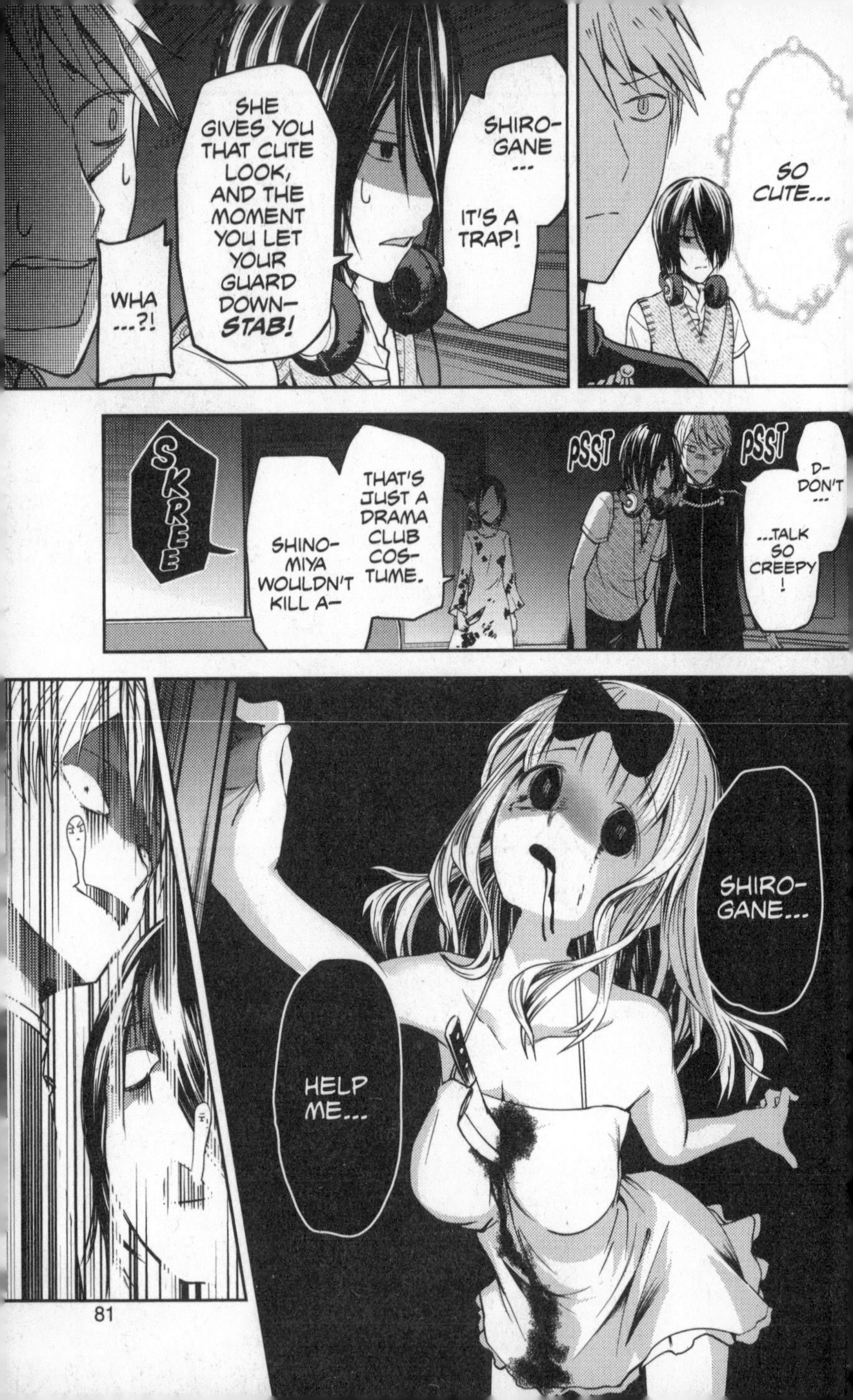
SO CUTE...
SHIRO-GANE...
IT'S A TRAP!
SHE GIVES YOU THAT CUTE LOOK, AND THE MOMENT YOU LET YOUR GUARD DOWN– STAB!
WHA...?!
D-DON'T...
...TALK SO CREEPY!
PSST
PSST
THAT'S JUST A DRAMA CLUB COSTUME.
SHINO-MIYA WOULDN'T KILL A–
SKREE
SHIRO-GANE...
HELP ME...

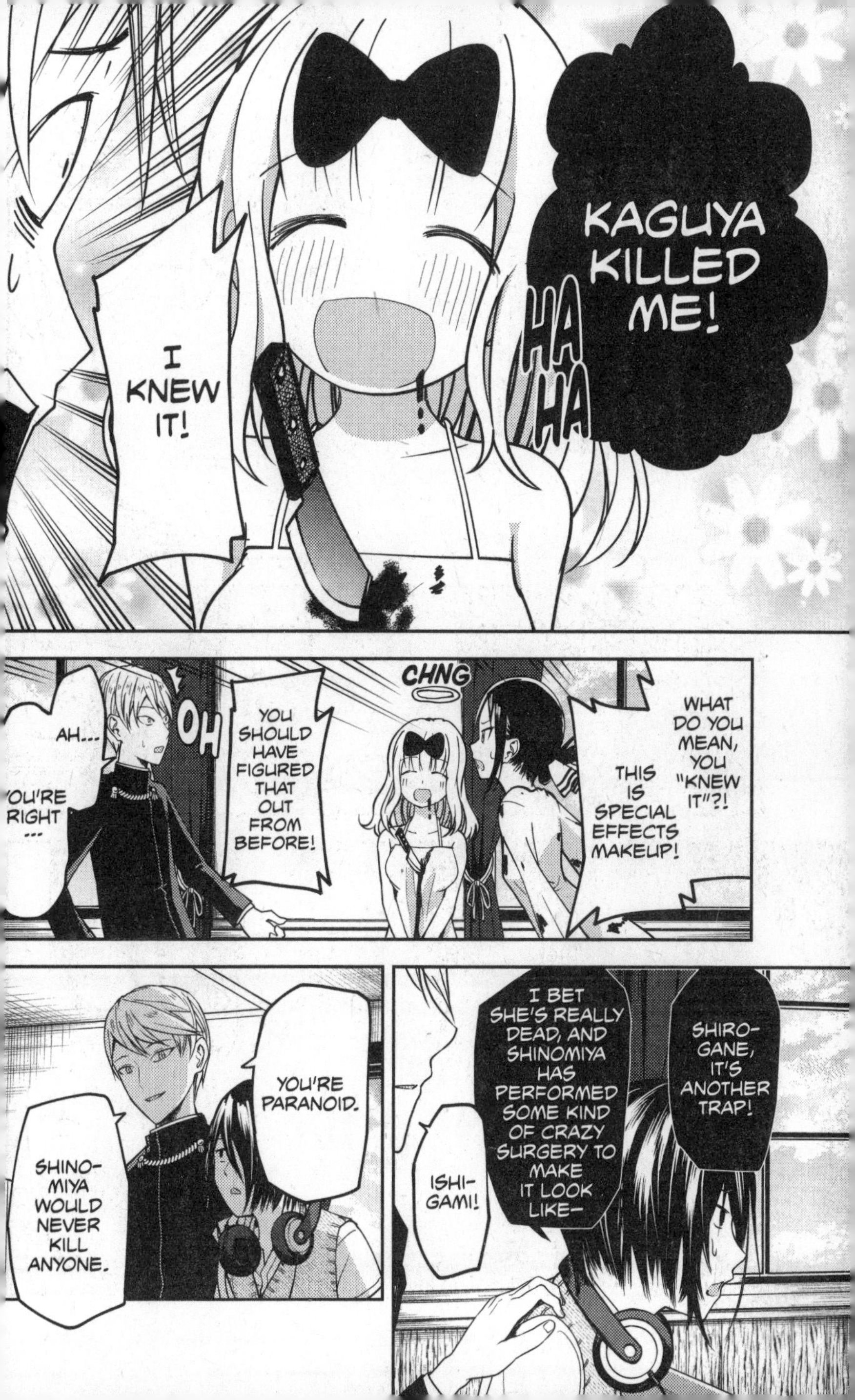

KAGUYA KILLED ME!
HA HA HA
I KNEW IT!
WHAT DO YOU MEAN, YOU "KNEW IT"?!
THIS IS SPECIAL EFFECTS MAKEUP!
CHNG
YOU SHOULD HAVE FIGURED THAT OUT FROM BEFORE!
OH
AH...
OU'RE RIGHT...
SHIRO-GANE, IT'S ANOTHER TRAP!
I BET SHE'S REALLY DEAD, AND SHINOMIYA HAS PERFORMED SOME KIND OF CRAZY SURGERY TO MAKE IT LOOK LIKE—
ISHI-GAMI!
YOU'RE PARANOID.
SHINO-MIYA WOULD NEVER KILL ANYONE.

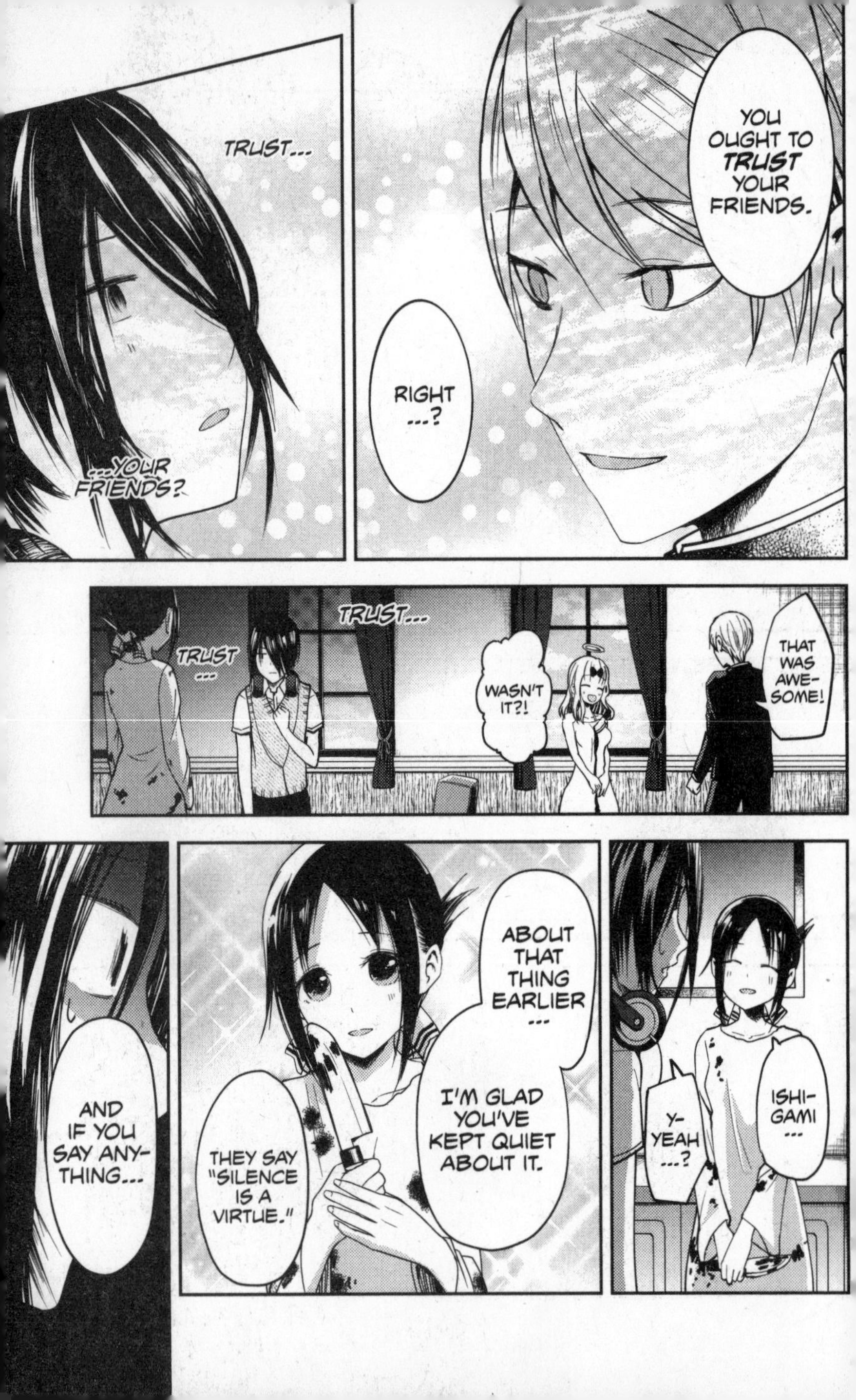
YOU OUGHT TO TRUST YOUR FRIENDS.
RIGHT...?
TRUST...
...YOUR FRIENDS?
THAT WAS AWE-SOME!
WASN'T IT?!
TRUST...
TRUST...
ISHI-GAMI...
Y-YEAH...?
ABOUT THAT THING EARLIER...
I'M GLAD YOU'VE KEPT QUIET ABOUT IT.
THEY SAY "SILENCE IS A VIRTUE."
AND IF YOU SAY ANY-THING...

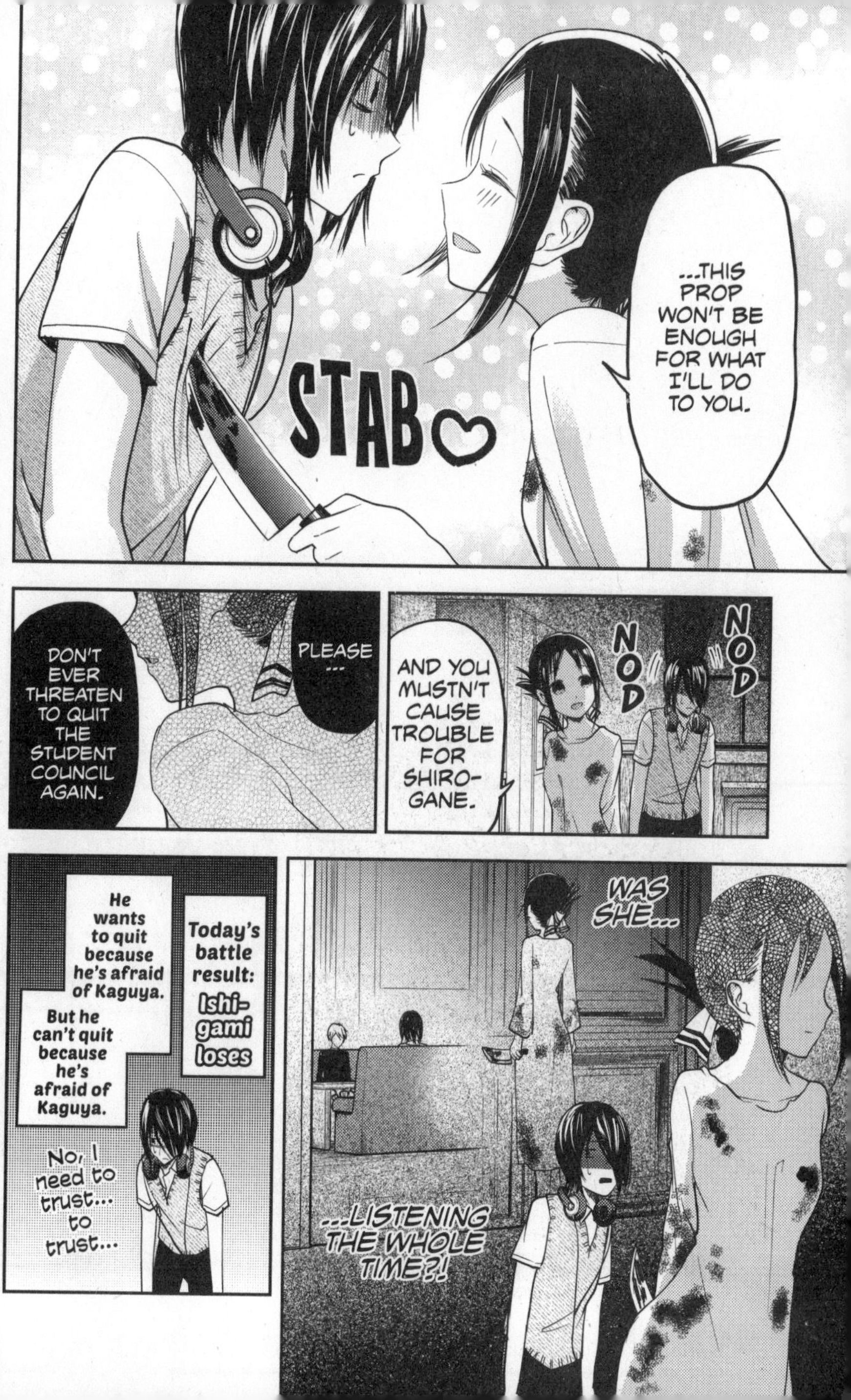
...THIS PROP WON'T BE ENOUGH FOR WHAT I'LL DO TO YOU.
STAB ♡
NOD NOD
AND YOU MUSTN'T CAUSE TROUBLE FOR SHIRO-GANE.
PLEASE...
DON'T EVER THREATEN TO QUIT THE STUDENT COUNCIL AGAIN.
WAS SHE...
...LISTENING THE WHOLE TIME?!
Today's battle result: Ishi-gami loses
He wants to quit because he's afraid of Kaguya.
But he can't quit because he's afraid of Kaguya.
No, I need to trust... to trust...

Shuchiin Academy Drama Club
Women in Love and Hate
First performance at 13:00
Second performance at 15:30

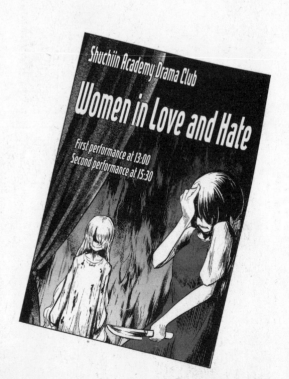

KAGUYA-SAMA
LOVE IS WAR

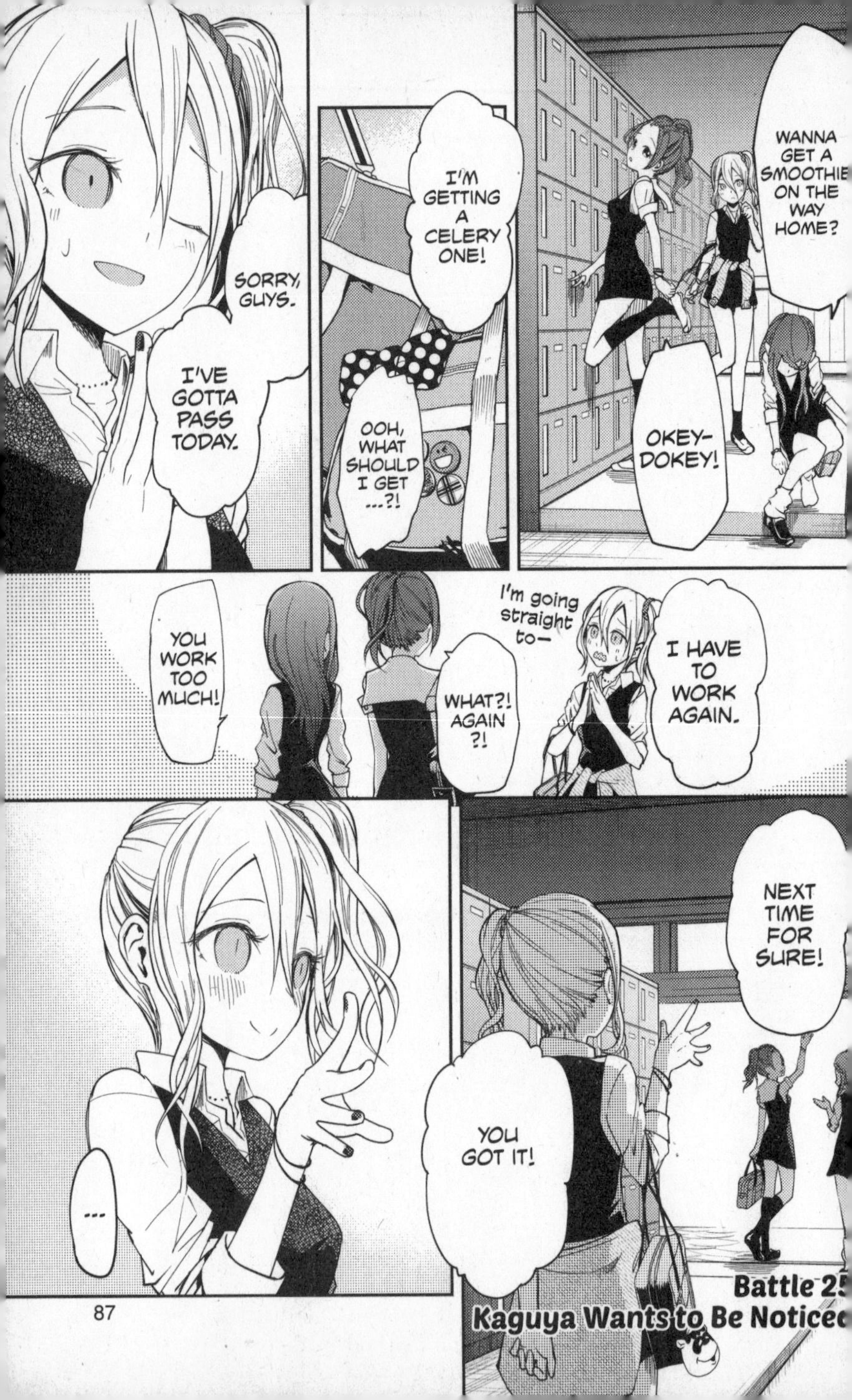
WANNA GET A SMOOTHIE ON THE WAY HOME?
OKEY-DOKEY!
I'M GETTING A CELERY ONE!
OOH, WHAT SHOULD I GET ...?!
SORRY, GUYS.
I'VE GOTTA PASS TODAY.
I HAVE TO WORK AGAIN.
I'm going straight to—
WHAT?! AGAIN?!
YOU WORK TOO MUCH!
NEXT TIME FOR SURE!
YOU GOT IT!
...

Battle 25 Kaguya Wants to Be Noticed

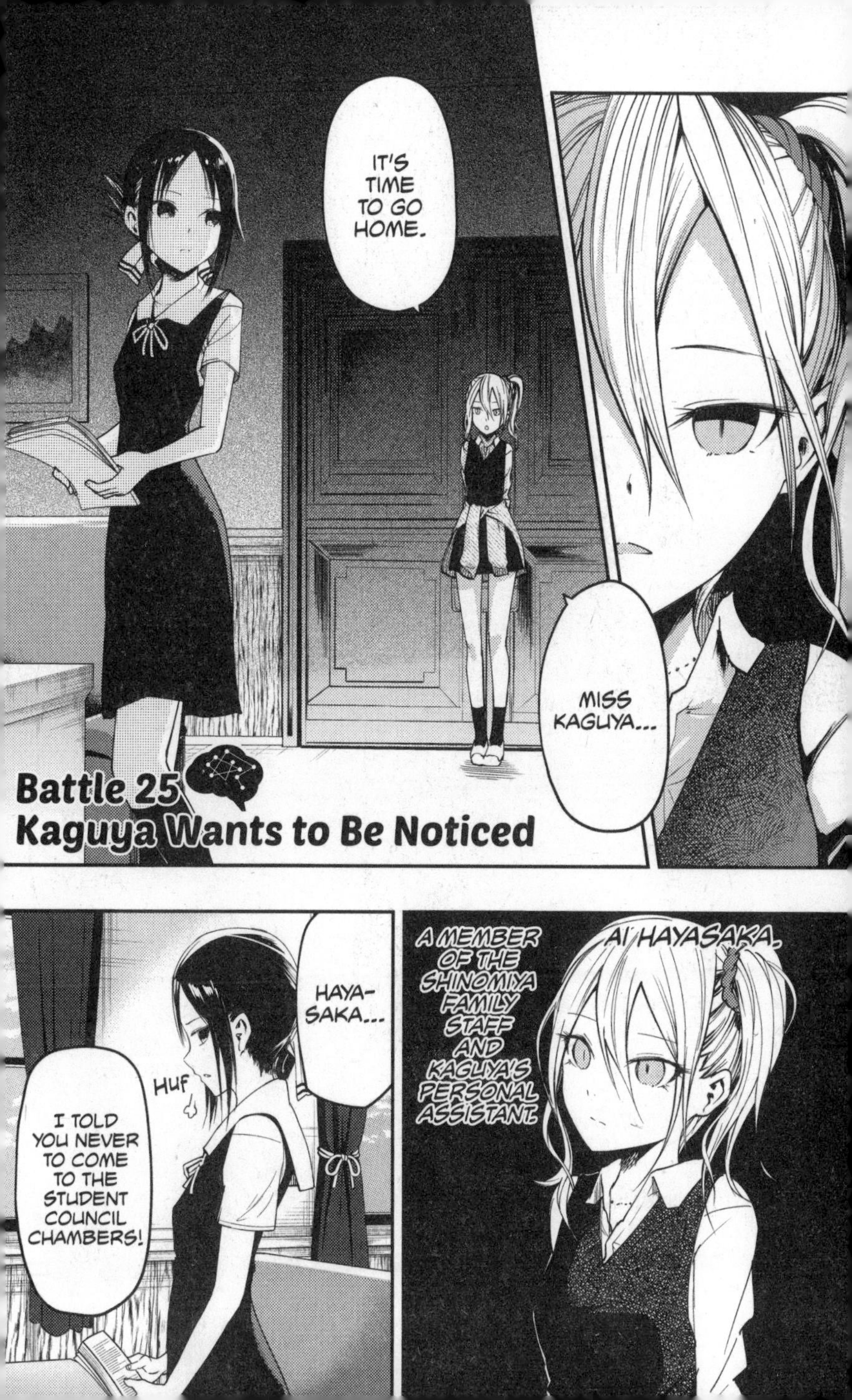
MISS KAGUYA...
IT'S TIME TO GO HOME.
Battle 25
Kaguya Wants to Be Noticed
AI HAYASAKA.
A MEMBER OF THE SHINOMIYA FAMILY STAFF AND KAGUYA'S PERSONAL ASSISTANT.
HAYA-SAKA...
HUF
I TOLD YOU NEVER TO COME TO THE STUDENT COUNCIL CHAMBERS!

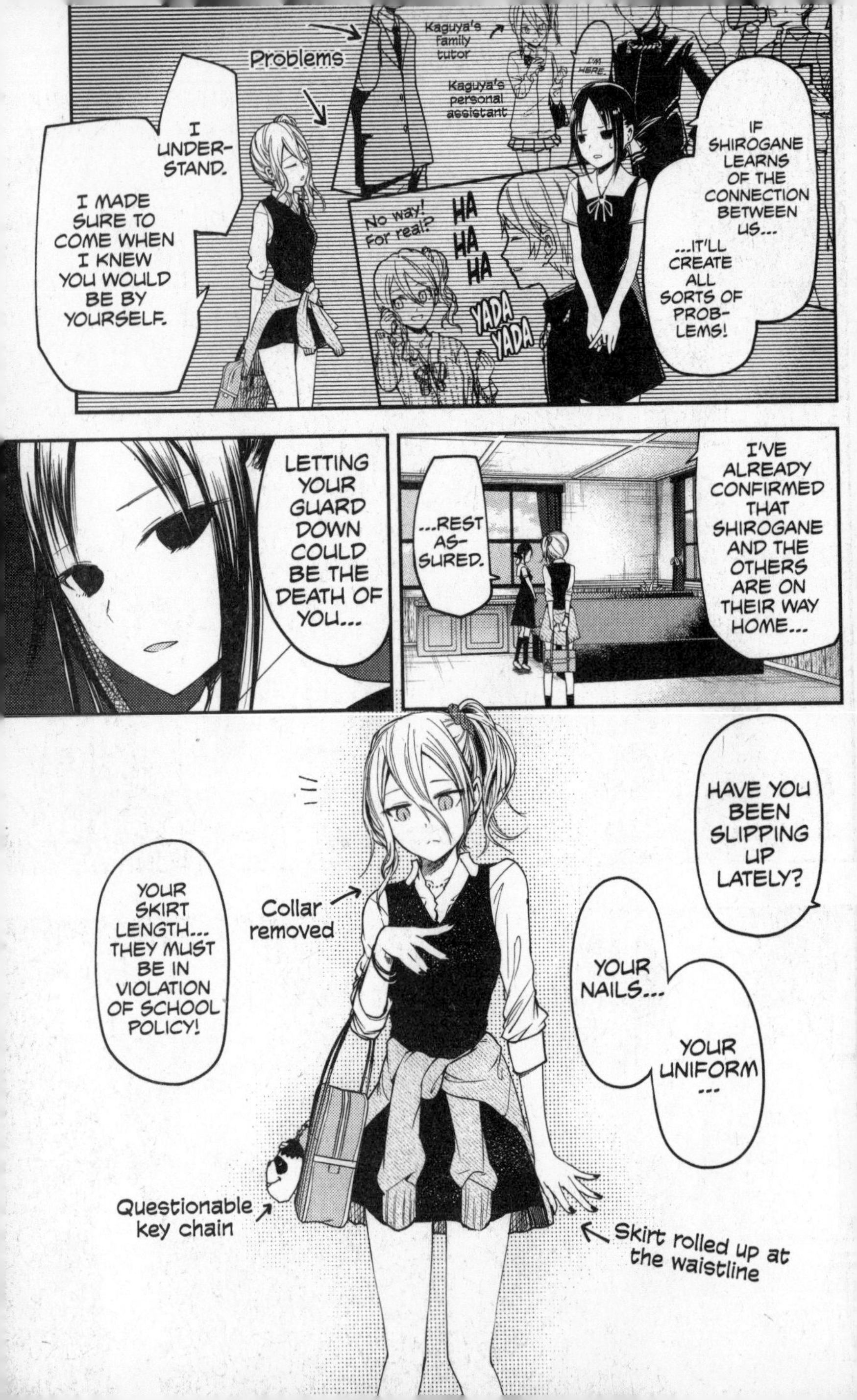
IF SHIROGANE LEARNS OF THE CONNECTION BETWEEN US...
...IT'LL CREATE ALL SORTS OF PROB-LEMS!
I'M HERE.
Kaguya's family tutor
Kaguya's personal assistant
Problems
No way! For real?
HA HA HA
YADA YADA
I UNDER-STAND.
I MADE SURE TO COME WHEN I KNEW YOU WOULD BE BY YOURSELF.
I'VE ALREADY CONFIRMED THAT SHIROGANE AND THE OTHERS ARE ON THEIR WAY HOME...
...REST AS-SURED.
LETTING YOUR GUARD DOWN COULD BE THE DEATH OF YOU...
HAVE YOU BEEN SLIPPING UP LATELY?
YOUR NAILS...
YOUR UNIFORM...
YOUR SKIRT LENGTH... THEY MUST BE IN VIOLATION OF SCHOOL POLICY!
Collar removed
Skirt rolled up at the waistline
Questionable key chain

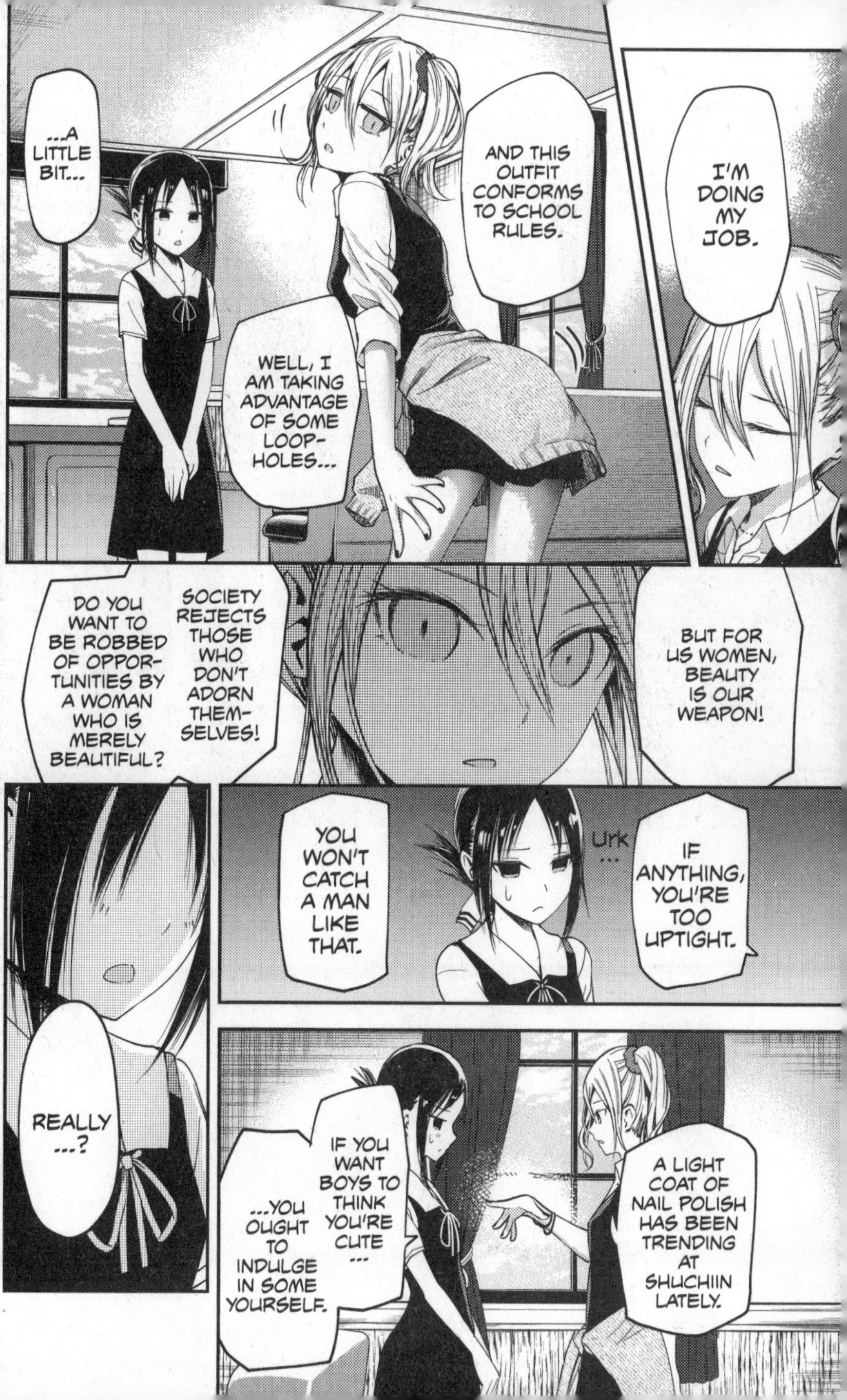
I'M DOING MY JOB.
AND THIS OUTFIT CONFORMS TO SCHOOL RULES.
WELL, I AM TAKING ADVANTAGE OF SOME LOOP-HOLES...
...A LITTLE BIT...
BUT FOR US WOMEN, BEAUTY IS OUR WEAPON!
SOCIETY REJECTS THOSE WHO DON'T ADORN THEM-SELVES!
DO YOU WANT TO BE ROBBED OF OPPOR-TUNITIES BY A WOMAN WHO IS MERELY BEAUTIFUL?
IF ANYTHING, YOU'RE TOO UPTIGHT.
Urk...
YOU WON'T CATCH A MAN LIKE THAT.
A LIGHT COAT OF NAIL POLISH HAS BEEN TRENDING AT SHUCHIIN LATELY.
IF YOU WANT BOYS TO THINK YOU'RE CUTE...
...YOU OUGHT TO INDULGE IN SOME YOURSELF.
REALLY...?

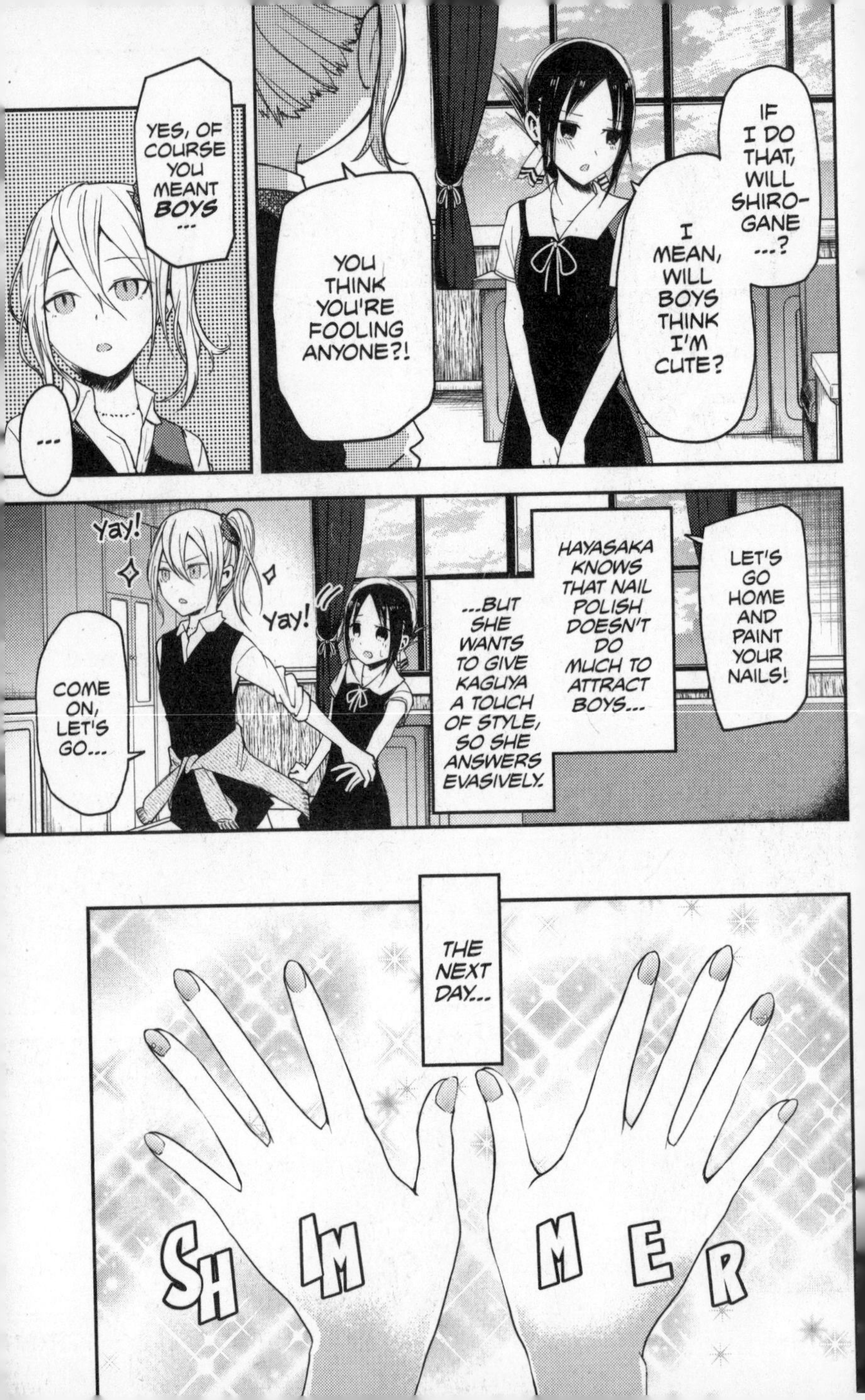
IF I DO THAT, WILL SHIRO-GANE...?
I MEAN, WILL BOYS THINK I'M CUTE?
YOU THINK YOU'RE FOOLING ANYONE?!
YES, OF COURSE YOU MEANT BOYS...
...
LET'S GO HOME AND PAINT YOUR NAILS!
HAYASAKA KNOWS THAT NAIL POLISH DOESN'T DO MUCH TO ATTRACT BOYS...
...BUT SHE WANTS TO GIVE KAGUYA A TOUCH OF STYLE, SO SHE ANSWERS EVASIVELY.
Yay!
Yay!
COME ON, LET'S GO...
THE NEXT DAY...
SHIMMER

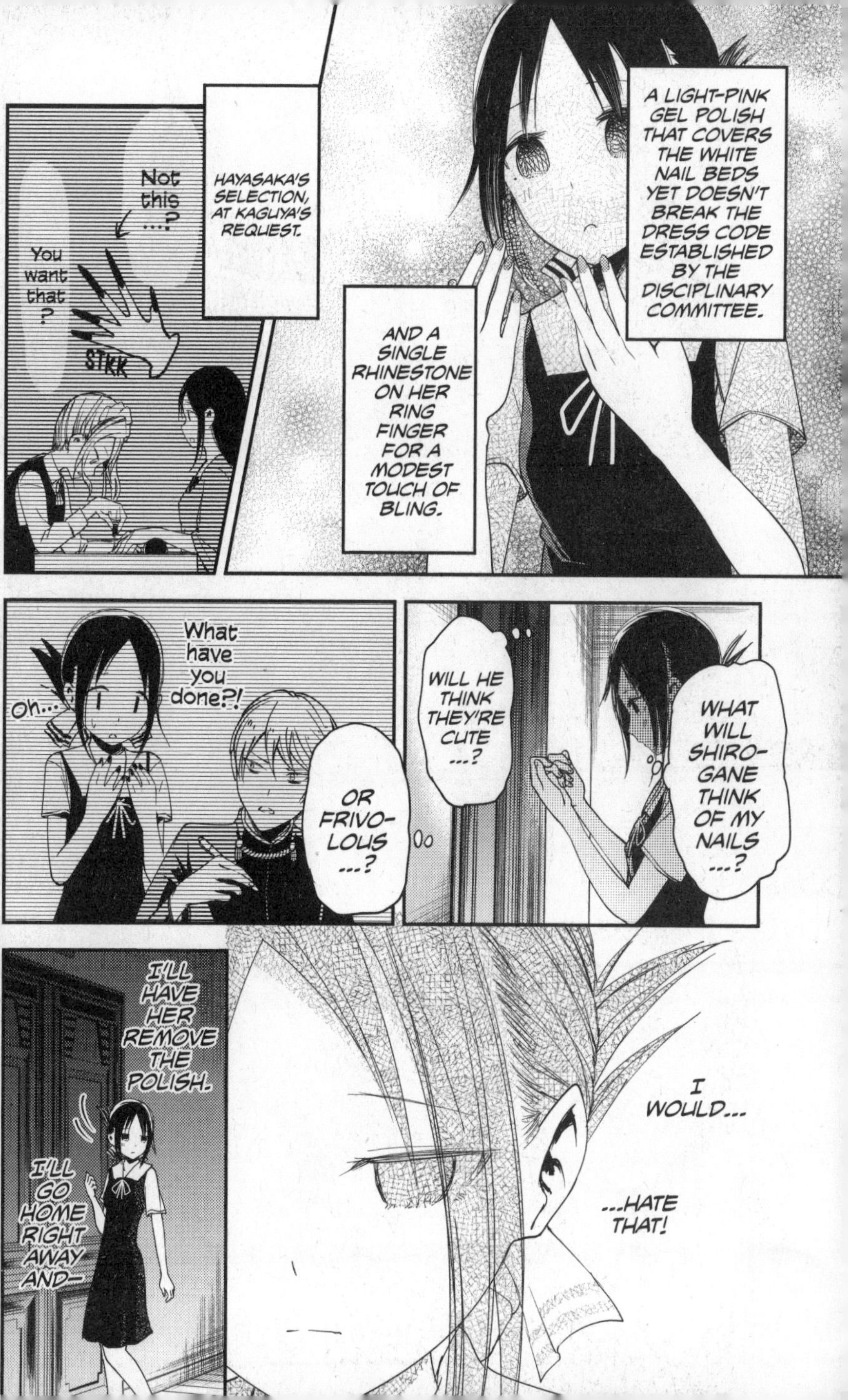
A LIGHT-PINK GEL POLISH THAT COVERS THE WHITE NAIL BEDS YET DOESN'T BREAK THE DRESS CODE ESTABLISHED BY THE DISCIPLINARY COMMITTEE.
AND A SINGLE RHINESTONE ON HER RING FINGER FOR A MODEST TOUCH OF BLING.
HAYASAKA'S SELECTION, AT KAGUYA'S REQUEST.
Not this ...?
You want that ?
STKK
WHAT WILL SHIRO-GANE THINK OF MY NAILS ...?
WILL HE THINK THEY'RE CUTE ...?
OR FRIVO-LOUS ...?
What have you done?!
Oh...
I WOULD...
...HATE THAT!
I'LL HAVE HER REMOVE THE POLISH.
I'LL GO HOME RIGHT AWAY AND-

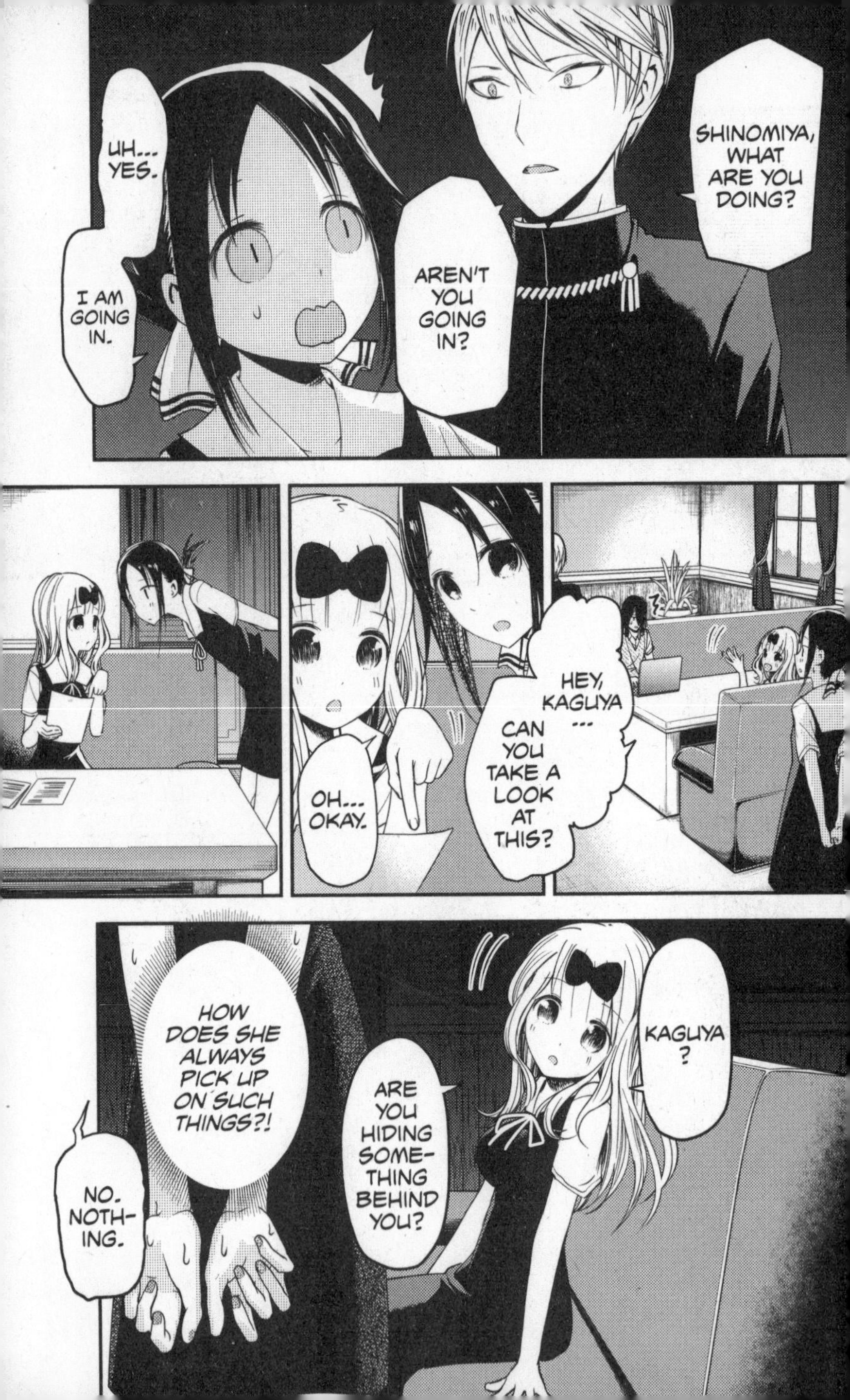
SHINOMIYA, WHAT ARE YOU DOING?
AREN'T YOU GOING IN?
UH... YES.
I AM GOING IN.
HEY, KAGUYA... CAN YOU TAKE A LOOK AT THIS?
OH... OKAY.
KAGUYA?
ARE YOU HIDING SOMETHING BEHIND YOU?
HOW DOES SHE ALWAYS PICK UP ON SUCH THINGS?!
NO. NOTHING.

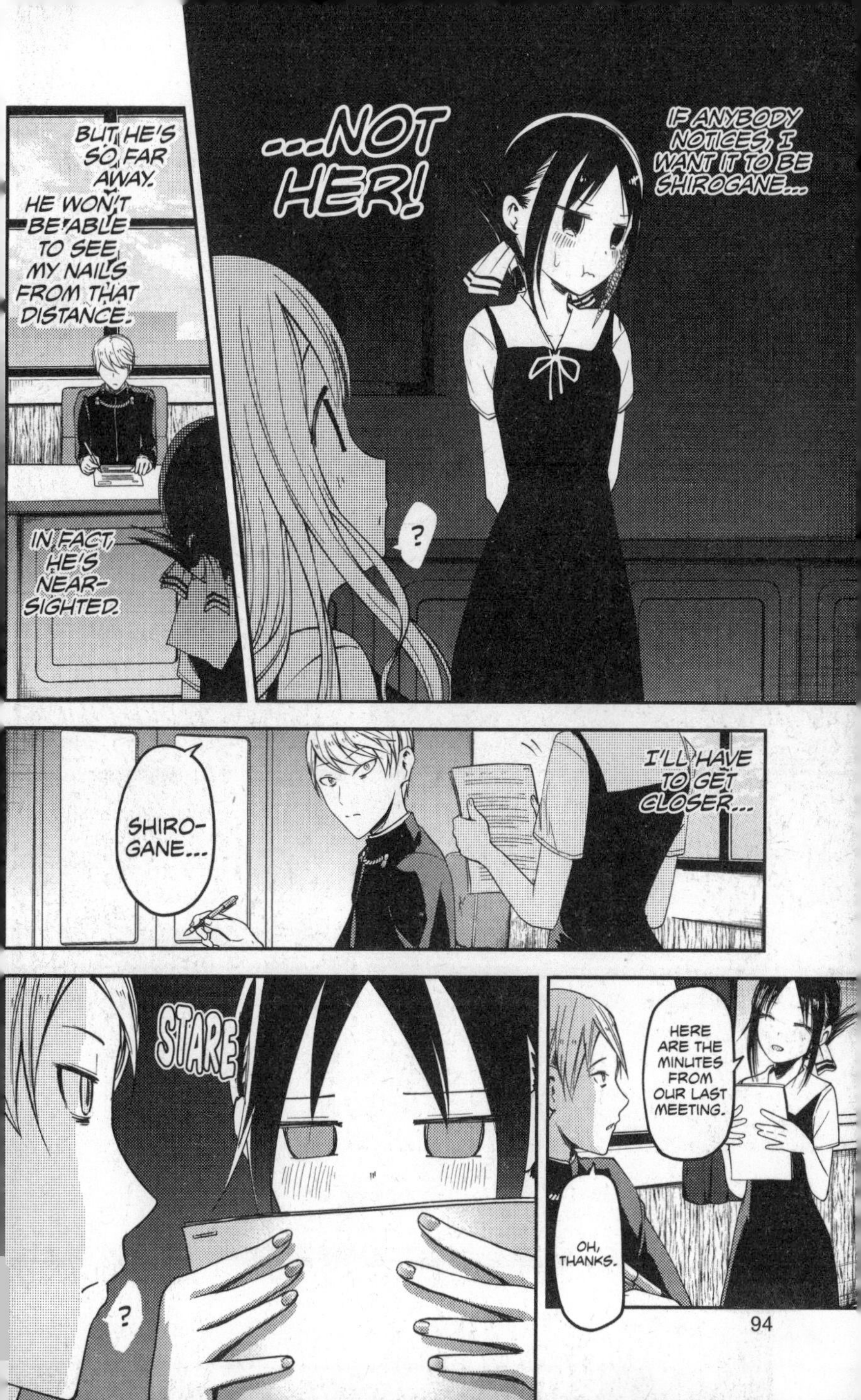

IF ANYBODY NOTICES, I WANT IT TO BE SHIROGANE...
...NOT HER!
?
BUT HE'S SO FAR AWAY. HE WON'T BE ABLE TO SEE MY NAILS FROM THAT DISTANCE.
IN FACT, HE'S NEAR-SIGHTED.
I'LL HAVE TO GET CLOSER...
SHIRO-GANE...
HERE ARE THE MINUTES FROM OUR LAST MEETING.
OH, THANKS.
STARE
?

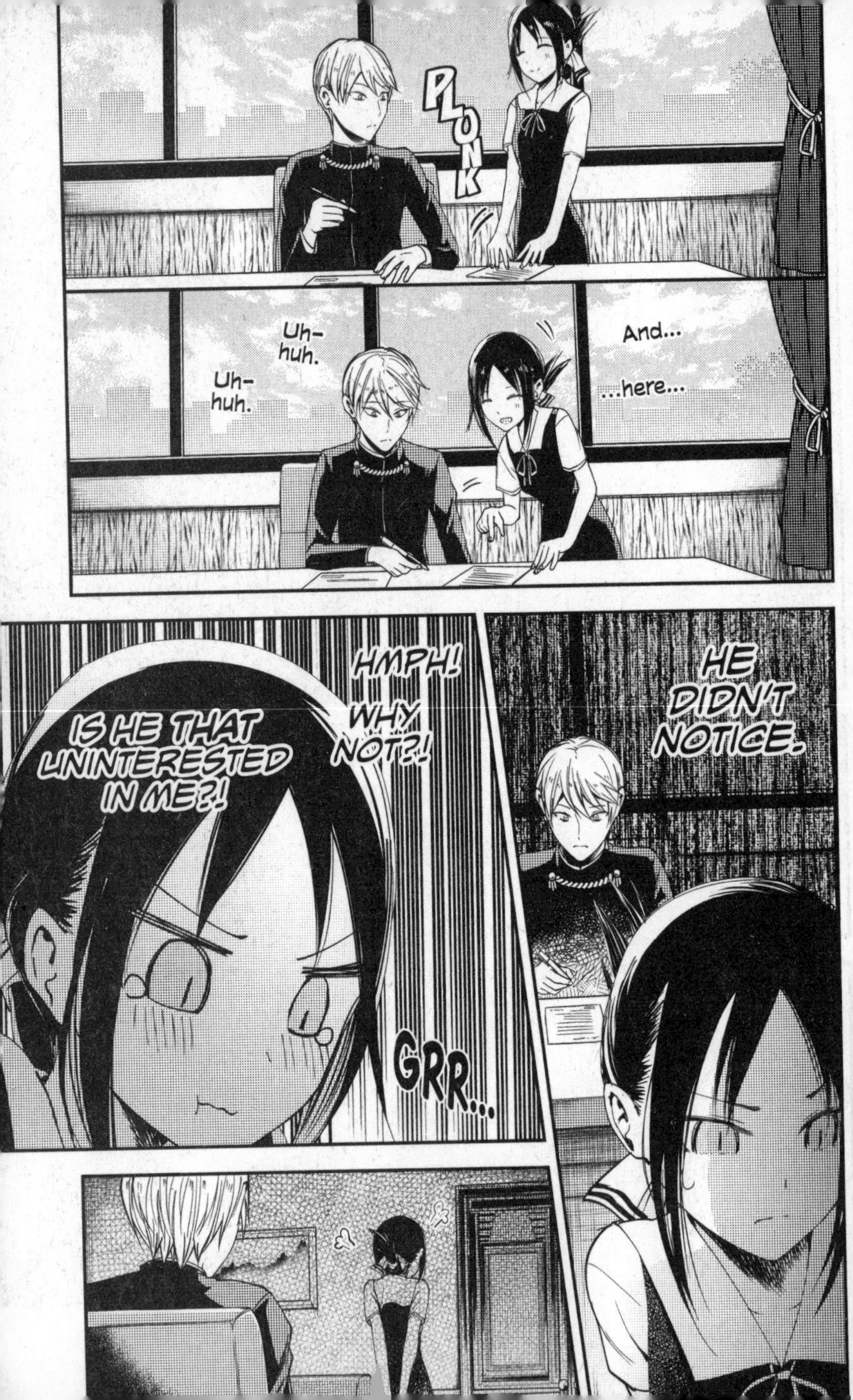
PLONK
And...
...here...
Uh-huh.
Uh-huh.
HE DIDN'T NOTICE.
HMPH! WHY NOT?!
IS HE THAT UNINTERESTED IN ME?!
GRR...

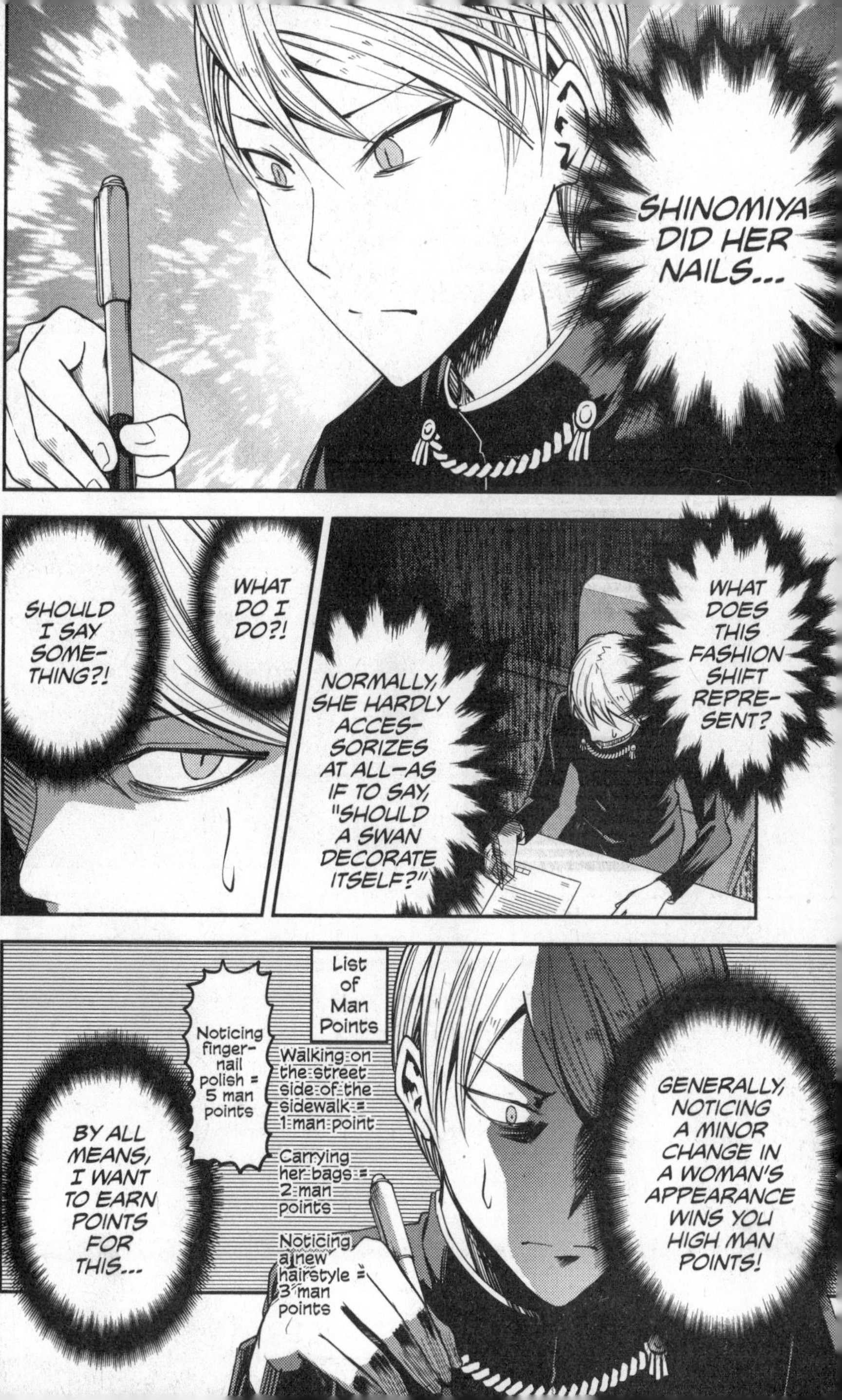
SHINOMIYA DID HER NAILS...
WHAT DOES THIS FASHION SHIFT REPRESENT?
NORMALLY, SHE HARDLY ACCESSORIZES AT ALL—AS IF TO SAY, "SHOULD A SWAN DECORATE ITSELF?"
WHAT DO I DO?!
SHOULD I SAY SOMETHING?!
GENERALLY, NOTICING A MINOR CHANGE IN A WOMAN'S APPEARANCE WINS YOU HIGH MAN POINTS!
List of Man Points
Walking on the street side of the sidewalk = 1 man point
Carrying her bags = 2 man points
Noticing a new hairstyle = 3 man points
Noticing fingernail polish = 5 man points
BY ALL MEANS, I WANT TO EARN POINTS FOR THIS...

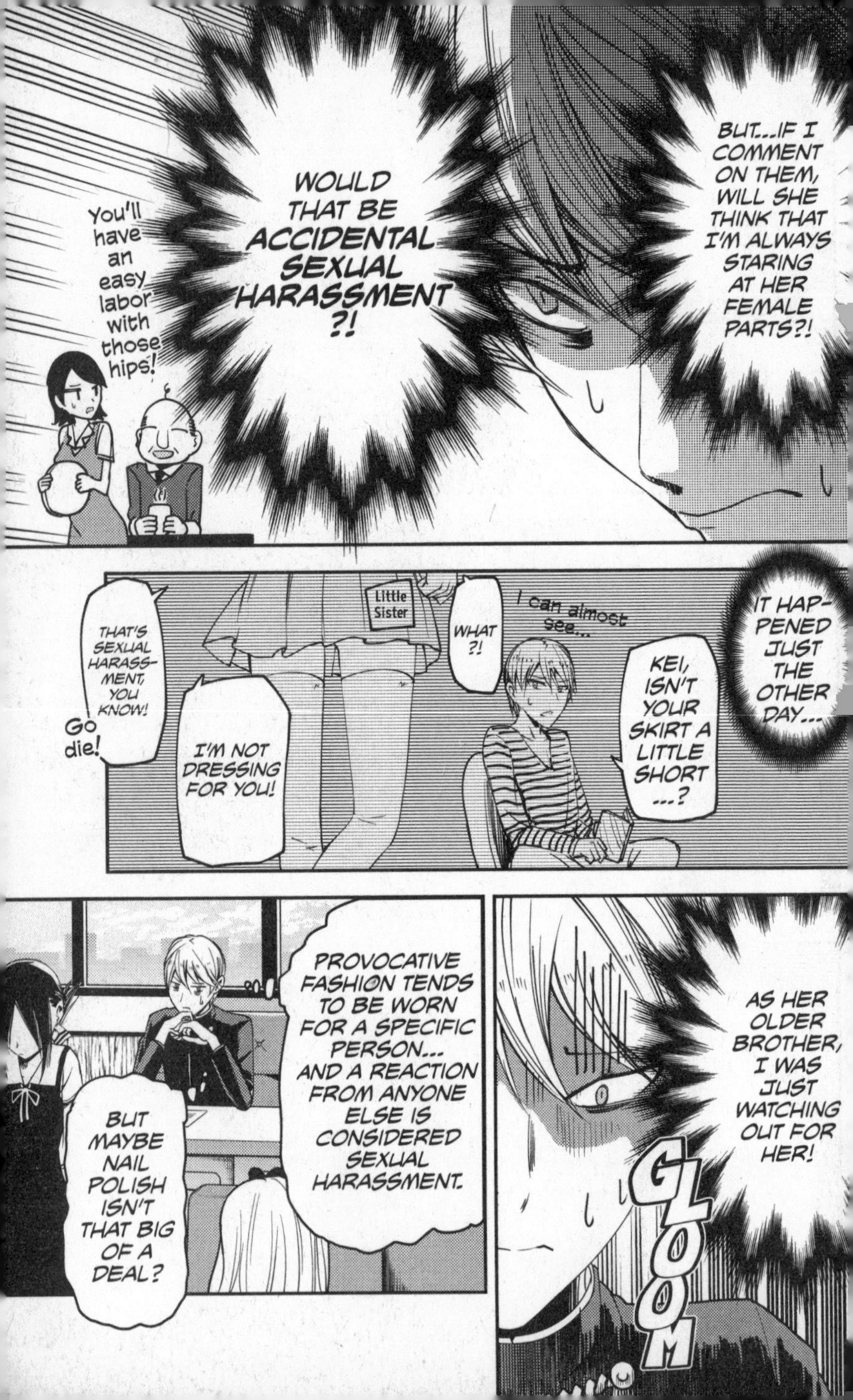
BUT...IF I COMMENT ON THEM, WILL SHE THINK THAT I'M ALWAYS STARING AT HER FEMALE PARTS?!
WOULD THAT BE ACCIDENTAL SEXUAL HARASSMENT ?!
You'll have an easy labor with those hips!
IT HAPPENED JUST THE OTHER DAY...
KEI, ISN'T YOUR SKIRT A LITTLE SHORT ...?
I can almost see...
WHAT ?!
Little Sister
I'M NOT DRESSING FOR YOU!
THAT'S SEXUAL HARASSMENT, YOU KNOW!
Go die!
AS HER OLDER BROTHER, I WAS JUST WATCHING OUT FOR HER!
GLOOM
PROVOCATIVE FASHION TENDS TO BE WORN FOR A SPECIFIC PERSON... AND A REACTION FROM ANYONE ELSE IS CONSIDERED SEXUAL HARASSMENT.
BUT MAYBE NAIL POLISH ISN'T THAT BIG OF A DEAL?

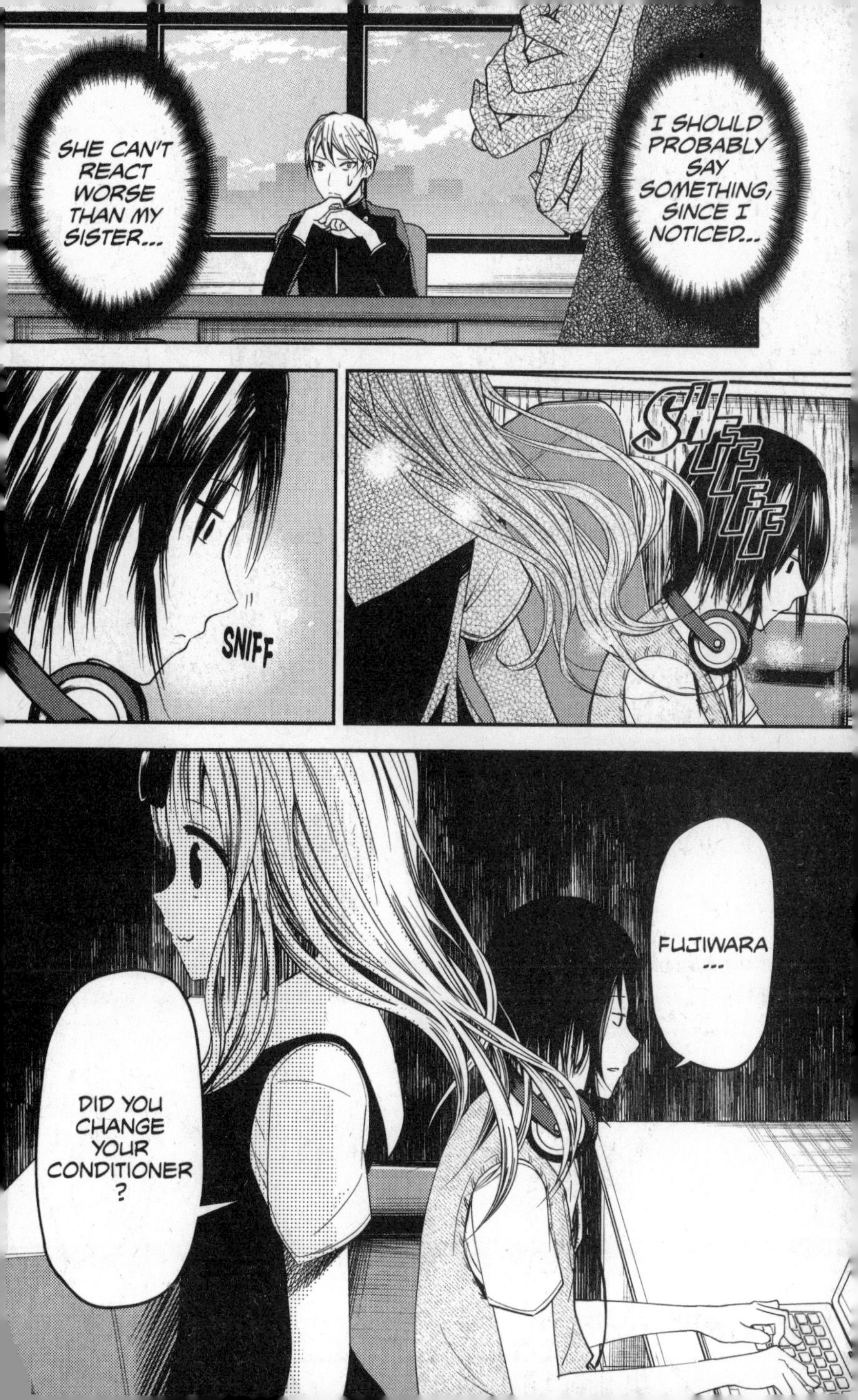
I SHOULD PROBABLY SAY SOMETHING, SINCE I NOTICED...
SHE CAN'T REACT WORSE THAN MY SISTER...
SHUFFUFF
SNIFF
FUJIWARA...
DID YOU CHANGE YOUR CONDITIONER?

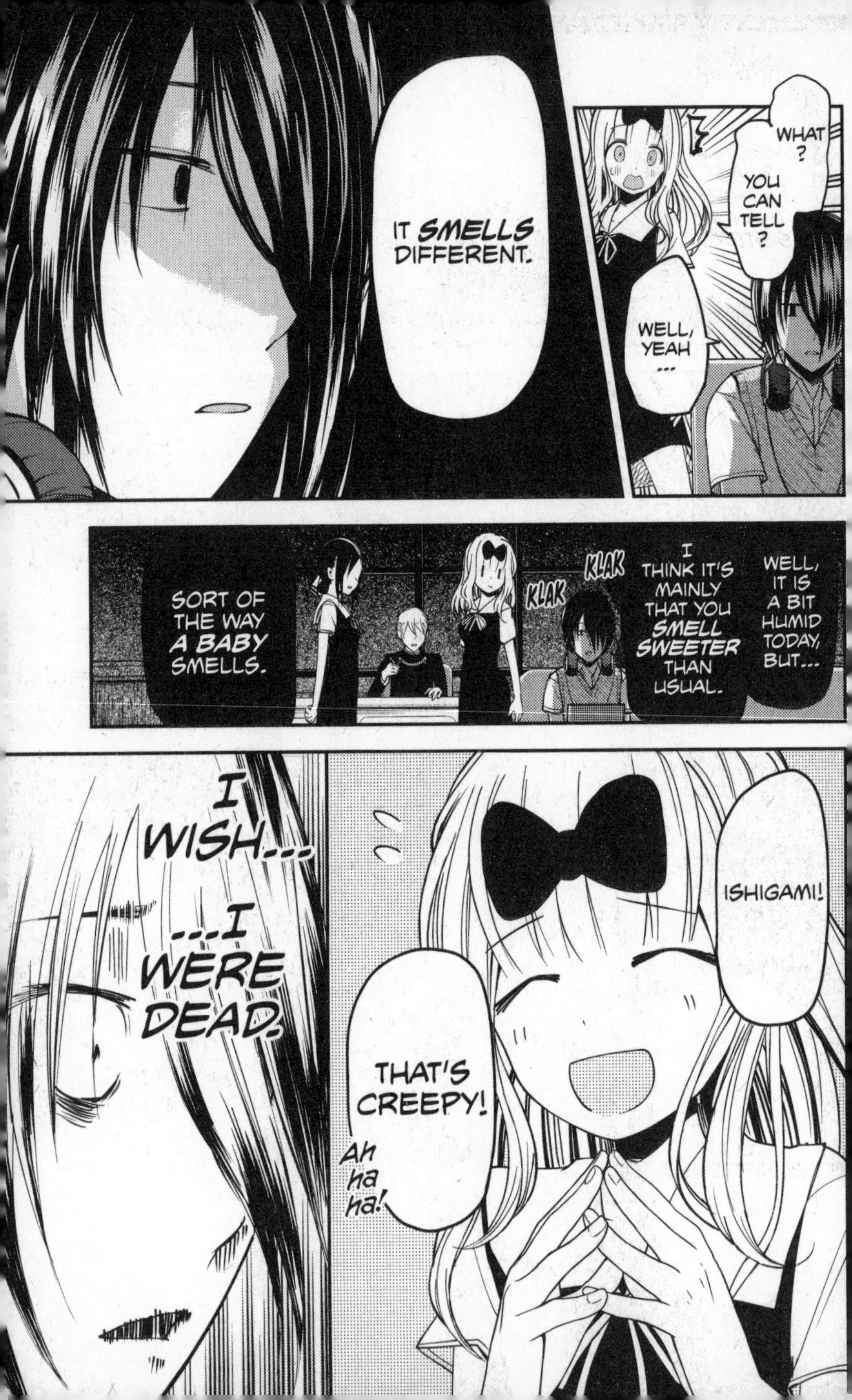
WHAT? YOU CAN TELL?
WELL, YEAH...
IT SMELLS DIFFERENT.
WELL, IT IS A BIT HUMID TODAY, BUT...
I THINK IT'S MAINLY THAT YOU SMELL SWEETER THAN USUAL.
KLAK
KLAK
SORT OF THE WAY A BABY SMELLS.
ISHIGAMI!
THAT'S CREEPY!
Ah ha ha!
I WISH...
...I WERE DEAD.

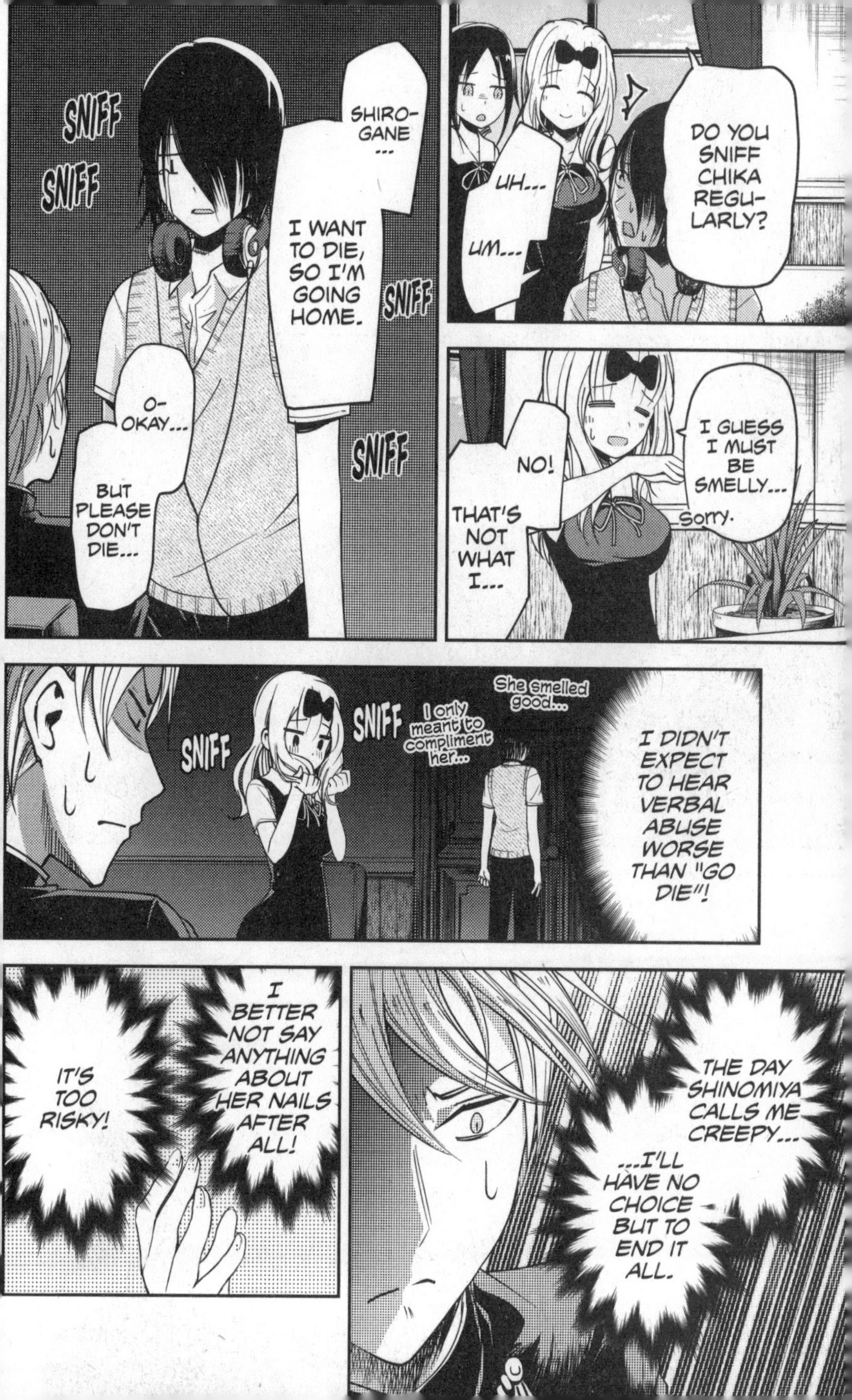
DO YOU SNIFF CHIKA REGULARLY?
UH...
UM...
I GUESS I MUST BE SMELLY...
Sorry.
NO!
THAT'S NOT WHAT I...
SHIRO-GANE...
I WANT TO DIE, SO I'M GOING HOME.
SNIFF
SNIFF
SNIFF
SNIFF
O-OKAY...
BUT PLEASE DON'T DIE...
I DIDN'T EXPECT TO HEAR VERBAL ABUSE WORSE THAN "GO DIE"!
She smelled good...
I only meant to compliment her...
SNIFF
SNIFF
THE DAY SHINOMIYA CALLS ME CREEPY...
...I'LL HAVE NO CHOICE BUT TO END IT ALL.
I BETTER NOT SAY ANYTHING ABOUT HER NAILS AFTER ALL!
IT'S TOO RISKY!

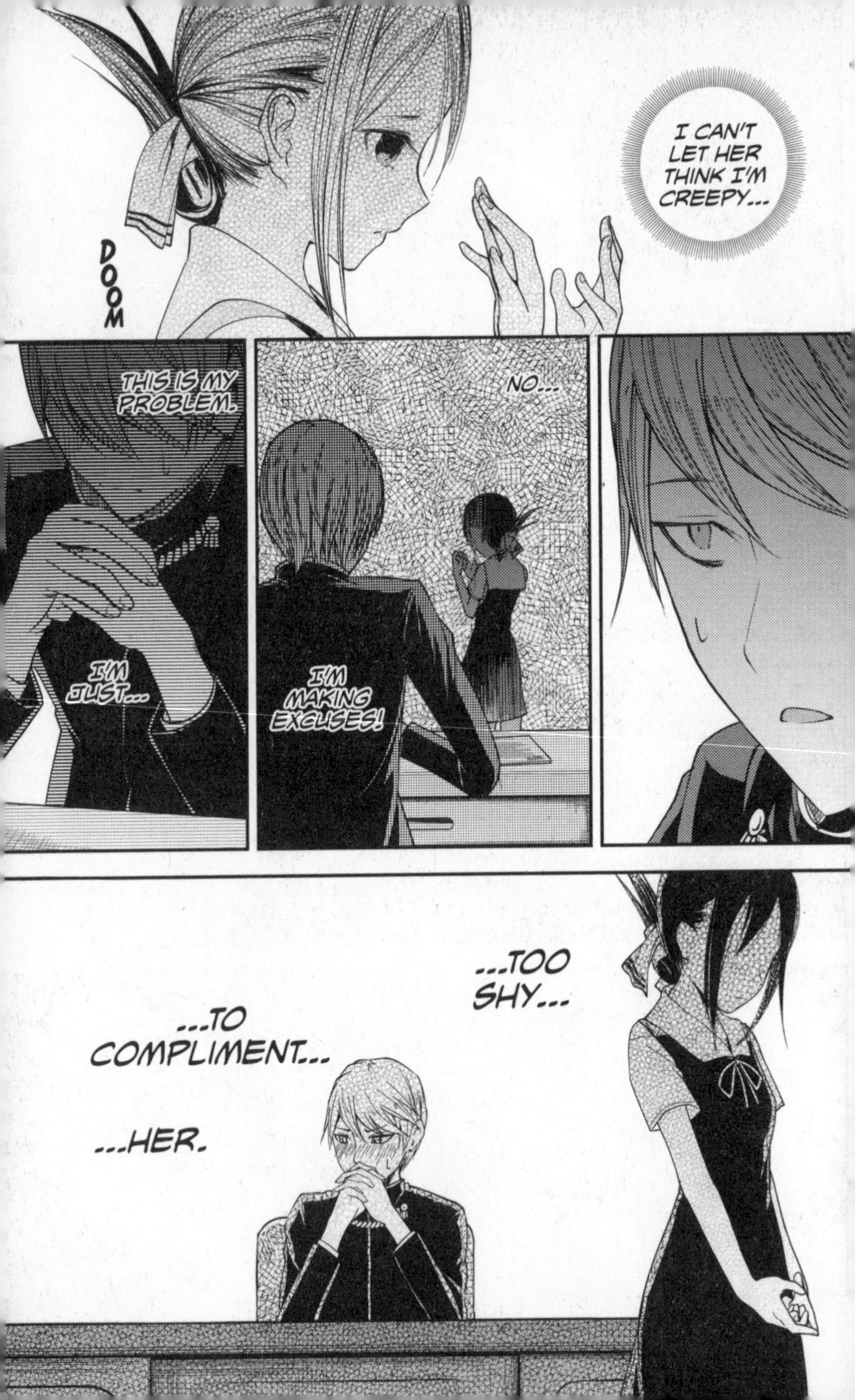
I CAN'T LET HER THINK I'M CREEPY...
DOOM
NO...
I'M MAKING EXCUSES!
THIS IS MY PROBLEM.
I'M JUST...
...TOO SHY...
...TO COMPLIMENT...
...HER.

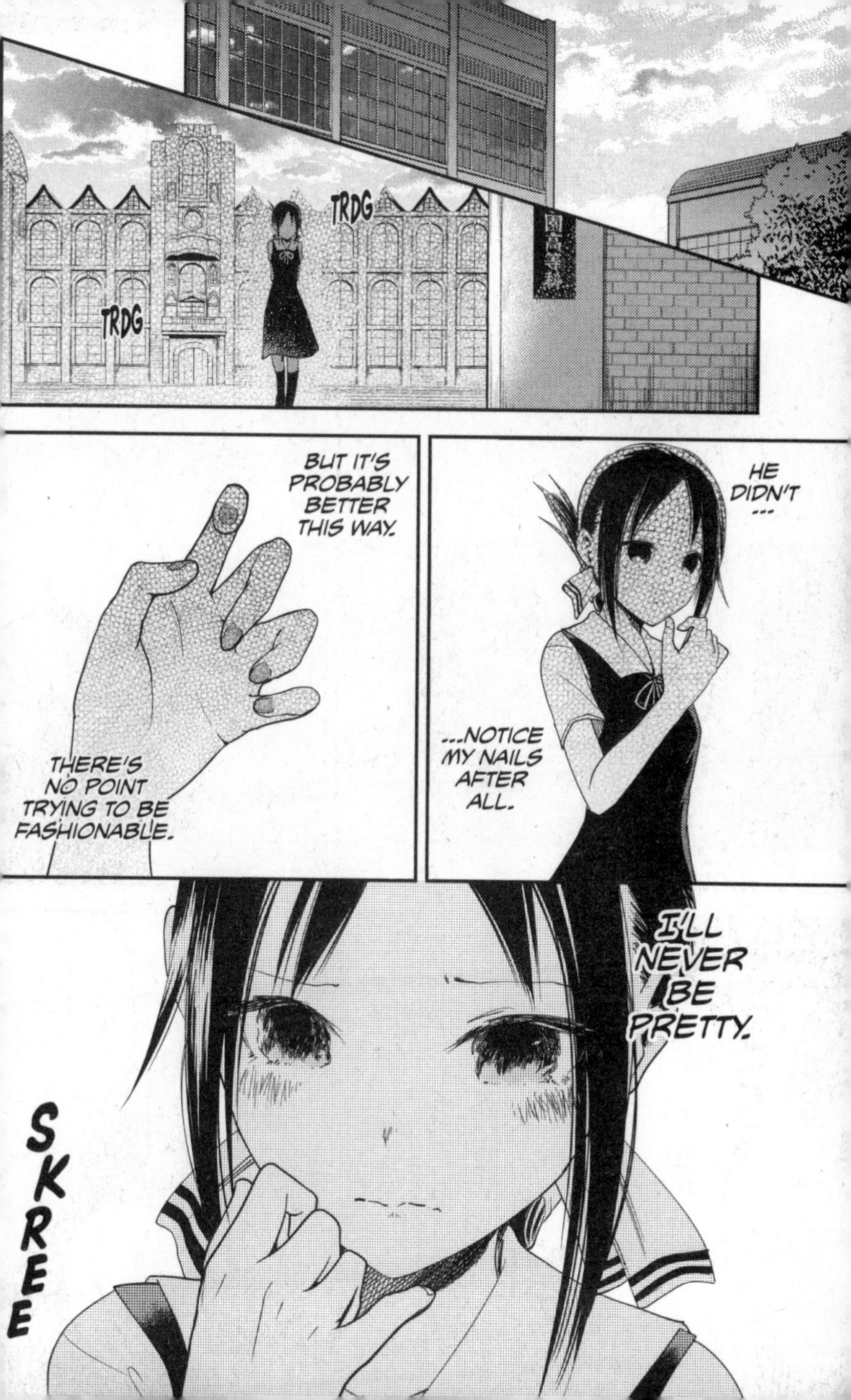
TRDG
TRDG
HE DIDN'T ---
...NOTICE MY NAILS AFTER ALL.
BUT IT'S PROBABLY BETTER THIS WAY.
THERE'S NO POINT TRYING TO BE FASHIONABLE.
I'LL NEVER BE PRETTY.
SKREE

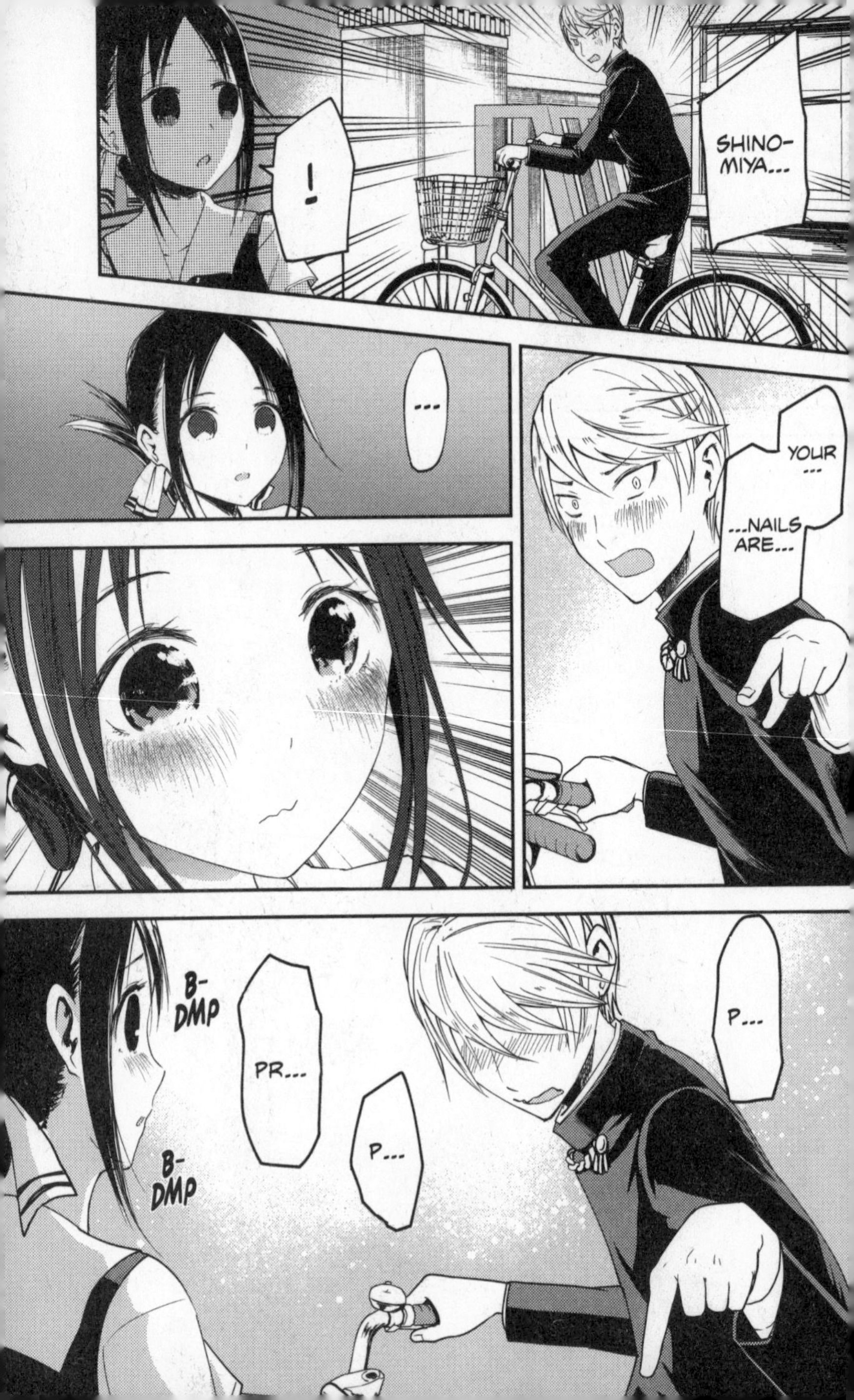
SHINO-MIYA...
!
YOUR...
...NAILS ARE...
...
P...
PR...
B-DMP
P...
B-DMP

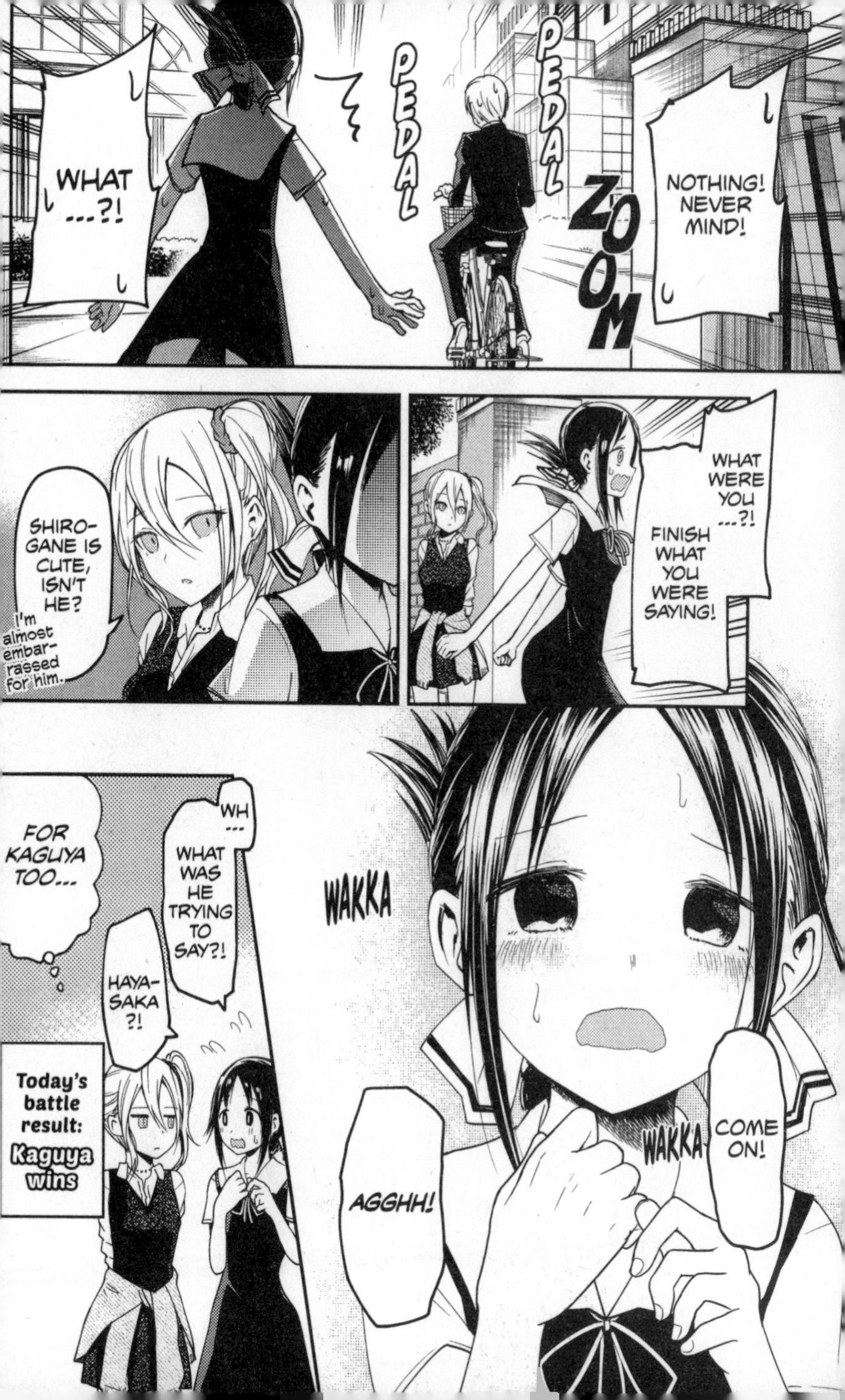
NOTHING! NEVER MIND!
ZOOM
PEDAL
PEDAL
WHAT ...?!
WHAT WERE YOU ...?!
FINISH WHAT YOU WERE SAYING!
SHIRO-GANE IS CUTE, ISN'T HE?
I'm almost embar-rassed for him.
COME ON!
AGGHH!
WAKKA
WAKKA
WH... WHAT WAS HE TRYING TO SAY?!
HAYA-SAKA?!
FOR KAGUYA TOO...
Today's battle result:
Kaguya wins

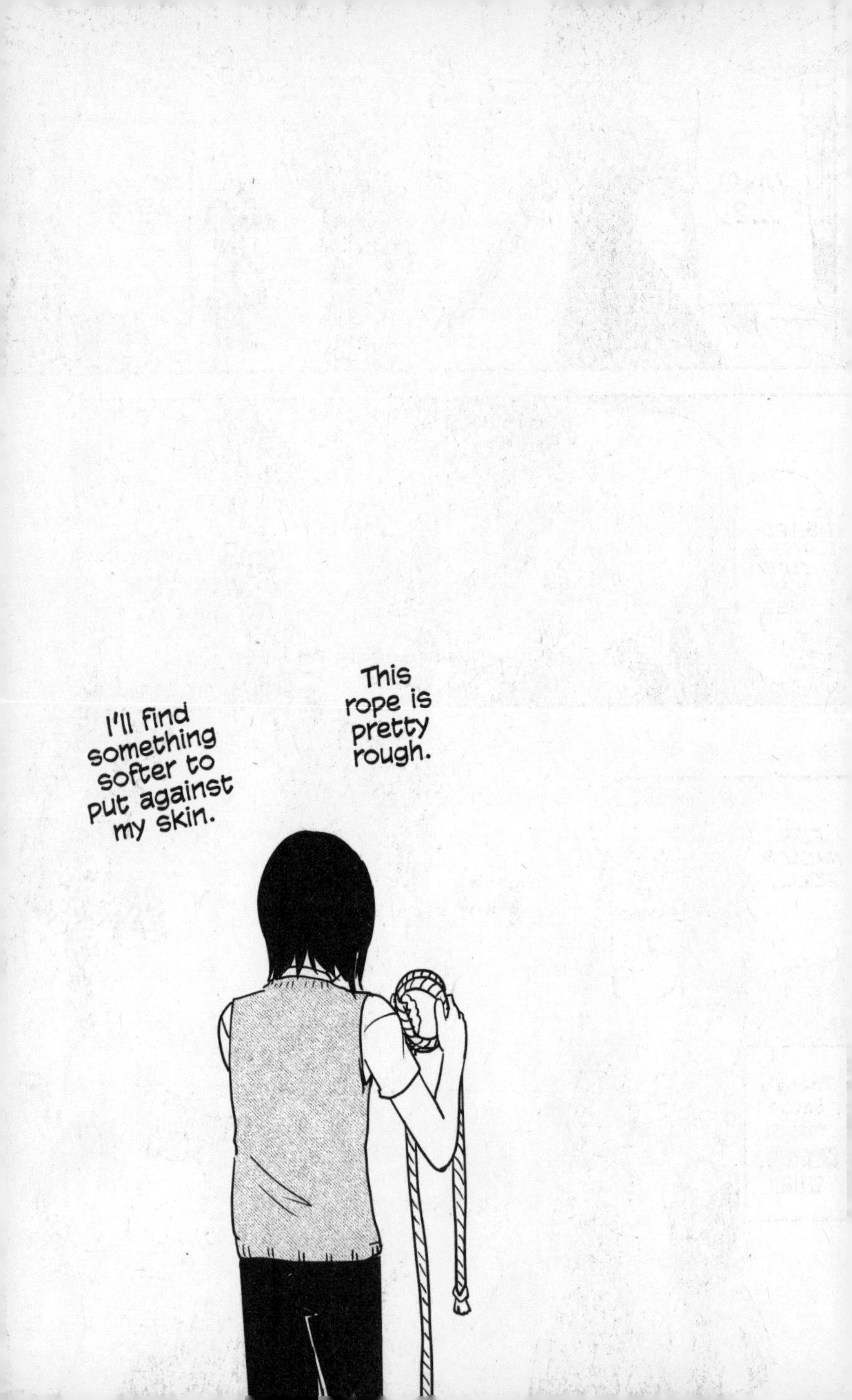
This rope is pretty rough.
I'll find something softer to put against my skin.

KAGUYA-SAMA

LOVE IS WAR

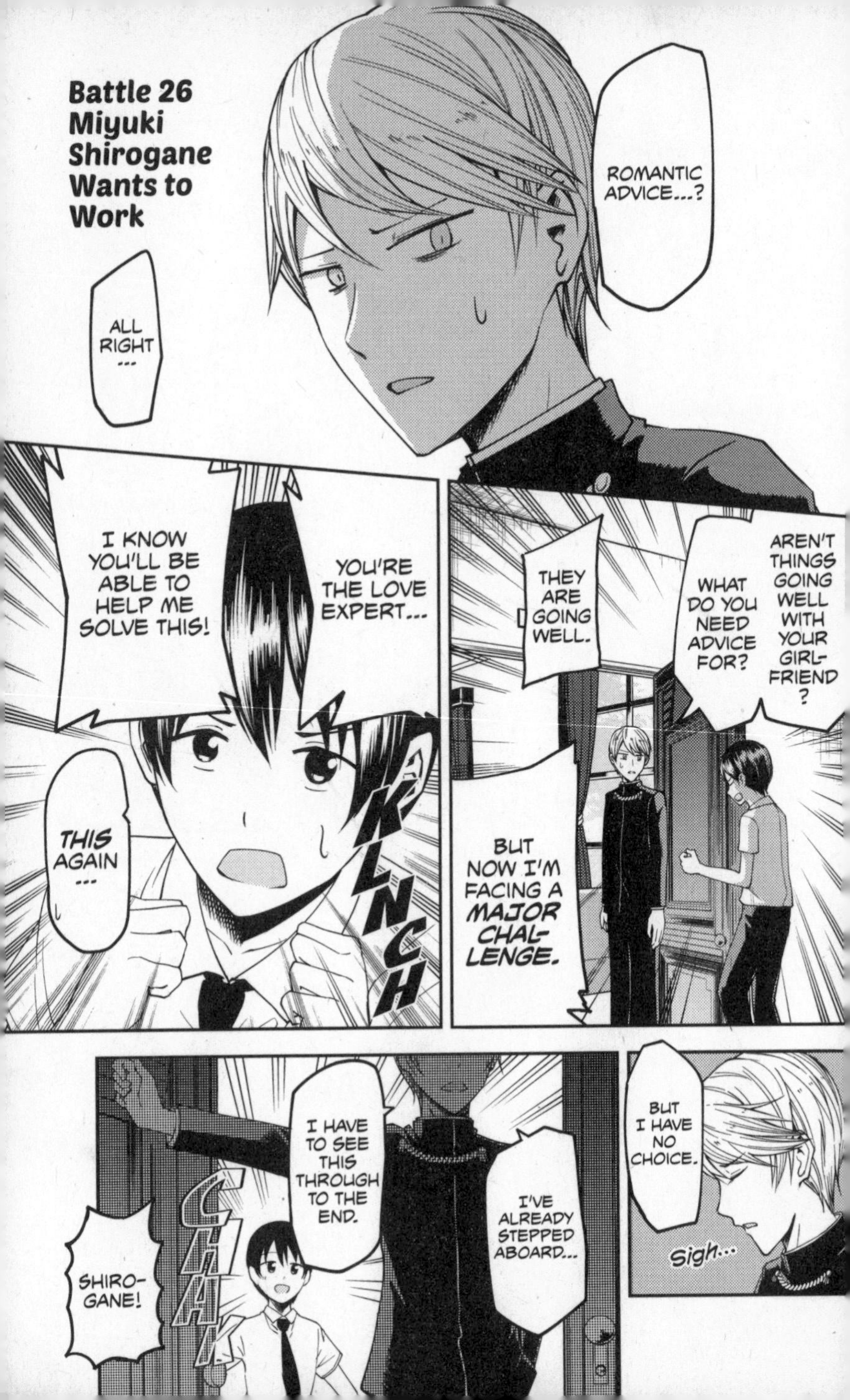
Battle 26 Miyuki Shirogane Wants to Work
ROMANTIC ADVICE...?
ALL RIGHT...
AREN'T THINGS GOING WELL WITH YOUR GIRL-FRIEND?
WHAT DO YOU NEED ADVICE FOR?
THEY ARE GOING WELL.
BUT NOW I'M FACING A MAJOR CHAL-LENGE.
YOU'RE THE LOVE EXPERT...
I KNOW YOU'LL BE ABLE TO HELP ME SOLVE THIS!
KLNCH
THIS AGAIN...
BUT I HAVE NO CHOICE.
Sigh...
I'VE ALREADY STEPPED ABOARD...
I HAVE TO SEE THIS THROUGH TO THE END.
CHAA
SHIRO-GANE!

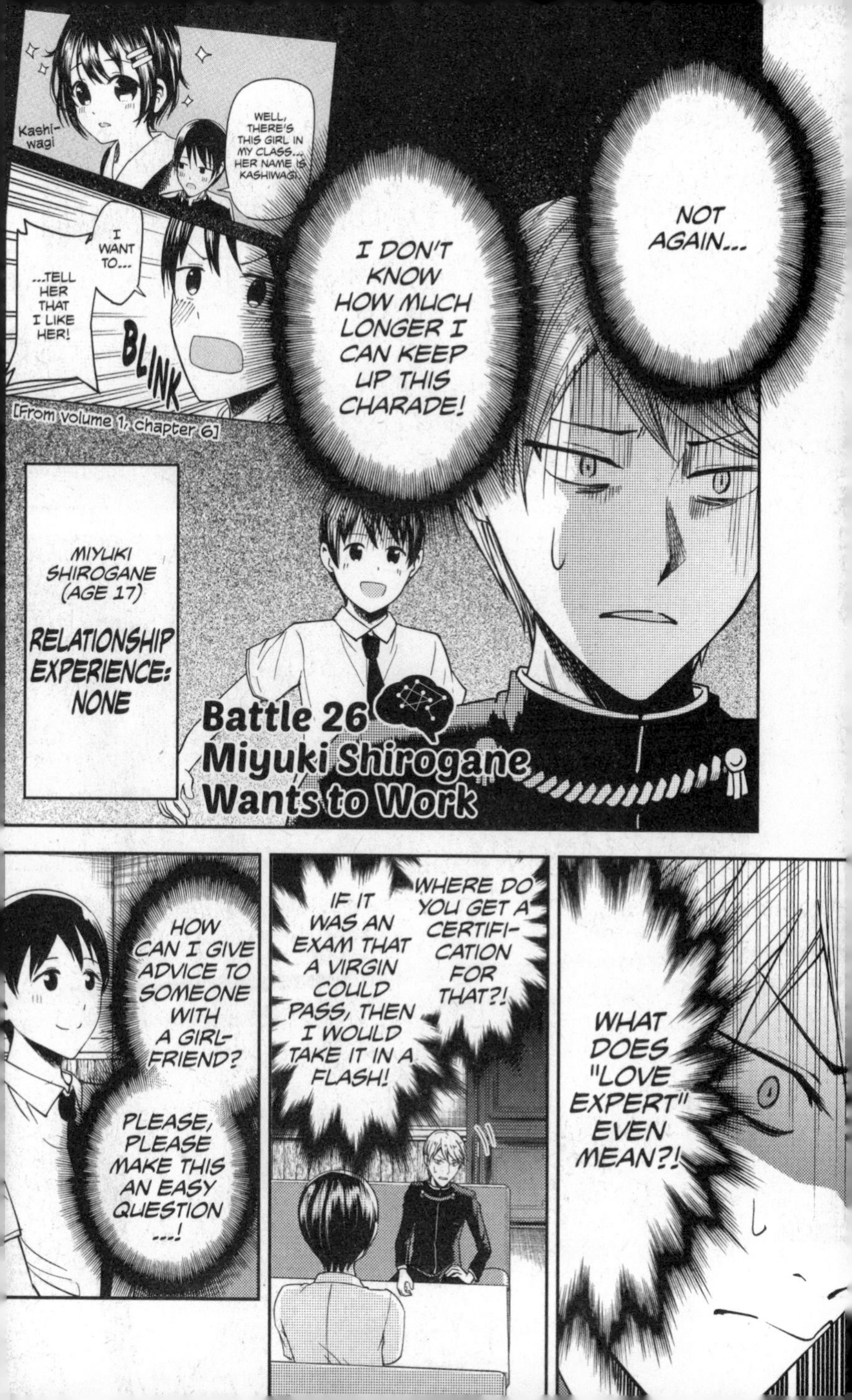
NOT AGAIN...
I DON'T KNOW HOW MUCH LONGER I CAN KEEP UP THIS CHARADE!
WELL, THERE'S THIS GIRL IN MY CLASS... HER NAME IS KASHIWAGI.
Kashi-wagi
I WANT TO...
...TELL HER THAT I LIKE HER!
BLINK
[From volume 1, chapter 6]
MIYUKI SHIROGANE (AGE 17)
RELATIONSHIP EXPERIENCE: NONE
Battle 26 Miyuki Shirogane Wants to Work
WHAT DOES "LOVE EXPERT" EVEN MEAN?!
WHERE DO YOU GET A CERTIFI-CATION FOR THAT?!
IF IT WAS AN EXAM THAT A VIRGIN COULD PASS, THEN I WOULD TAKE IT IN A FLASH!
HOW CAN I GIVE ADVICE TO SOMEONE WITH A GIRL-FRIEND?
PLEASE, PLEASE MAKE THIS AN EASY QUESTION ...!

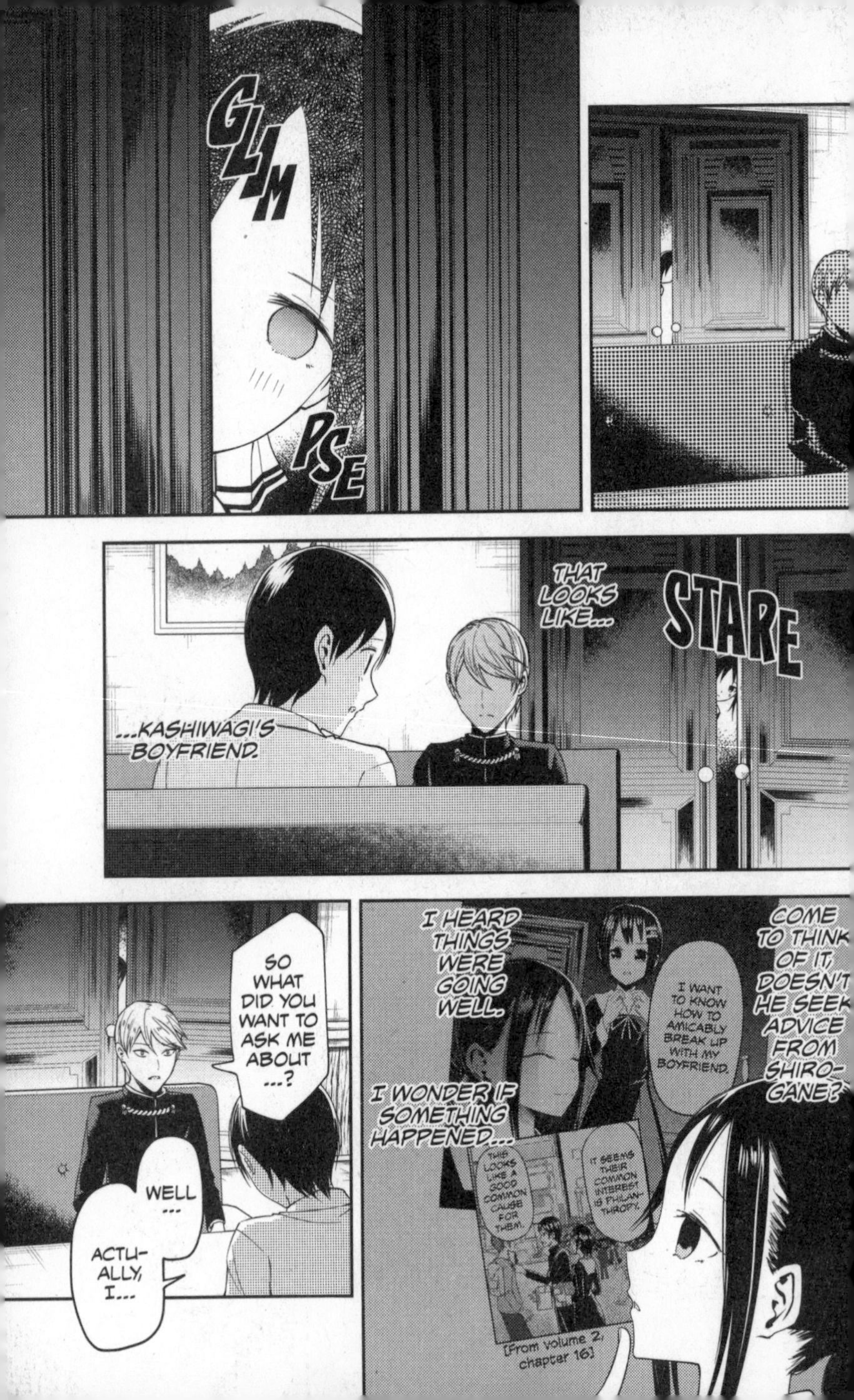
GLIMPSE
STARE
THAT LOOKS LIKE...
...KASHIWAGI'S BOYFRIEND.
COME TO THINK OF IT, DOESN'T HE SEEK ADVICE FROM SHIRO-GANE?
I WANT TO KNOW HOW TO AMICABLY BREAK UP WITH MY BOYFRIEND.
I HEARD THINGS WERE GOING WELL.
IT SEEMS THEIR COMMON INTEREST IS PHILAN-THROPY.
THIS LOOKS LIKE A GOOD COMMON CAUSE FOR THEM.
I WONDER IF SOMETHING HAPPENED...
[From volume 2, chapter 16]
SO WHAT DID YOU WANT TO ASK ME ABOUT...?
WELL...
ACTU-ALLY, I...

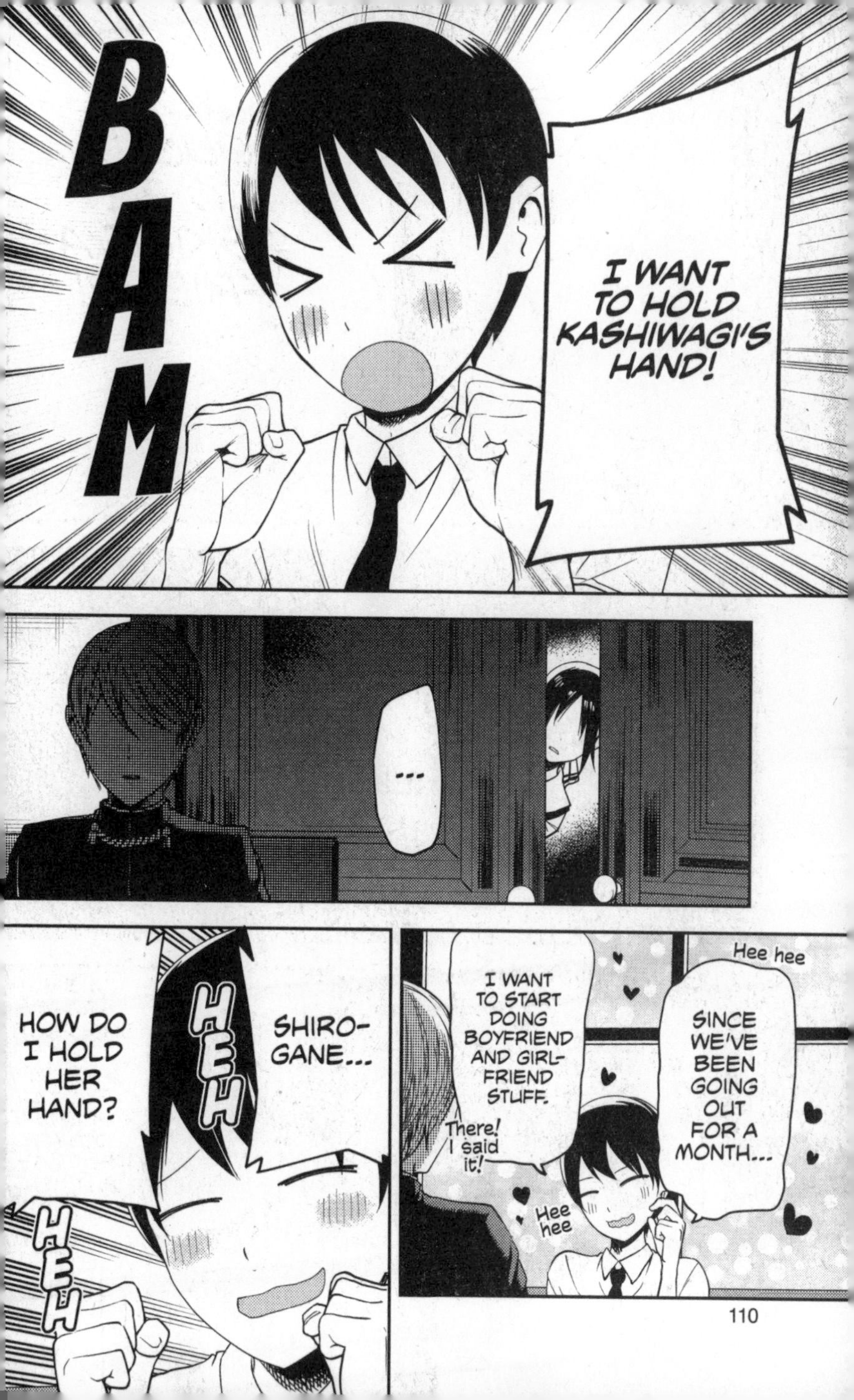
I WANT TO HOLD KASHIWAGI'S HAND!
BAM
...
Hee hee
SINCE WE'VE BEEN GOING OUT FOR A MONTH...
I WANT TO START DOING BOYFRIEND AND GIRL-FRIEND STUFF.
There! I said it!
Hee hee
SHIRO-GANE...
HEH
HOW DO I HOLD HER HAND?
HEH

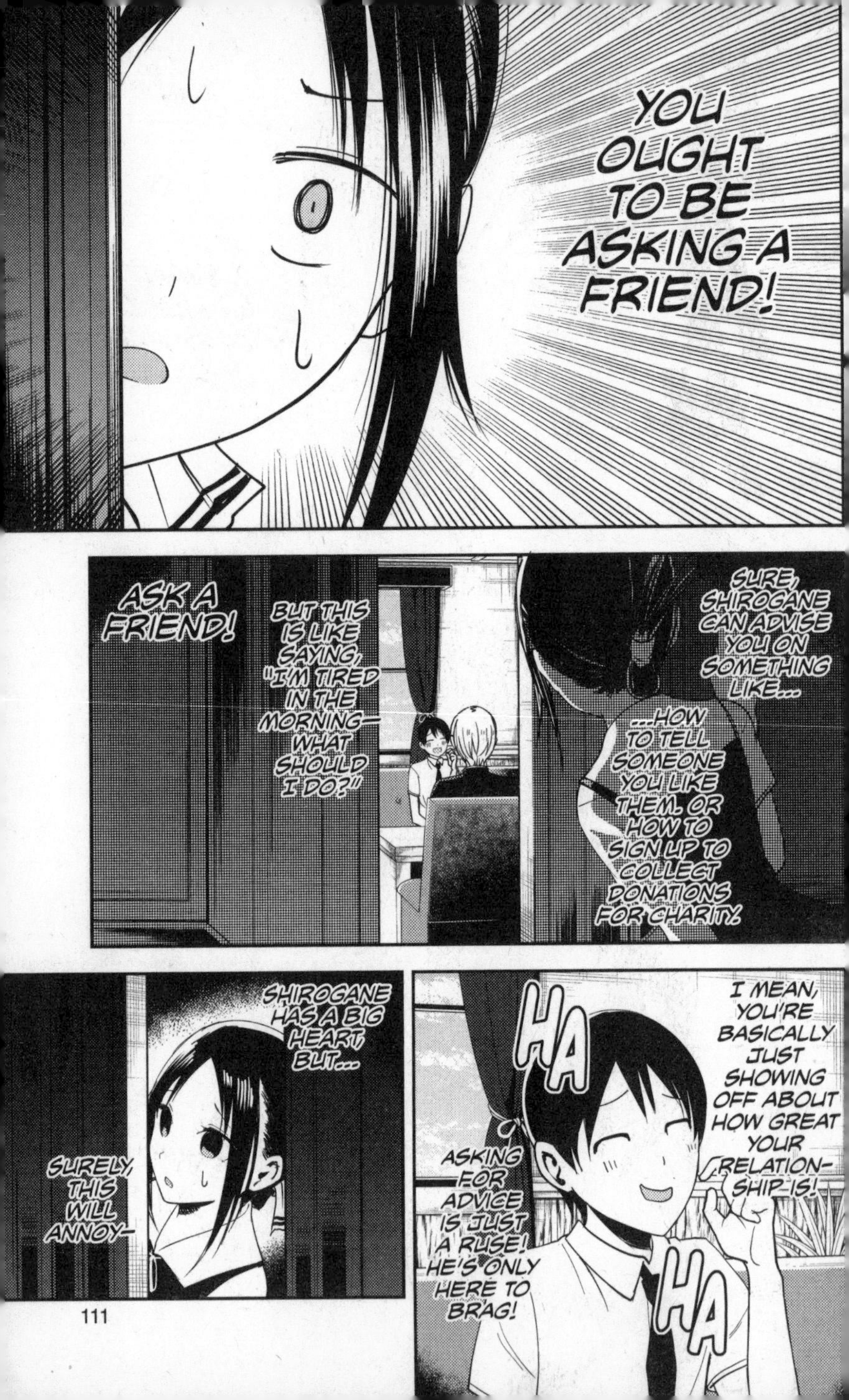

YOU OUGHT TO BE ASKING A FRIEND!
SURE, SHIROGANE CAN ADVISE YOU ON SOMETHING LIKE...
...HOW TO TELL SOMEONE YOU LIKE THEM, OR HOW TO SIGN UP TO COLLECT DONATIONS FOR CHARITY.
ASK A FRIEND!
BUT THIS IS LIKE SAYING, "I'M TIRED IN THE MORNING—WHAT SHOULD I DO?"
HA
I MEAN, YOU'RE BASICALLY JUST SHOWING OFF ABOUT HOW GREAT YOUR RELATIONSHIP IS!
ASKING FOR ADVICE IS JUST A RUSE! HE'S ONLY HERE TO BRAG!
HA
SHIROGANE HAS A BIG HEART, BUT...
SURELY, THIS WILL ANNOY—

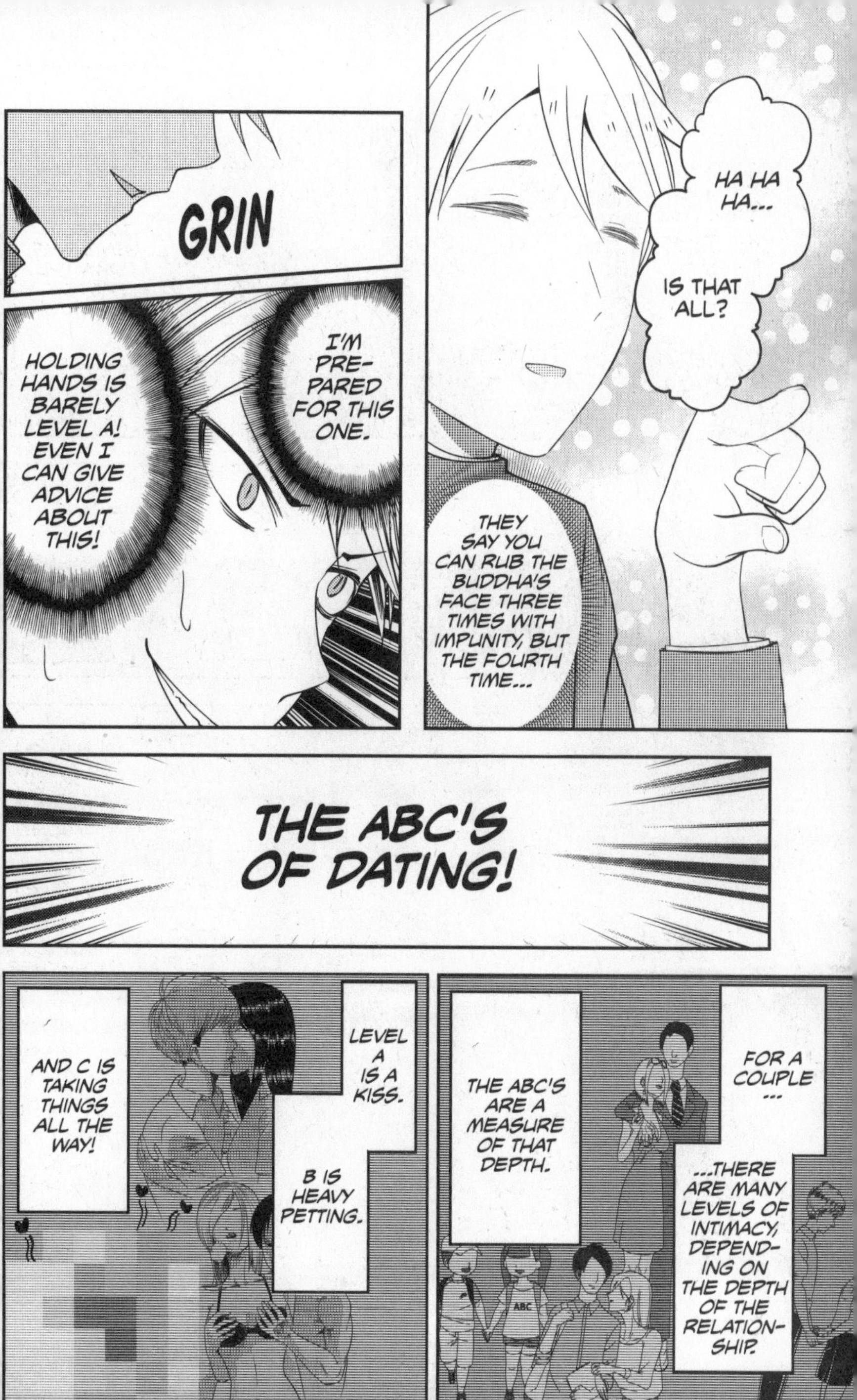
HA HA HA...
IS THAT ALL?
THEY SAY YOU CAN RUB THE BUDDHA'S FACE THREE TIMES WITH IMPUNITY, BUT THE FOURTH TIME...
GRIN
I'M PRE-PARED FOR THIS ONE.
HOLDING HANDS IS BARELY LEVEL A! EVEN I CAN GIVE ADVICE ABOUT THIS!
THE ABC'S OF DATING!
FOR A COUPLE...
...THERE ARE MANY LEVELS OF INTIMACY, DEPEND-ING ON THE DEPTH OF THE RELATION-SHIP.
THE ABC'S ARE A MEASURE OF THAT DEPTH.
ABC
LEVEL A IS A KISS.
B IS HEAVY PETTING.
AND C IS TAKING THINGS ALL THE WAY!

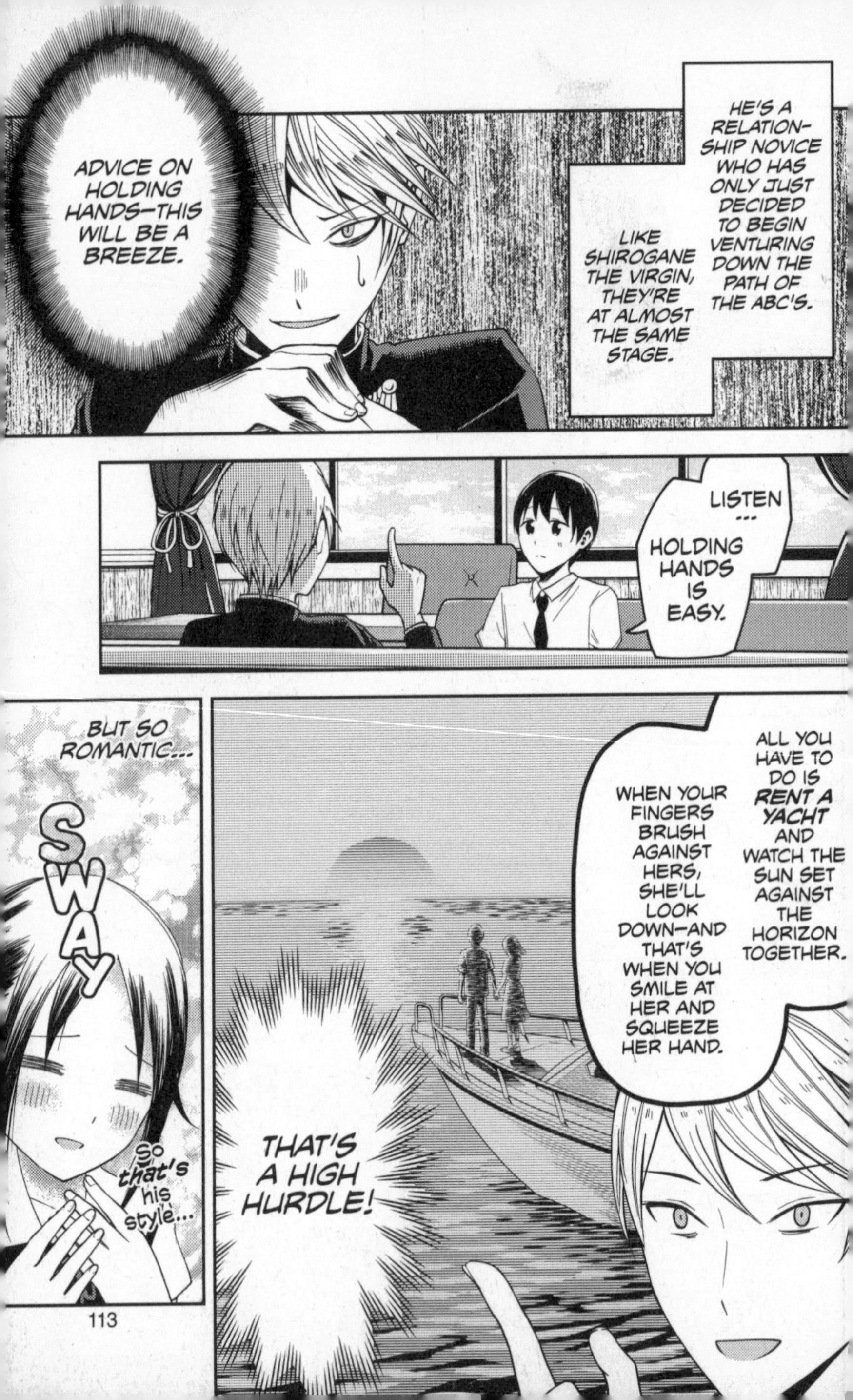
HE'S A RELATIONSHIP NOVICE WHO HAS ONLY JUST DECIDED TO BEGIN VENTURING DOWN THE PATH OF THE ABC'S.
LIKE SHIROGANE THE VIRGIN, THEY'RE AT ALMOST THE SAME STAGE.
ADVICE ON HOLDING HANDS—THIS WILL BE A BREEZE.
LISTEN... HOLDING HANDS IS EASY.
ALL YOU HAVE TO DO IS **RENT A YACHT** AND WATCH THE SUN SET AGAINST THE HORIZON TOGETHER.
WHEN YOUR FINGERS BRUSH AGAINST HERS, SHE'LL LOOK DOWN—AND THAT'S WHEN YOU SMILE AT HER AND SQUEEZE HER HAND.
THAT'S A HIGH HURDLE!
BUT SO ROMANTIC...
SWAY
So *that*'s his style...

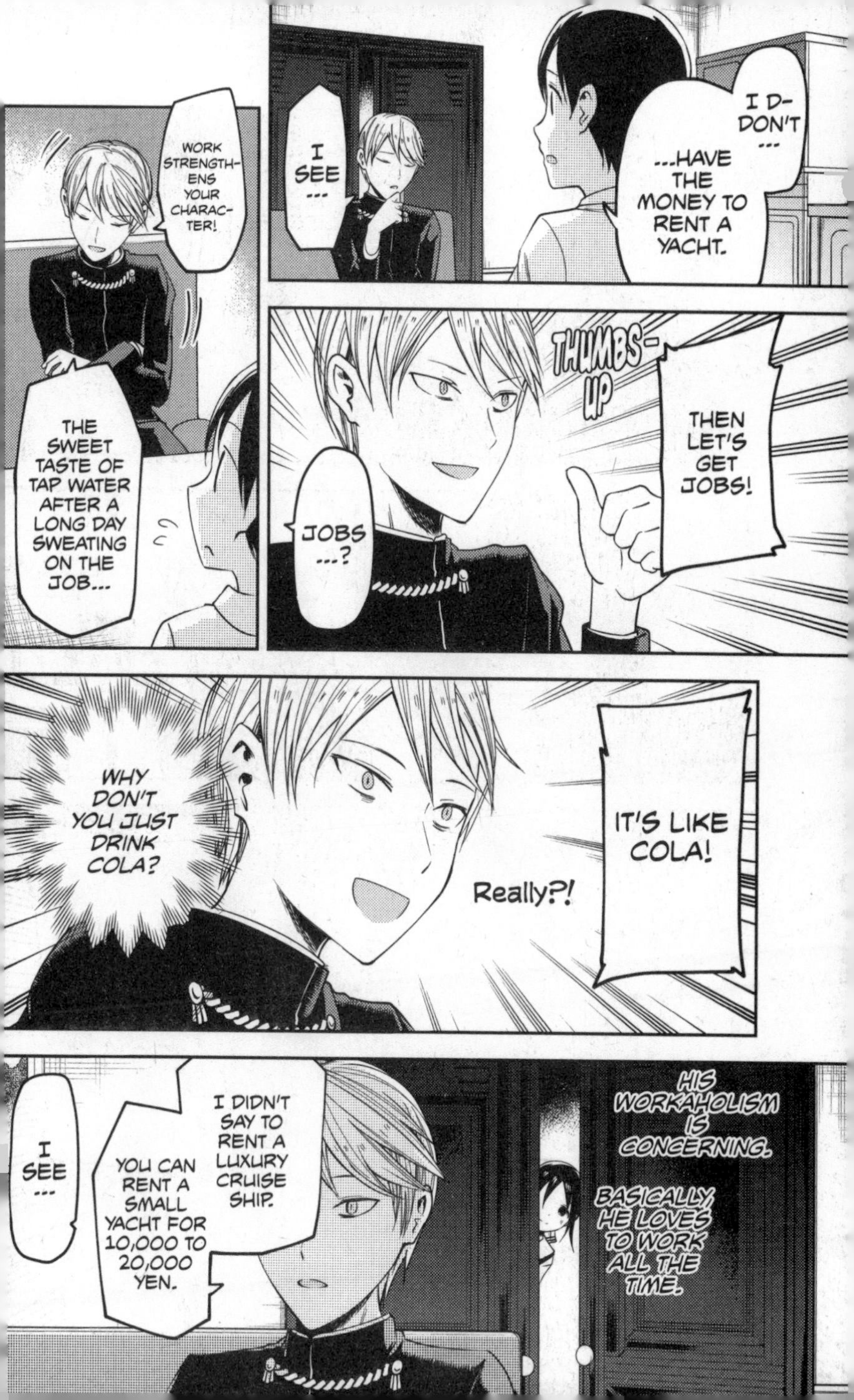
I D-DON'T...
...HAVE THE MONEY TO RENT A YACHT.
I SEE...
THEN LET'S GET JOBS!
THUMBS-UP
JOBS...?
WORK STRENGTHENS YOUR CHARACTER!
THE SWEET TASTE OF TAP WATER AFTER A LONG DAY SWEATING ON THE JOB...
IT'S LIKE COLA!
Really?!
WHY DON'T YOU JUST DRINK COLA?
HIS WORKAHOLISM IS CONCERNING.
BASICALLY, HE LOVES TO WORK ALL THE TIME.
I DIDN'T SAY TO RENT A LUXURY CRUISE SHIP.
YOU CAN RENT A SMALL YACHT FOR 10,000 TO 20,000 YEN.
I SEE...

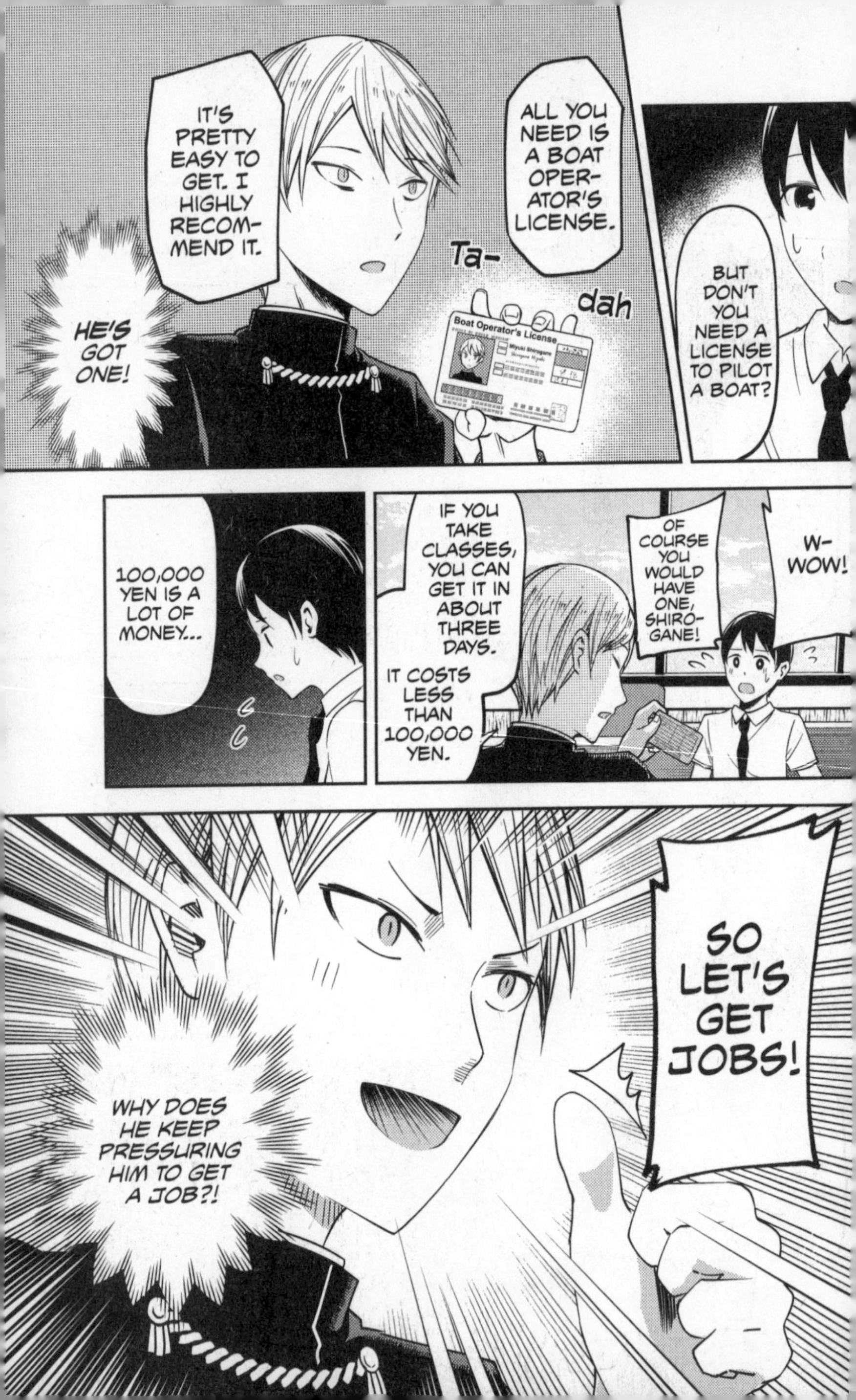
BUT DON'T YOU NEED A LICENSE TO PILOT A BOAT?
ALL YOU NEED IS A BOAT OPERATOR'S LICENSE.
Ta-
dah
Boat Operator's License
Miyuki Shirogane
IT'S PRETTY EASY TO GET. I HIGHLY RECOMMEND IT.
HE'S GOT ONE!
W-WOW!
OF COURSE YOU WOULD HAVE ONE, SHIROGANE!
IF YOU TAKE CLASSES, YOU CAN GET IT IN ABOUT THREE DAYS.
IT COSTS LESS THAN 100,000 YEN.
100,000 YEN IS A LOT OF MONEY...
SO LET'S GET JOBS!
WHY DOES HE KEEP PRESSURING HIM TO GET A JOB?!

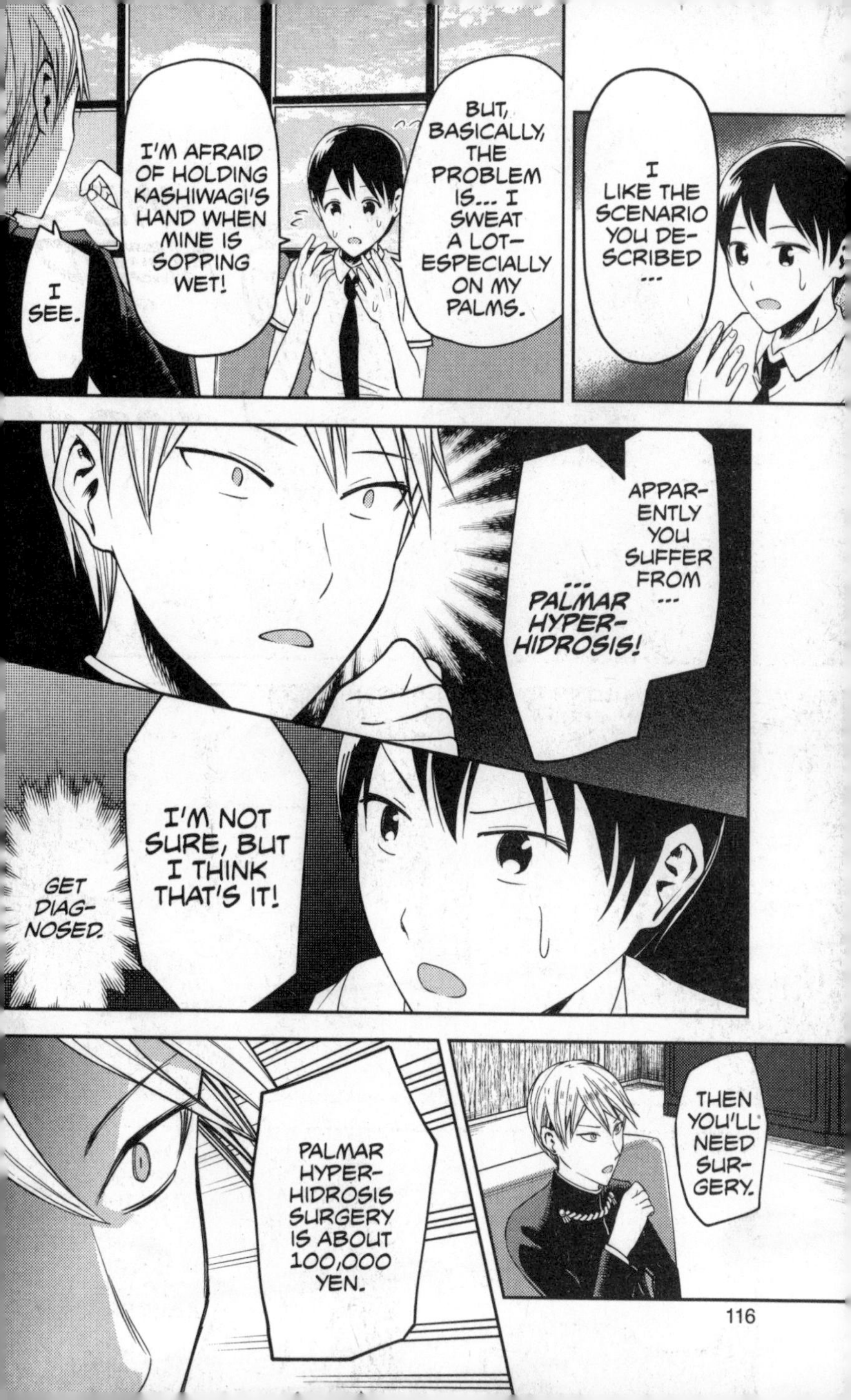
I LIKE THE SCENARIO YOU DESCRIBED...
BUT, BASICALLY, THE PROBLEM IS... I SWEAT A LOT—ESPECIALLY ON MY PALMS.
I'M AFRAID OF HOLDING KASHIWAGI'S HAND WHEN MINE IS SOPPING WET!
I SEE.
APPARENTLY YOU SUFFER FROM... ...PALMAR HYPERHIDROSIS!
I'M NOT SURE, BUT I THINK THAT'S IT!
GET DIAGNOSED.
THEN YOU'LL NEED SURGERY.
PALMAR HYPERHIDROSIS SURGERY IS ABOUT 100,000 YEN.

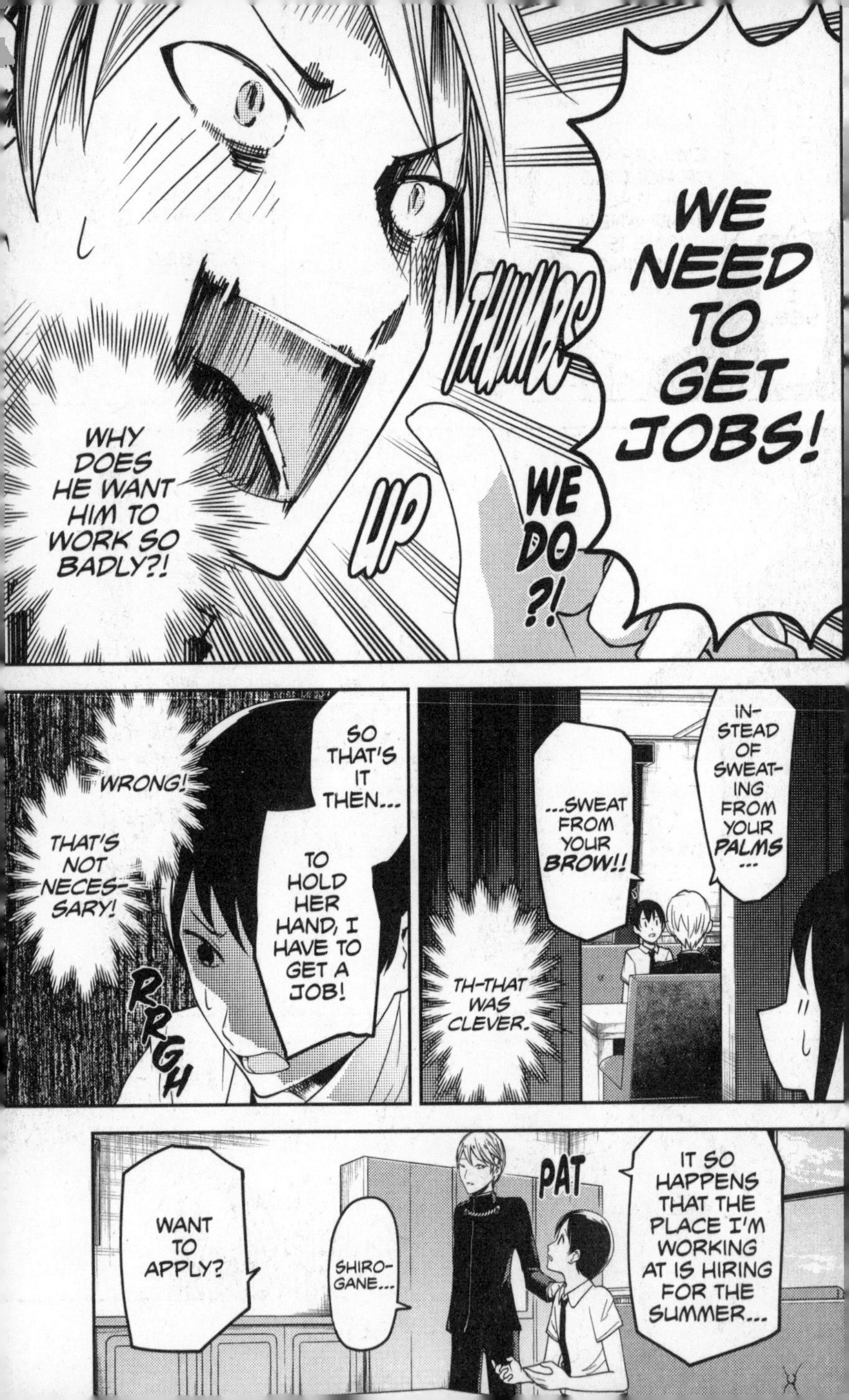
WE NEED TO GET JOBS!
WE DO?!
UP
WHY DOES HE WANT HIM TO WORK SO BADLY?!
INSTEAD OF SWEATING FROM YOUR PALMS...
...SWEAT FROM YOUR BROW!!
TH-THAT WAS CLEVER.
SO THAT'S IT THEN...
TO HOLD HER HAND, I HAVE TO GET A JOB!
WRONG!
THAT'S NOT NECES-SARY!
RRRGH
IT SO HAPPENS THAT THE PLACE I'M WORKING AT IS HIRING FOR THE SUMMER...
PAT
SHIRO-GANE...
WANT TO APPLY?

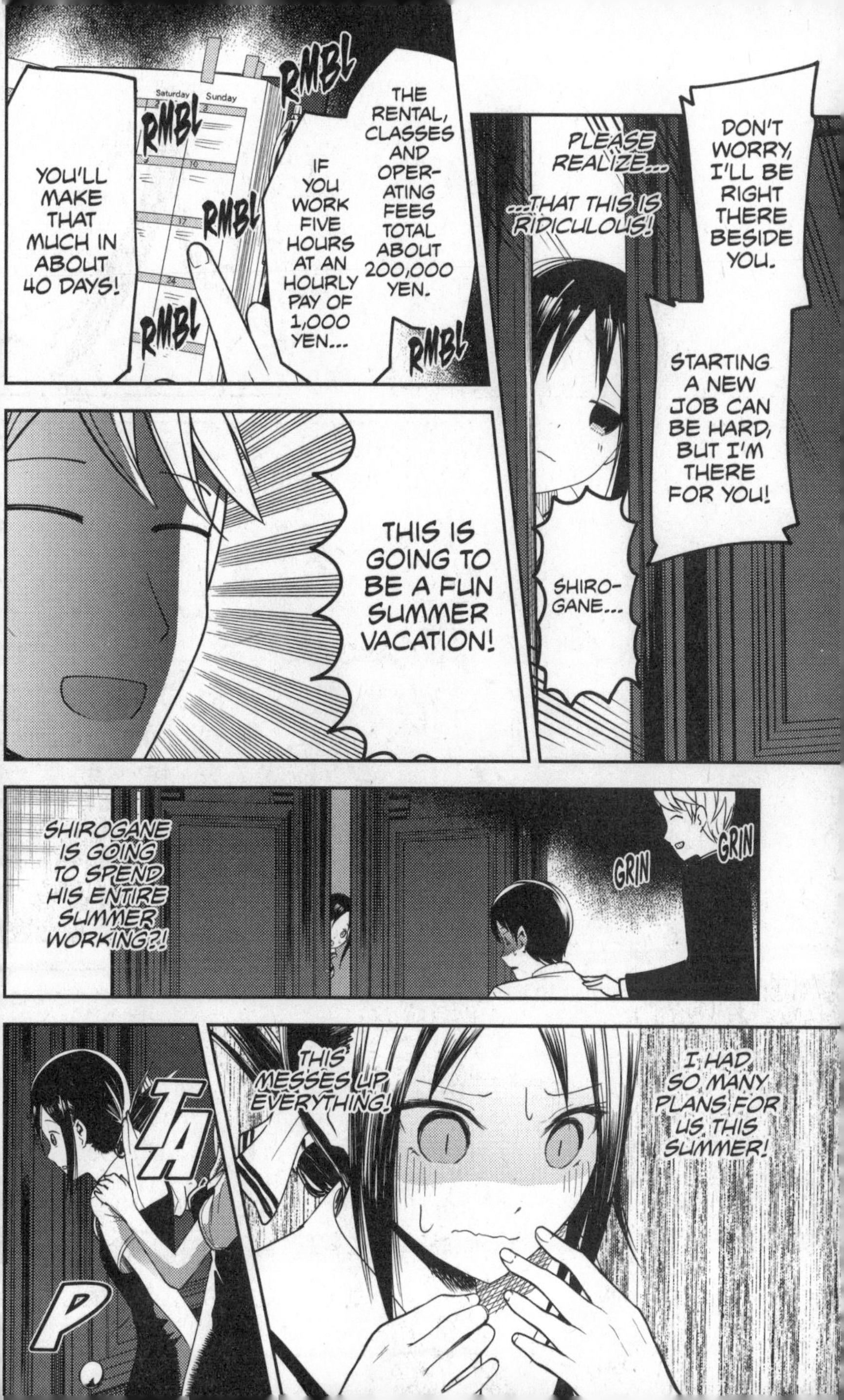
RMBL
THE RENTAL, CLASSES AND OPER-ATING FEES TOTAL ABOUT 200,000 YEN.
IF YOU WORK FIVE HOURS AT AN HOURLY PAY OF 1,000 YEN...
RMBL
RMBL
RMBL
RMBL
YOU'LL MAKE THAT MUCH IN ABOUT 40 DAYS!
Saturday
Sunday
DON'T WORRY, I'LL BE RIGHT THERE BESIDE YOU.
PLEASE REALIZE...
...THAT THIS IS RIDICULOUS!
STARTING A NEW JOB CAN BE HARD, BUT I'M THERE FOR YOU!
SHIRO-GANE...
THIS IS GOING TO BE A FUN SUMMER VACATION!
GRIN
GRIN
SHIROGANE IS GOING TO SPEND HIS ENTIRE SUMMER WORKING?!
I HAD SO MANY PLANS FOR US THIS SUMMER!
THIS MESSES UP EVERYTHING!
TA
P

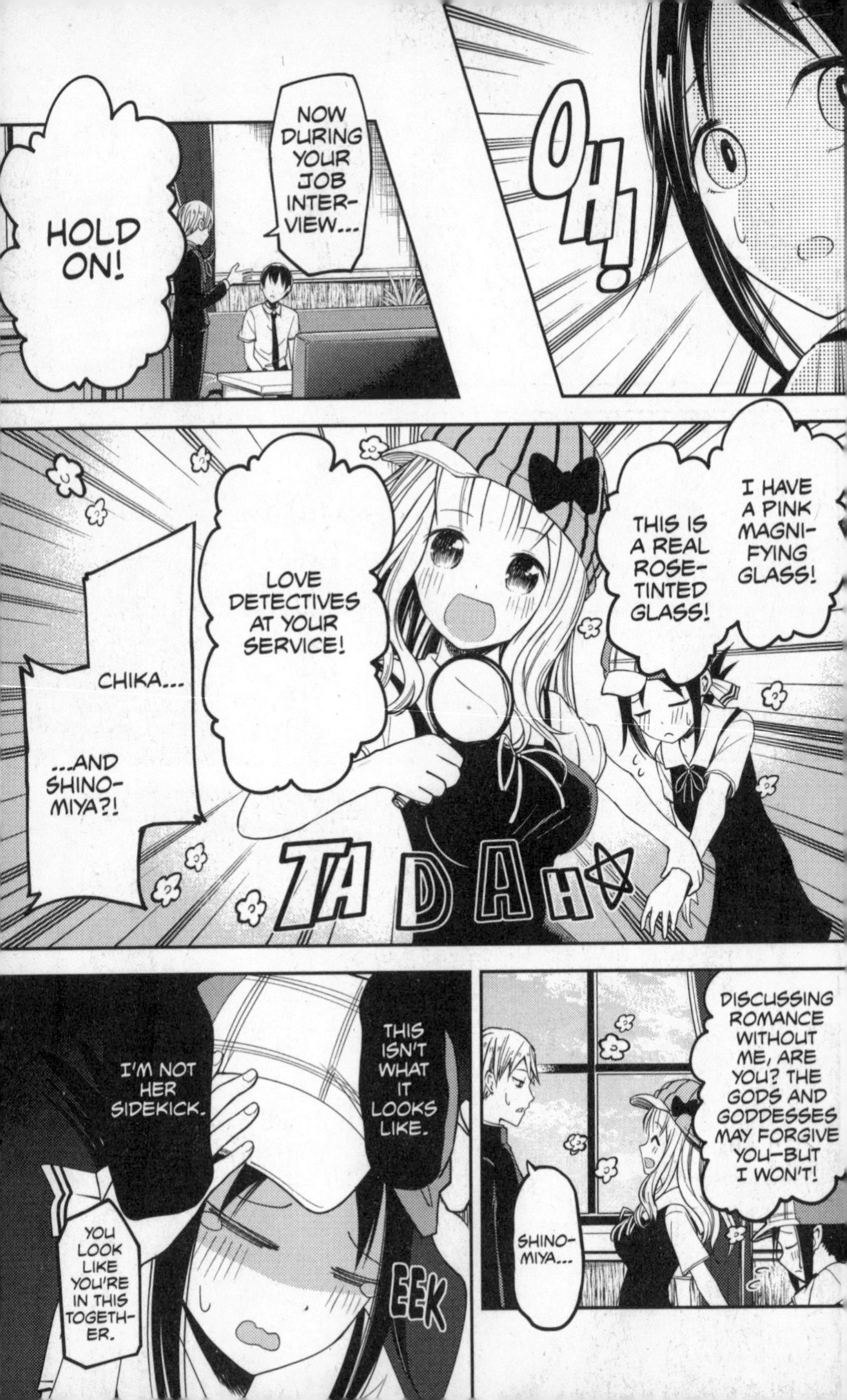
OH!
NOW DURING YOUR JOB INTERVIEW...
HOLD ON!
I HAVE A PINK MAGNIFYING GLASS!
THIS IS A REAL ROSE-TINTED GLASS!
LOVE DETECTIVES AT YOUR SERVICE!
TADAH
CHIKA...
...AND SHINOMIYA?!
DISCUSSING ROMANCE WITHOUT ME, ARE YOU? THE GODS AND GODDESSES MAY FORGIVE YOU—BUT I WON'T!
SHINOMIYA...
THIS ISN'T WHAT IT LOOKS LIKE.
I'M NOT HER SIDEKICK.
EEK
YOU LOOK LIKE YOU'RE IN THIS TOGETHER.

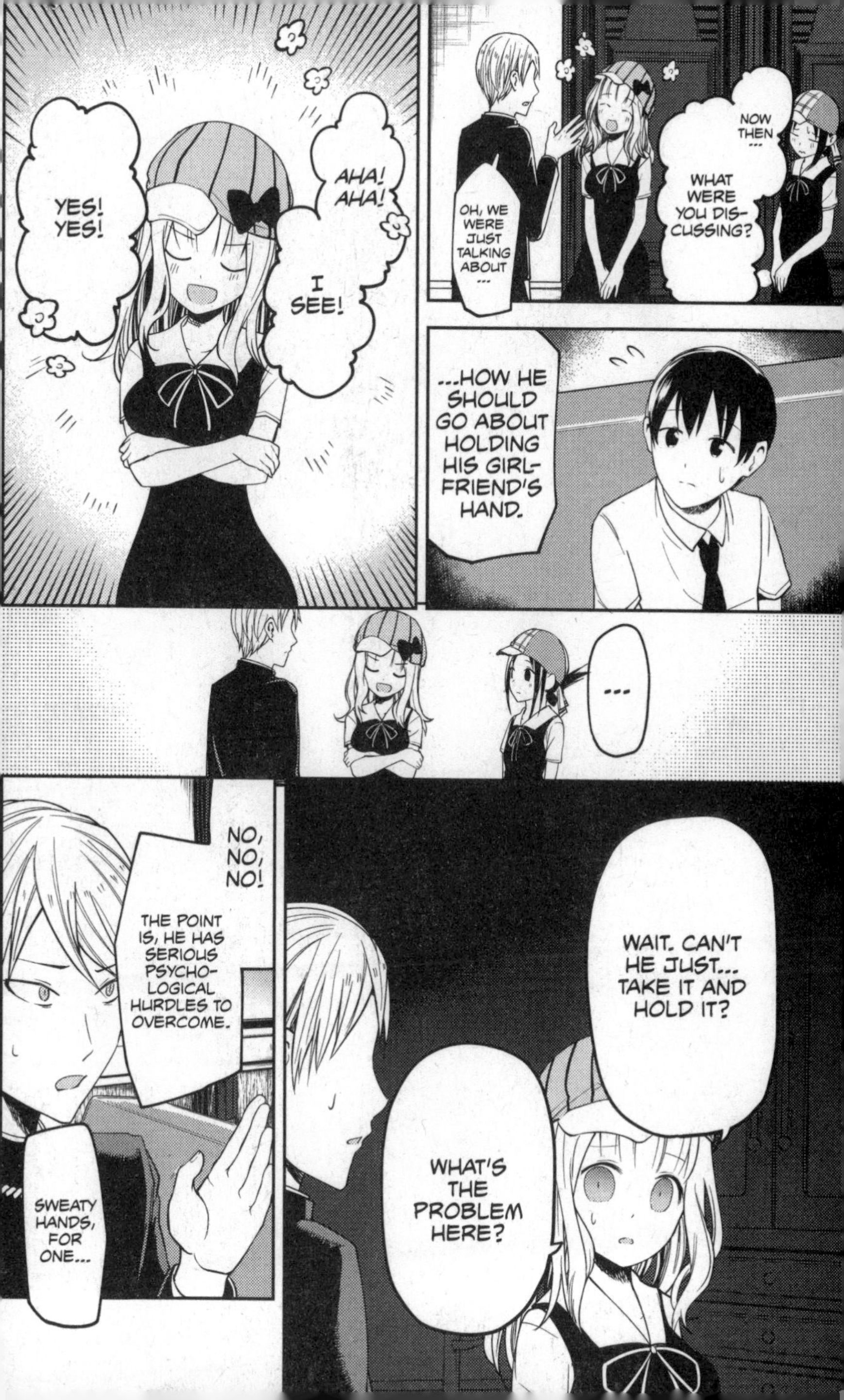
NOW THEN...
WHAT WERE YOU DISCUSSING?
OH, WE WERE JUST TALKING ABOUT...
...HOW HE SHOULD GO ABOUT HOLDING HIS GIRLFRIEND'S HAND.
AHA! AHA!
I SEE!
YES! YES!
...
WAIT. CAN'T HE JUST... TAKE IT AND HOLD IT?
WHAT'S THE PROBLEM HERE?
NO, NO, NO!
THE POINT IS, HE HAS SERIOUS PSYCHOLOGICAL HURDLES TO OVERCOME.
SWEATY HANDS, FOR ONE...

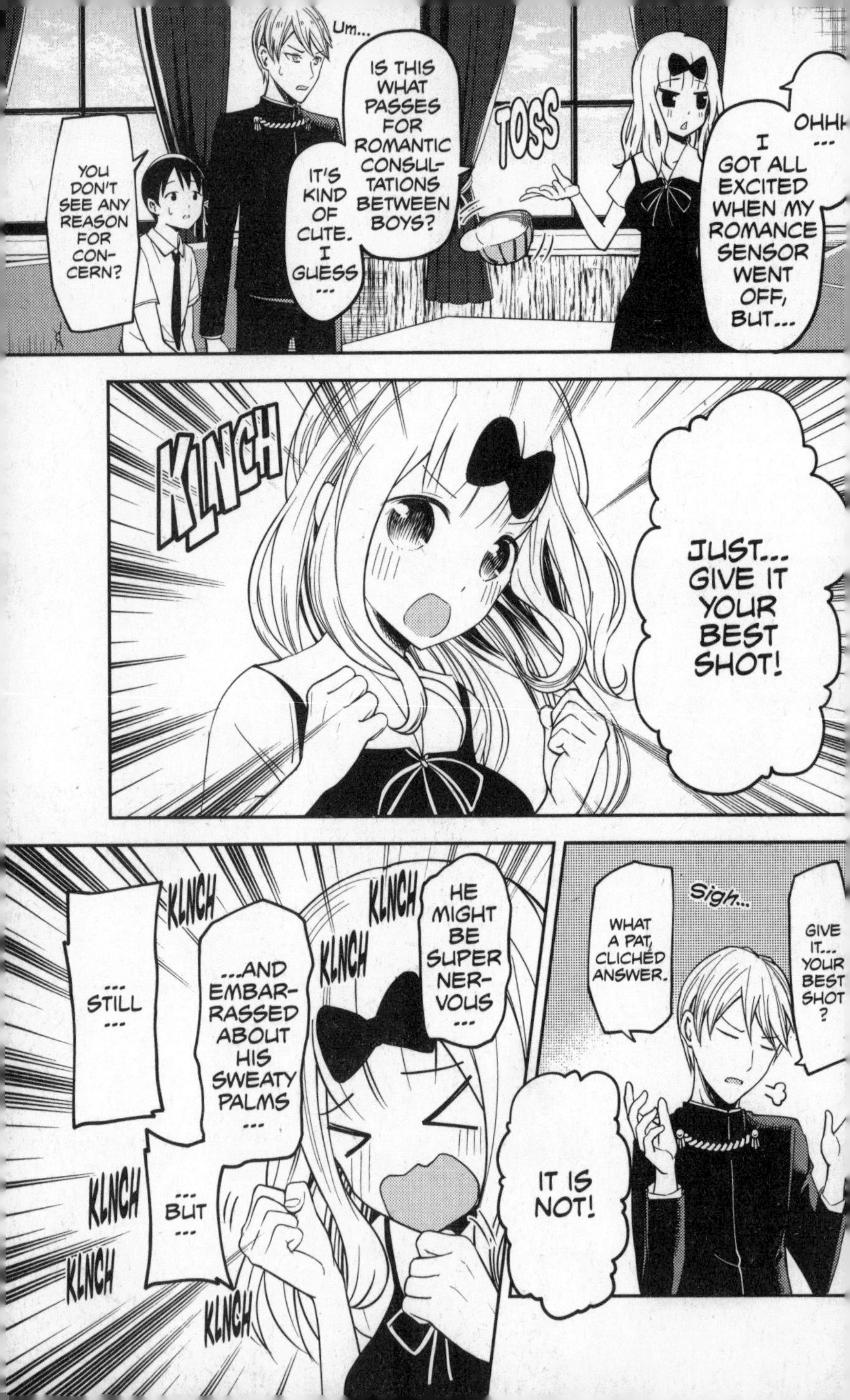
OHH...
I GOT ALL EXCITED WHEN MY ROMANCE SENSOR WENT OFF, BUT...
TOSS
Um...
IS THIS WHAT PASSES FOR ROMANTIC CONSULTATIONS BETWEEN BOYS?
IT'S KIND OF CUTE. I GUESS...
YOU DON'T SEE ANY REASON FOR CONCERN?
JUST... GIVE IT YOUR BEST SHOT!
KLNCH
GIVE IT... YOUR BEST SHOT?
Sigh...
WHAT A PAT, CLICHÉD ANSWER.
IT IS NOT!
HE MIGHT BE SUPER NERVOUS...
KLNCH
KLNCH
...AND EMBARRASSED ABOUT HIS SWEATY PALMS...
KLNCH
...STILL...
...BUT...
KLNCH
KLNCH
KLNCH

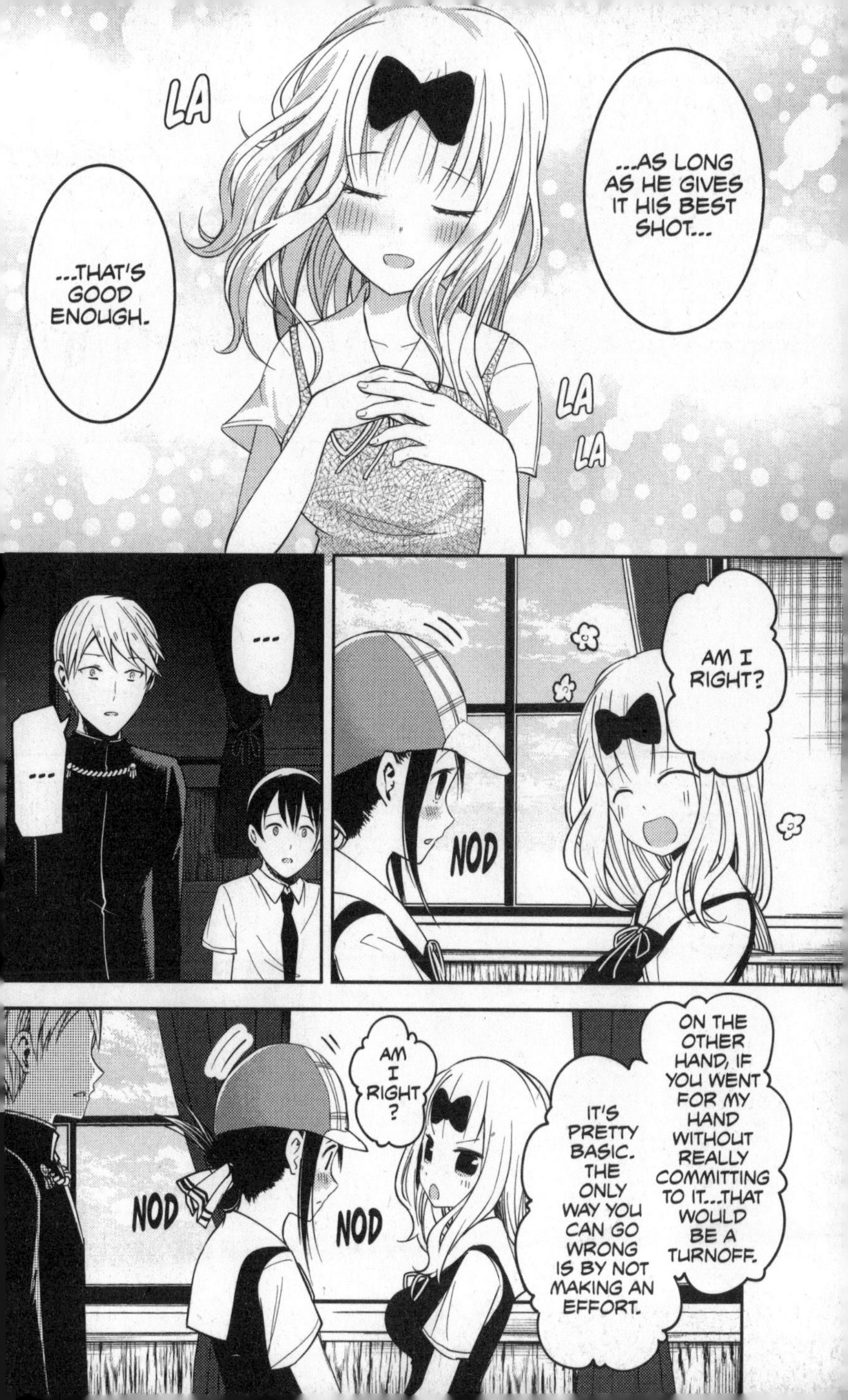
...AS LONG AS HE GIVES IT HIS BEST SHOT...
LA
LA
LA
...THAT'S GOOD ENOUGH.
AM I RIGHT?
NOD
...
...
ON THE OTHER HAND, IF YOU WENT FOR MY HAND WITHOUT REALLY COMMITTING TO IT...THAT WOULD BE A TURNOFF.
IT'S PRETTY BASIC. THE ONLY WAY YOU CAN GO WRONG IS BY NOT MAKING AN EFFORT.
AM I RIGHT?
NOD
NOD

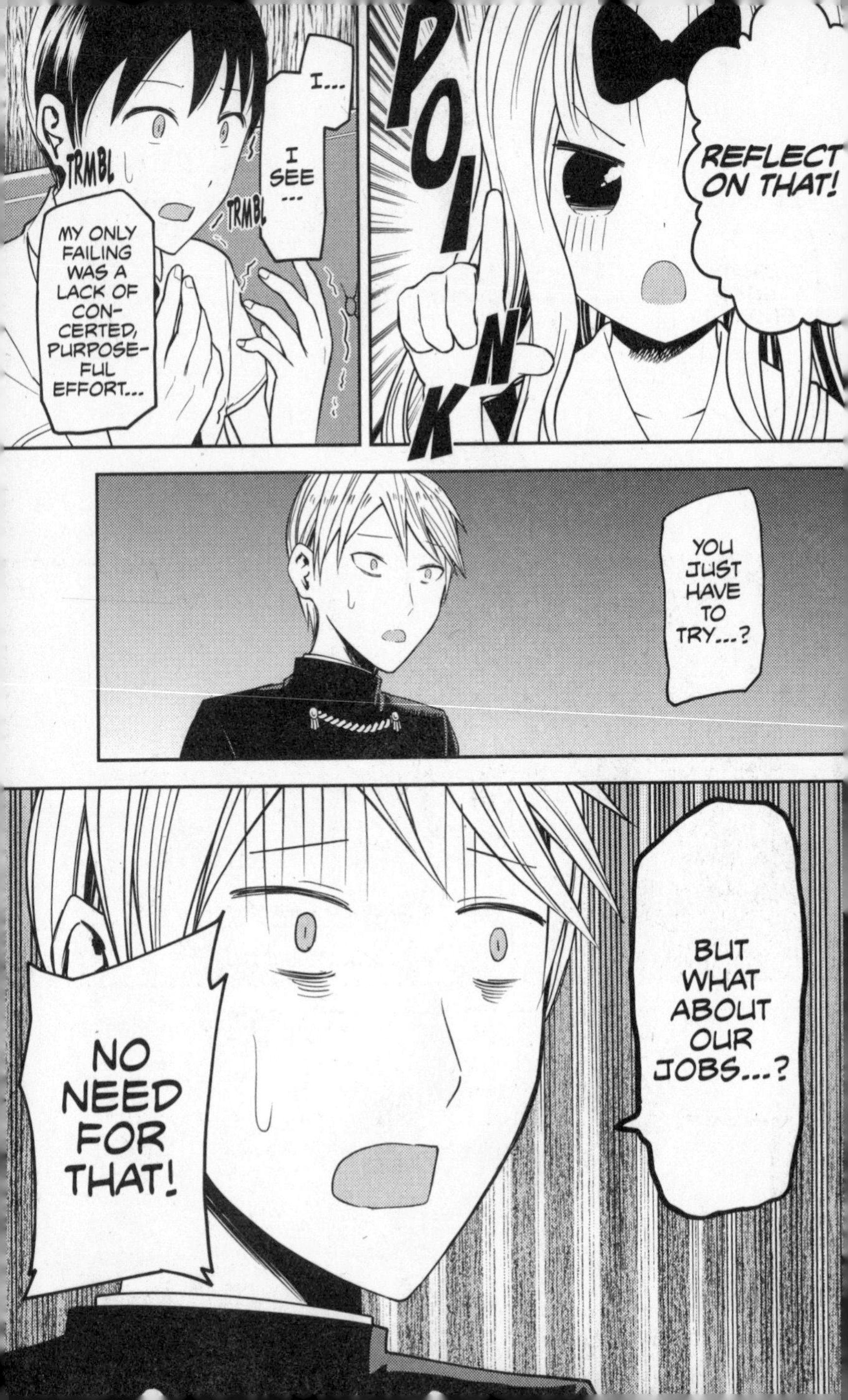
REFLECT ON THAT!
POINK
I...
I SEE...
TRMBL
TRMBL
MY ONLY FAILING WAS A LACK OF CON-CERTED, PURPOSE-FUL EFFORT...
YOU JUST HAVE TO TRY...?
BUT WHAT ABOUT OUR JOBS...?
NO NEED FOR THAT!

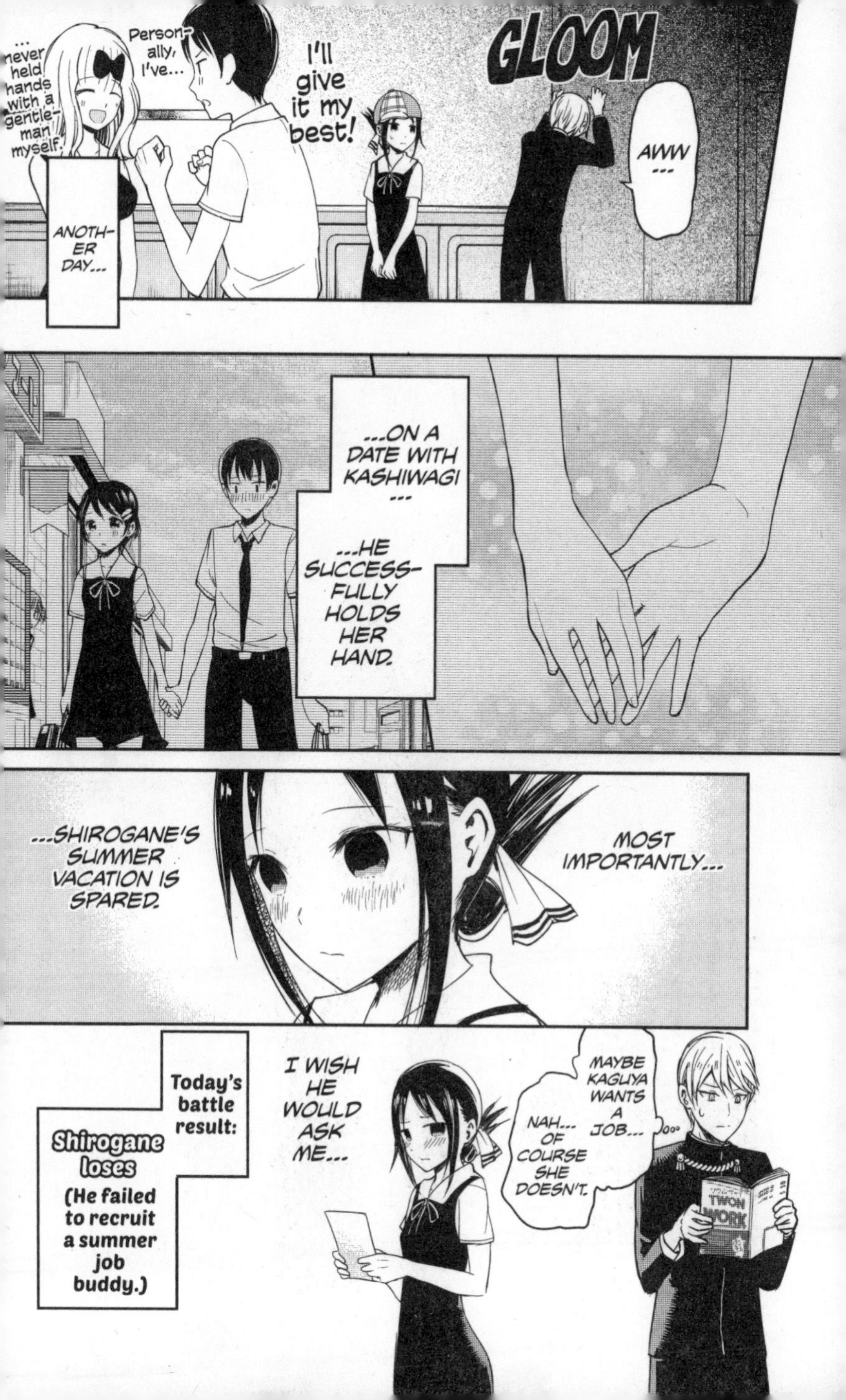
GLOOM
AWW ...
I'll give it my best!
Personally, I've...
... never held hands with a gentleman myself.
ANOTHER DAY...
...ON A DATE WITH KASHIWAGI ...
...HE SUCCESSFULLY HOLDS HER HAND.
MOST IMPORTANTLY...
...SHIROGANE'S SUMMER VACATION IS SPARED.
MAYBE KAGUYA WANTS A JOB...
NAH... OF COURSE SHE DOESN'T.
TWON WORK
I WISH HE WOULD ASK ME...
Today's battle result:
Shirogane loses
(He failed to recruit a summer job buddy.)

 Zoom In

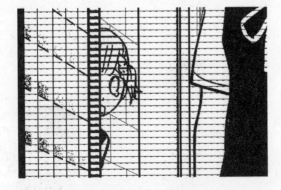

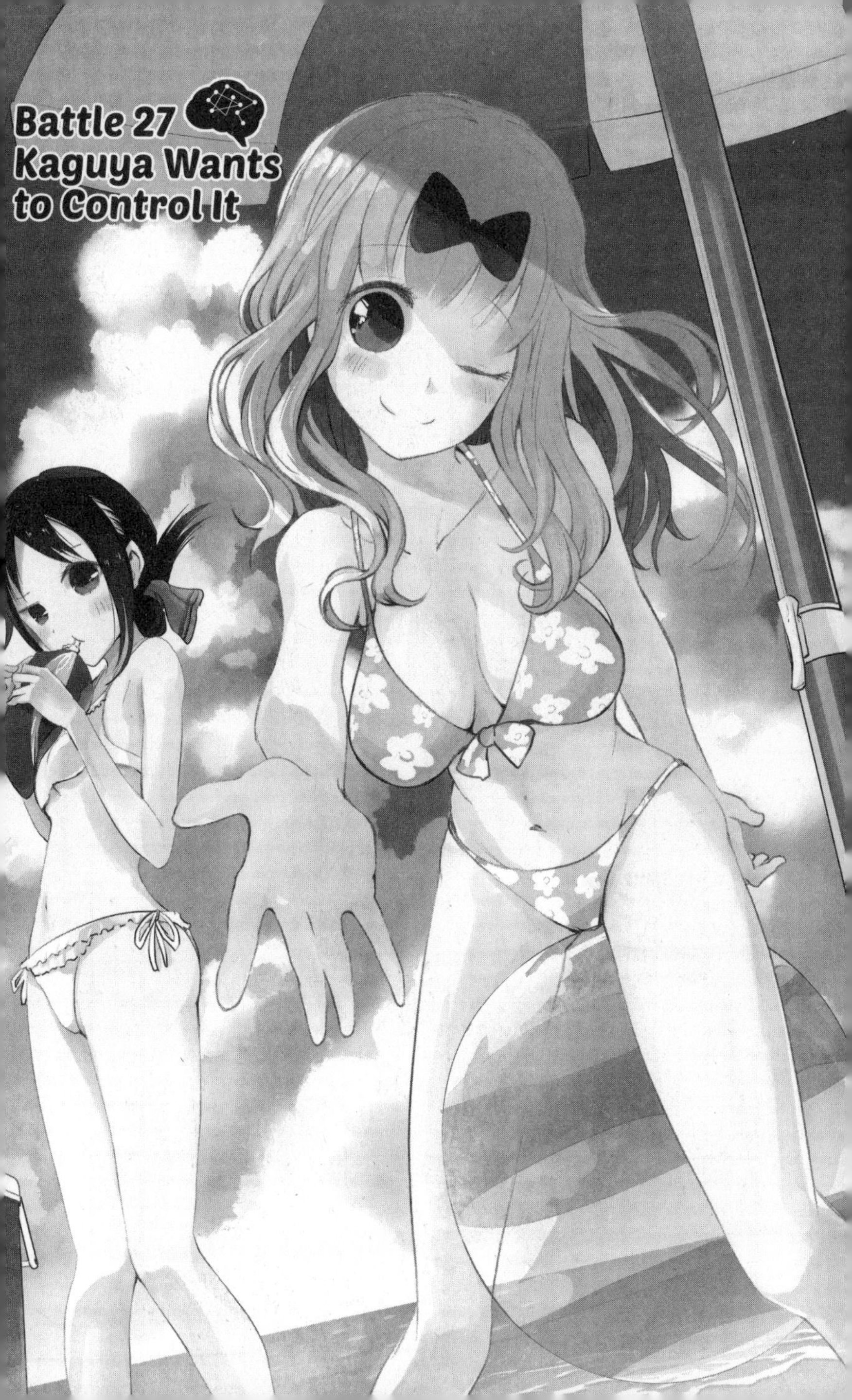
Battle 27
Kaguya Wants to Control It

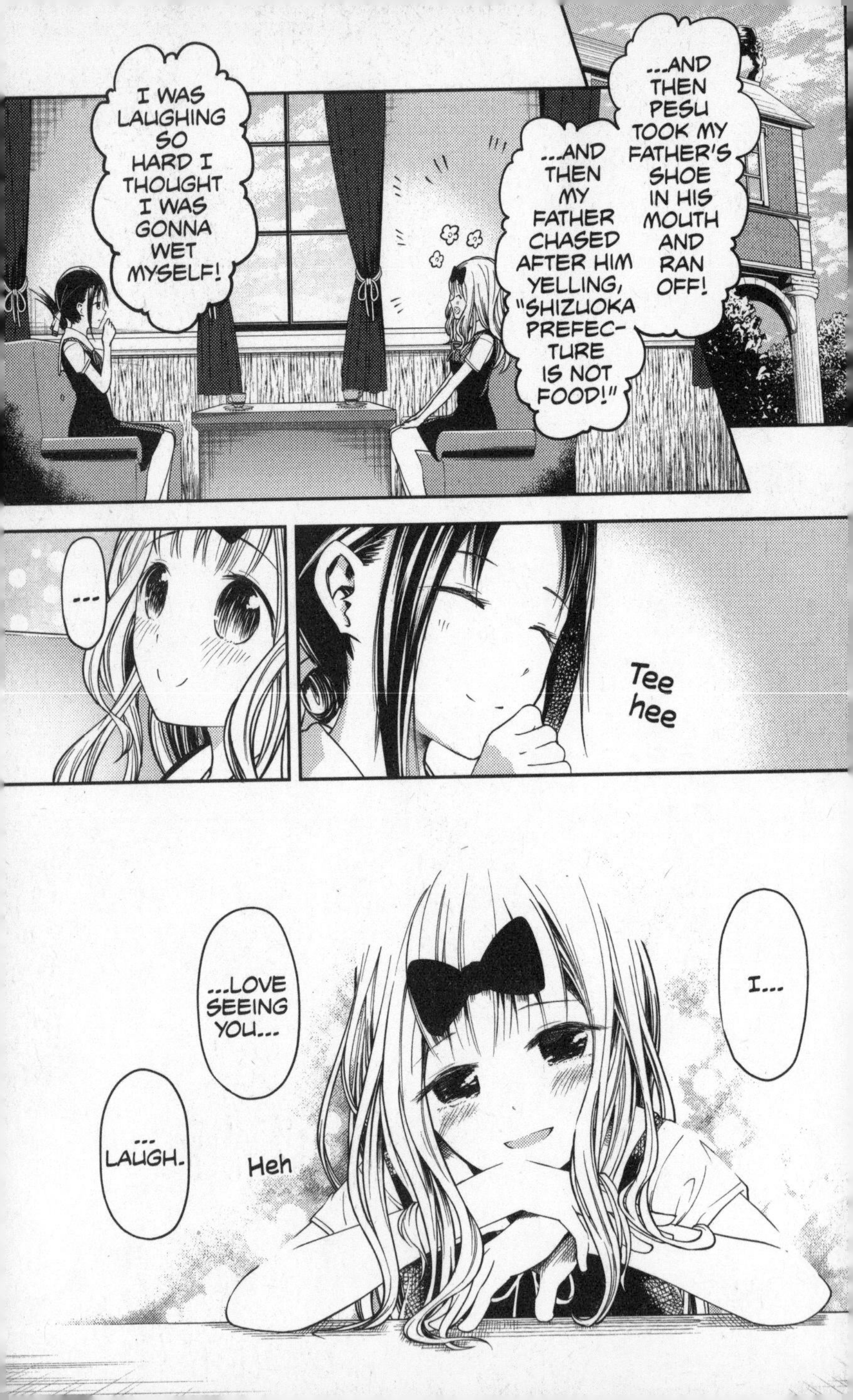
...AND THEN PESU TOOK MY FATHER'S SHOE IN HIS MOUTH AND RAN OFF!
...AND THEN MY FATHER CHASED AFTER HIM YELLING, "SHIZUOKA PREFECTURE IS NOT FOOD!"
I WAS LAUGHING SO HARD I THOUGHT I WAS GONNA WET MYSELF!
Tee hee
...
I...
...LOVE SEEING YOU...
Heh
...LAUGH.

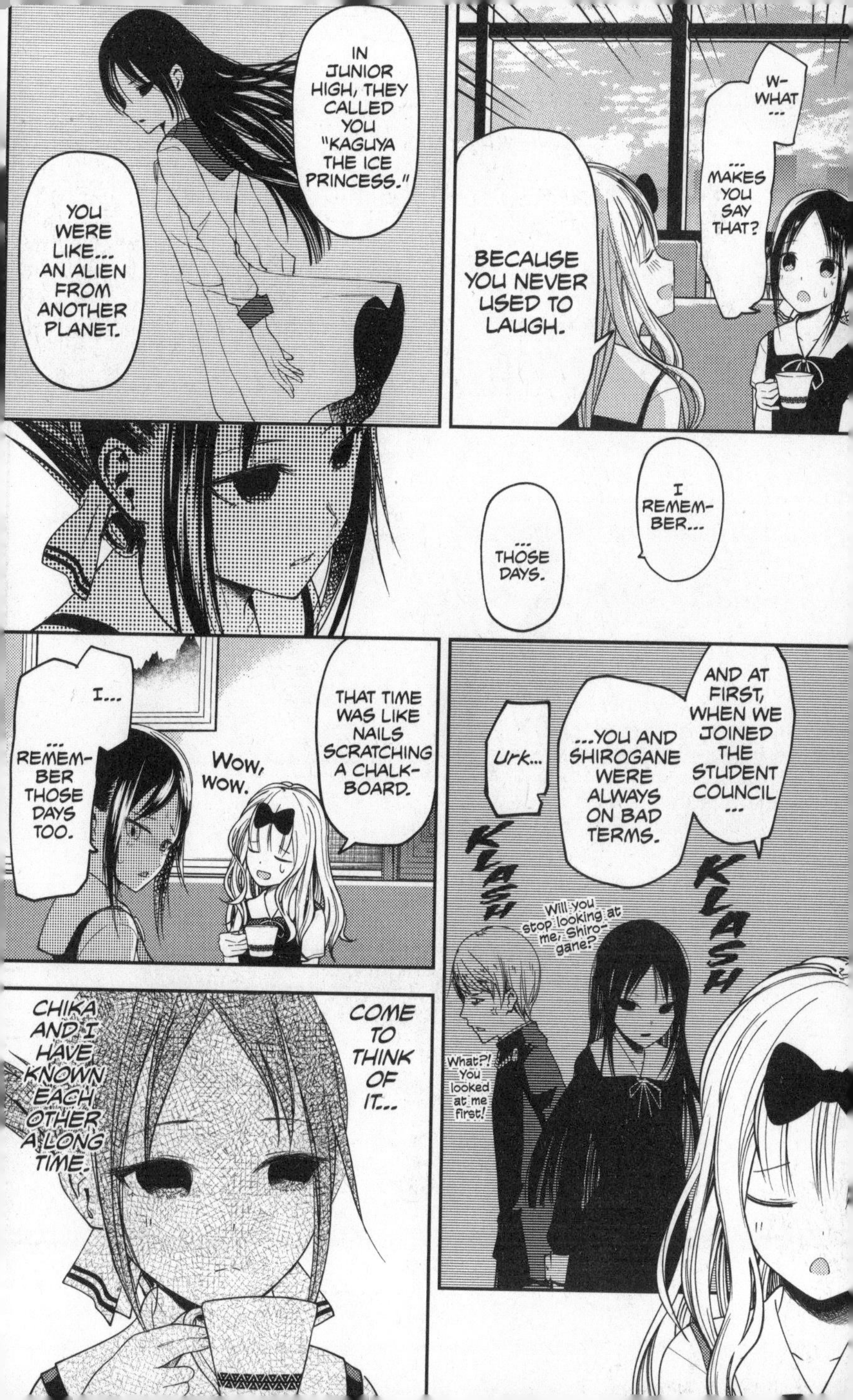

W-WHAT...
...MAKES YOU SAY THAT?
BECAUSE YOU NEVER USED TO LAUGH.
IN JUNIOR HIGH, THEY CALLED YOU "KAGUYA THE ICE PRINCESS."
YOU WERE LIKE... AN ALIEN FROM ANOTHER PLANET.
I REMEMBER...
...THOSE DAYS.
AND AT FIRST, WHEN WE JOINED THE STUDENT COUNCIL...
...YOU AND SHIROGANE WERE ALWAYS ON BAD TERMS.
Urk...
KLASH
Will you stop looking at me, Shirogane?
What?! You looked at me first!
KLASH
THAT TIME WAS LIKE NAILS SCRATCHING A CHALKBOARD.
Wow, wow.
I...
...REMEMBER THOSE DAYS TOO.
COME TO THINK OF IT...
CHIKA AND I HAVE KNOWN EACH OTHER A LONG TIME.

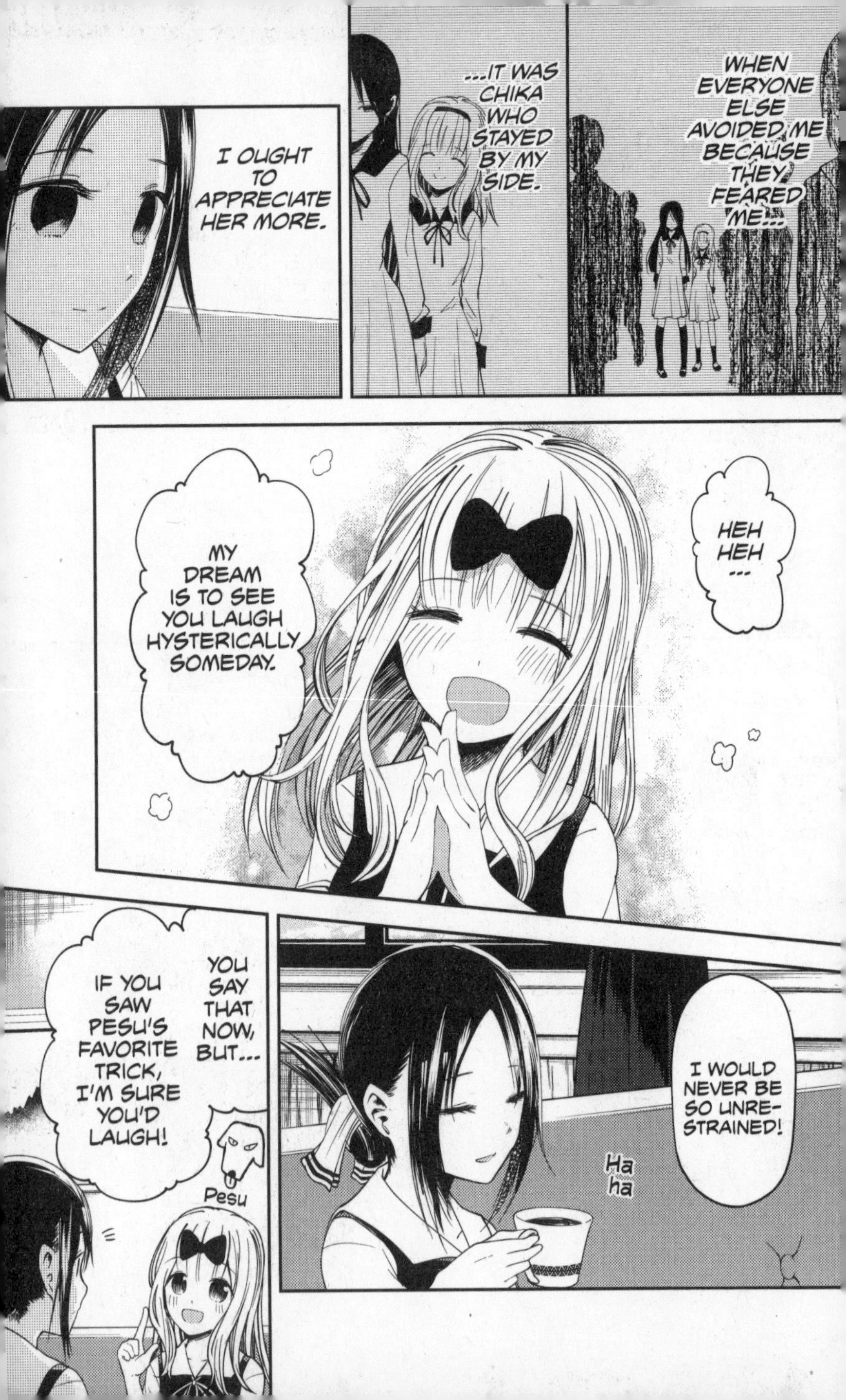
WHEN EVERYONE ELSE AVOIDED ME BECAUSE THEY FEARED ME...
...IT WAS CHIKA WHO STAYED BY MY SIDE.
I OUGHT TO APPRECIATE HER MORE.
HEH HEH...
MY DREAM IS TO SEE YOU LAUGH HYSTERICALLY SOMEDAY.
I WOULD NEVER BE SO UNRE-STRAINED!
Ha ha
YOU SAY THAT NOW, BUT...
IF YOU SAW PESU'S FAVORITE TRICK, I'M SURE YOU'D LAUGH!
Pesu

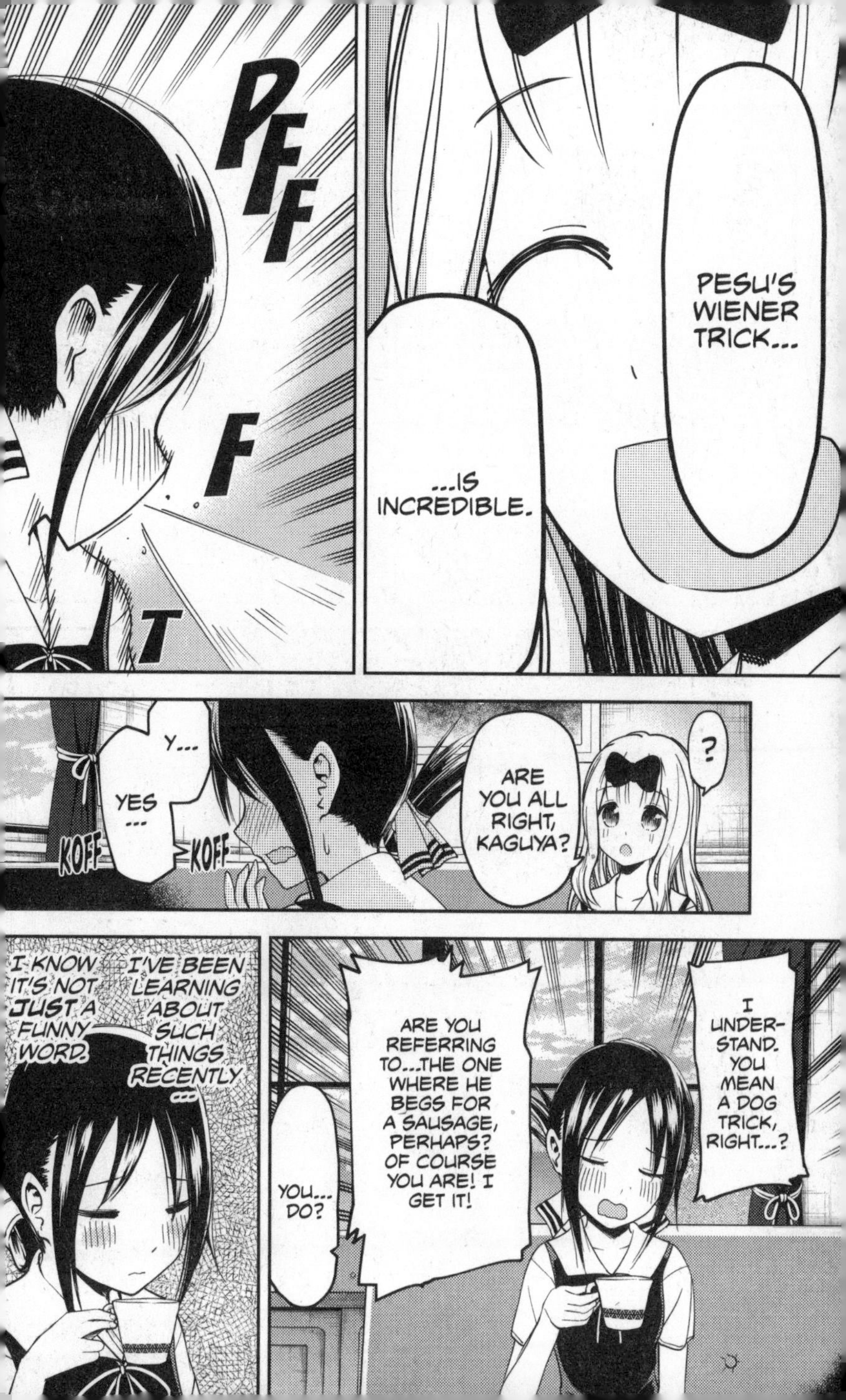
PESU'S WIENER TRICK...
...IS INCREDIBLE.
PFFFT
?
ARE YOU ALL RIGHT, KAGUYA?
Y... YES ...
KOFF KOFF
I UNDER-STAND. YOU MEAN A DOG TRICK, RIGHT...?
ARE YOU REFERRING TO...THE ONE WHERE HE BEGS FOR A SAUSAGE, PERHAPS? OF COURSE YOU ARE! I GET IT!
YOU... DO?
I'VE BEEN LEARNING ABOUT SUCH THINGS RECENTLY ...
I KNOW IT'S NOT JUST A FUNNY WORD.

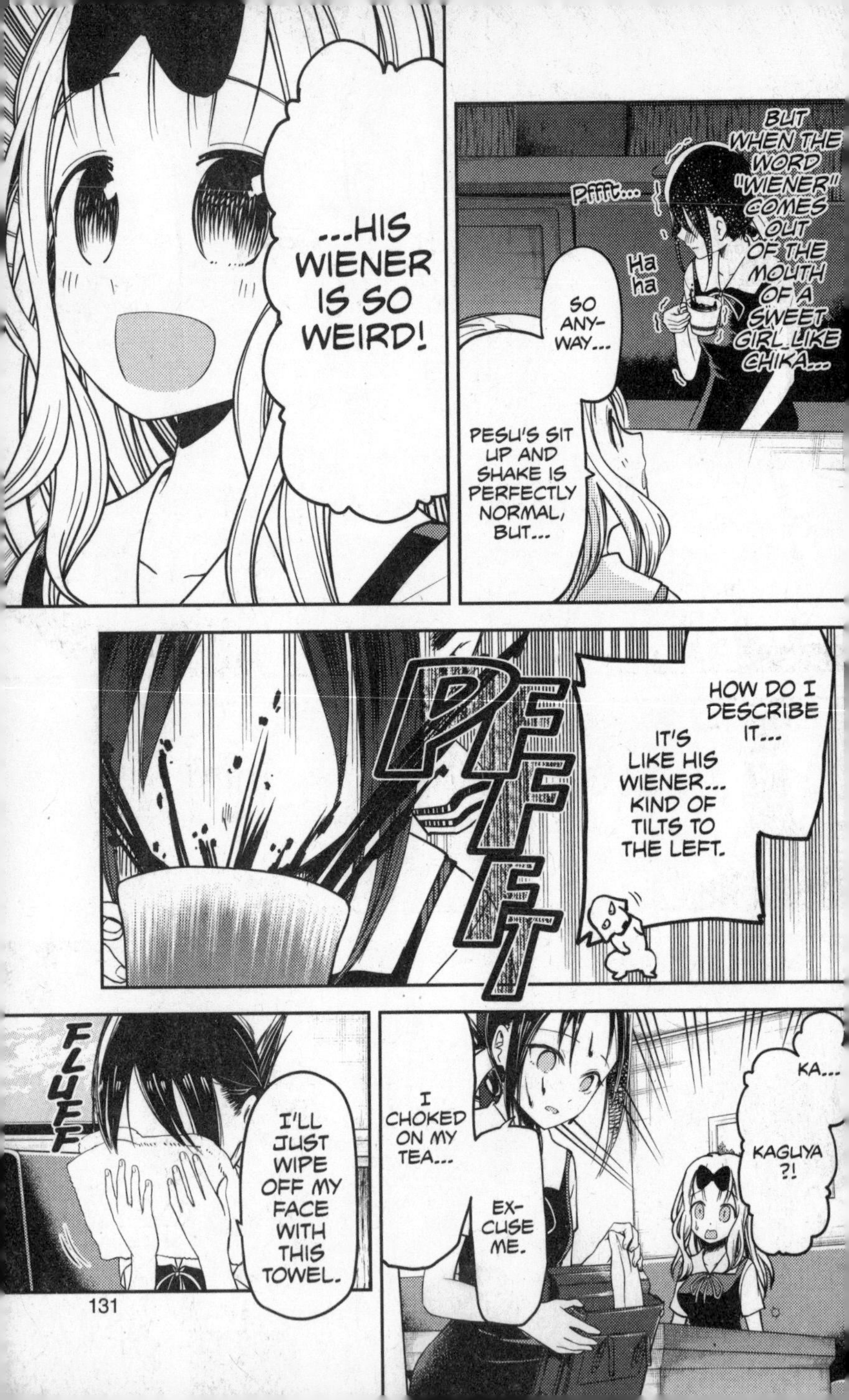
BUT WHEN THE WORD "WIENER" COMES OUT OF THE MOUTH OF A SWEET GIRL LIKE CHIKA...
Pffft...
Ha ha
SO ANYWAY...
PESU'S SIT UP AND SHAKE IS PERFECTLY NORMAL, BUT...
...HIS WIENER IS SO WEIRD!
HOW DO I DESCRIBE IT...
IT'S LIKE HIS WIENER... KIND OF TILTS TO THE LEFT.
PFFFT
KA...
KAGUYA?!
I CHOKED ON MY TEA...
EXCUSE ME.
FLUFF
I'LL JUST WIPE OFF MY FACE WITH THIS TOWEL.

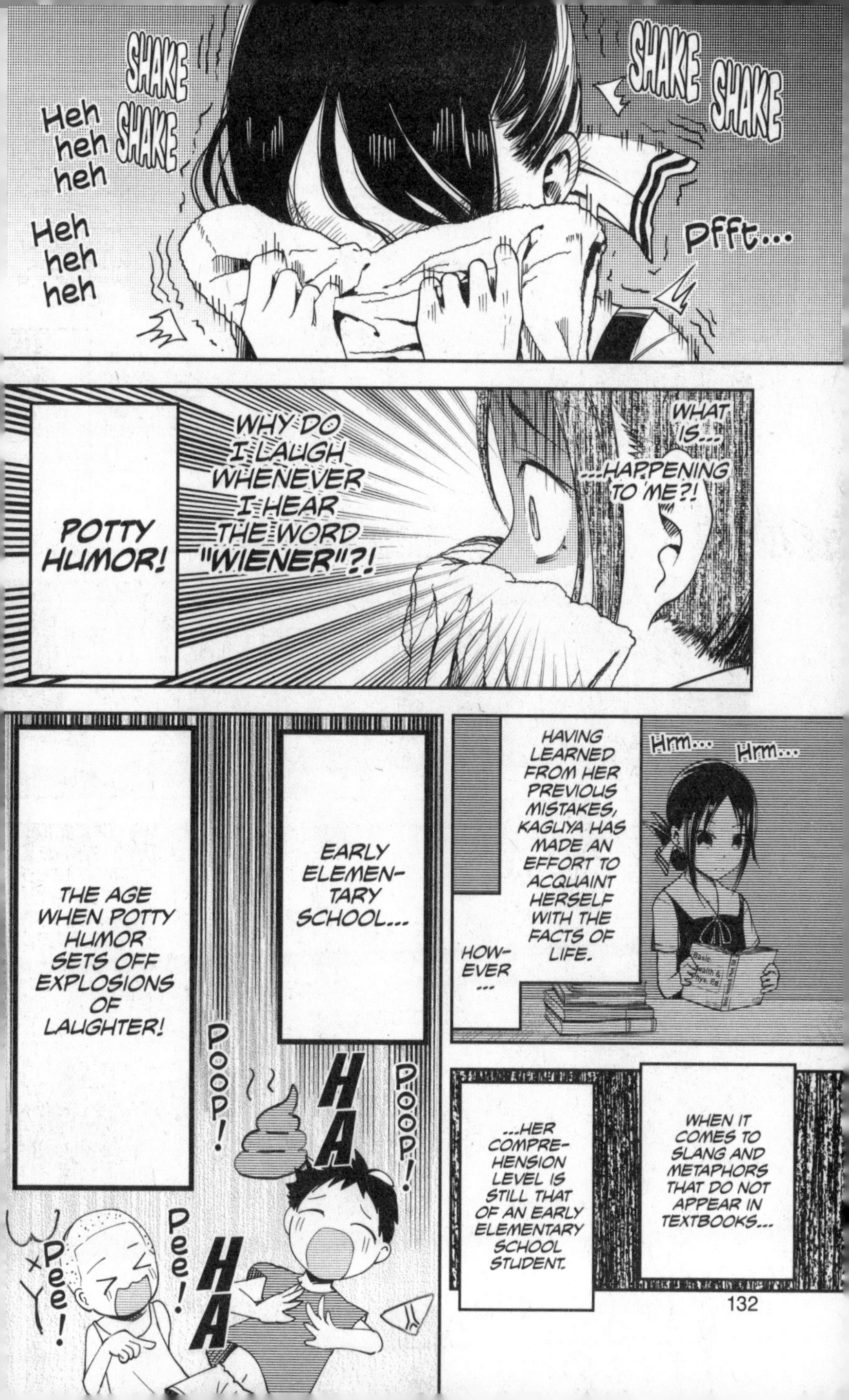
SHAKE SHAKE
Pfft...
SHAKE SHAKE
Heh heh heh
Heh heh heh
WHAT IS...
...HAPPENING TO ME?!
WHY DO I LAUGH WHENEVER I HEAR THE WORD "WIENER"?!
POTTY HUMOR!
Hrm... Hrm...
HAVING LEARNED FROM HER PREVIOUS MISTAKES, KAGUYA HAS MADE AN EFFORT TO ACQUAINT HERSELF WITH THE FACTS OF LIFE.
HOW-EVER...
Basic Health & Phys Ed
WHEN IT COMES TO SLANG AND METAPHORS THAT DO NOT APPEAR IN TEXTBOOKS...
...HER COMPREHENSION LEVEL IS STILL THAT OF AN EARLY ELEMENTARY SCHOOL STUDENT.
EARLY ELEMENTARY SCHOOL...
THE AGE WHEN POTTY HUMOR SETS OFF EXPLOSIONS OF LAUGHTER!
POOP!
HA HA HA
POOP!
Pee!
Pee!

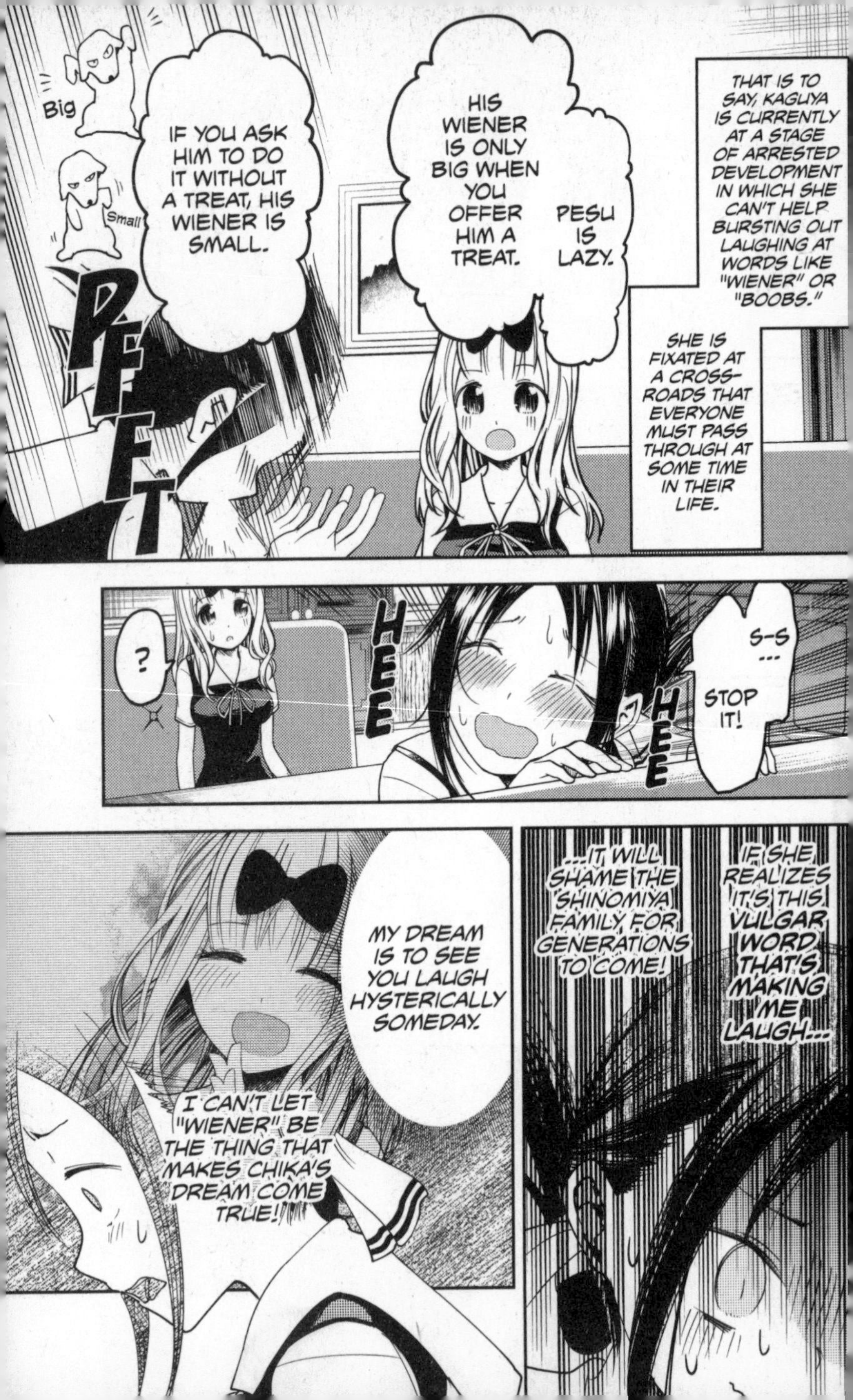
THAT IS TO SAY, KAGUYA IS CURRENTLY AT A STAGE OF ARRESTED DEVELOPMENT IN WHICH SHE CAN'T HELP BURSTING OUT LAUGHING AT WORDS LIKE "WIENER" OR "BOOBS."
SHE IS FIXATED AT A CROSS-ROADS THAT EVERYONE MUST PASS THROUGH AT SOME TIME IN THEIR LIFE.
PESU IS LAZY.
HIS WIENER IS ONLY BIG WHEN YOU OFFER HIM A TREAT.
IF YOU ASK HIM TO DO IT WITHOUT A TREAT, HIS WIENER IS SMALL.
Big
Small
PFFFT
S-S... STOP IT!
HEE
HEE
?
IF SHE REALIZES IT'S THIS VULGAR WORD THAT'S MAKING ME LAUGH...
...IT WILL SHAME THE SHINOMIYA FAMILY FOR GENERATIONS TO COME!
MY DREAM IS TO SEE YOU LAUGH HYSTERICALLY SOMEDAY.
I CAN'T LET "WIENER" BE THE THING THAT MAKES CHIKA'S DREAM COME TRUE!

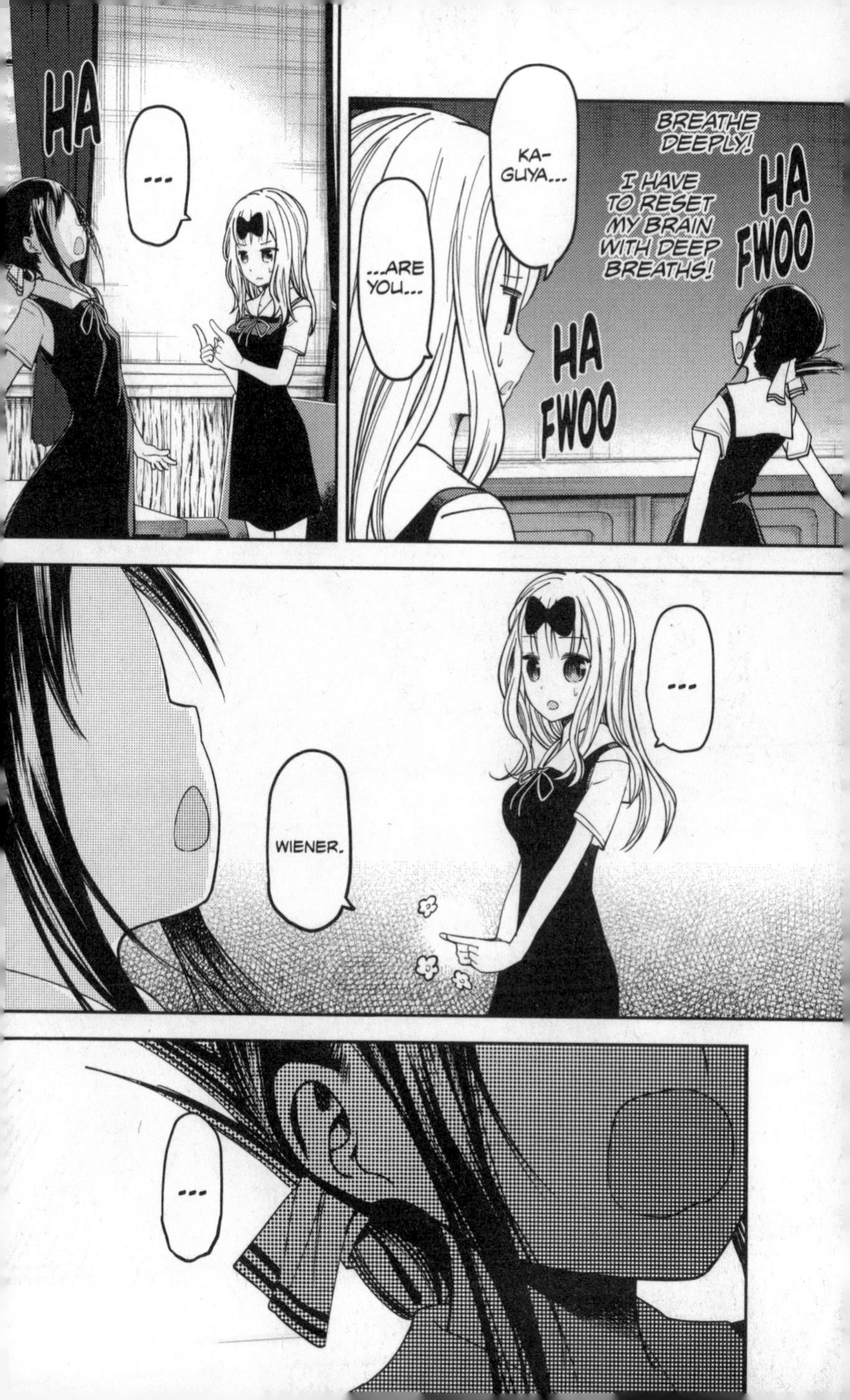
BREATHE DEEPLY!
HA FWOO
I HAVE TO RESET MY BRAIN WITH DEEP BREATHS!
KA-GUYA...
HA FWOO
...ARE YOU...
...
HA
...
WIENER.
...

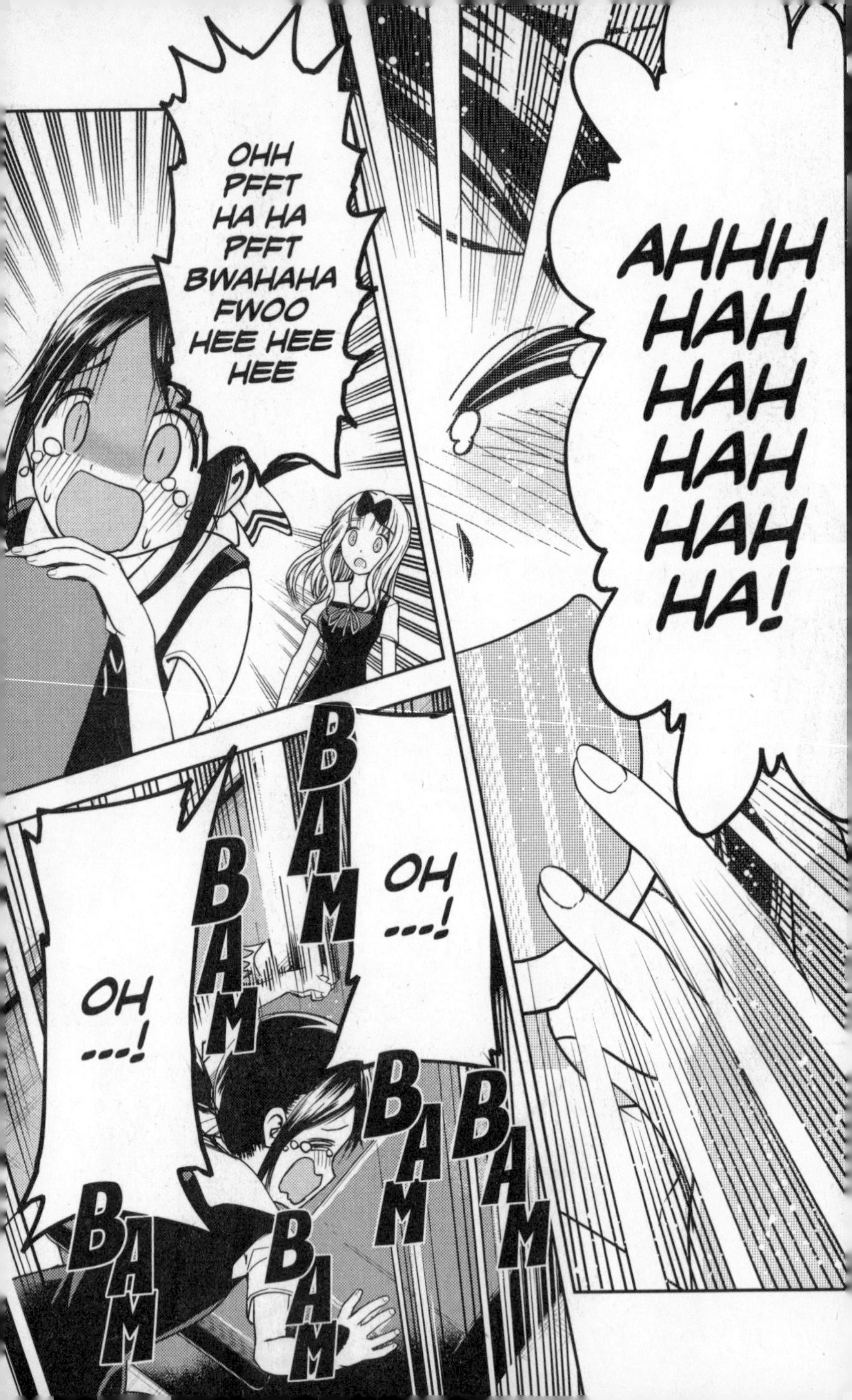
AHHH HAH HAH HAH HAH HA!
OHH PFFT HA HA PFFT BWAHAHA FWOO HEE HEE HEE
BAM
OH ...!
BAM
OH ...!
BAM
BAM
BAM
BAM

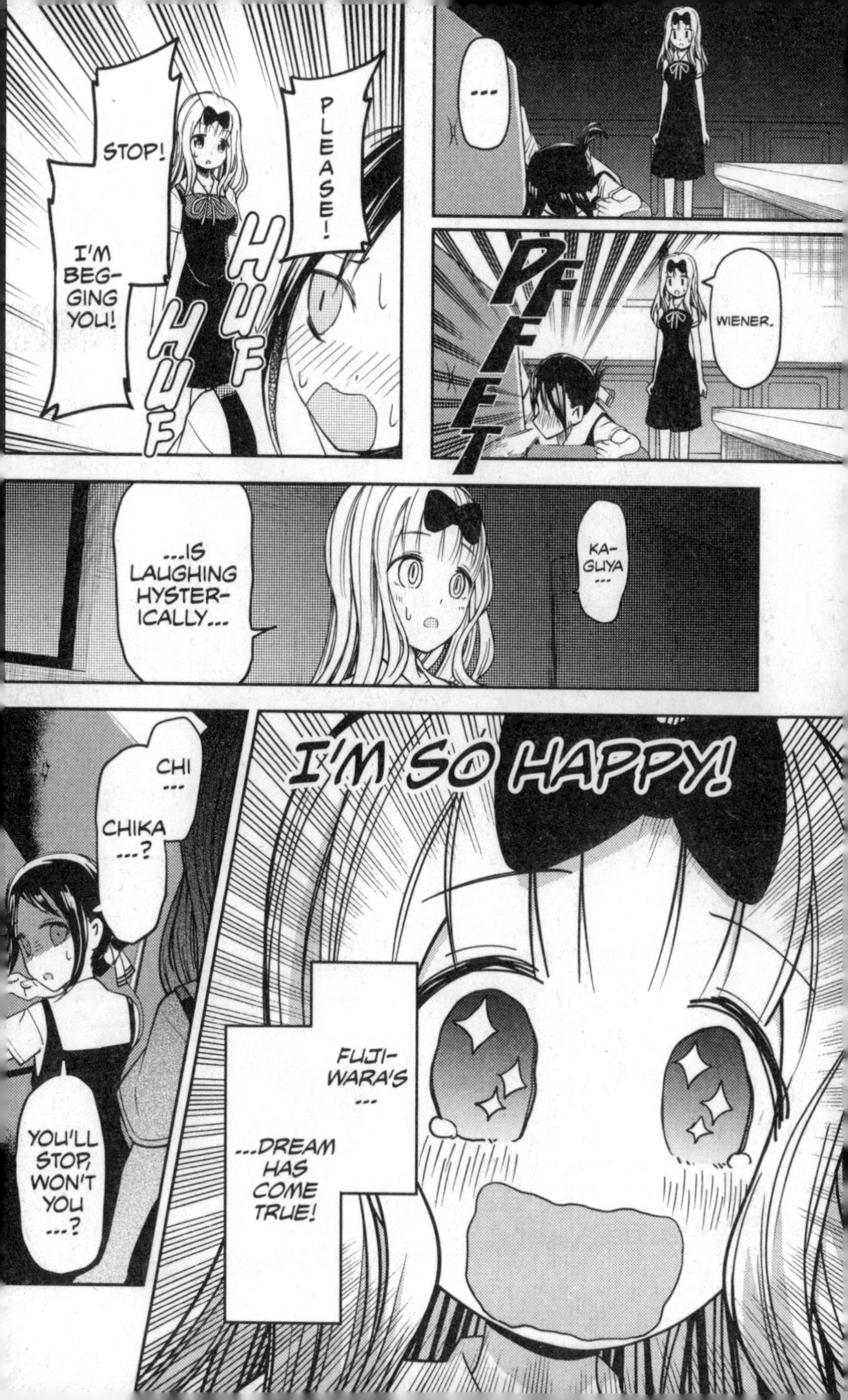
...
WIENER.
PFFFFT
PLEASE!
STOP!
I'M BEG-GING YOU!
HUFF HUFF
KA-GUYA...
...IS LAUGHING HYSTER-ICALLY...
I'M SO HAPPY!
FUJI-WARA'S...
...DREAM HAS COME TRUE!
CHI... CHIKA...?
YOU'LL STOP, WON'T YOU...?

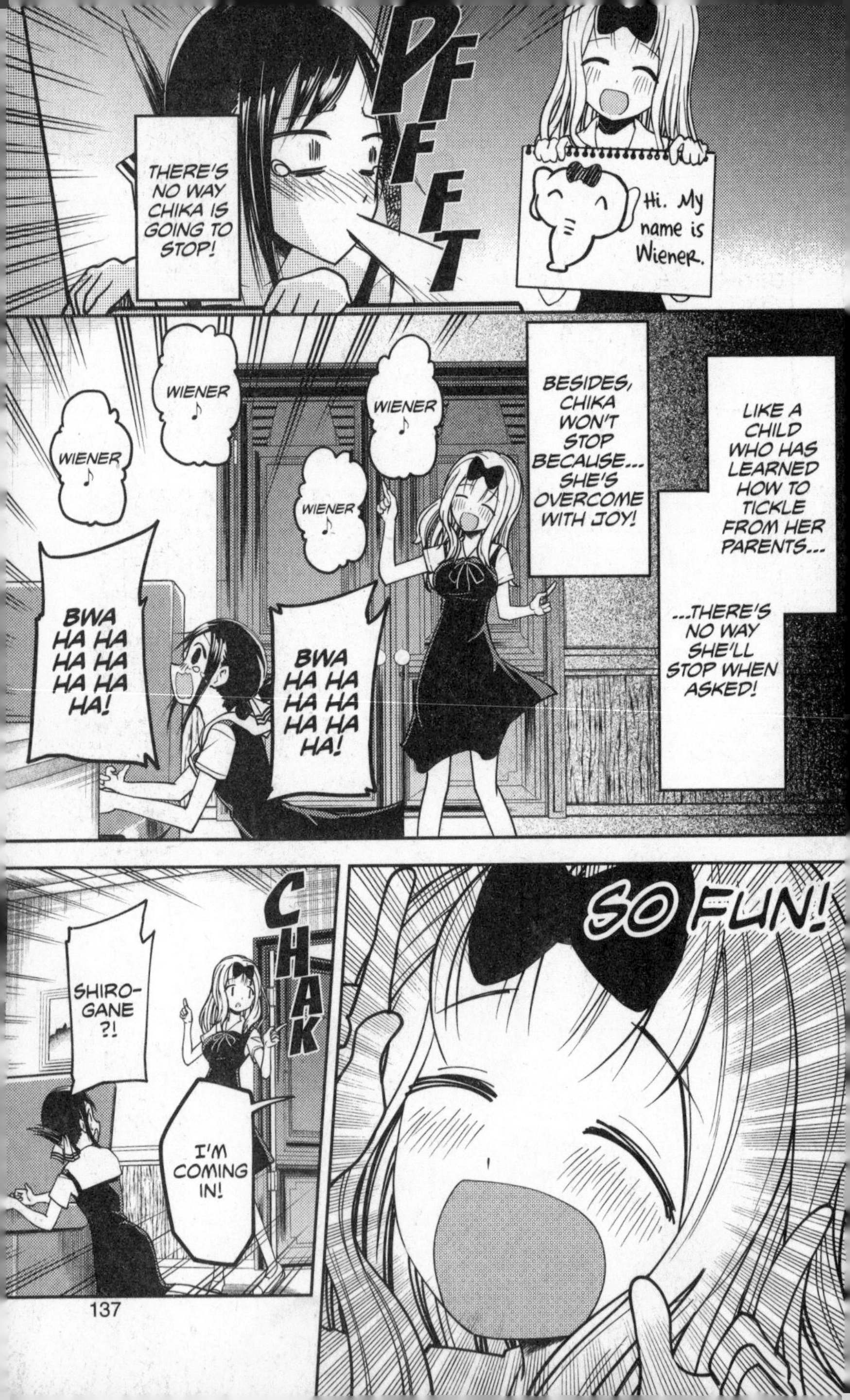
Hi. My name is Wiener.
PFFFT
THERE'S NO WAY CHIKA IS GOING TO STOP!
LIKE A CHILD WHO HAS LEARNED HOW TO TICKLE FROM HER PARENTS...
...THERE'S NO WAY SHE'LL STOP WHEN ASKED!
BESIDES, CHIKA WON'T STOP BECAUSE... SHE'S OVERCOME WITH JOY!
WIENER ♪
WIENER ♪
WIENER ♪
WIENER ♪
BWA HA HA HA HA HA HA HA!
BWA HA HA HA HA HA HA HA!
SO FUN!
CHAK
I'M COMING IN!
SHIRO-GANE ?!

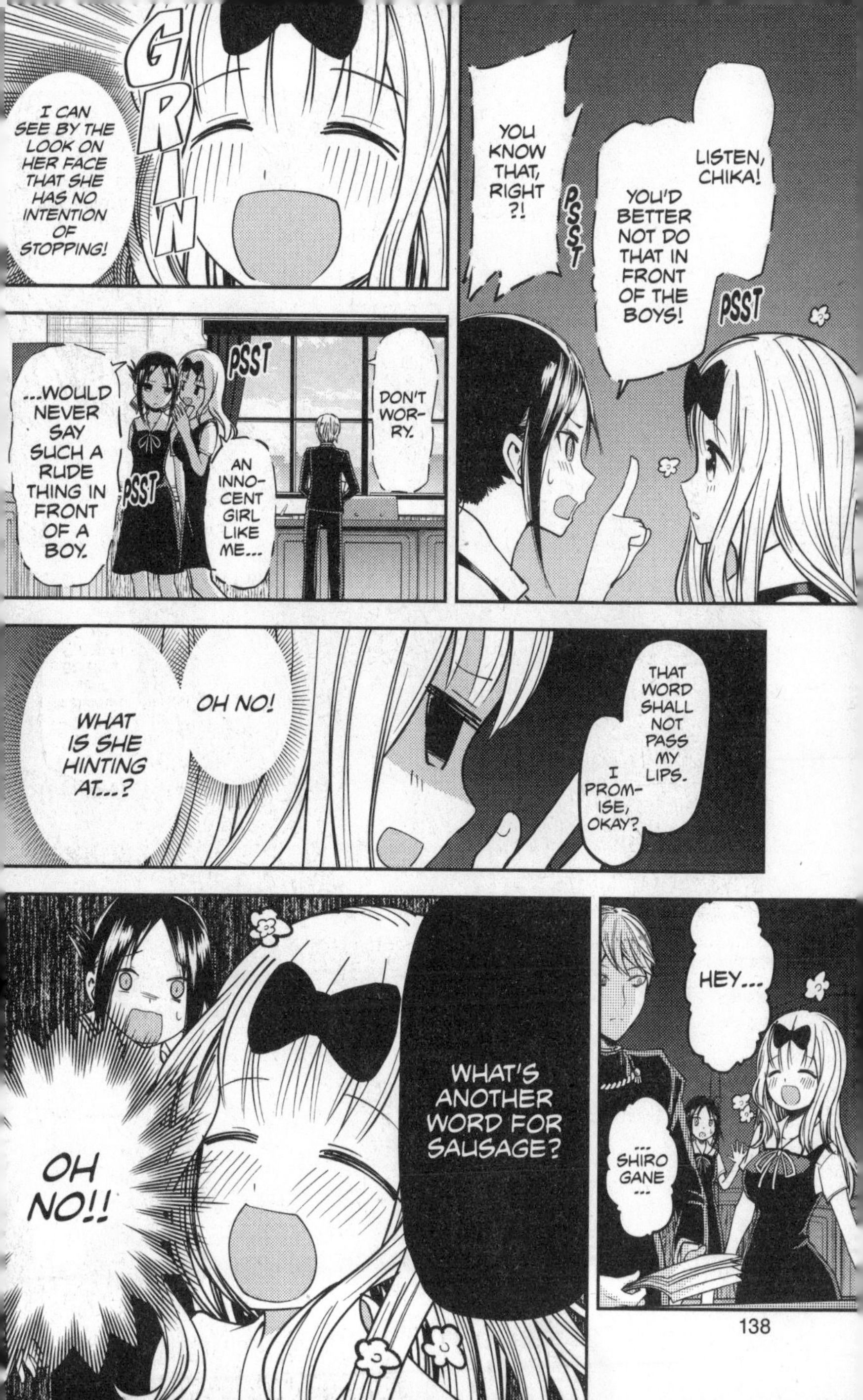
LISTEN, CHIKA!
YOU'D BETTER NOT DO THAT IN FRONT OF THE BOYS!
PSST
YOU KNOW THAT, RIGHT?!
PSST
GRIN
I CAN SEE BY THE LOOK ON HER FACE THAT SHE HAS NO INTENTION OF STOPPING!
DON'T WORRY.
PSST
AN INNOCENT GIRL LIKE ME...
PSST
...WOULD NEVER SAY SUCH A RUDE THING IN FRONT OF A BOY.
THAT WORD SHALL NOT PASS MY LIPS.
I PROMISE, OKAY?
OH NO!
WHAT IS SHE HINTING AT...?
HEY...
...SHIROGANE...
WHAT'S ANOTHER WORD FOR SAUSAGE?
OH NO!!

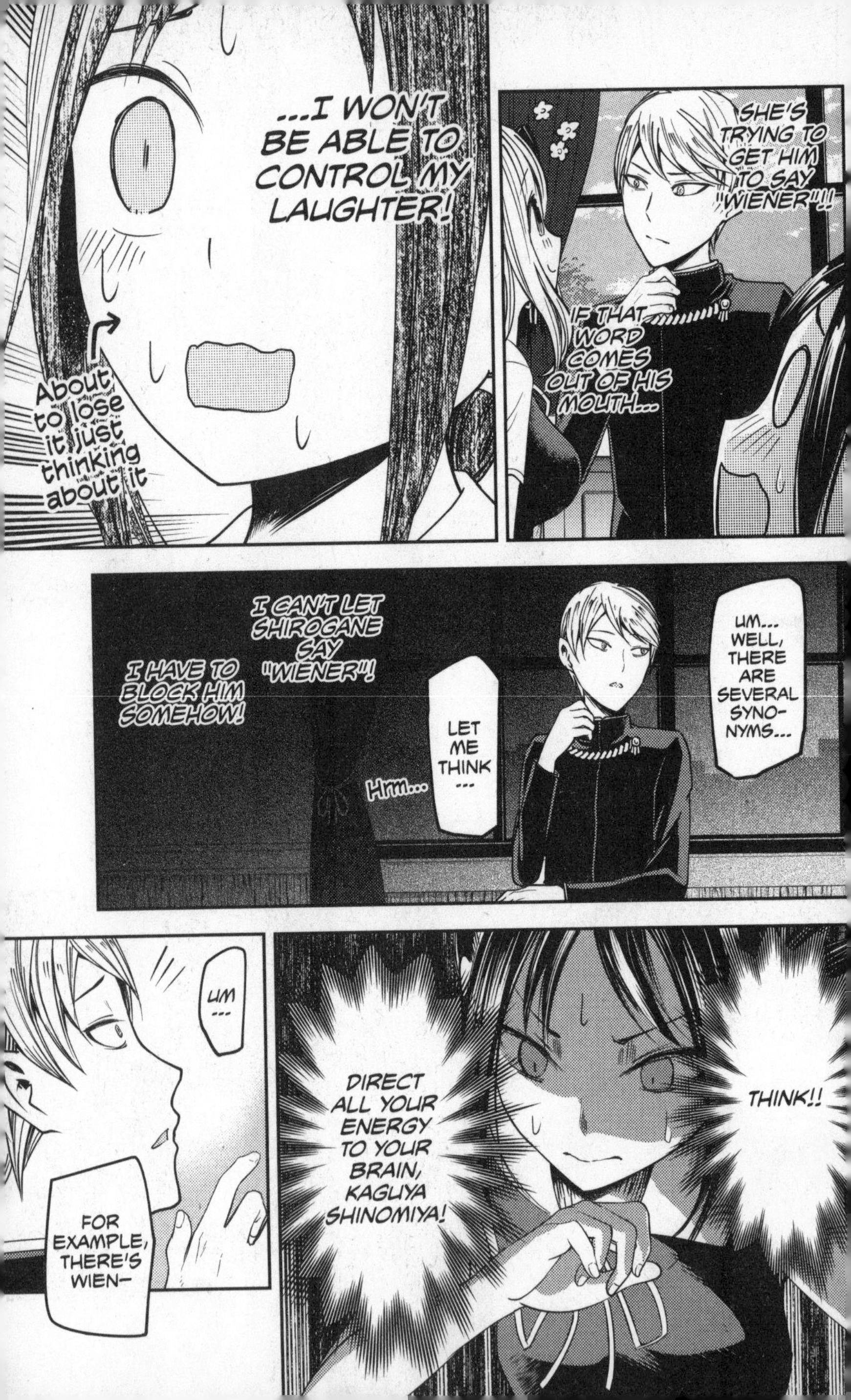
SHE'S TRYING TO GET HIM TO SAY "WIENER"!!
IF THAT WORD COMES OUT OF HIS MOUTH...
...I WON'T BE ABLE TO CONTROL MY LAUGHTER!
About to lose it just thinking about it
UM... WELL, THERE ARE SEVERAL SYNONYMS...
LET ME THINK...
Hrm...
I CAN'T LET SHIROGANE SAY "WIENER"!
I HAVE TO BLOCK HIM SOMEHOW!
THINK!!
DIRECT ALL YOUR ENERGY TO YOUR BRAIN, KAGUYA SHINOMIYA!
UM...
FOR EXAMPLE, THERE'S WIEN—

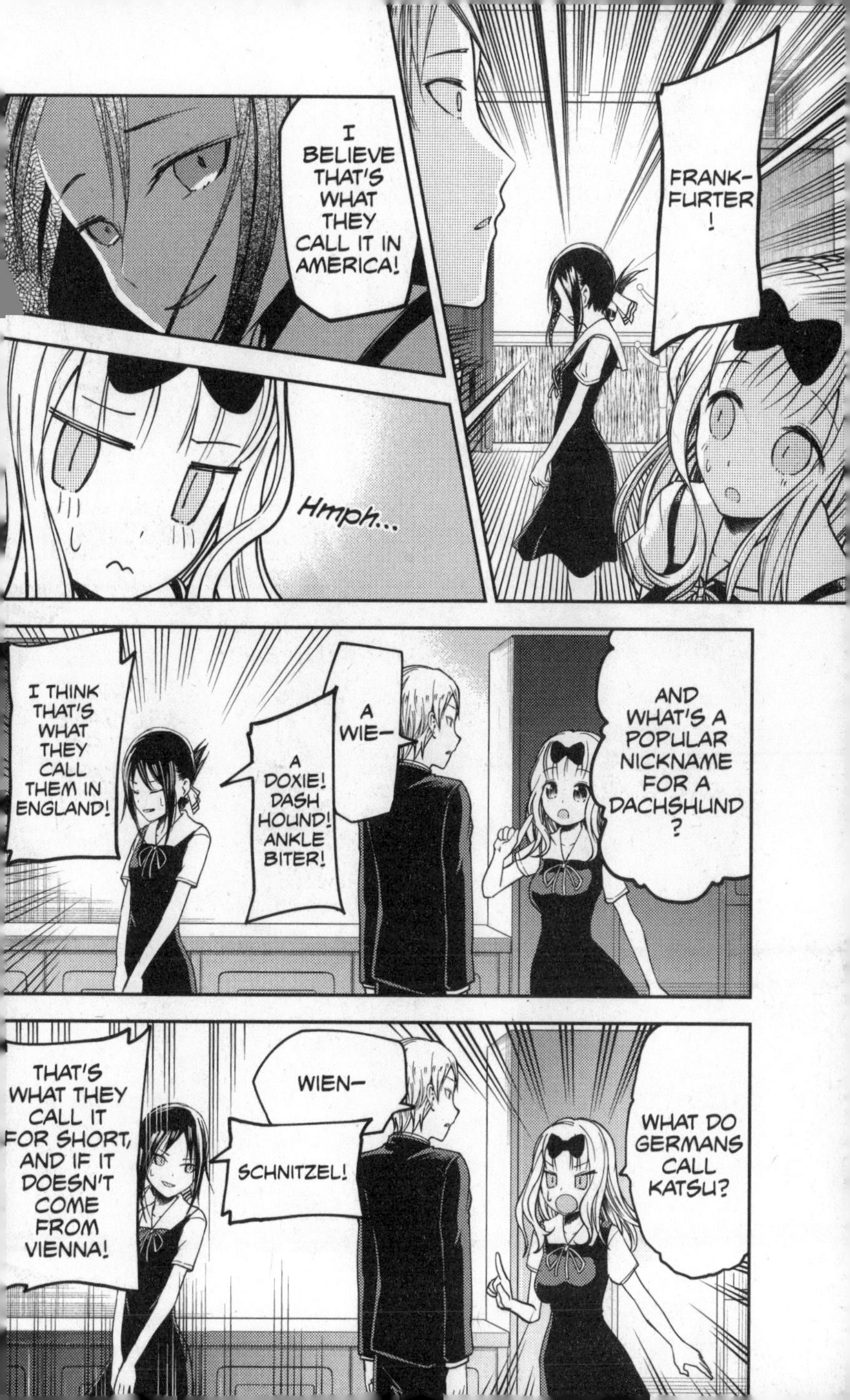
FRANK-FURTER!
I BELIEVE THAT'S WHAT THEY CALL IT IN AMERICA!
Hmph...
AND WHAT'S A POPULAR NICKNAME FOR A DACHSHUND?
A WIE—
A DOXIE! DASH HOUND! ANKLE BITER!
I THINK THAT'S WHAT THEY CALL THEM IN ENGLAND!
WHAT DO GERMANS CALL KATSU?
WIEN—
SCHNITZEL!
THAT'S WHAT THEY CALL IT FOR SHORT, AND IF IT DOESN'T COME FROM VIENNA!

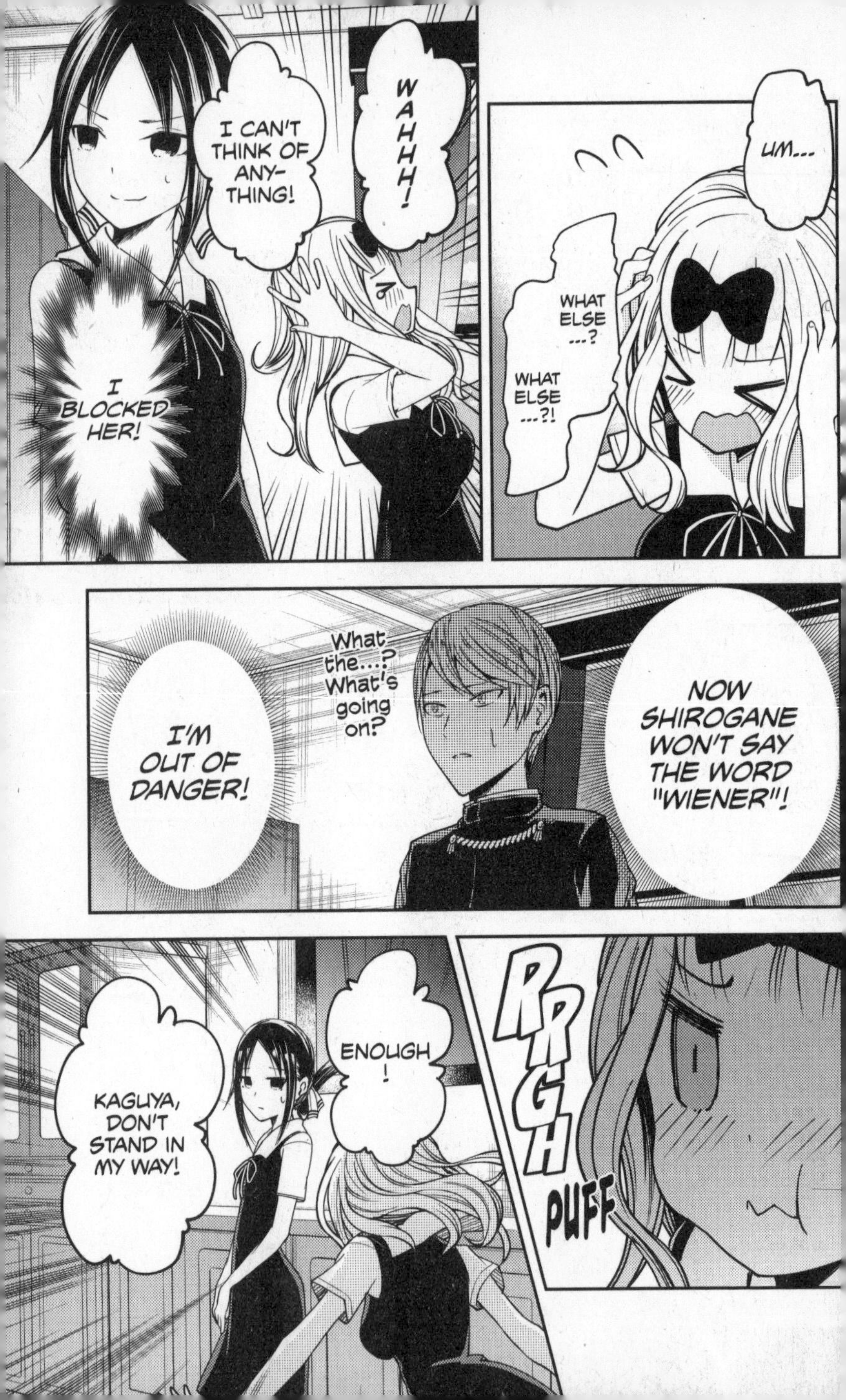
UM...
WHAT ELSE ...?
WHAT ELSE ...?!
WAHHH!
I CAN'T THINK OF ANY-THING!
I BLOCKED HER!
NOW SHIROGANE WON'T SAY THE WORD "WIENER"!
What the...? What's going on?
I'M OUT OF DANGER!
RRRGH
PUFF
ENOUGH!
KAGUYA, DON'T STAND IN MY WAY!

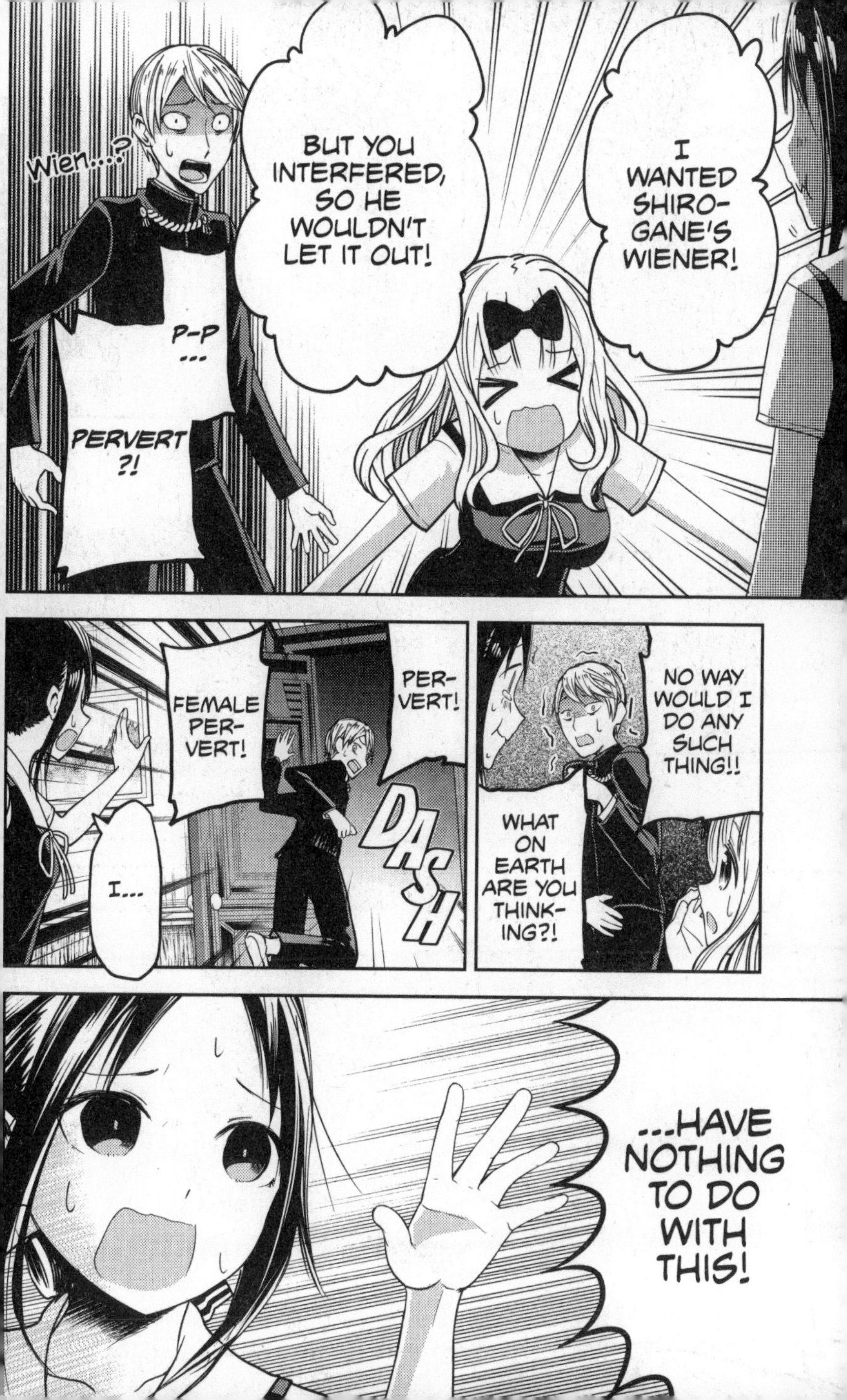
I WANTED SHIROGANE'S WIENER!
BUT YOU INTERFERED, SO HE WOULDN'T LET IT OUT!
Wien...?
P-P...
PERVERT?!
NO WAY WOULD I DO ANY SUCH THING!!
WHAT ON EARTH ARE YOU THINKING?!
PER-VERT!
FEMALE PER-VERT!
DASH
I...
...HAVE NOTHING TO DO WITH THIS!

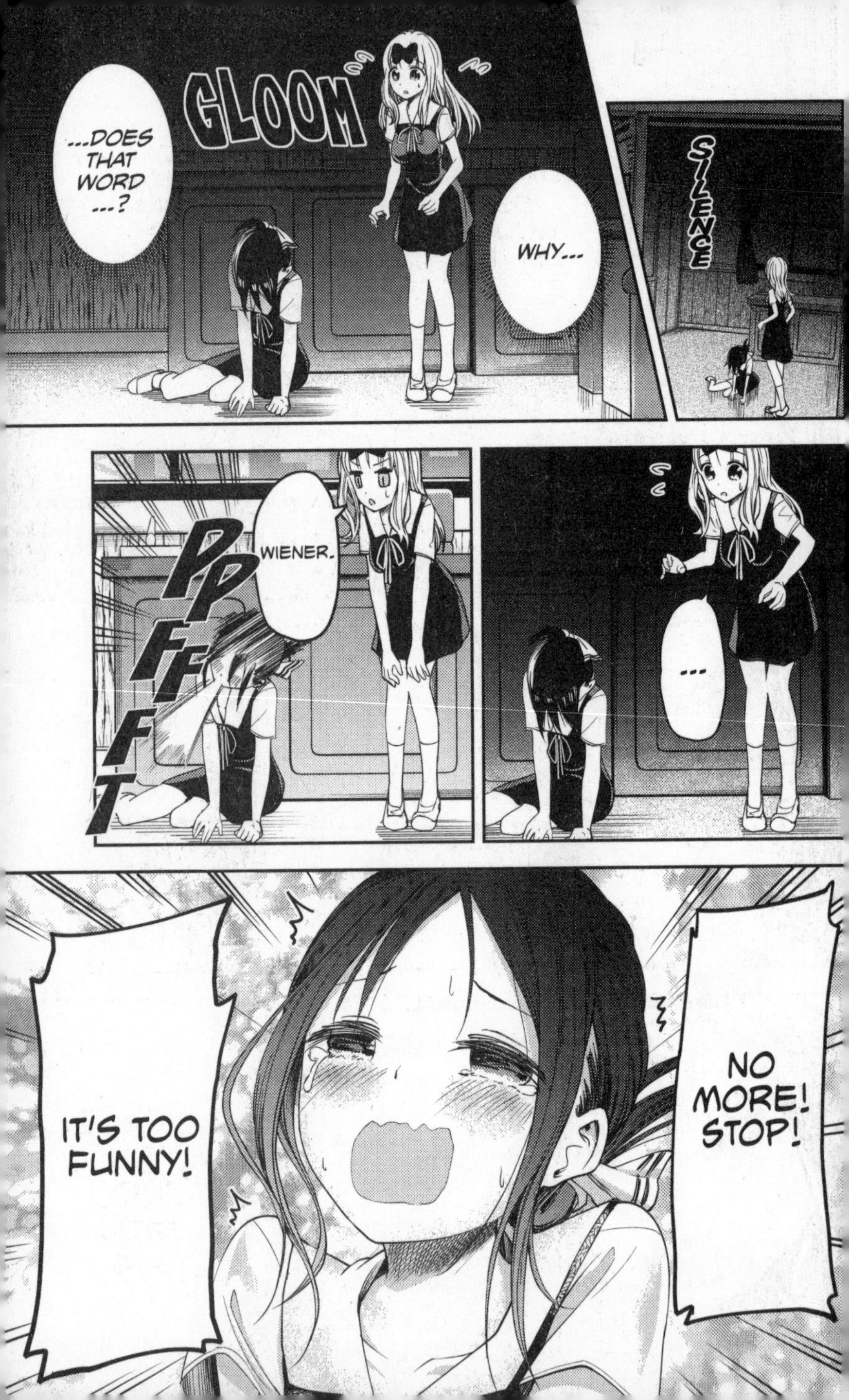
SILENCE
WHY...
GLOOM
...DOES THAT WORD ...?
...
WIENER.
PPFFFT
NO MORE! STOP!
IT'S TOO FUNNY!

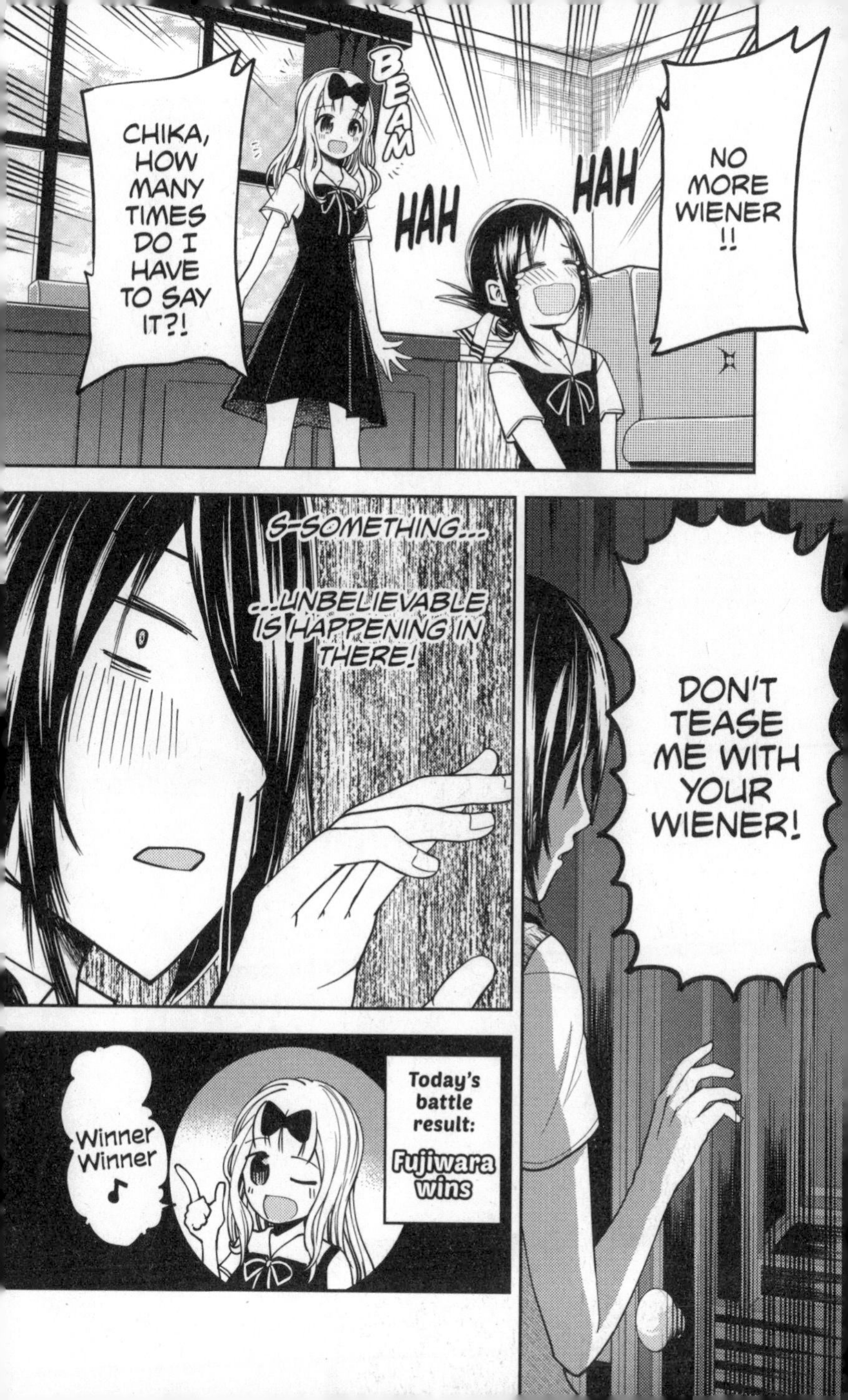
NO MORE WIENER !!
HAH
HAH
BEAM
CHIKA, HOW MANY TIMES DO I HAVE TO SAY IT?!
DON'T TEASE ME WITH YOUR WIENER!
S-SOMETHING...
...UNBELIEVABLE IS HAPPENING IN THERE!
Today's battle result:
Fujiwara wins
Winner Winner ♪

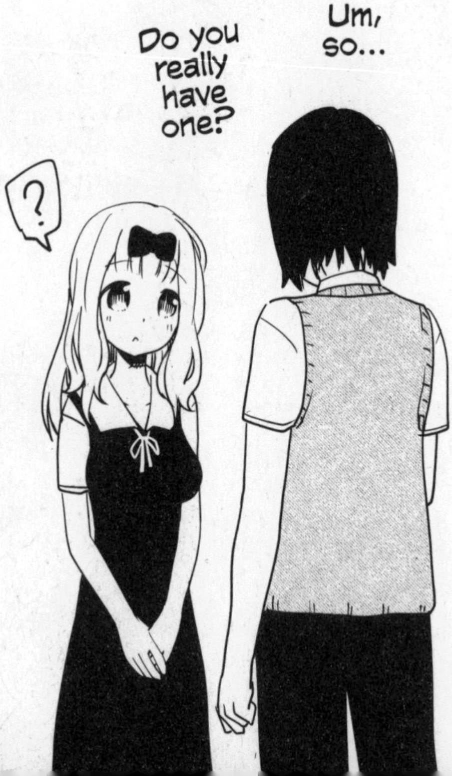
Um, so...
Do you really have one?
?

KAGUYA-SAMA
LOVE IS WAR

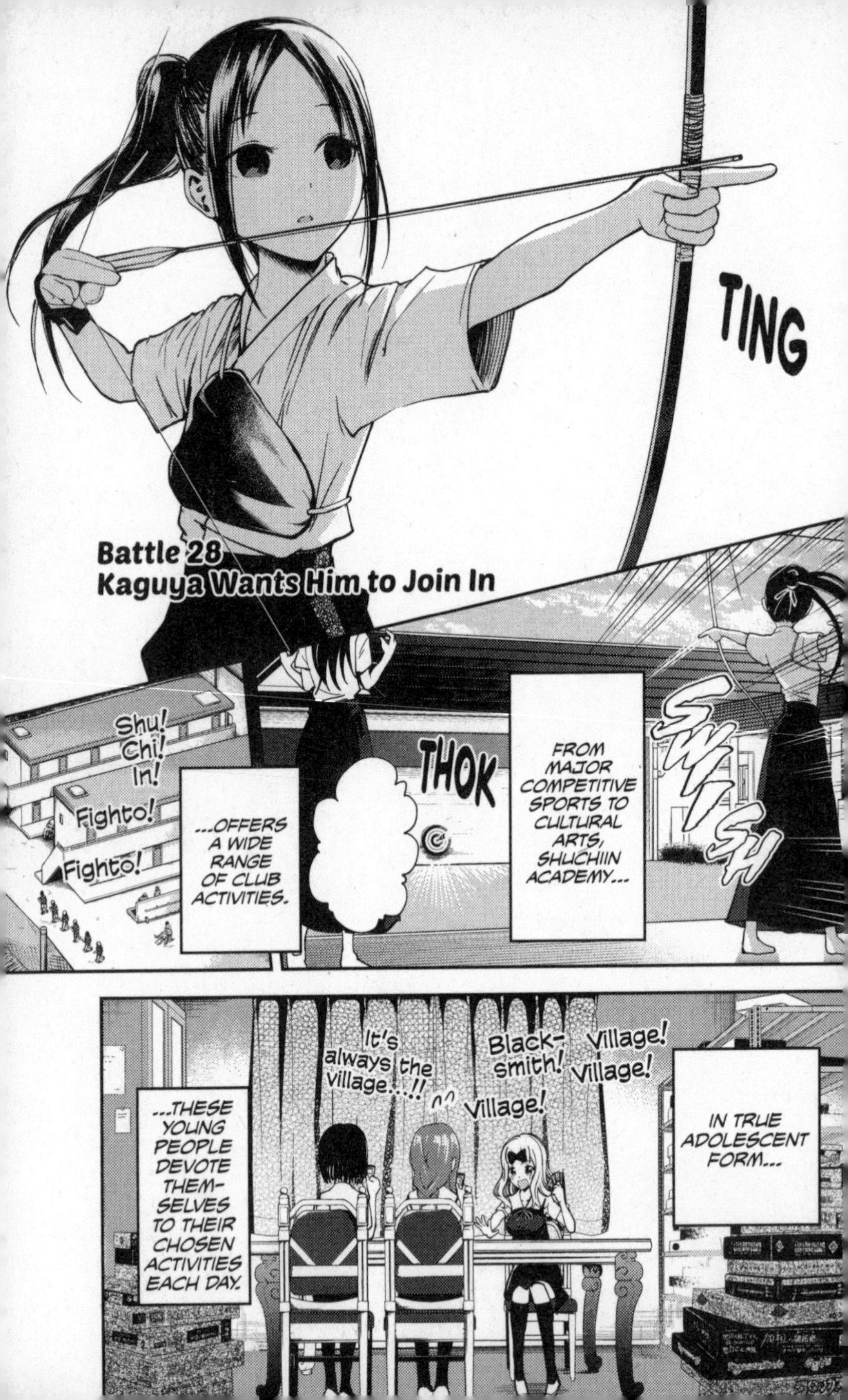
TING
Battle 28
Kaguya Wants Him to Join In
SWISH
FROM MAJOR COMPETITIVE SPORTS TO CULTURAL ARTS, SHUCHIIN ACADEMY...
THOK
...OFFERS A WIDE RANGE OF CLUB ACTIVITIES.
Shu! Chi! In!
Fighto!
Fighto!
IN TRUE ADOLESCENT FORM...
Village! Village!
Black-smith!
Village!
It's always the village...!!
...THESE YOUNG PEOPLE DEVOTE THEM-SELVES TO THEIR CHOSEN ACTIVITIES EACH DAY.

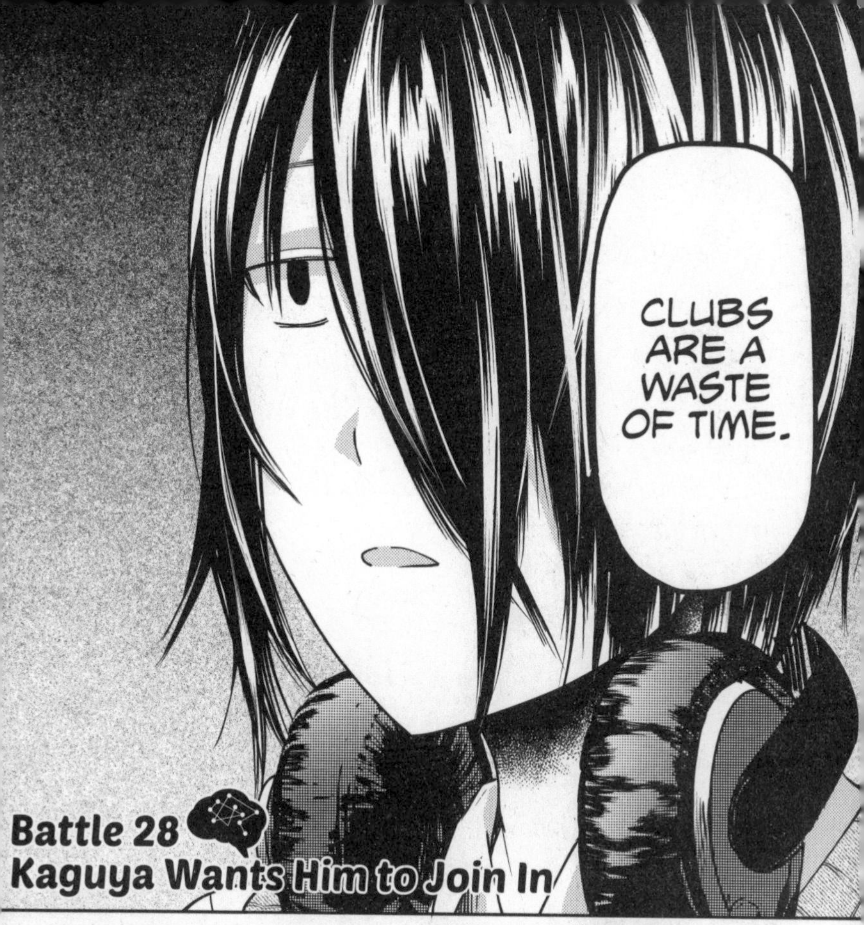
CLUBS ARE A WASTE OF TIME.

Battle 28
Kaguya Wants Him to Join In

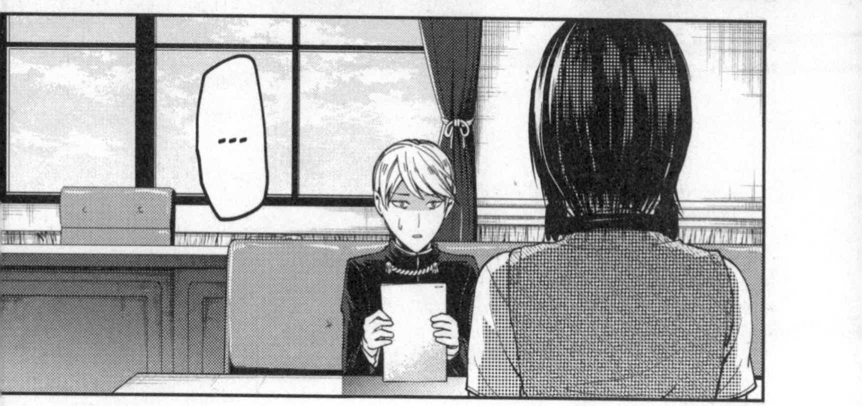
...

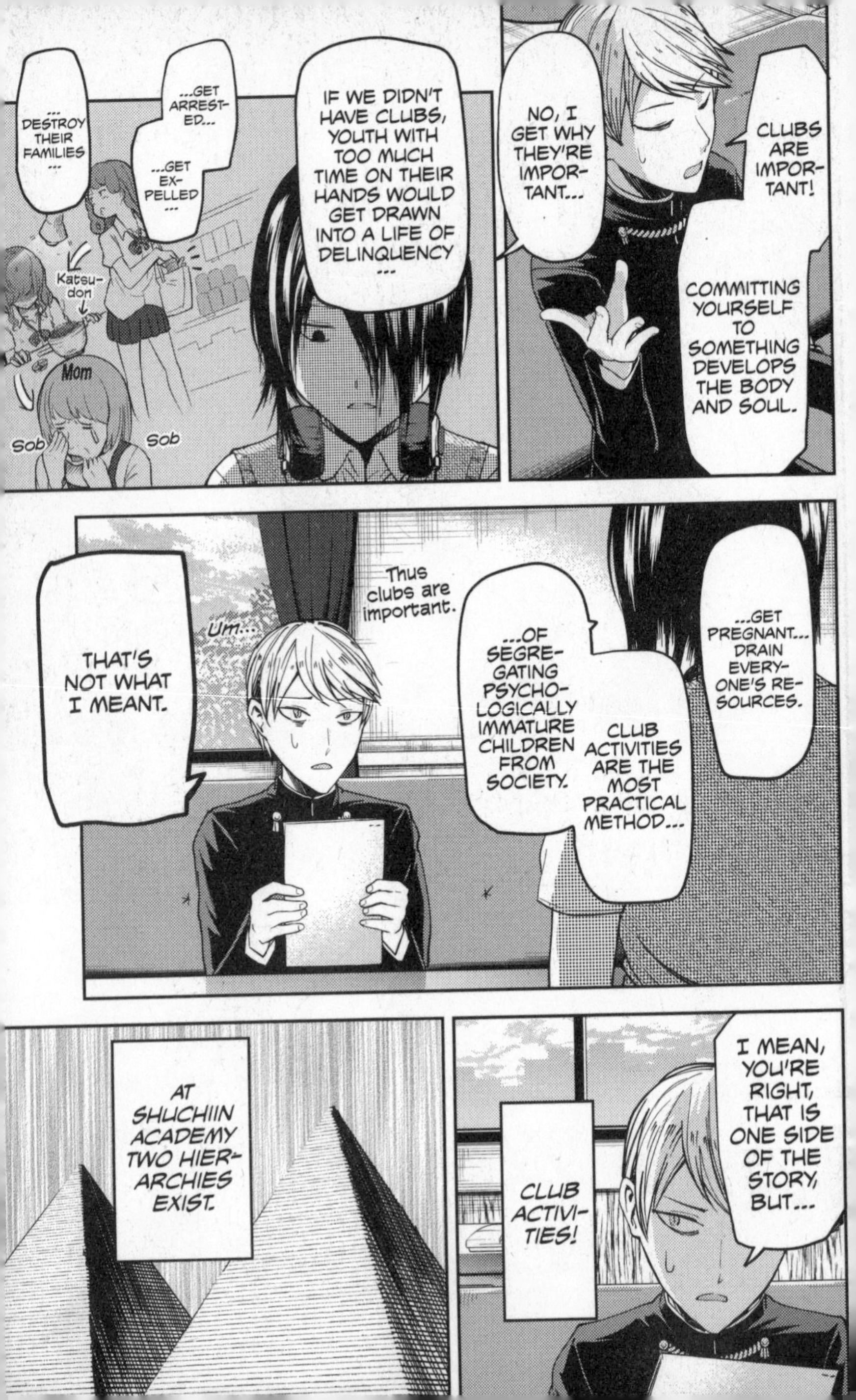
CLUBS ARE IMPORTANT!
COMMITTING YOURSELF TO SOMETHING DEVELOPS THE BODY AND SOUL.
NO, I GET WHY THEY'RE IMPORTANT...
IF WE DIDN'T HAVE CLUBS, YOUTH WITH TOO MUCH TIME ON THEIR HANDS WOULD GET DRAWN INTO A LIFE OF DELINQUENCY...
...GET ARRESTED...
...GET EXPELLED...
...DESTROY THEIR FAMILIES...
Katsu-don
Mom
Sob
Sob
...GET PREGNANT... DRAIN EVERYONE'S RESOURCES.
CLUB ACTIVITIES ARE THE MOST PRACTICAL METHOD...
...OF SEGREGATING PSYCHOLOGICALLY IMMATURE CHILDREN FROM SOCIETY.
Thus clubs are important.
Um...
THAT'S NOT WHAT I MEANT.
I MEAN, YOU'RE RIGHT, THAT IS ONE SIDE OF THE STORY, BUT...
CLUB ACTIVITIES!
AT SHUCHIIN ACADEMY TWO HIERARCHIES EXIST.

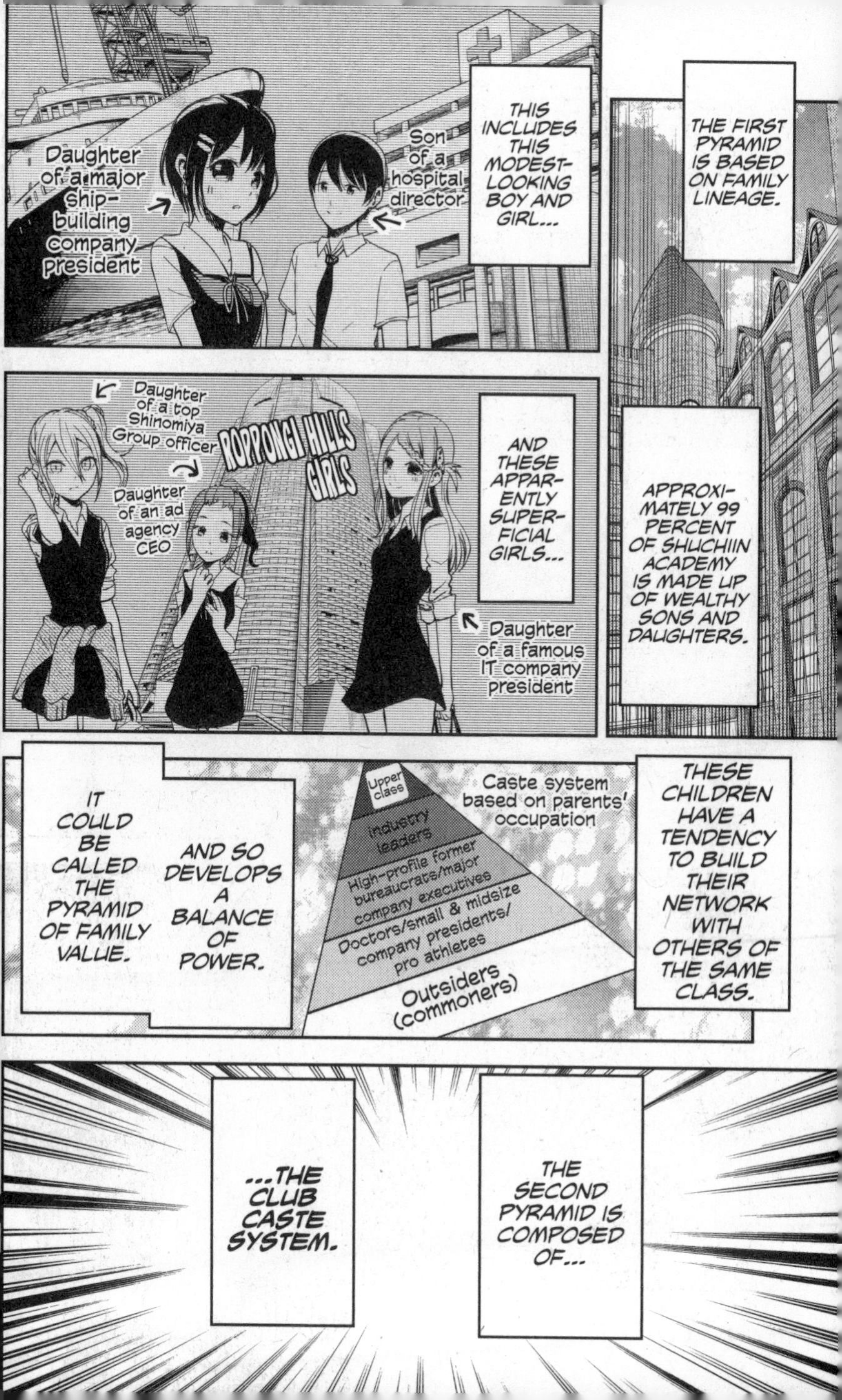
THE FIRST PYRAMID IS BASED ON FAMILY LINEAGE.
APPROXIMATELY 99 PERCENT OF SHUCHIIN ACADEMY IS MADE UP OF WEALTHY SONS AND DAUGHTERS.
THIS INCLUDES THIS MODEST-LOOKING BOY AND GIRL...
Son of a hospital director
Daughter of a major ship-building company president
AND THESE APPARENTLY SUPERFICIAL GIRLS...
Daughter of a famous IT company president
ROPPONGI HILLS GIRLS
Daughter of a top Shinomiya Group officer
Daughter of an ad agency CEO
THESE CHILDREN HAVE A TENDENCY TO BUILD THEIR NETWORK WITH OTHERS OF THE SAME CLASS.
Caste system based on parents' occupation
Upper class
Industry leaders
High-profile former bureaucrats/major company executives
Doctors/small & midsize company presidents/pro athletes
Outsiders (commoners)
AND SO DEVELOPS A BALANCE OF POWER.
IT COULD BE CALLED THE PYRAMID OF FAMILY VALUE.
THE SECOND PYRAMID IS COMPOSED OF...
...THE CLUB CASTE SYSTEM.

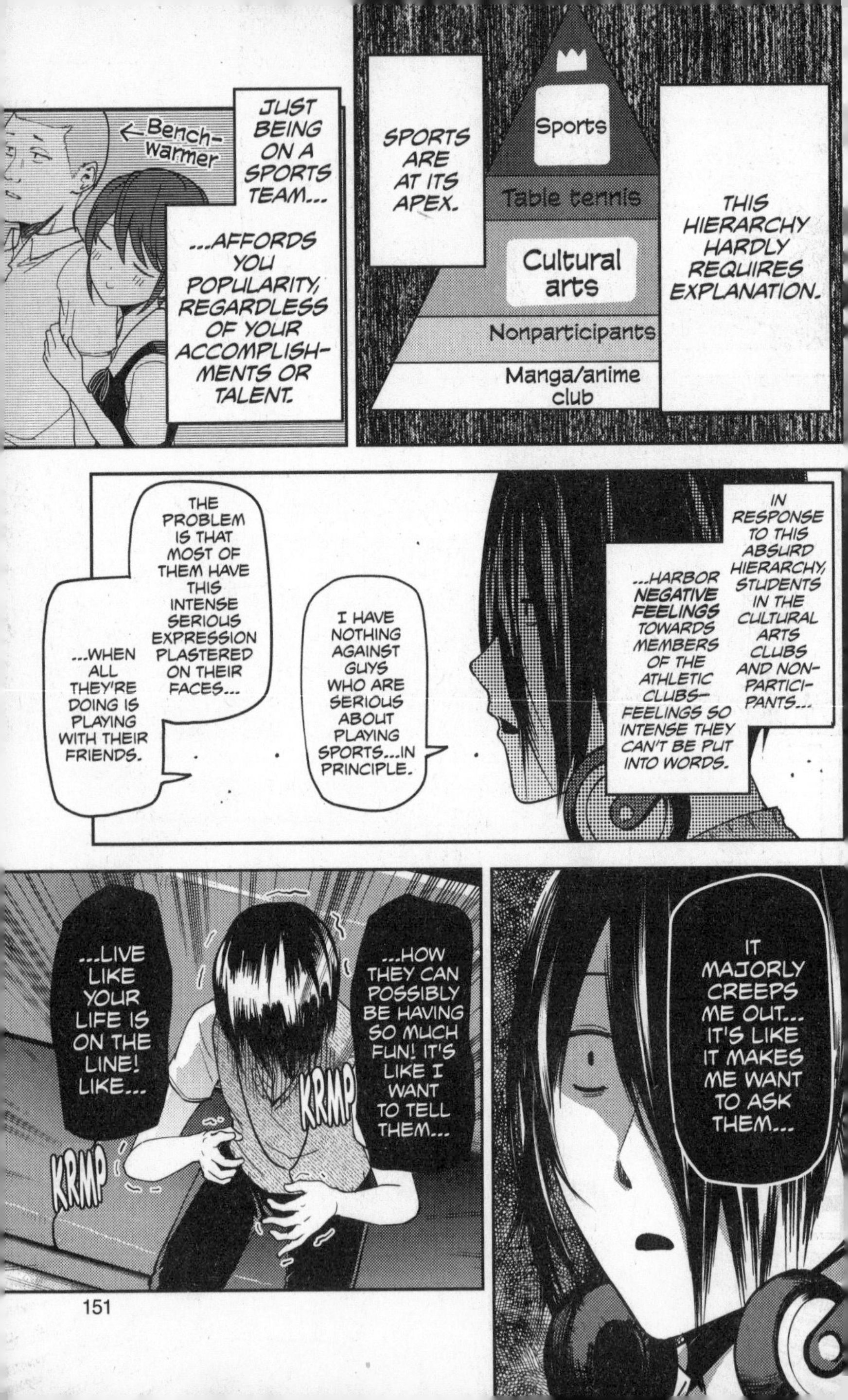
SPORTS ARE AT ITS APEX.
Sports
Table tennis
Cultural arts
Nonparticipants
Manga/anime club
THIS HIERARCHY HARDLY REQUIRES EXPLANATION.
JUST BEING ON A SPORTS TEAM...
...AFFORDS YOU POPULARITY, REGARDLESS OF YOUR ACCOMPLISHMENTS OR TALENT.
← Bench-warmer
IN RESPONSE TO THIS ABSURD HIERARCHY, STUDENTS IN THE CULTURAL ARTS CLUBS AND NON-PARTICIPANTS...
...HARBOR NEGATIVE FEELINGS TOWARDS MEMBERS OF THE ATHLETIC CLUBS—FEELINGS SO INTENSE THEY CAN'T BE PUT INTO WORDS.
I HAVE NOTHING AGAINST GUYS WHO ARE SERIOUS ABOUT PLAYING SPORTS...IN PRINCIPLE.
THE PROBLEM IS THAT MOST OF THEM HAVE THIS INTENSE SERIOUS EXPRESSION PLASTERED ON THEIR FACES...
...WHEN ALL THEY'RE DOING IS PLAYING WITH THEIR FRIENDS.
IT MAJORLY CREEPS ME OUT... IT'S LIKE IT MAKES ME WANT TO ASK THEM...
...HOW THEY CAN POSSIBLY BE HAVING SO MUCH FUN! IT'S LIKE I WANT TO TELL THEM...
...LIVE LIKE YOUR LIFE IS ON THE LINE! LIKE...
KRMP
KRMP

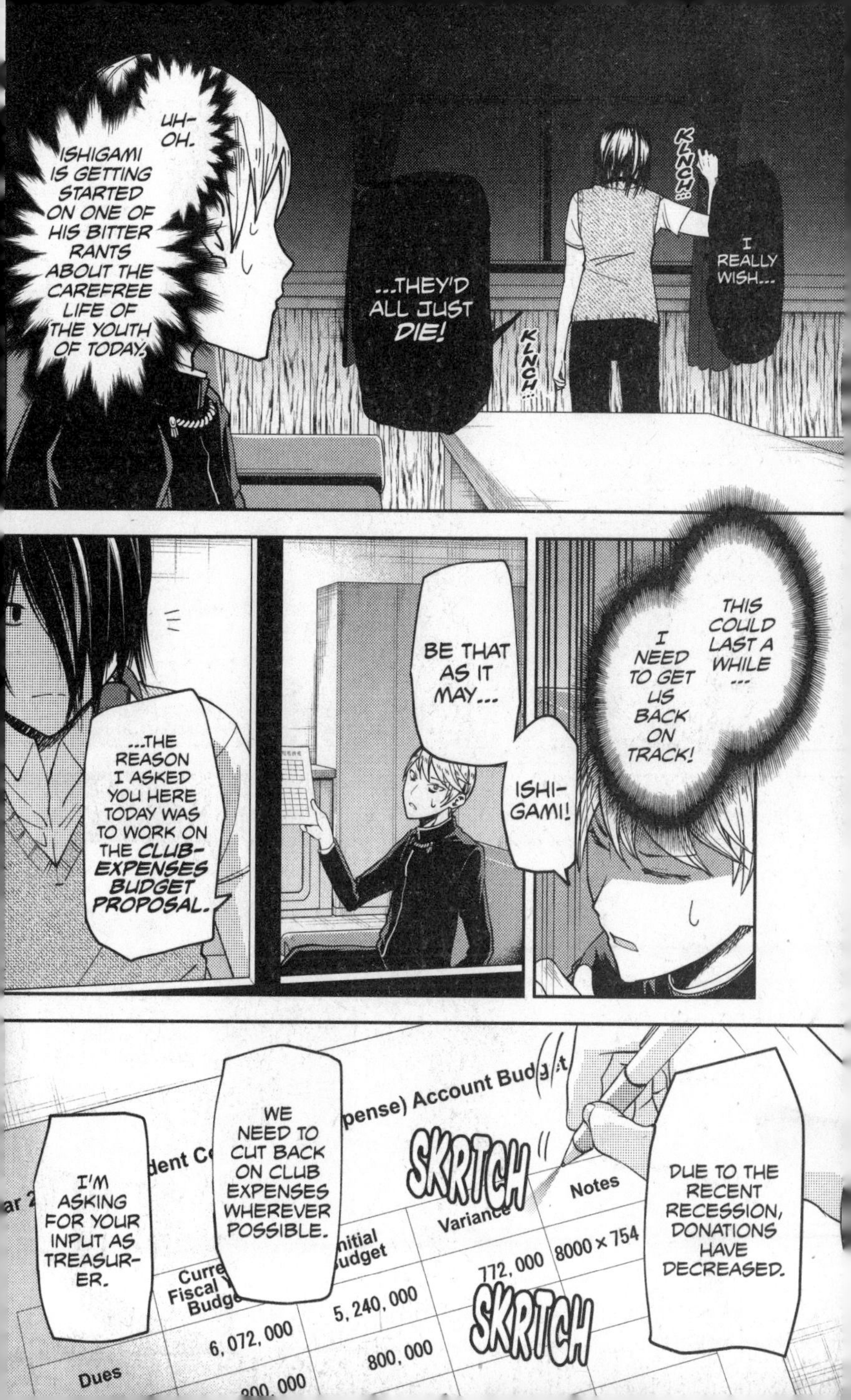
KLNCH..
I REALLY WISH...
KLNCH..
...THEY'D ALL JUST DIE!
UH-OH.
ISHIGAMI IS GETTING STARTED ON ONE OF HIS BITTER RANTS ABOUT THE CAREFREE LIFE OF THE YOUTH OF TODAY.
THIS COULD LAST A WHILE...
I NEED TO GET US BACK ON TRACK!
ISHI-GAMI!
BE THAT AS IT MAY...
...THE REASON I ASKED YOU HERE TODAY WAS TO WORK ON THE CLUB-EXPENSES BUDGET PROPOSAL.
DUE TO THE RECENT RECESSION, DONATIONS HAVE DECREASED.
SKRTCH
SKRTCH
WE NEED TO CUT BACK ON CLUB EXPENSES WHEREVER POSSIBLE.
I'M ASKING FOR YOUR INPUT AS TREASURER.
Notes
Variance
8000 × 754
772,000
5,240,000
6,072,000
800,000
Dues

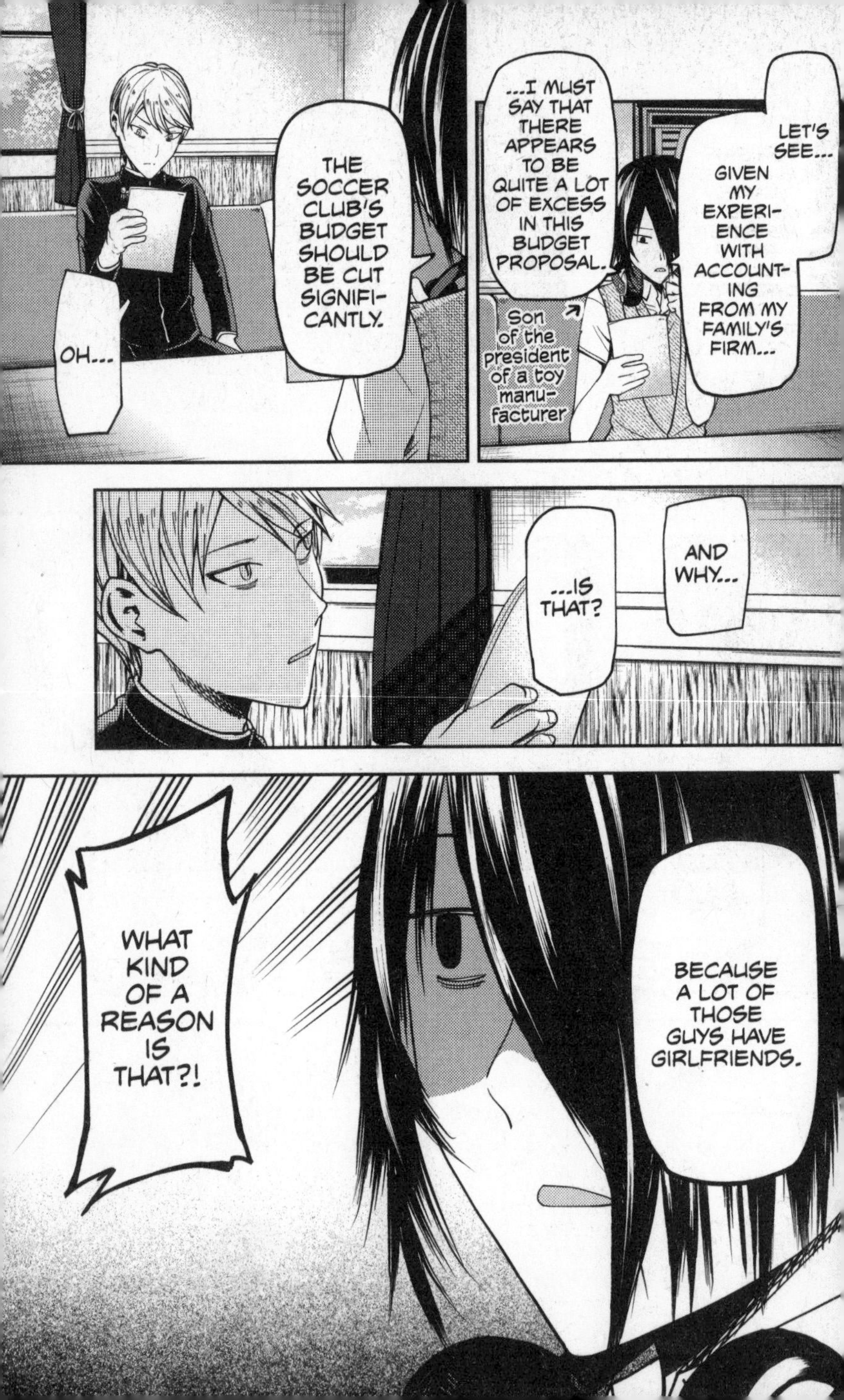
LET'S SEE... GIVEN MY EXPERIENCE WITH ACCOUNTING FROM MY FAMILY'S FIRM...
...I MUST SAY THAT THERE APPEARS TO BE QUITE A LOT OF EXCESS IN THIS BUDGET PROPOSAL.
Son of the president of a toy manufacturer
THE SOCCER CLUB'S BUDGET SHOULD BE CUT SIGNIFICANTLY.
OH...
AND WHY...
...IS THAT?
BECAUSE A LOT OF THOSE GUYS HAVE GIRLFRIENDS.
WHAT KIND OF A REASON IS THAT?!

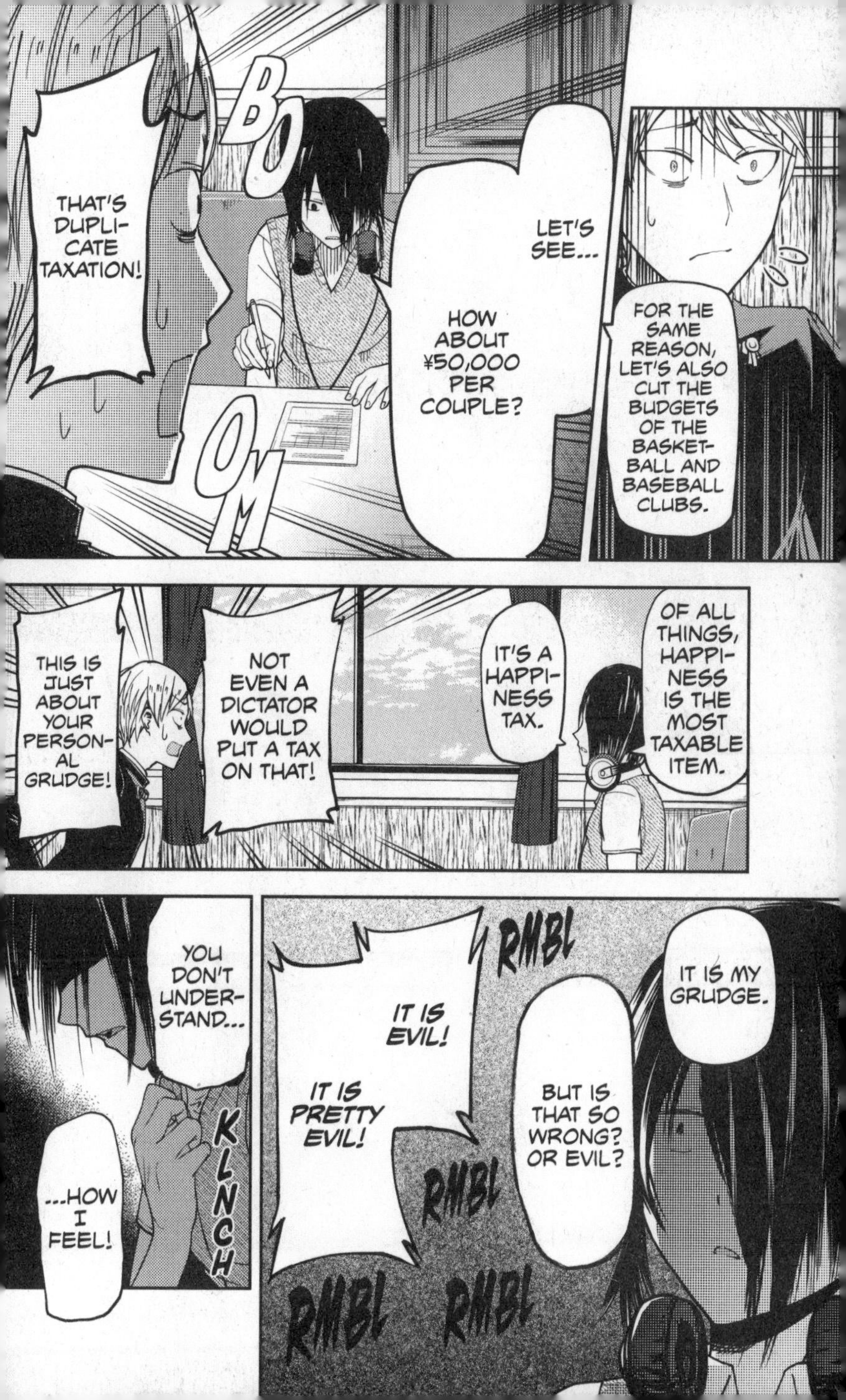
FOR THE SAME REASON, LET'S ALSO CUT THE BUDGETS OF THE BASKETBALL AND BASEBALL CLUBS.
LET'S SEE...
HOW ABOUT ¥50,000 PER COUPLE?
BOOM
THAT'S DUPLICATE TAXATION!
OF ALL THINGS, HAPPINESS IS THE MOST TAXABLE ITEM.
IT'S A HAPPINESS TAX.
NOT EVEN A DICTATOR WOULD PUT A TAX ON THAT!
THIS IS JUST ABOUT YOUR PERSONAL GRUDGE!
IT IS MY GRUDGE.
BUT IS THAT SO WRONG? OR EVIL?
RMBL
IT IS EVIL!
IT IS PRETTY EVIL!
RMBL
RMBL
RMBL
YOU DON'T UNDERSTAND...
KLNCH
...HOW I FEEL!

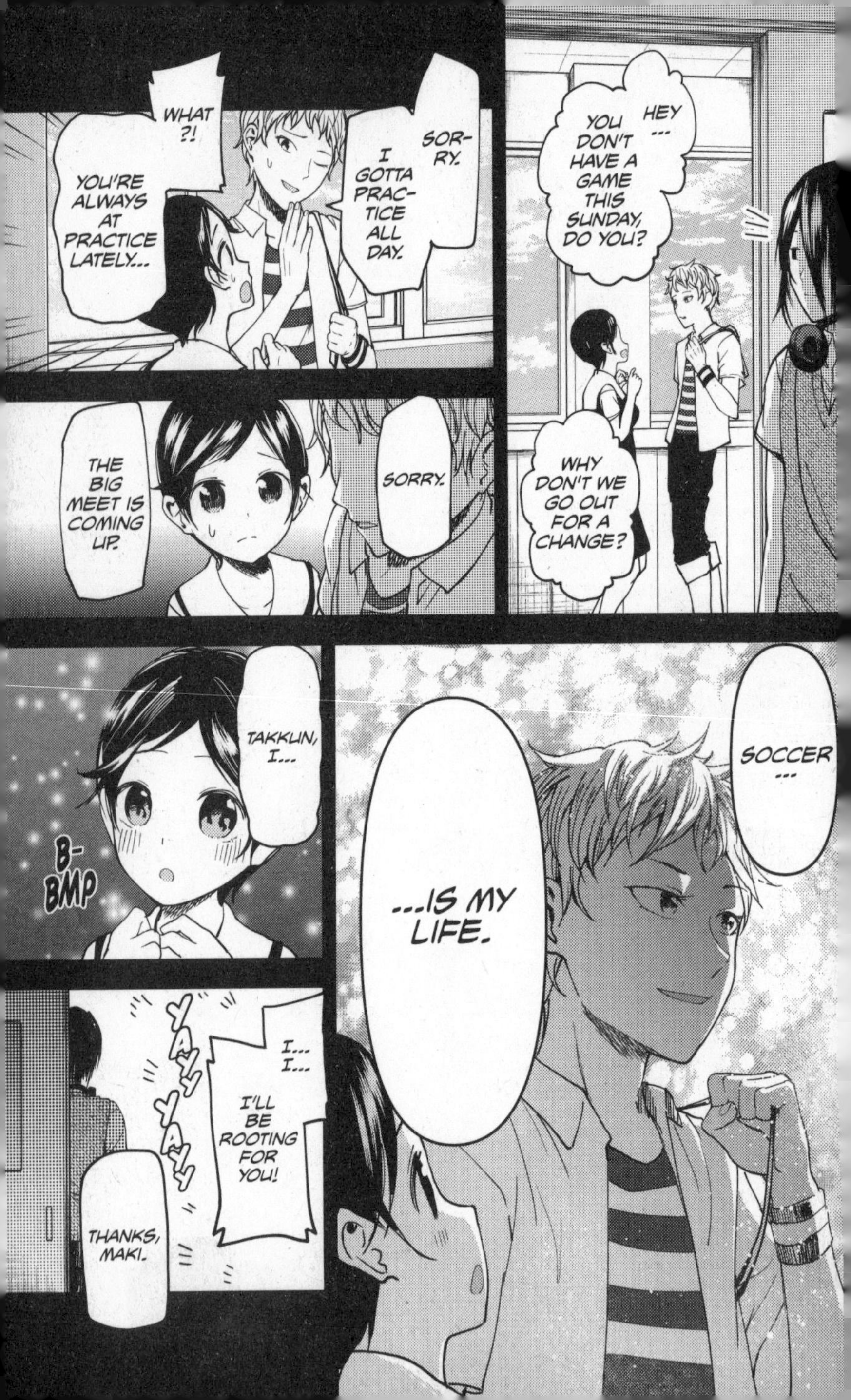
HEY ... YOU DON'T HAVE A GAME THIS SUNDAY, DO YOU?
WHY DON'T WE GO OUT FOR A CHANGE?
SORRY. I GOTTA PRACTICE ALL DAY.
WHAT?! YOU'RE ALWAYS AT PRACTICE LATELY...
SORRY.
THE BIG MEET IS COMING UP.
SOCCER ...
...IS MY LIFE.
TAKKUN, I...
B-BMP
I... I... I'LL BE ROOTING FOR YOU!
YAY YAY YAY
THANKS, MAKI.

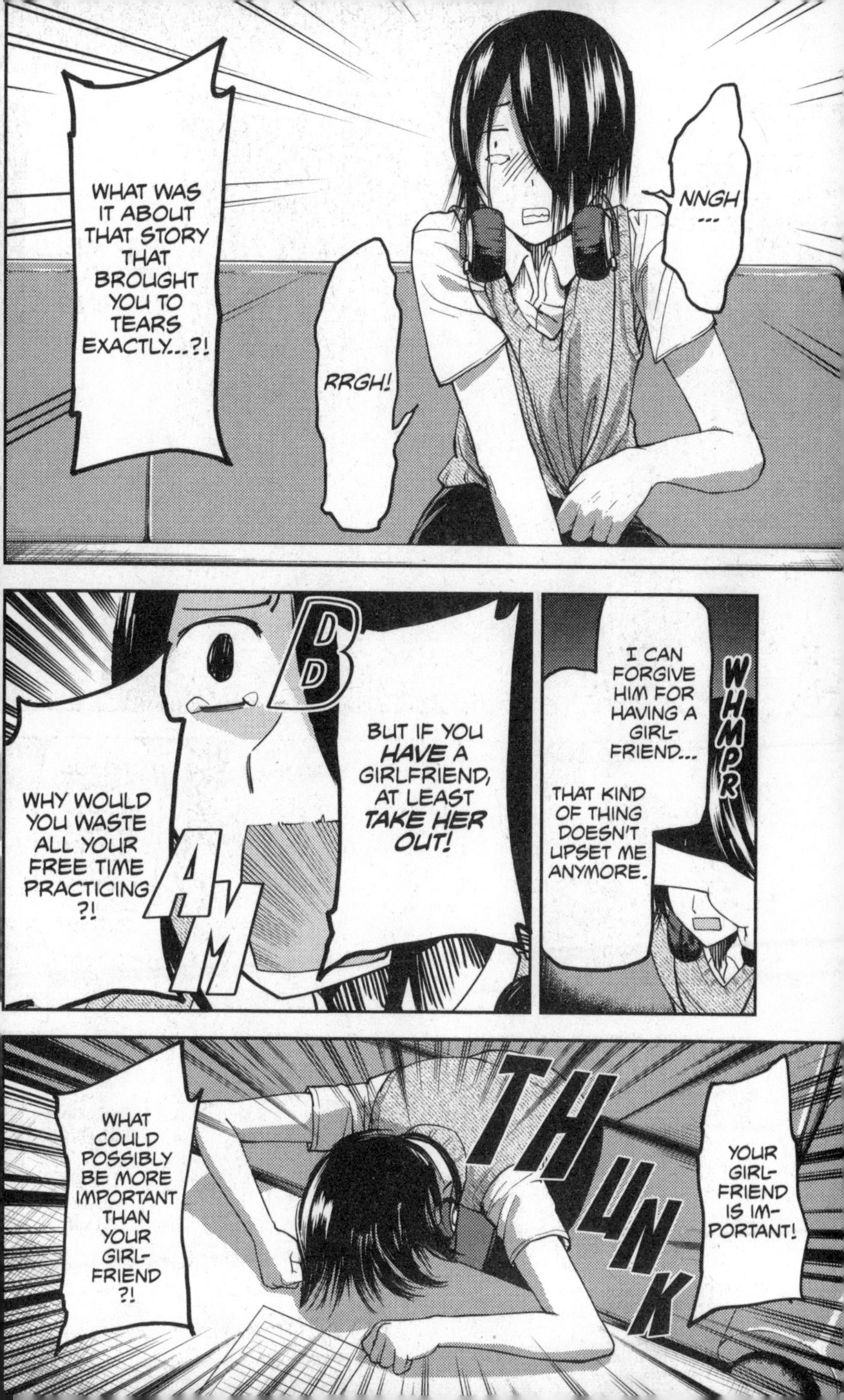
NNGH ...
WHAT WAS IT ABOUT THAT STORY THAT BROUGHT YOU TO TEARS EXACTLY...?!
RRGH!
I CAN FORGIVE HIM FOR HAVING A GIRL-FRIEND...
WHMPR
THAT KIND OF THING DOESN'T UPSET ME ANYMORE.
BDD
BUT IF YOU *HAVE* A GIRLFRIEND, AT LEAST *TAKE HER OUT!*
WHY WOULD YOU WASTE ALL YOUR FREE TIME PRACTICING?!
AM
YOUR GIRL-FRIEND IS IM-PORTANT!
THUNK
WHAT COULD POSSIBLY BE MORE IMPORTANT THAN YOUR GIRL-FRIEND?!

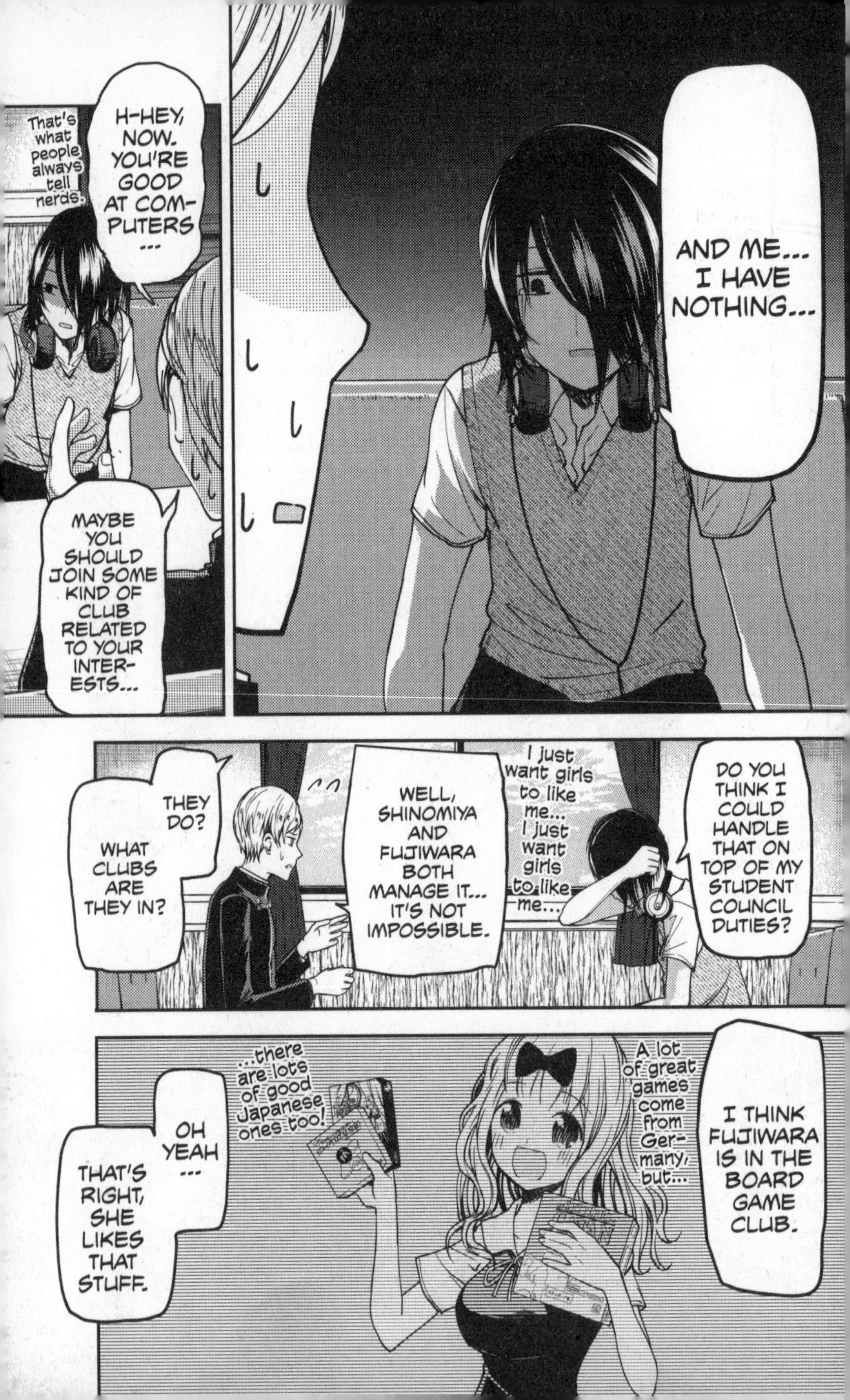
AND ME... I HAVE NOTHING...
H-HEY, NOW. YOU'RE GOOD AT COMPUTERS...
That's what people always tell nerds.
MAYBE YOU SHOULD JOIN SOME KIND OF CLUB RELATED TO YOUR INTERESTS...
DO YOU THINK I COULD HANDLE THAT ON TOP OF MY STUDENT COUNCIL DUTIES?
I just want girls to like me... I just want girls to like me...
WELL, SHINOMIYA AND FUJIWARA BOTH MANAGE IT... IT'S NOT IMPOSSIBLE.
THEY DO? WHAT CLUBS ARE THEY IN?
I THINK FUJIWARA IS IN THE BOARD GAME CLUB.
A lot of great games come from Germany, but...
...there are lots of good Japanese ones too!
OH YEAH... THAT'S RIGHT, SHE LIKES THAT STUFF.

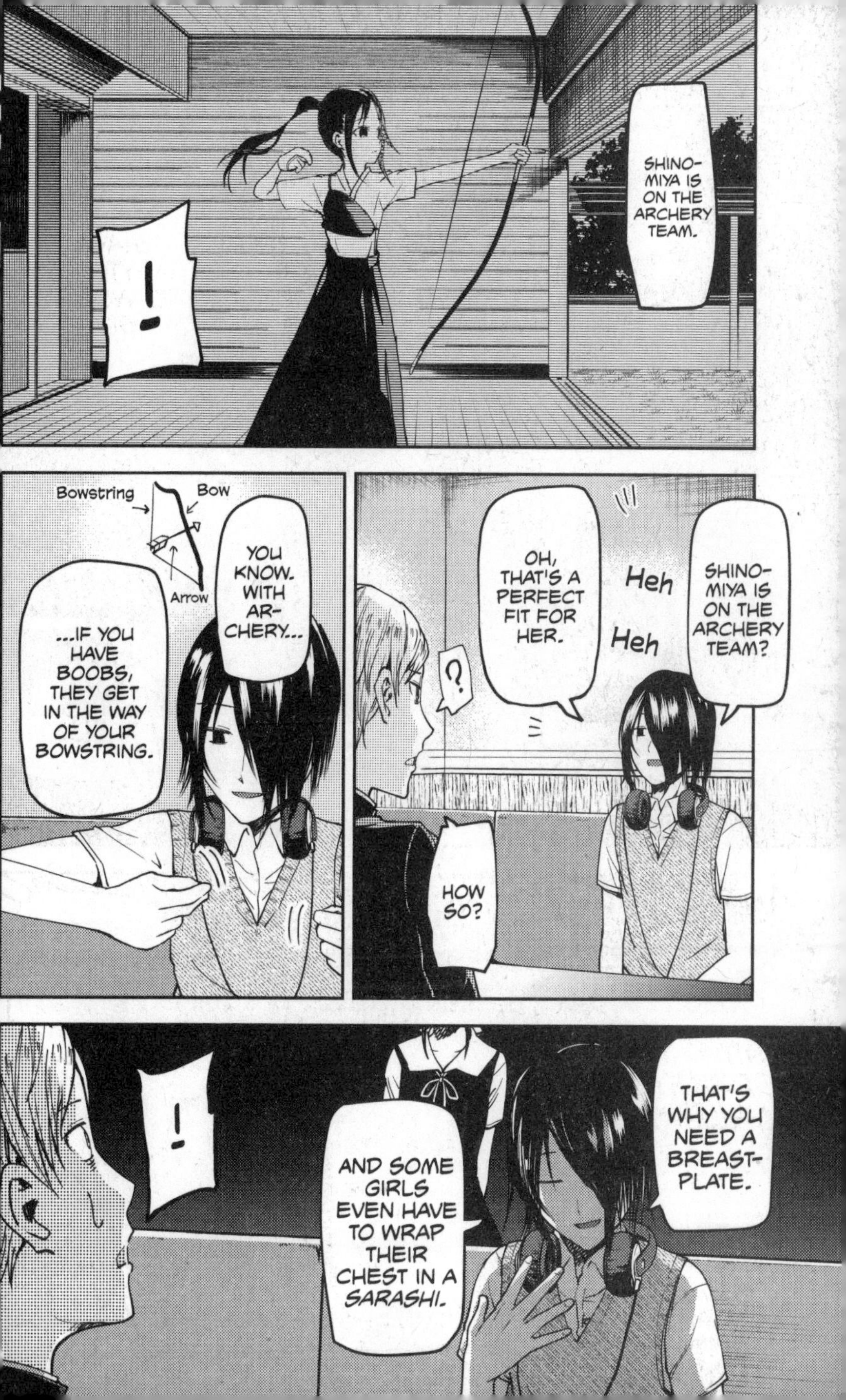

SHINO-MIYA IS ON THE ARCHERY TEAM.
!
SHINO-MIYA IS ON THE ARCHERY TEAM?
Heh
Heh
OH, THAT'S A PERFECT FIT FOR HER.
?
HOW SO?
YOU KNOW. WITH AR-CHERY...
Bowstring
Bow
Arrow
...IF YOU HAVE BOOBS, THEY GET IN THE WAY OF YOUR BOWSTRING.
THAT'S WHY YOU NEED A BREAST-PLATE.
AND SOME GIRLS EVEN HAVE TO WRAP THEIR CHEST IN A SARASHI.
!

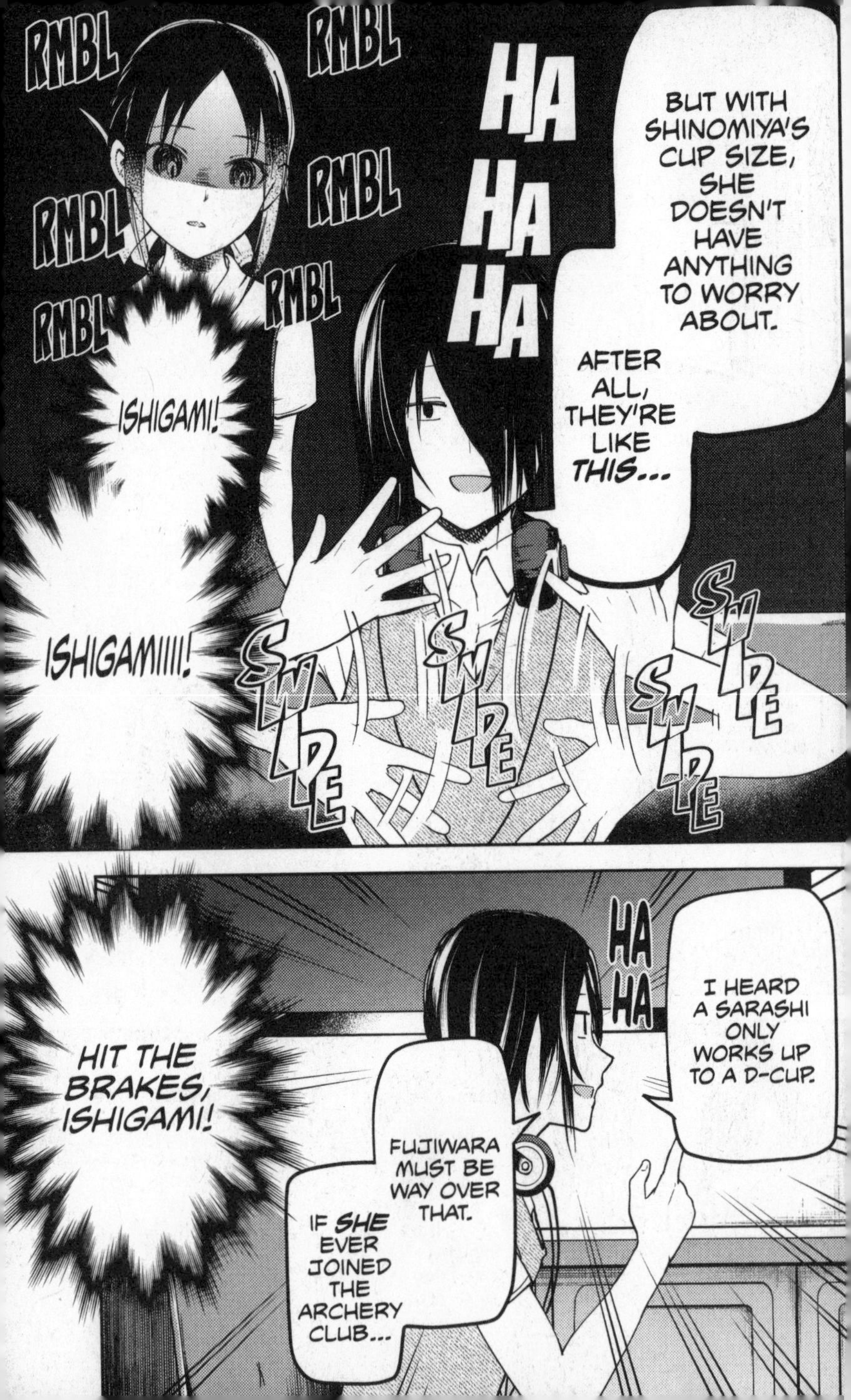
BUT WITH SHINOMIYA'S CUP SIZE, SHE DOESN'T HAVE ANYTHING TO WORRY ABOUT.
HA HA HA
AFTER ALL, THEY'RE LIKE *THIS*...
SWIPE SWIPE SWIPE SWIPE
RMBL RMBL RMBL RMBL RMBL RMBL
ISHIGAMI!
ISHIGAMIIIII!
I HEARD A SARASHI ONLY WORKS UP TO A D-CUP.
HA HA
FUJIWARA MUST BE WAY OVER THAT.
IF *SHE* EVER JOINED THE ARCHERY CLUB...
HIT THE BRAKES, ISHIGAMI!

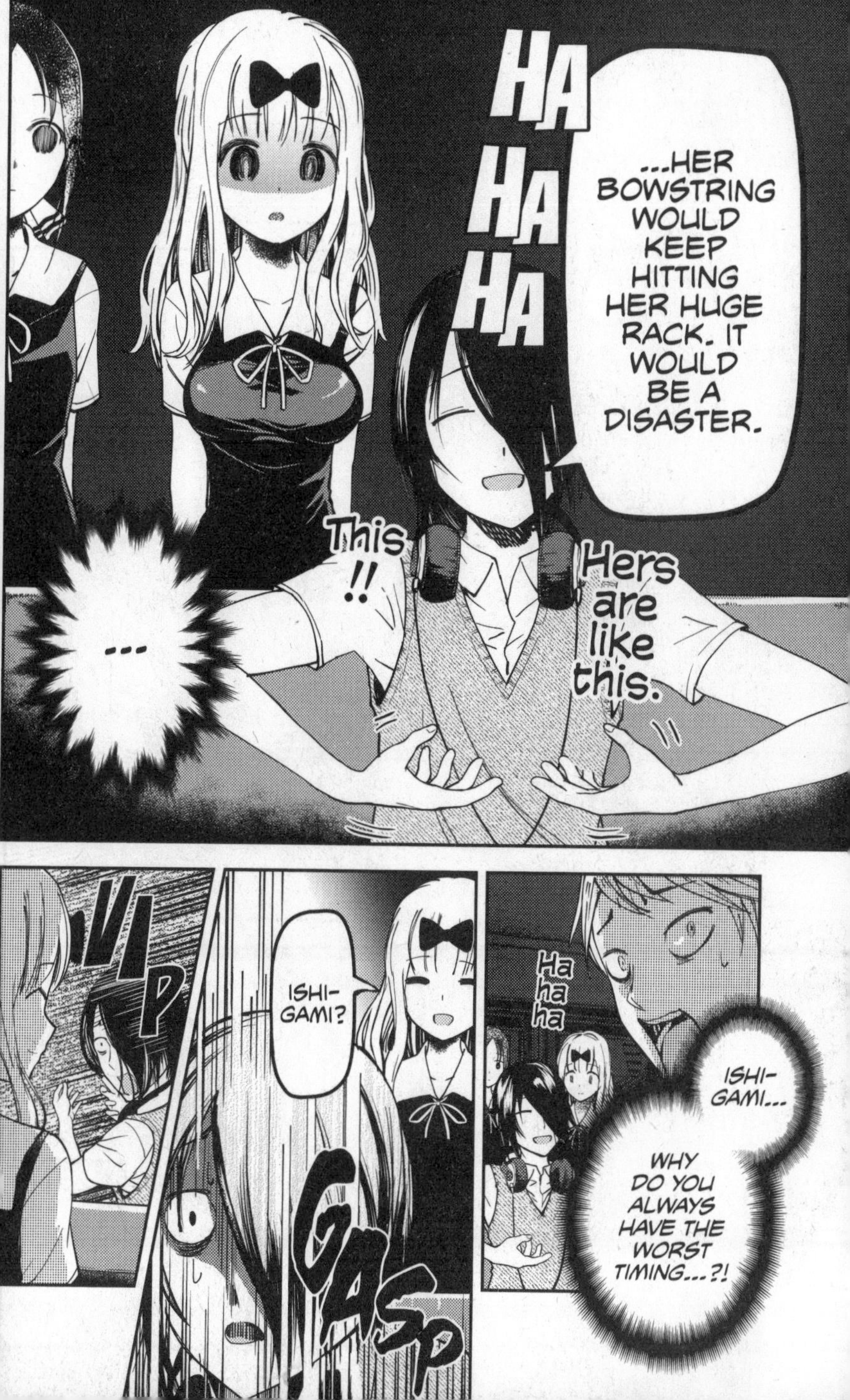
HA HA HA
...HER BOWSTRING WOULD KEEP HITTING HER HUGE RACK. IT WOULD BE A DISASTER.
Hers are like this.
This!!
...
Ha ha ha
ISHI-GAMI...
WHY DO YOU ALWAYS HAVE THE WORST TIMING...?!
ISHI-GAMI?
GASP

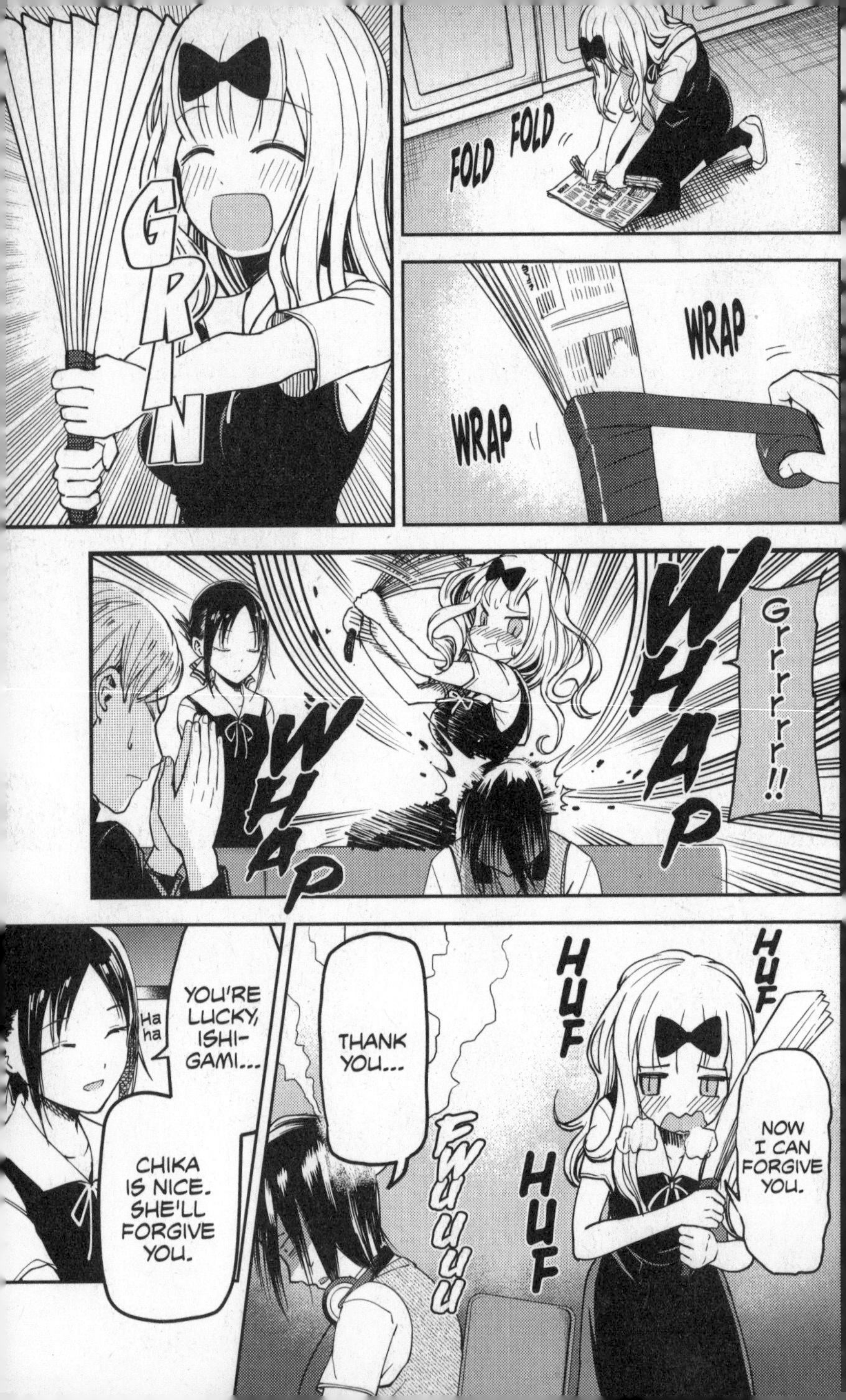
FOLD FOLD
WRAP
WRAP
GRIN
Grrrrr!!
WHAP
WHAP
HUF HUF
NOW I CAN FORGIVE YOU.
HUF HUF
THANK YOU...
Fwuuuu
YOU'RE LUCKY, ISHI-GAMI...
Ha ha
CHIKA IS NICE. SHE'LL FORGIVE YOU.

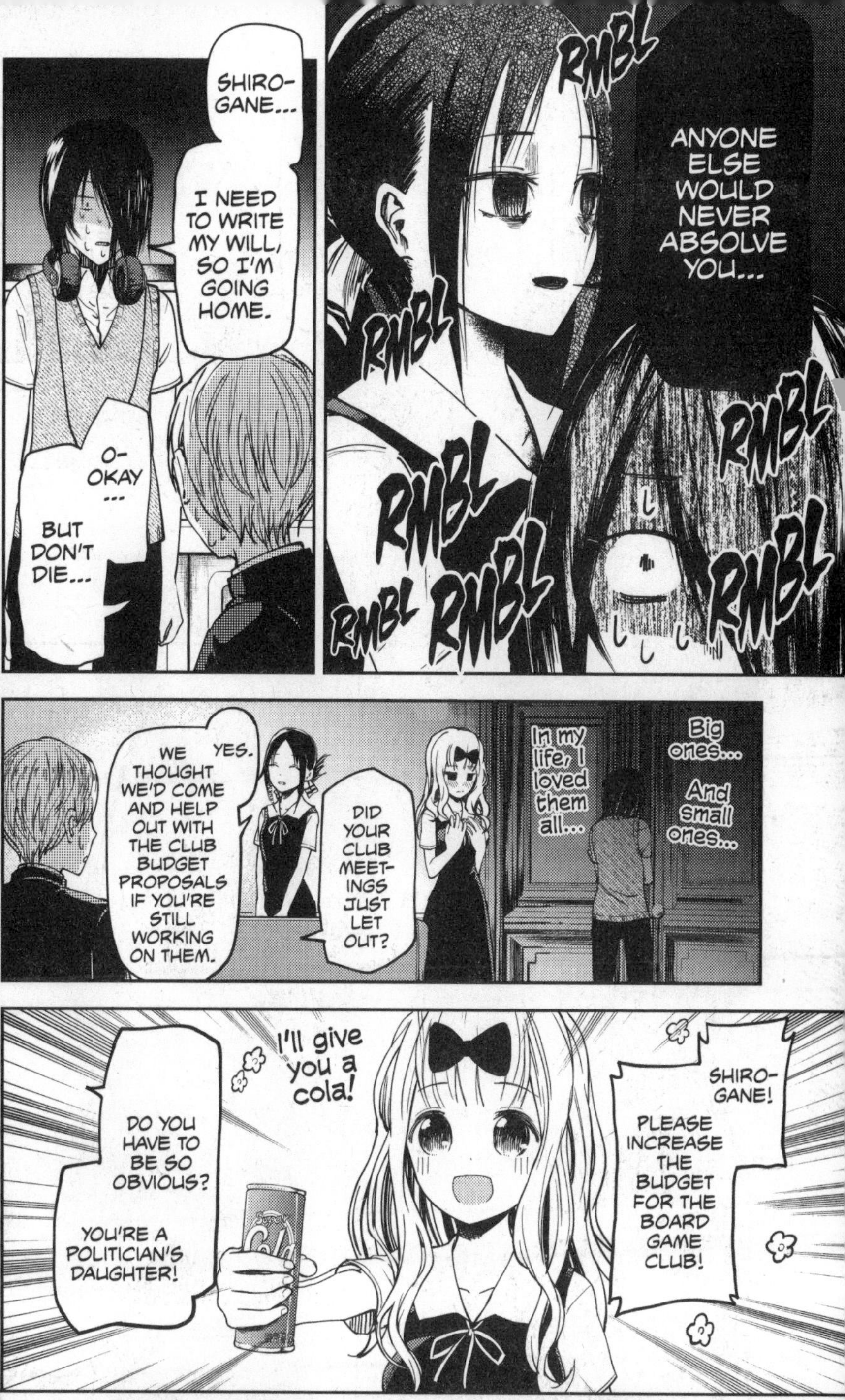
RMBL
ANYONE ELSE WOULD NEVER ABSOLVE YOU...
RMBL
RMBL
RMBL
RMBL
RMBL
RMBL
RMBL
SHIRO-GANE...
I NEED TO WRITE MY WILL, SO I'M GOING HOME.
O-OKAY... BUT DON'T DIE...
Big ones... And small ones...
In my life, I loved them all...
DID YOUR CLUB MEETINGS JUST LET OUT?
YES.
WE THOUGHT WE'D COME AND HELP OUT WITH THE CLUB BUDGET PROPOSALS IF YOU'RE STILL WORKING ON THEM.
SHIRO-GANE! PLEASE INCREASE THE BUDGET FOR THE BOARD GAME CLUB!
I'll give you a cola!
DO YOU HAVE TO BE SO OBVIOUS? YOU'RE A POLITICIAN'S DAUGHTER!

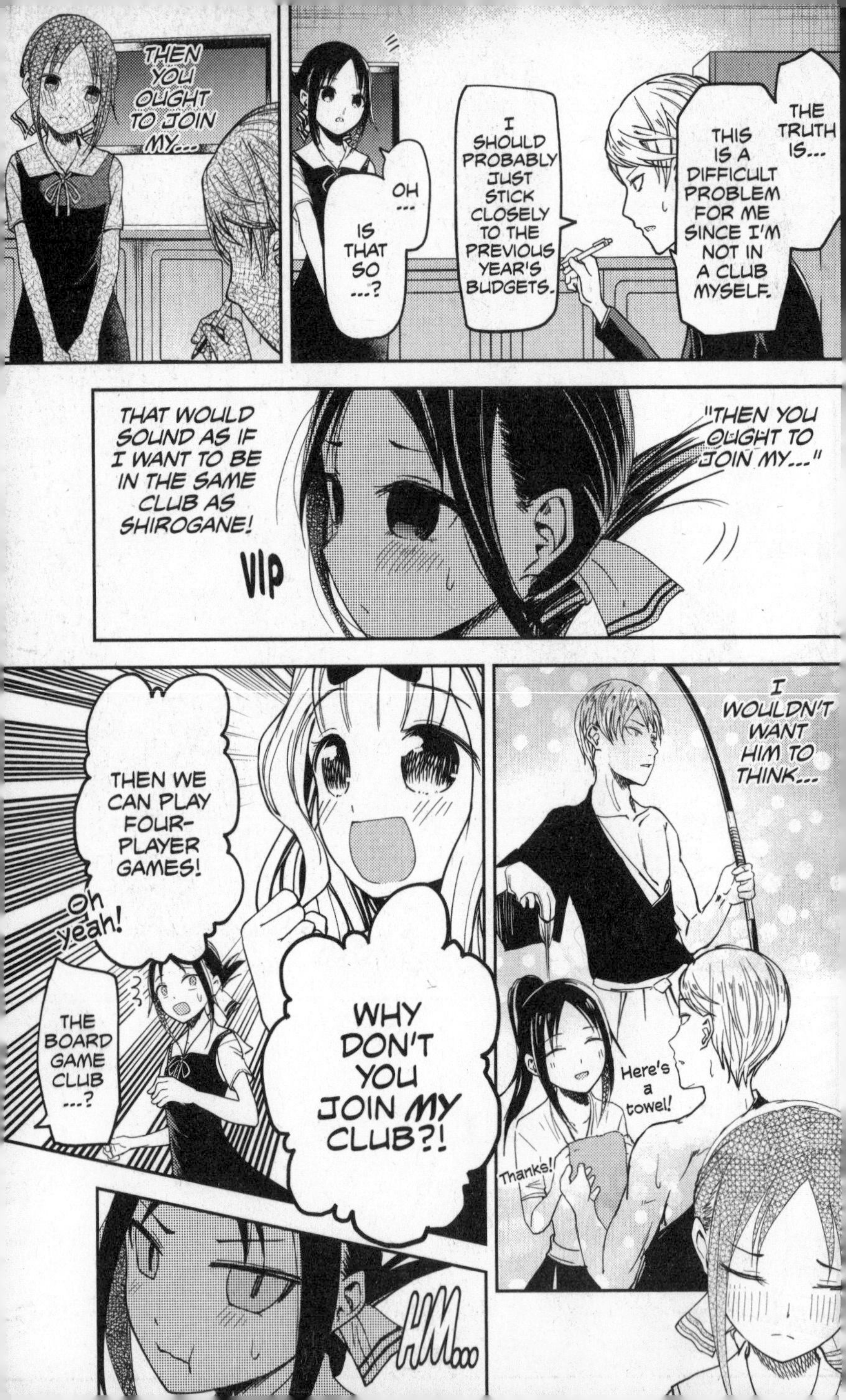
THE TRUTH IS...
THIS IS A DIFFICULT PROBLEM FOR ME SINCE I'M NOT IN A CLUB MYSELF.
I SHOULD PROBABLY JUST STICK CLOSELY TO THE PREVIOUS YEAR'S BUDGETS.
OH... IS THAT SO...?
THEN YOU OUGHT TO JOIN MY...
"THEN YOU OUGHT TO JOIN MY..."
THAT WOULD SOUND AS IF I WANT TO BE IN THE SAME CLUB AS SHIROGANE!
VIP
I WOULDN'T WANT HIM TO THINK...
Here's a towel!
Thanks!
WHY DON'T YOU JOIN MY CLUB?!
THEN WE CAN PLAY FOUR-PLAYER GAMES!
Oh yeah!
THE BOARD GAME CLUB...?
HM...

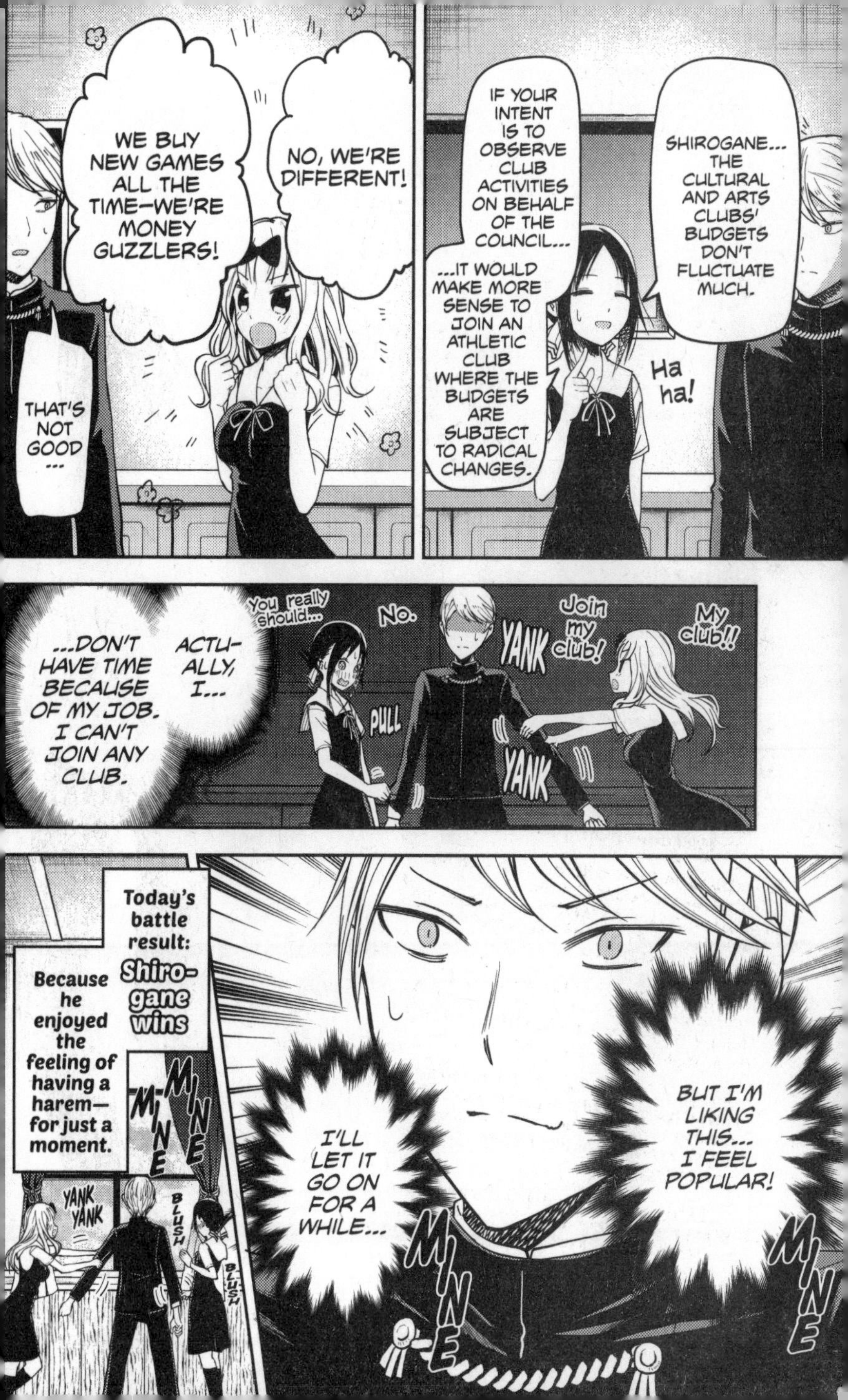
SHIROGANE... THE CULTURAL AND ARTS CLUBS' BUDGETS DON'T FLUCTUATE MUCH.
Ha ha!
IF YOUR INTENT IS TO OBSERVE CLUB ACTIVITIES ON BEHALF OF THE COUNCIL...
...IT WOULD MAKE MORE SENSE TO JOIN AN ATHLETIC CLUB WHERE THE BUDGETS ARE SUBJECT TO RADICAL CHANGES.
NO, WE'RE DIFFERENT!
WE BUY NEW GAMES ALL THE TIME—WE'RE MONEY GUZZLERS!
THAT'S NOT GOOD...
My club!!
Join my club!
YANK
No.
You really should...
PULL
YANK
ACTU-ALLY, I...
...DON'T HAVE TIME BECAUSE OF MY JOB. I CAN'T JOIN ANY CLUB.
BUT I'M LIKING THIS... I FEEL POPULAR!
I'LL LET IT GO ON FOR A WHILE...
MINE
MINE
Today's battle result:
Shiro-gane wins
Because he enjoyed the feeling of having a harem—for just a moment.
MINE
MINE
YANK YANK
BLUSH
BLUSH

YU ISHIGAMI

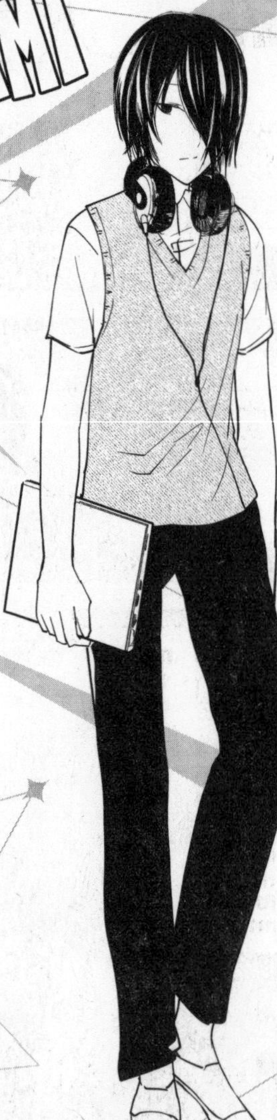

Yu Ishigami

- Shuchiin Academy High School First-Year
- Student Council Treasurer
- Notable characteristics: emo bangs
- Background character

The second son of a small toy manufacturer. He was forced to attend Shuchiin Academy by his father, who only graduated from high school, to uphold the family reputation. Yu's motivation to learn is low, and he only puts effort into subjects he enjoys.

His observational skills are noteworthy. As easily as one might notice what another person is wearing, he notices the things they do not wish to reveal—their personal land mines.

However, he does not touch the land mines obvious to everyone but the hidden ones. Problems arise when he trips over a land mine without realizing it.

Though Yu used to have a high truancy rate, Miyuki pulled him out of the habit and soon after Yu entered high school, Miyuki recruited him to serve as student council treasurer.

Yu's long bangs are a physical barrier that prevent him from seeing too much, and they also represent his fear of others.

It's possible that this series will become the story of his development.

KAGUYA-SAMA

LOVE IS WAR

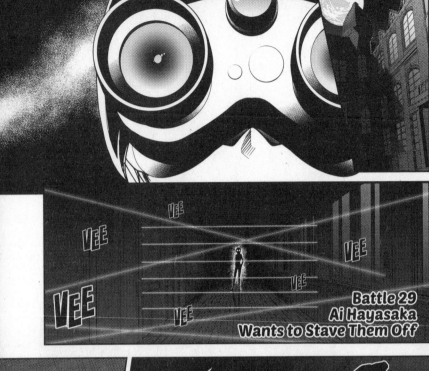

VEE VEE VEE VEE VEE VEE

Battle 29
Ai Hayasaka
Wants to Stave Them Off

Student Council

TAP

TAP

SHFT

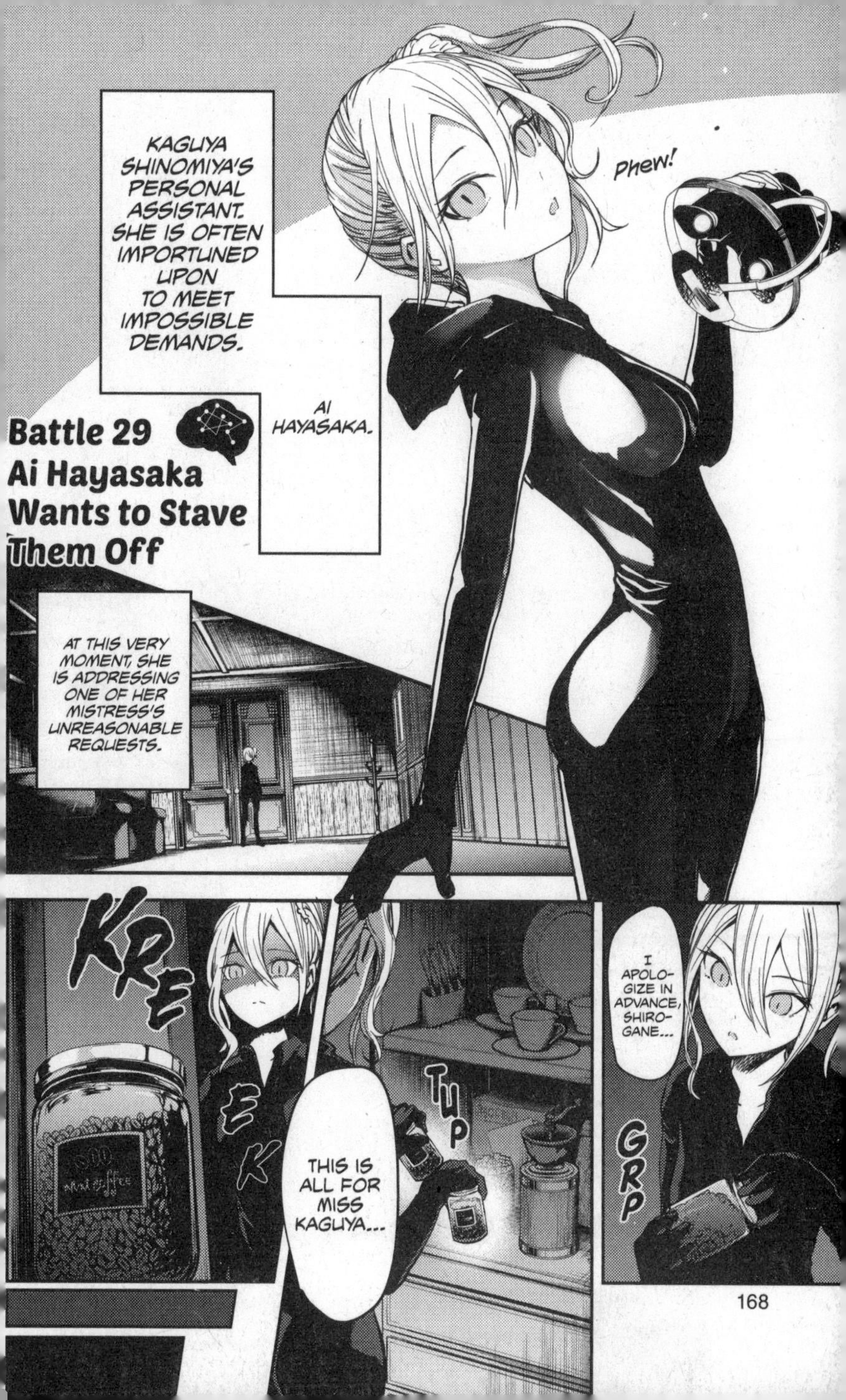
Phew!
KAGUYA SHINOMIYA'S PERSONAL ASSISTANT. SHE IS OFTEN IMPORTUNED UPON TO MEET IMPOSSIBLE DEMANDS.
AI HAYASAKA.
Battle 29
Ai Hayasaka Wants to Stave Them Off
AT THIS VERY MOMENT, SHE IS ADDRESSING ONE OF HER MISTRESS'S UNREASONABLE REQUESTS.
I APOLO-GIZE IN ADVANCE, SHIRO-GANE...
GRP
TUP
THIS IS ALL FOR MISS KAGUYA...
KREEK

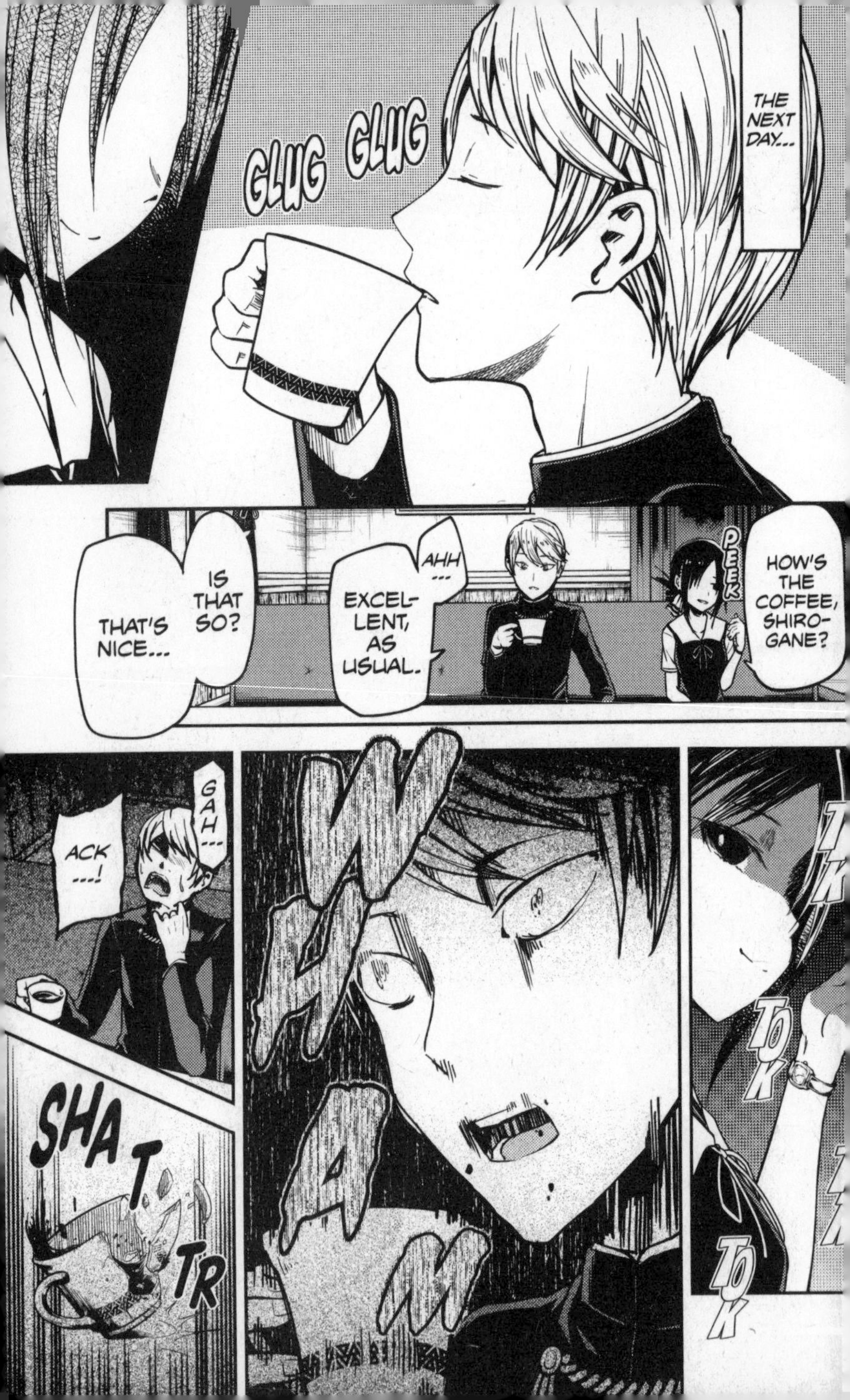
THE NEXT DAY...
GLUG GLUG
HOW'S THE COFFEE, SHIROGANE?
PEEK
AHH... EXCEL-LENT, AS USUAL.
IS THAT SO?
THAT'S NICE...
TOK
TOK
GAH...
ACK...!
SHATTR

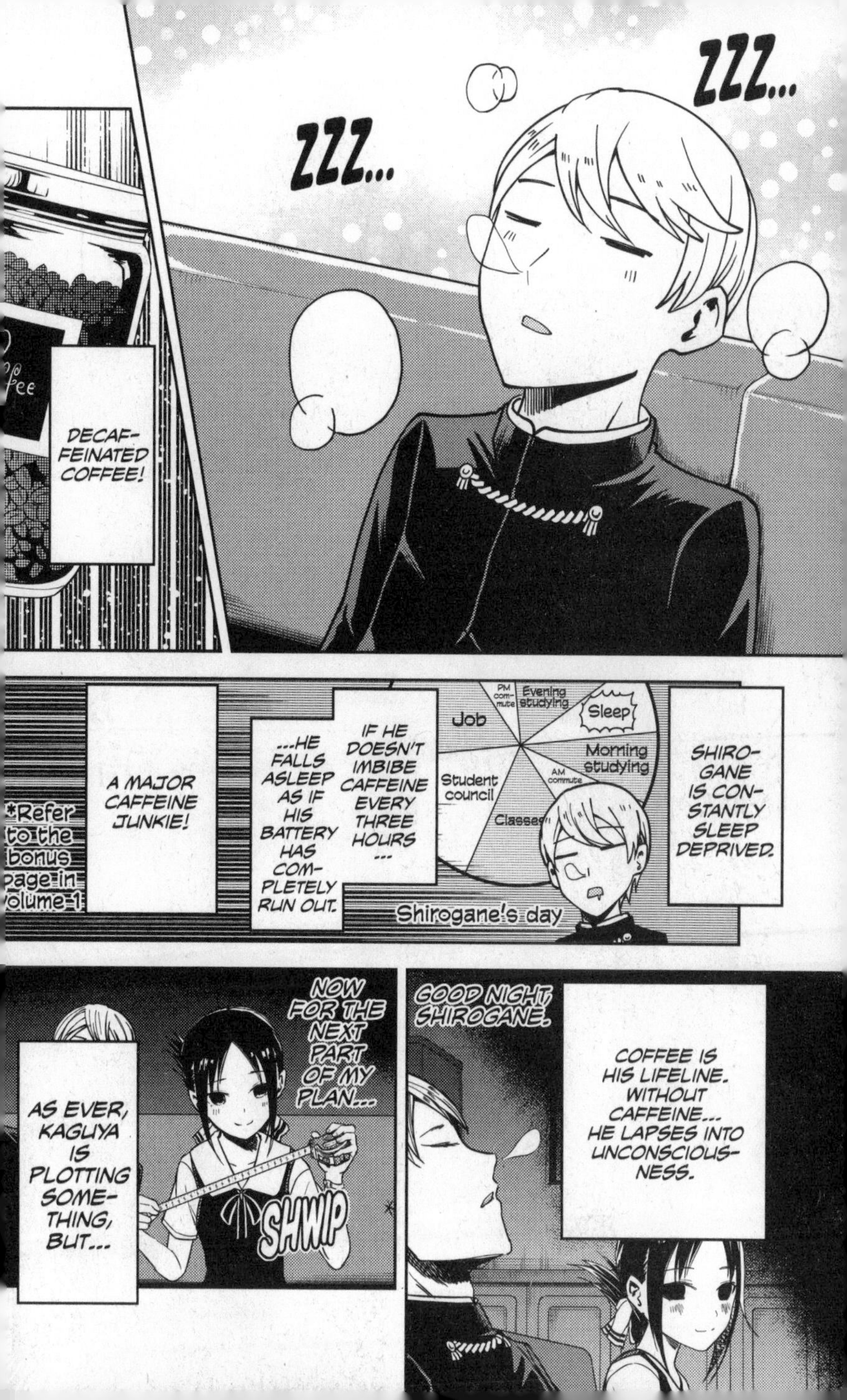
ZZZ...
ZZZ...
DECAF-FEINATED COFFEE!
SHIRO-GANE IS CON-STANTLY SLEEP DEPRIVED.
Sleep
Evening studying
PM commute
Job
Morning studying
AM commute
Student council
Classes
Shirogane's day
IF HE DOESN'T IMBIBE CAFFEINE EVERY THREE HOURS ...
...HE FALLS ASLEEP AS IF HIS BATTERY HAS COM-PLETELY RUN OUT.
A MAJOR CAFFEINE JUNKIE!
*Refer to the bonus page in volume 1
COFFEE IS HIS LIFELINE. WITHOUT CAFFEINE... HE LAPSES INTO UNCONSCIOUS-NESS.
GOOD NIGHT, SHIROGANE.
NOW FOR THE NEXT PART OF MY PLAN...
SHWIP
AS EVER, KAGUYA IS PLOTTING SOME-THING, BUT...

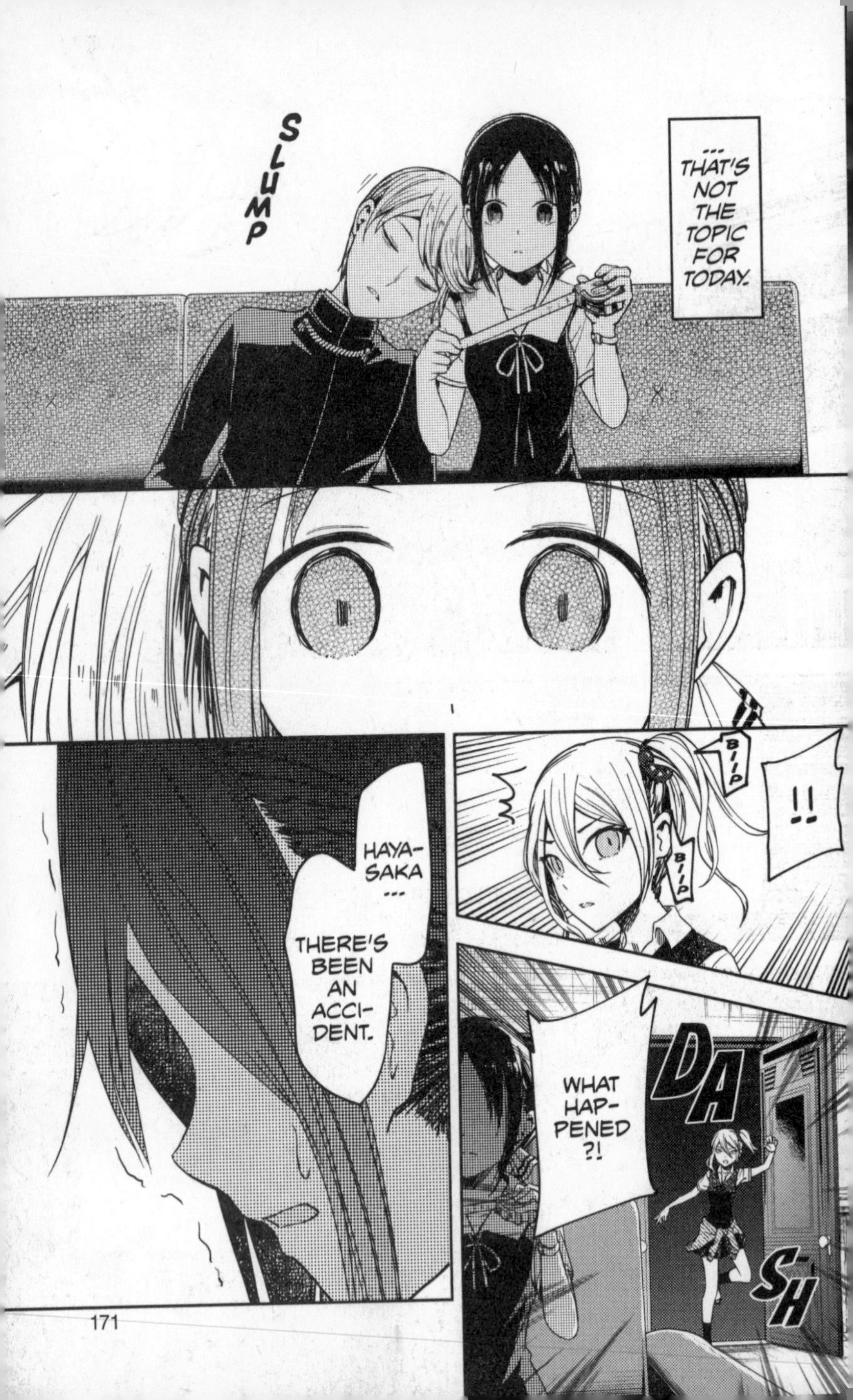
...THAT'S NOT THE TOPIC FOR TODAY.
SLUMP
BIIP
BIIP
!!
WHAT HAPPENED?!
DA-
SH
HAYASAKA...
THERE'S BEEN AN ACCIDENT.

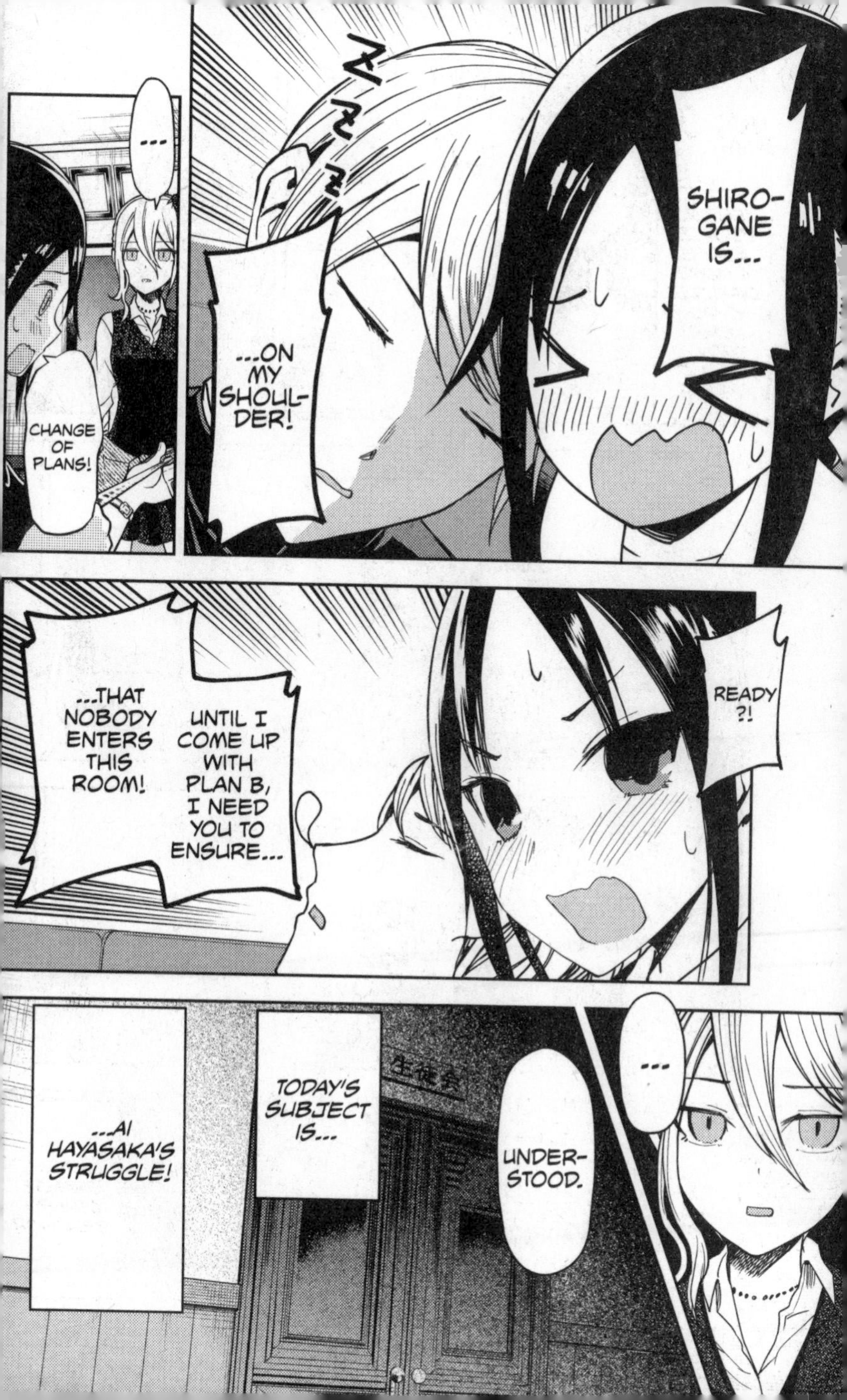
SHIRO-GANE IS...
...ON MY SHOULDER!
...
CHANGE OF PLANS!
READY?!
UNTIL I COME UP WITH PLAN B, I NEED YOU TO ENSURE...
...THAT NOBODY ENTERS THIS ROOM!
...
UNDER-STOOD.
生徒会
TODAY'S SUBJECT IS...
...AI HAYASAKA'S STRUGGLE!

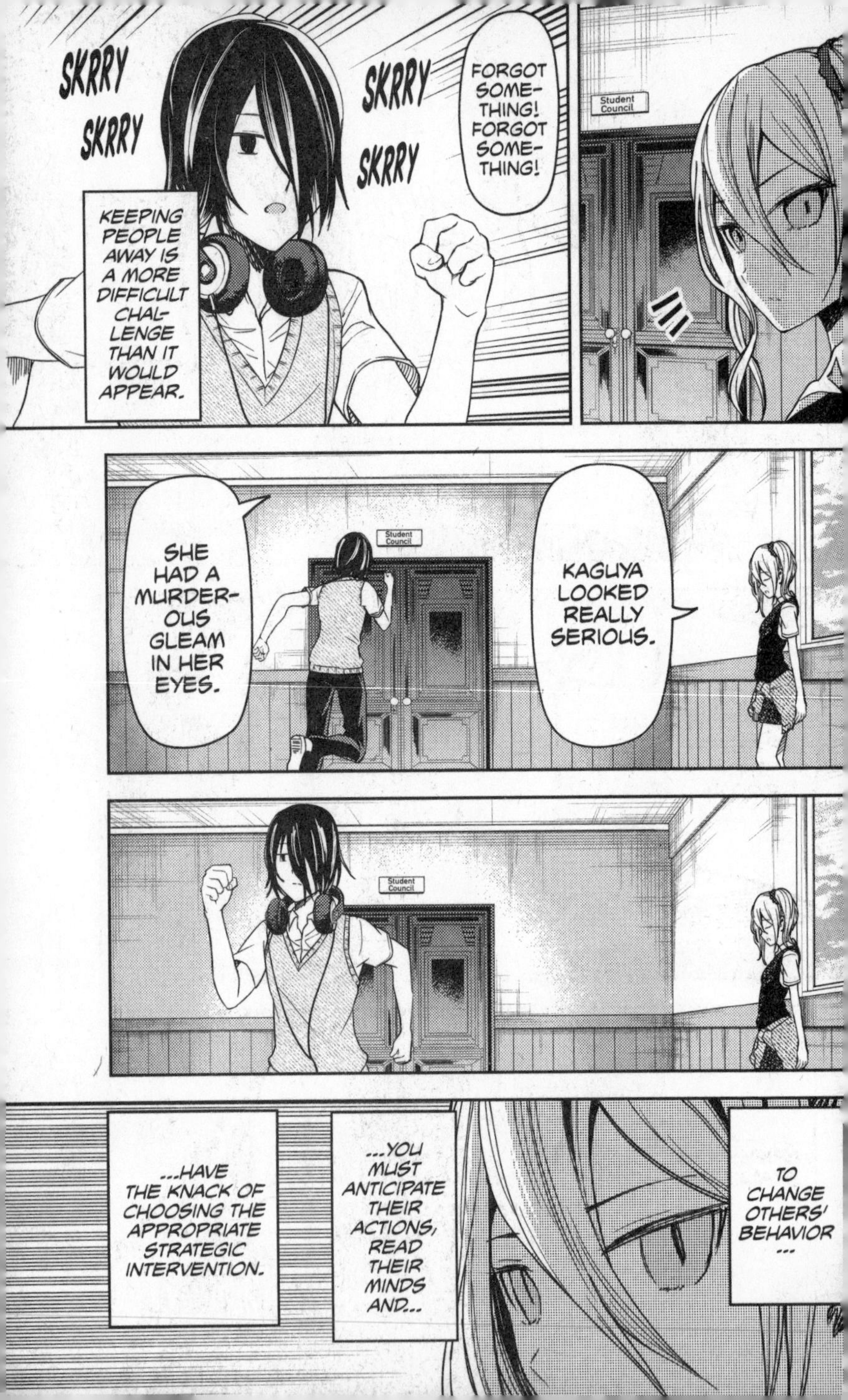
FORGOT SOME-THING! FORGOT SOME-THING!
SKRRY SKRRY
SKRRY SKRRY
KEEPING PEOPLE AWAY IS A MORE DIFFICULT CHAL-LENGE THAN IT WOULD APPEAR.
Student Council
KAGUYA LOOKED REALLY SERIOUS.
SHE HAD A MURDER-OUS GLEAM IN HER EYES.
Student Council
Student Council
TO CHANGE OTHERS' BEHAVIOR...
...YOU MUST ANTICIPATE THEIR ACTIONS, READ THEIR MINDS AND...
...HAVE THE KNACK OF CHOOSING THE APPROPRIATE STRATEGIC INTERVENTION.

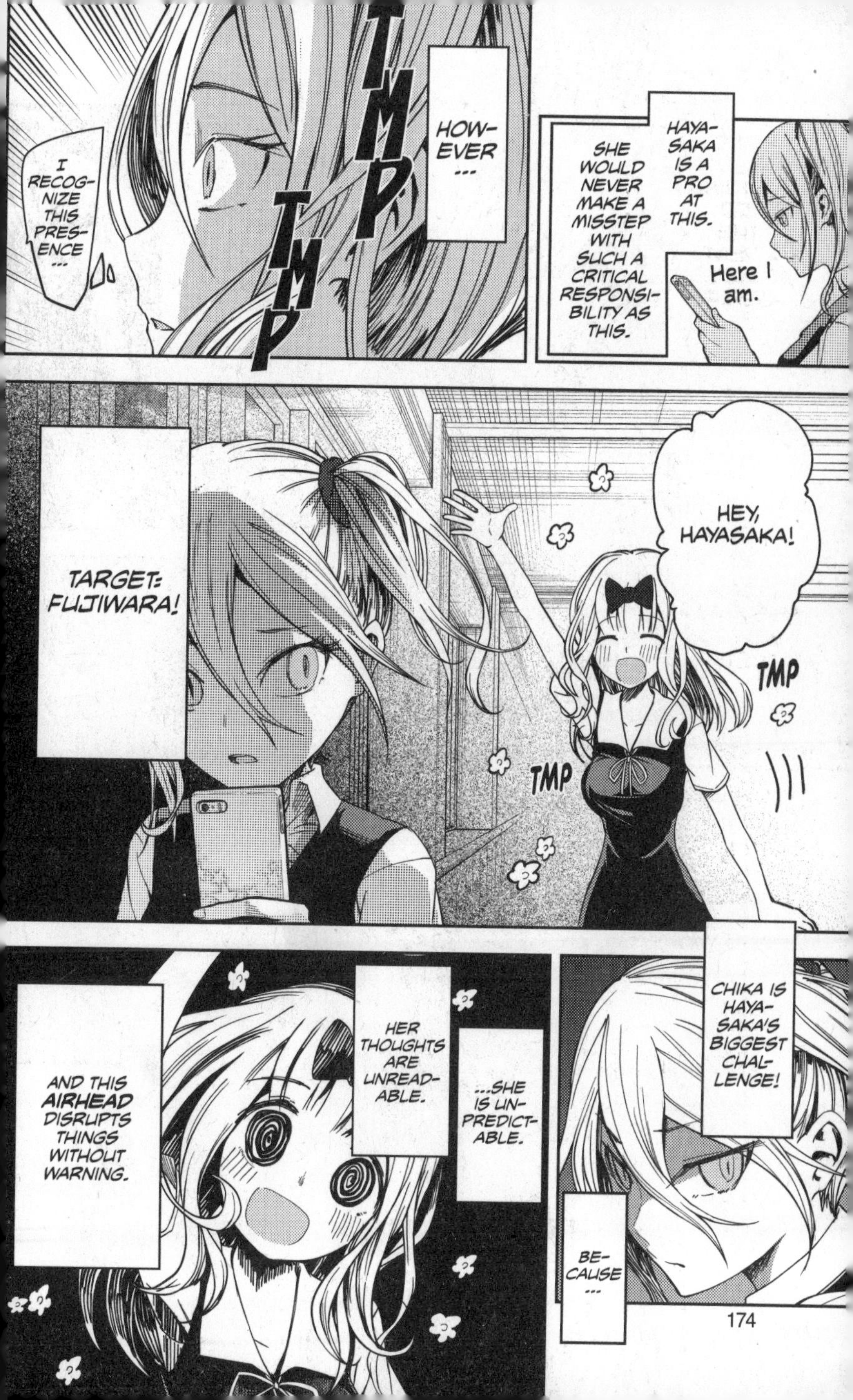
HAYA-SAKA IS A PRO AT THIS.
SHE WOULD NEVER MAKE A MISSTEP WITH SUCH A CRITICAL RESPONSI-BILITY AS THIS.
Here I am.
HOW-EVER...
TMP TMP
I RECOG-NIZE THIS PRES-ENCE...
HEY, HAYASAKA!
TMP
TMP
TARGET: FUJIWARA!
CHIKA IS HAYA-SAKA'S BIGGEST CHAL-LENGE!
BE-CAUSE...
HER THOUGHTS ARE UNREAD-ABLE.
...SHE IS UN-PREDICT-ABLE.
AND THIS **AIRHEAD** DISRUPTS THINGS WITHOUT WARNING.

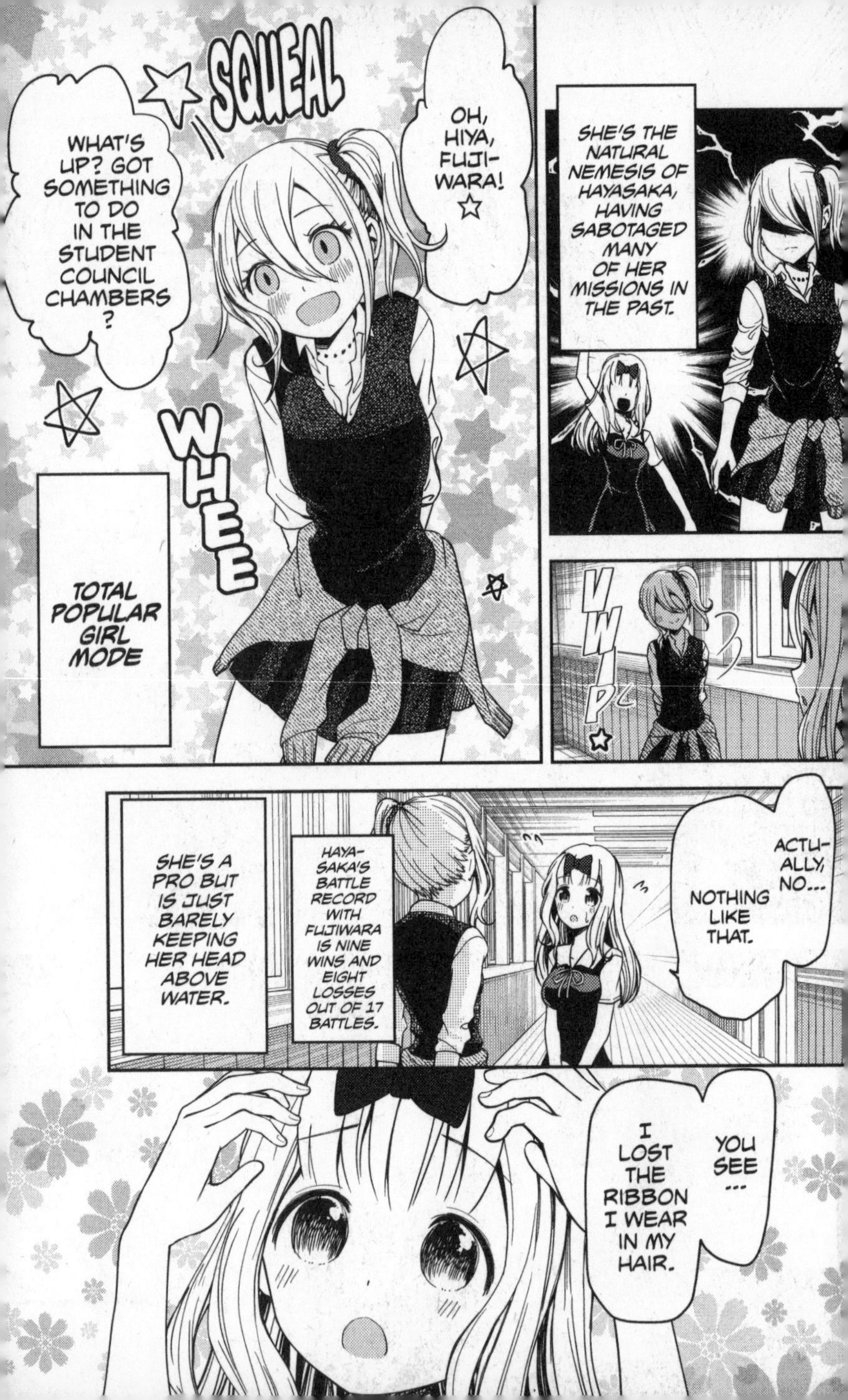
SHE'S THE NATURAL NEMESIS OF HAYASAKA, HAVING SABOTAGED MANY OF HER MISSIONS IN THE PAST.
VWIP ☆
OH, HIYA, FUJIWARA! ☆
SQUEAL
WHAT'S UP? GOT SOMETHING TO DO IN THE STUDENT COUNCIL CHAMBERS?
WHEE
TOTAL POPULAR GIRL MODE
ACTUALLY, NO...
NOTHING LIKE THAT.
HAYASAKA'S BATTLE RECORD WITH FUJIWARA IS NINE WINS AND EIGHT LOSSES OUT OF 17 BATTLES.
SHE'S A PRO BUT IS JUST BARELY KEEPING HER HEAD ABOVE WATER.
YOU SEE...
I LOST THE RIBBON I WEAR IN MY HAIR.

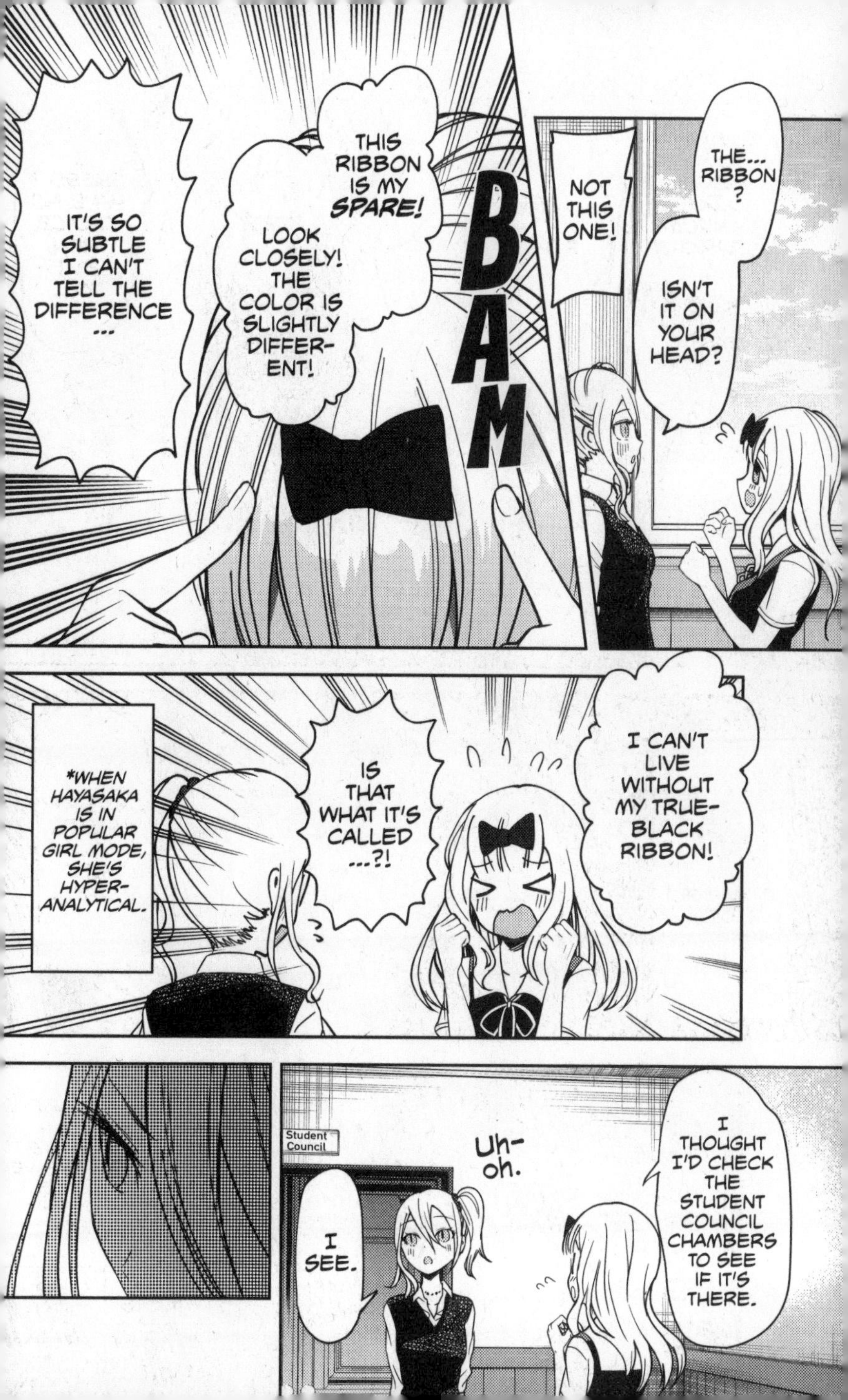
THE... RIBBON?
ISN'T IT ON YOUR HEAD?
NOT THIS ONE!
THIS RIBBON IS MY SPARE!
BAM
LOOK CLOSELY! THE COLOR IS SLIGHTLY DIFFER-ENT!
IT'S SO SUBTLE I CAN'T TELL THE DIFFERENCE...
I CAN'T LIVE WITHOUT MY TRUE-BLACK RIBBON!
IS THAT WHAT IT'S CALLED...?!
*WHEN HAYASAKA IS IN POPULAR GIRL MODE, SHE'S HYPER-ANALYTICAL.
I THOUGHT I'D CHECK THE STUDENT COUNCIL CHAMBERS TO SEE IF IT'S THERE.
Uh-oh.
Student Council
I SEE.

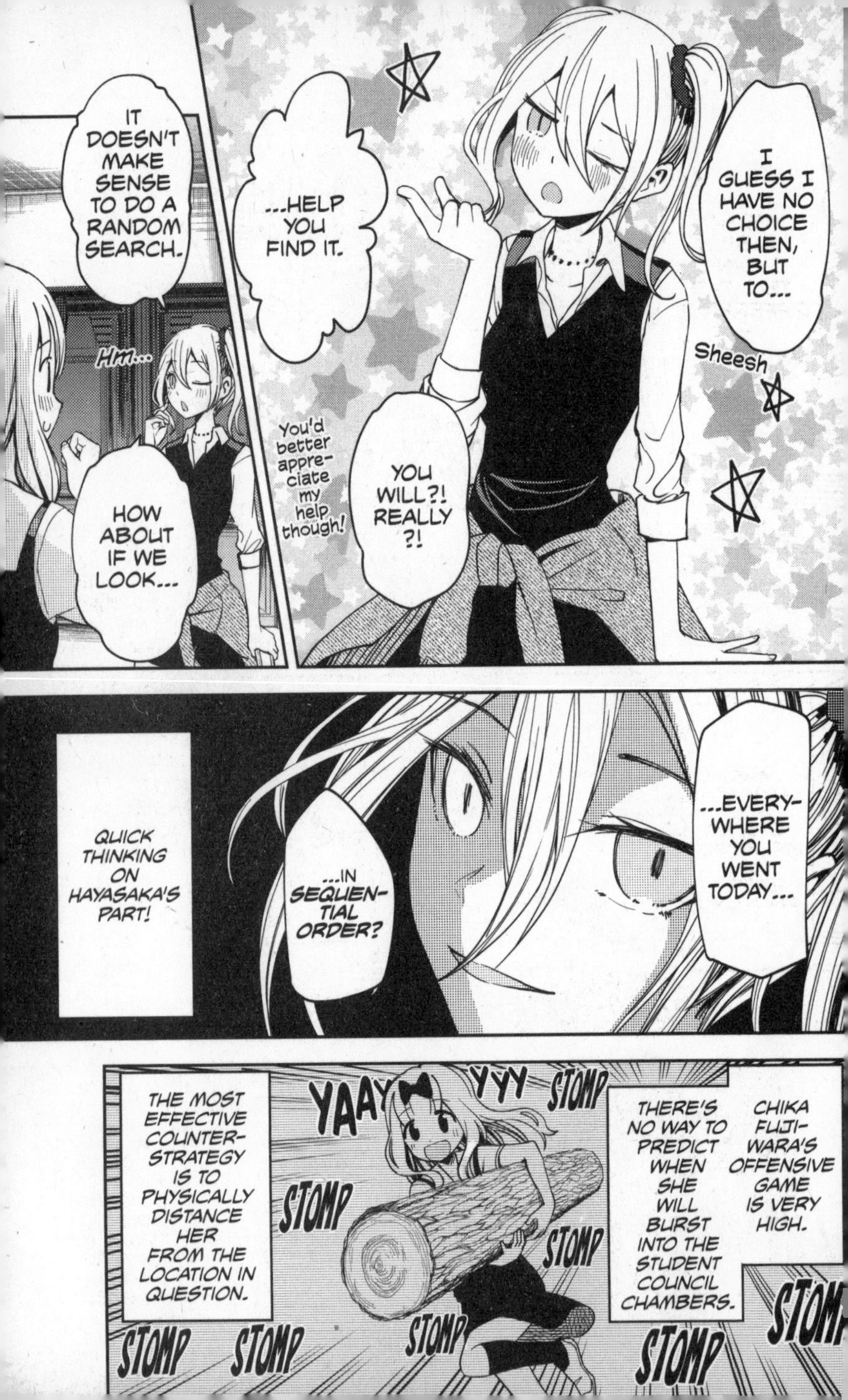
I GUESS I HAVE NO CHOICE THEN, BUT TO...
...HELP YOU FIND IT.
Sheesh
YOU WILL?! REALLY?!
You'd better appreciate my help though!
IT DOESN'T MAKE SENSE TO DO A RANDOM SEARCH.
Hm...
HOW ABOUT IF WE LOOK...
...EVERY-WHERE YOU WENT TODAY...
...IN SEQUEN-TIAL ORDER?
QUICK THINKING ON HAYASAKA'S PART!
CHIKA FUJI-WARA'S OFFENSIVE GAME IS VERY HIGH.
THERE'S NO WAY TO PREDICT WHEN SHE WILL BURST INTO THE STUDENT COUNCIL CHAMBERS.
YAAYYYY
STOMP STOMP STOMP STOMP STOMP STOMP STOMP STOMP
THE MOST EFFECTIVE COUNTER-STRATEGY IS TO PHYSICALLY DISTANCE HER FROM THE LOCATION IN QUESTION.

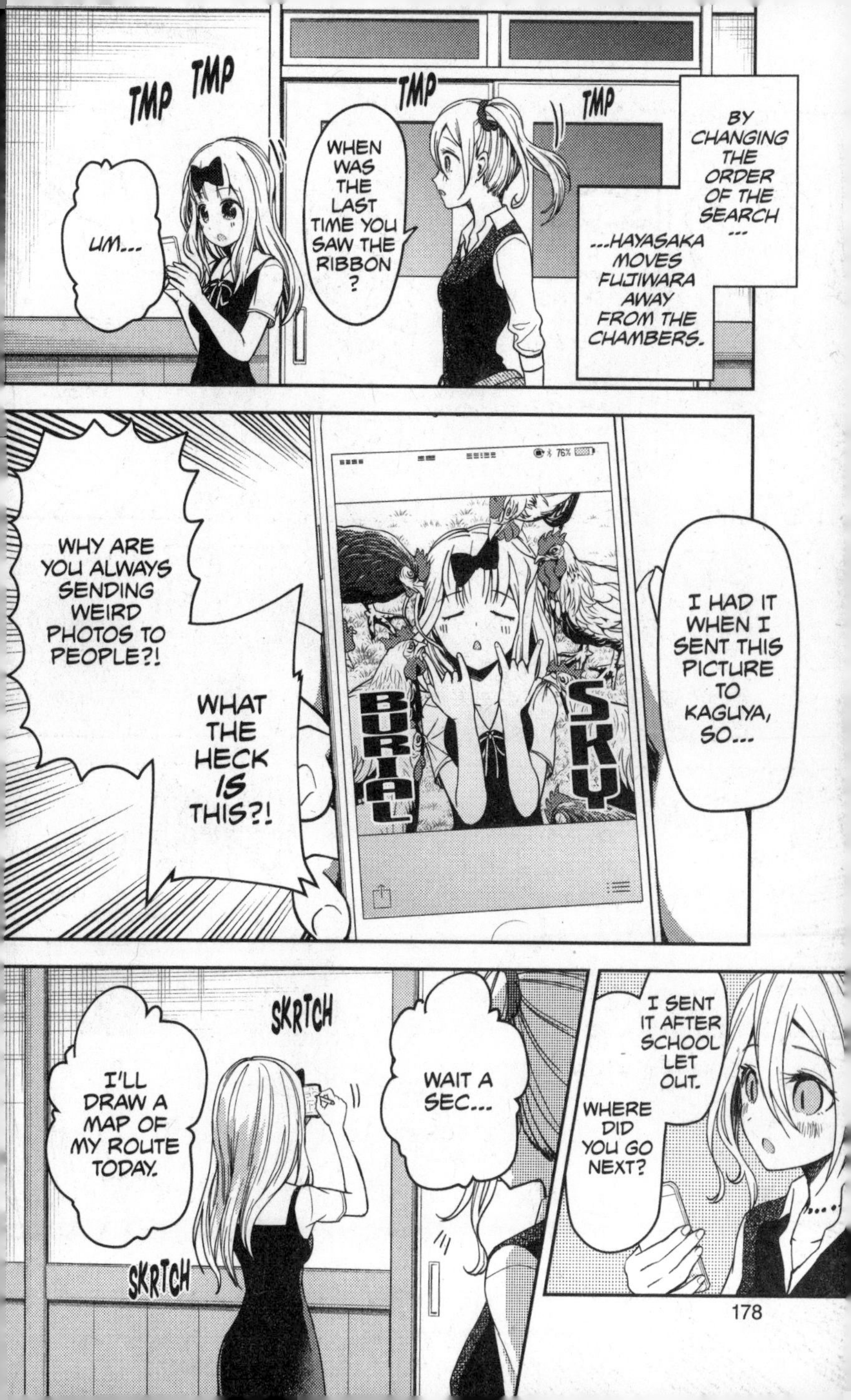
BY CHANGING THE ORDER OF THE SEARCH ...
...HAYASAKA MOVES FUJIWARA AWAY FROM THE CHAMBERS.
TMP
TMP
WHEN WAS THE LAST TIME YOU SAW THE RIBBON?
TMP
TMP
UM...
I HAD IT WHEN I SENT THIS PICTURE TO KAGUYA, SO...
76%
SKY
BURIAL
WHY ARE YOU ALWAYS SENDING WEIRD PHOTOS TO PEOPLE?!
WHAT THE HECK *IS* THIS?!
I SENT IT AFTER SCHOOL LET OUT.
WHERE DID YOU GO NEXT?
...
WAIT A SEC...
SKRTCH
I'LL DRAW A MAP OF MY ROUTE TODAY.
SKRTCH

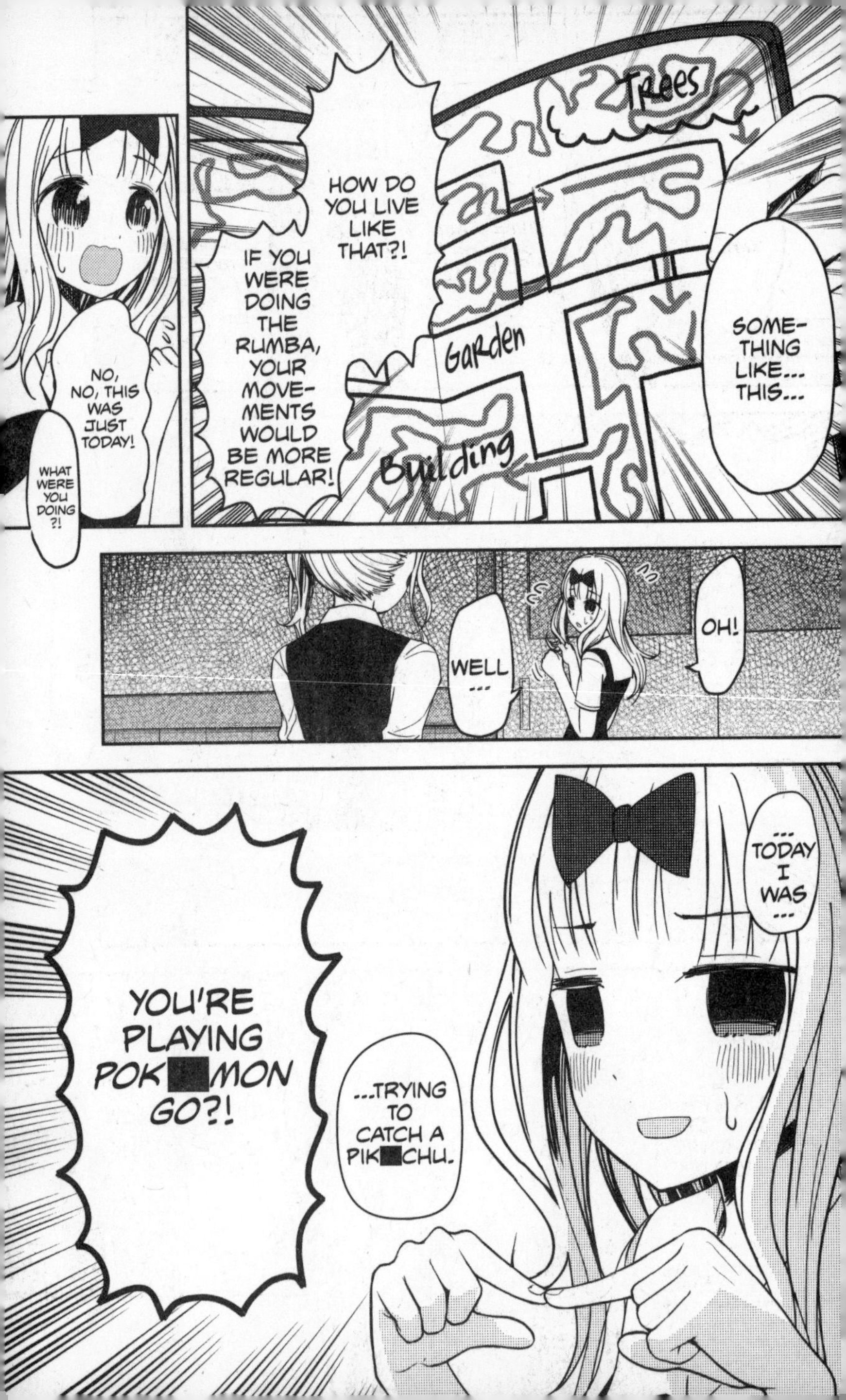
Trees
Garden
Building
SOMETHING LIKE... THIS...
HOW DO YOU LIVE LIKE THAT?!
IF YOU WERE DOING THE RUMBA, YOUR MOVEMENTS WOULD BE MORE REGULAR!
NO, NO, THIS WAS JUST TODAY!
WHAT WERE YOU DOING?!
OH!
WELL...
...TODAY I WAS...
...TRYING TO CATCH A PIK[redacted]CHU.
YOU'RE PLAYING POK[redacted]MON GO?!

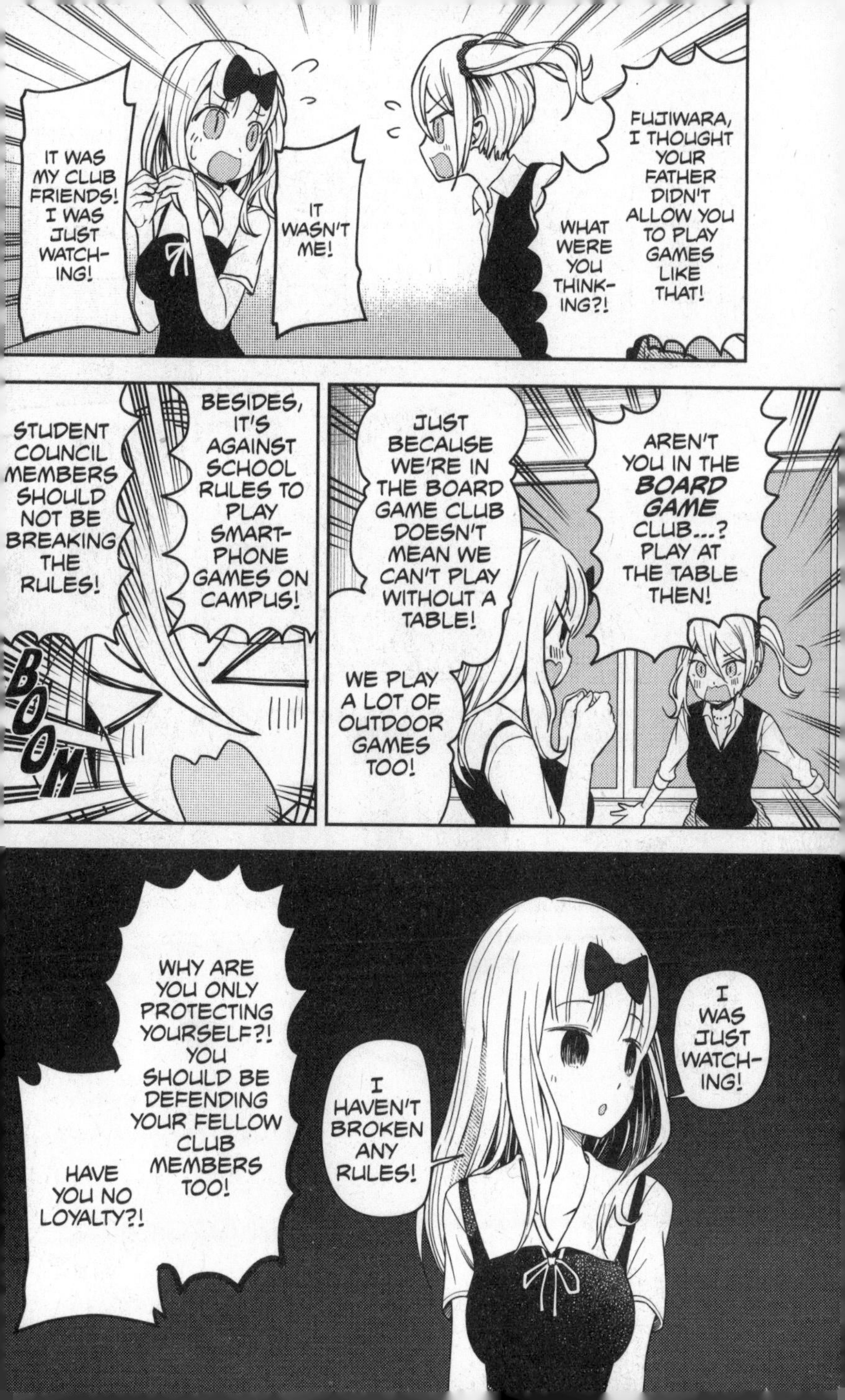
FUJIWARA, I THOUGHT YOUR FATHER DIDN'T ALLOW YOU TO PLAY GAMES LIKE THAT!
WHAT WERE YOU THINKING?!
IT WASN'T ME!
IT WAS MY CLUB FRIENDS! I WAS JUST WATCHING!
AREN'T YOU IN THE BOARD GAME CLUB...? PLAY AT THE TABLE THEN!
JUST BECAUSE WE'RE IN THE BOARD GAME CLUB DOESN'T MEAN WE CAN'T PLAY WITHOUT A TABLE!
WE PLAY A LOT OF OUTDOOR GAMES TOO!
BESIDES, IT'S AGAINST SCHOOL RULES TO PLAY SMARTPHONE GAMES ON CAMPUS!
STUDENT COUNCIL MEMBERS SHOULD NOT BE BREAKING THE RULES!
BOOM
I WAS JUST WATCHING!
I HAVEN'T BROKEN ANY RULES!
WHY ARE YOU ONLY PROTECTING YOURSELF?! YOU SHOULD BE DEFENDING YOUR FELLOW CLUB MEMBERS TOO!
HAVE YOU NO LOYALTY?!

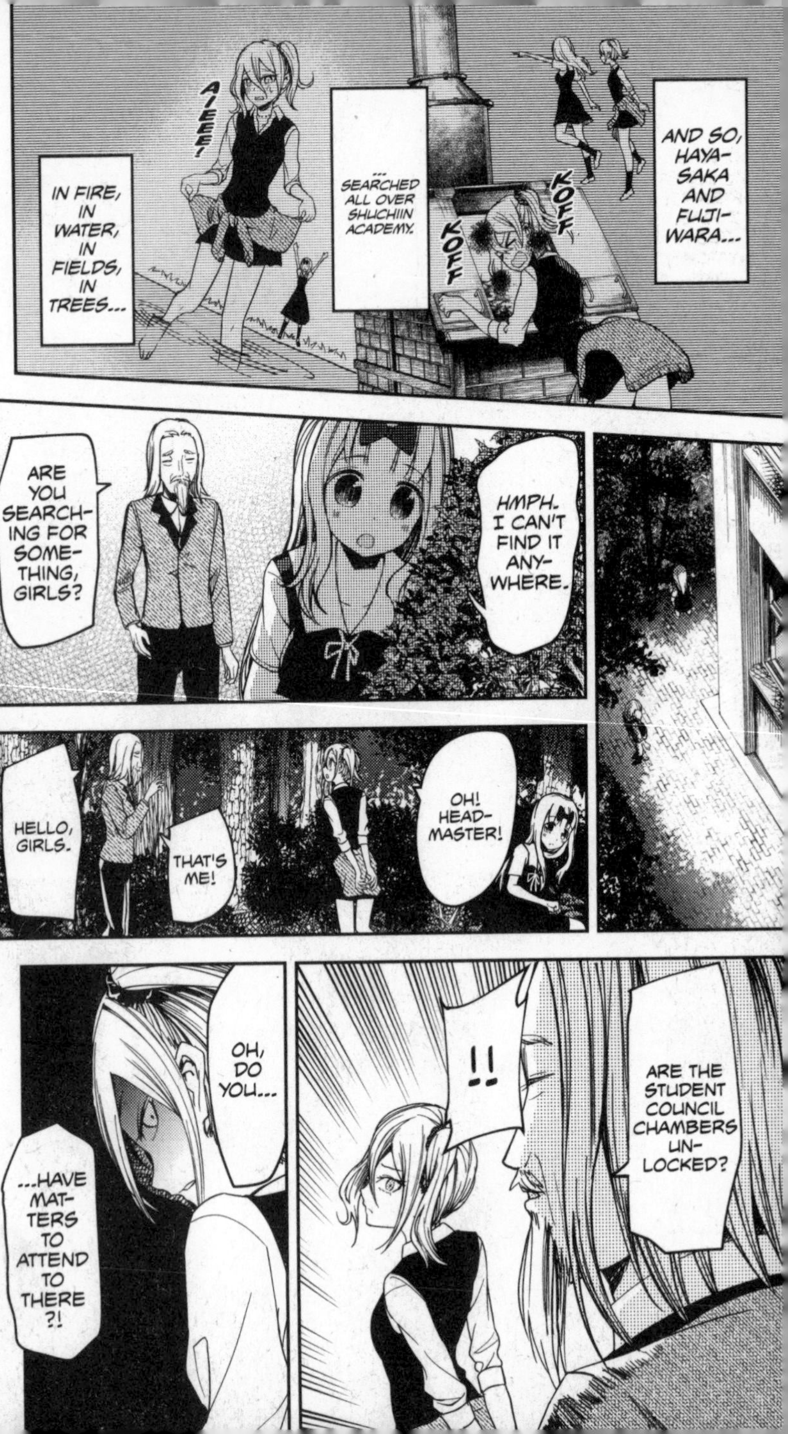
AND SO, HAYA-SAKA AND FUJI-WARA...
KOFF
KOFF
...SEARCHED ALL OVER SHUCHIIN ACADEMY.
AIEEE!
IN FIRE, IN WATER, IN FIELDS, IN TREES...
HMPH. I CAN'T FIND IT ANY-WHERE.
ARE YOU SEARCH-ING FOR SOME-THING, GIRLS?
OH! HEAD-MASTER!
THAT'S ME!
HELLO, GIRLS.
ARE THE STUDENT COUNCIL CHAMBERS UN-LOCKED?
!!
OH, DO YOU...
...HAVE MAT-TERS TO ATTEND TO THERE?!

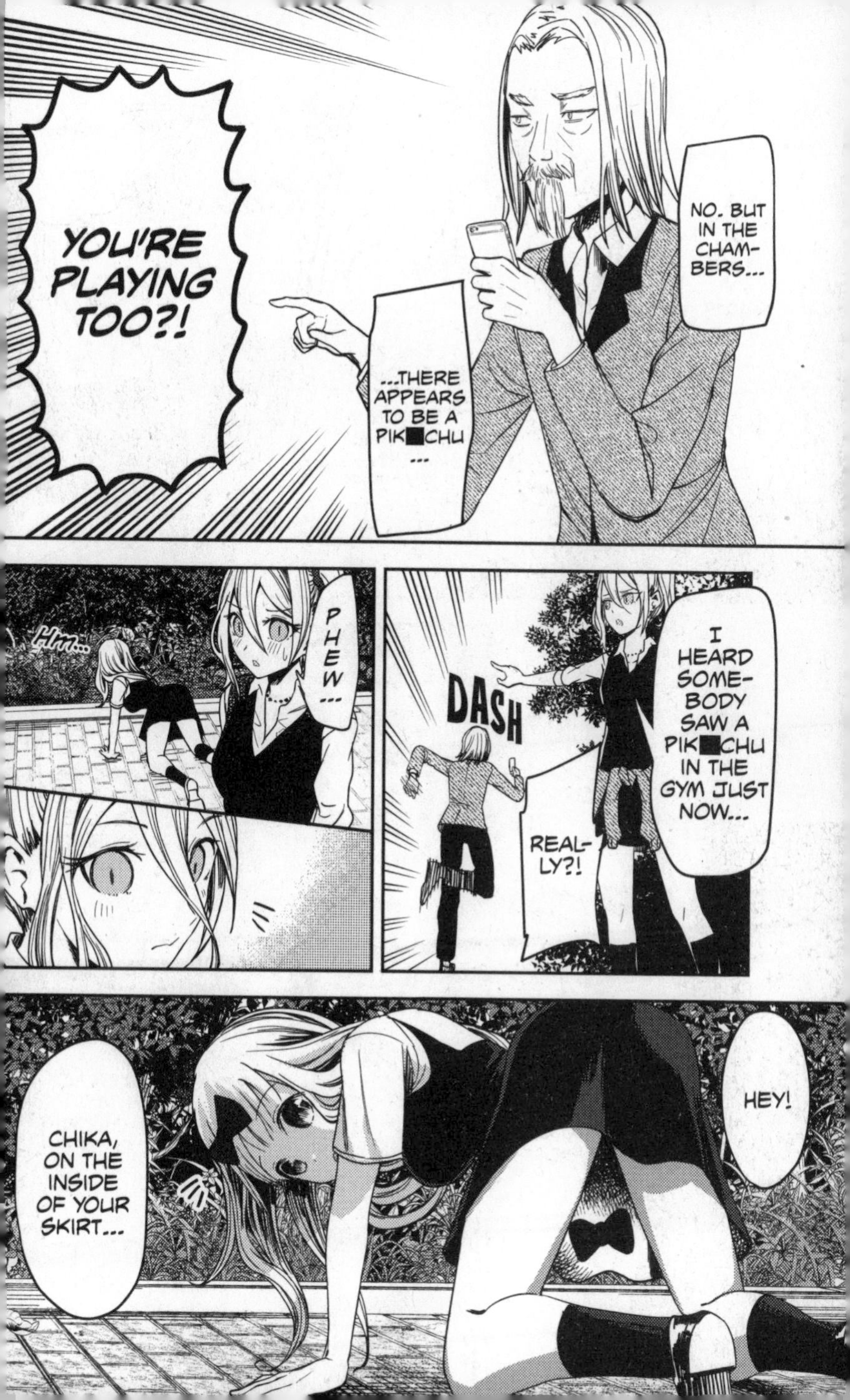
NO. BUT IN THE CHAMBERS...
...THERE APPEARS TO BE A PIK[redacted]CHU ...
YOU'RE PLAYING TOO?!
I HEARD SOMEBODY SAW A PIK[redacted]CHU IN THE GYM JUST NOW...
REALLY?!
DASH
PHEW...
Hm...
HEY!
CHIKA, ON THE INSIDE OF YOUR SKIRT...

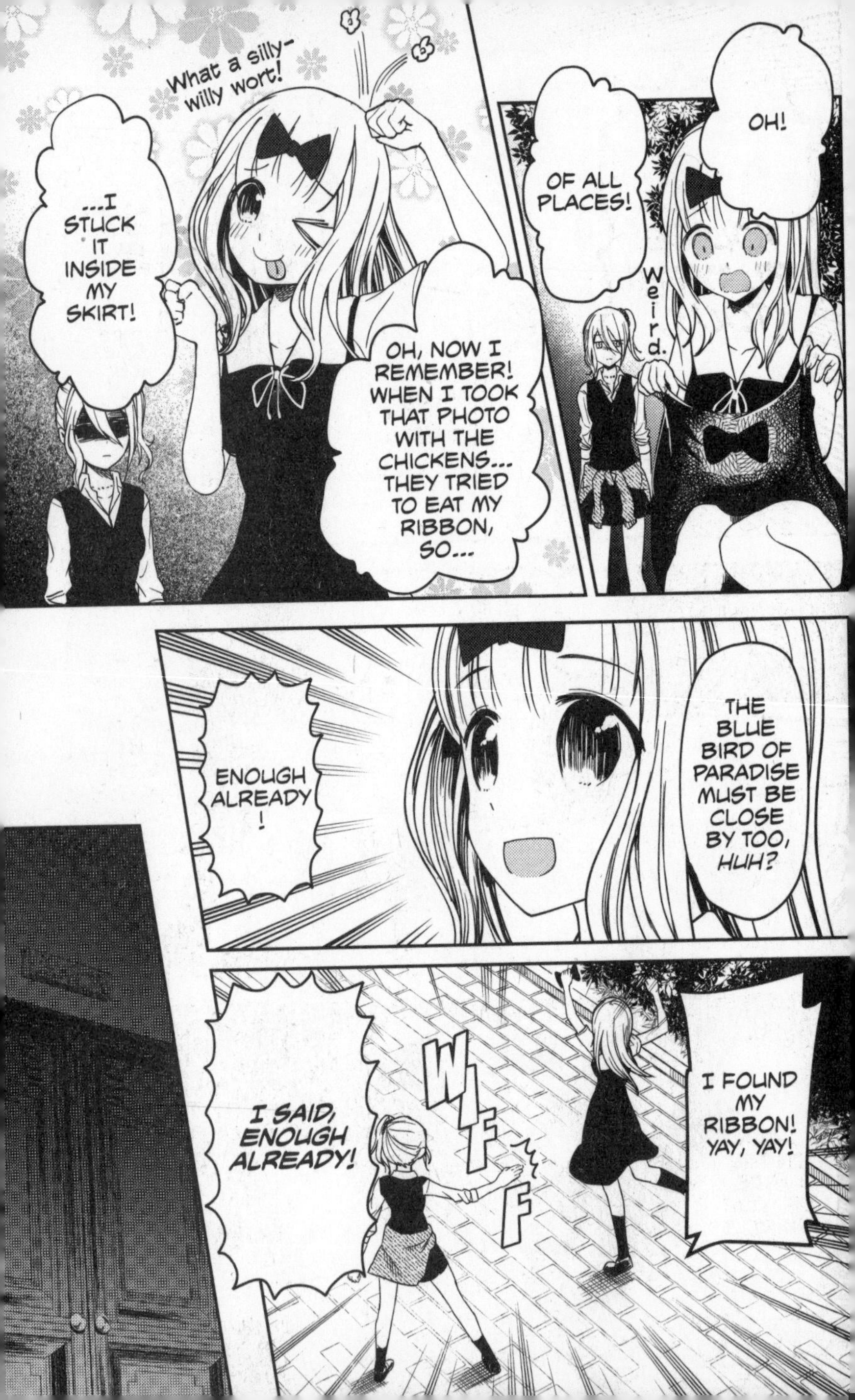
OH!
OF ALL PLACES!
Weird.
OH, NOW I REMEMBER! WHEN I TOOK THAT PHOTO WITH THE CHICKENS... THEY TRIED TO EAT MY RIBBON, SO...
What a silly-willy wort!
...I STUCK IT INSIDE MY SKIRT!
THE BLUE BIRD OF PARADISE MUST BE CLOSE BY TOO, HUH?
ENOUGH ALREADY!
I FOUND MY RIBBON! YAY, YAY!
WHFF
I SAID, ENOUGH ALREADY!

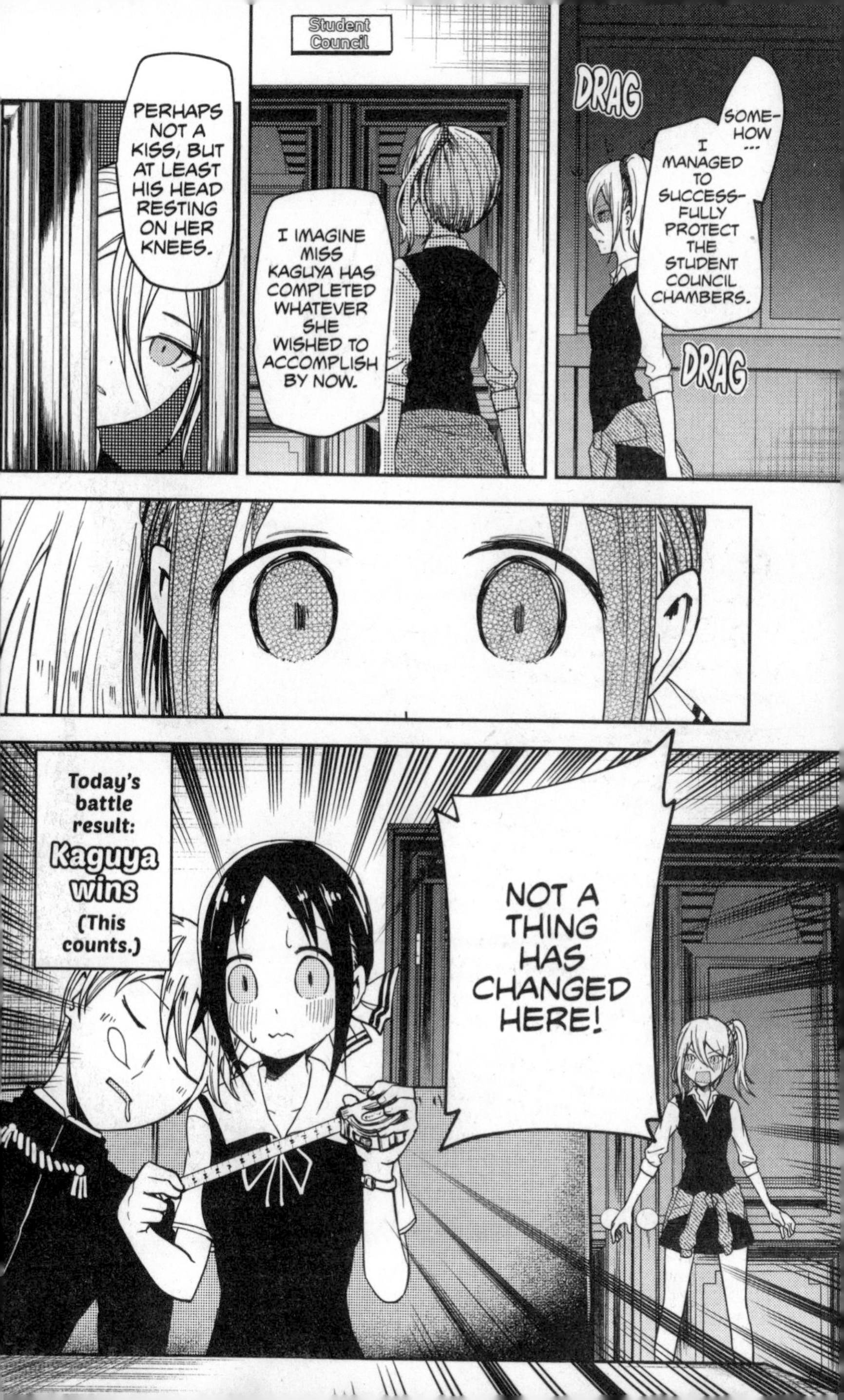
DRAG
SOME-HOW... I MANAGED TO SUCCESSFULLY PROTECT THE STUDENT COUNCIL CHAMBERS.
DRAG
Student Council
I IMAGINE MISS KAGUYA HAS COMPLETED WHATEVER SHE WISHED TO ACCOMPLISH BY NOW.
PERHAPS NOT A KISS, BUT AT LEAST HIS HEAD RESTING ON HER KNEES.
NOT A THING HAS CHANGED HERE!
Today's battle result:
Kaguya wins
(This counts.)

AI HAYASAKA

Ai Hayasaka

◆ Shuchiin Academy
  High School Second-Year

◆ Notable characteristics: one-quarter Irish

◆ Profession: Kaguya Shinomiya's personal assistant

The once-distinguished Hayasaka clan was conquered by the Shinomiya clan. However, in recognition of their excellent bloodlines, the Hayasakas were taken in by the Shinomiya family.

Ai was born in the Shinomiya home. She is a pedigreed servant who receives schooling for the gifted. Like Kaguya, she was born and raised in isolation, but she is nevertheless considerably more worldly than Kaguya.

Ai adapts as needed to circumstances. Personal assistant mode and popular girl mode are her most common personas. Few know the true Hayasaka, whom Kaguya considers a coward and a crybaby.

Hayasaka's father is the one who named Kaguya, and Hayasaka's mother was Kaguya's nanny. After the girls were born, they were raised together for some time, but when Kaguya turned two, she returned to the main Shinomiya household. They were not reunited until the age of seven, when Ai officially entered into domestic service.

Although Ai's relationship with Kaguya is technically that of master and servant, in reality, the two girls share a profound connection, much like sisters.

KAGUYA-SAMA

LOVE IS WAR

Battle 30 Miyuki Shirogane Can't Lose

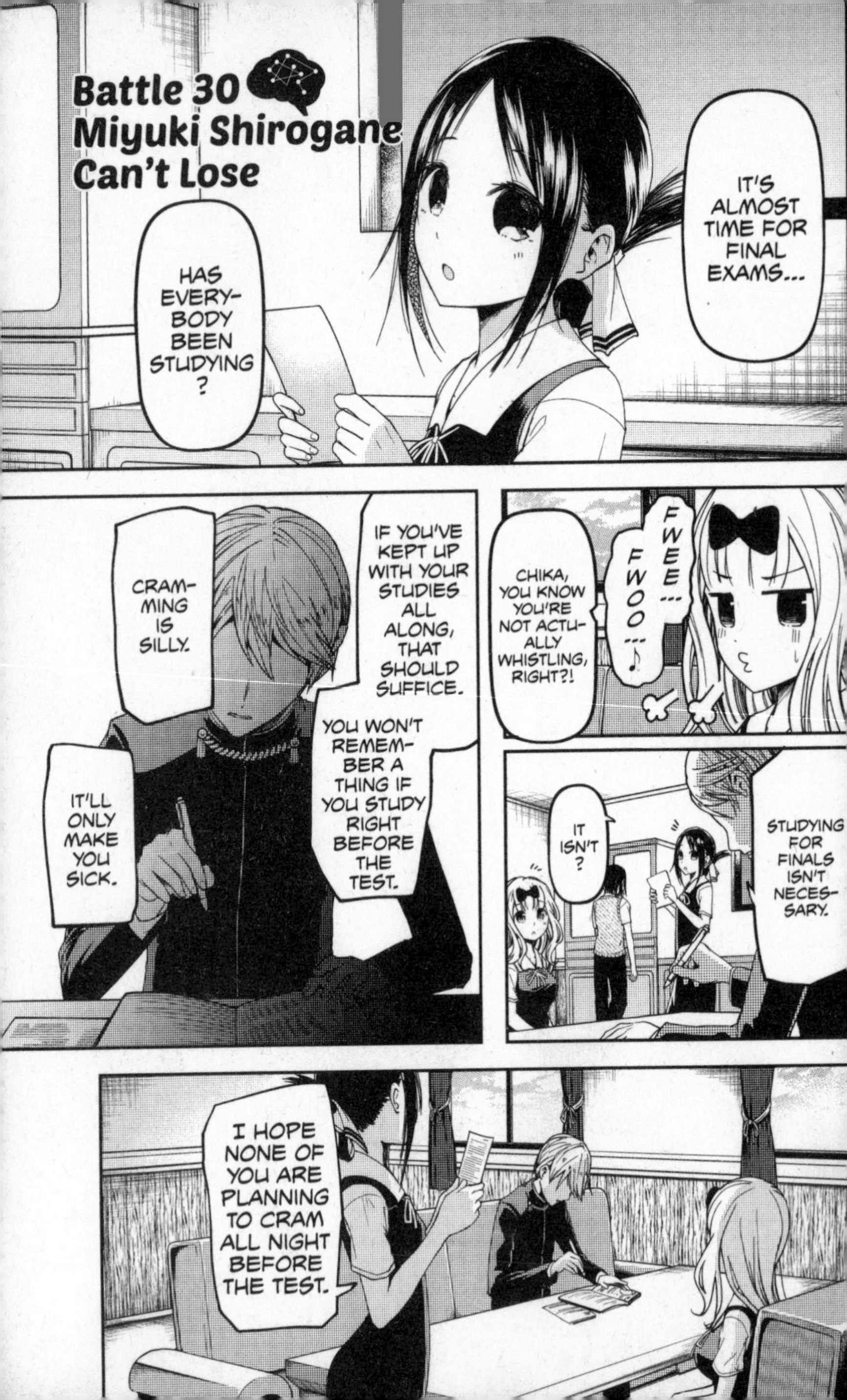
IT'S ALMOST TIME FOR FINAL EXAMS...
HAS EVERY-BODY BEEN STUDYING?
FWEE... FWOO... ♪
CHIKA, YOU KNOW YOU'RE NOT ACTU-ALLY WHISTLING, RIGHT?!
STUDYING FOR FINALS ISN'T NECES-SARY.
IT ISN'T?
IF YOU'VE KEPT UP WITH YOUR STUDIES ALL ALONG, THAT SHOULD SUFFICE.
CRAM-MING IS SILLY.
YOU WON'T REMEM-BER A THING IF YOU STUDY RIGHT BEFORE THE TEST.
IT'LL ONLY MAKE YOU SICK.
I HOPE NONE OF YOU ARE PLANNING TO CRAM ALL NIGHT BEFORE THE TEST.

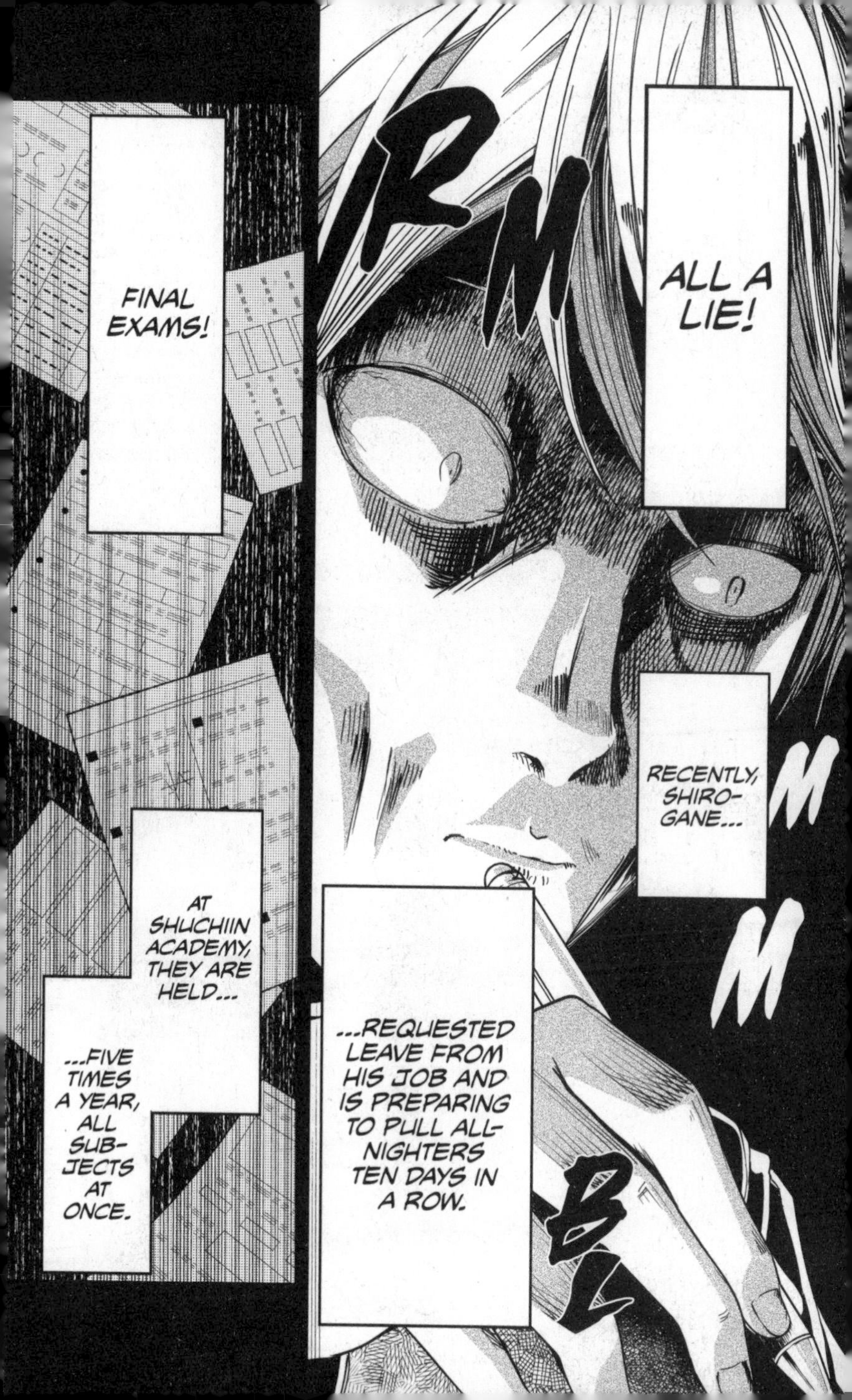
ALL A LIE!
RM
RECENTLY, SHIRO-GANE...
MM
...REQUESTED LEAVE FROM HIS JOB AND IS PREPARING TO PULL ALL-NIGHTERS TEN DAYS IN A ROW.
FINAL EXAMS!
AT SHUCHIIN ACADEMY, THEY ARE HELD...
...FIVE TIMES A YEAR, ALL SUB-JECTS AT ONCE.

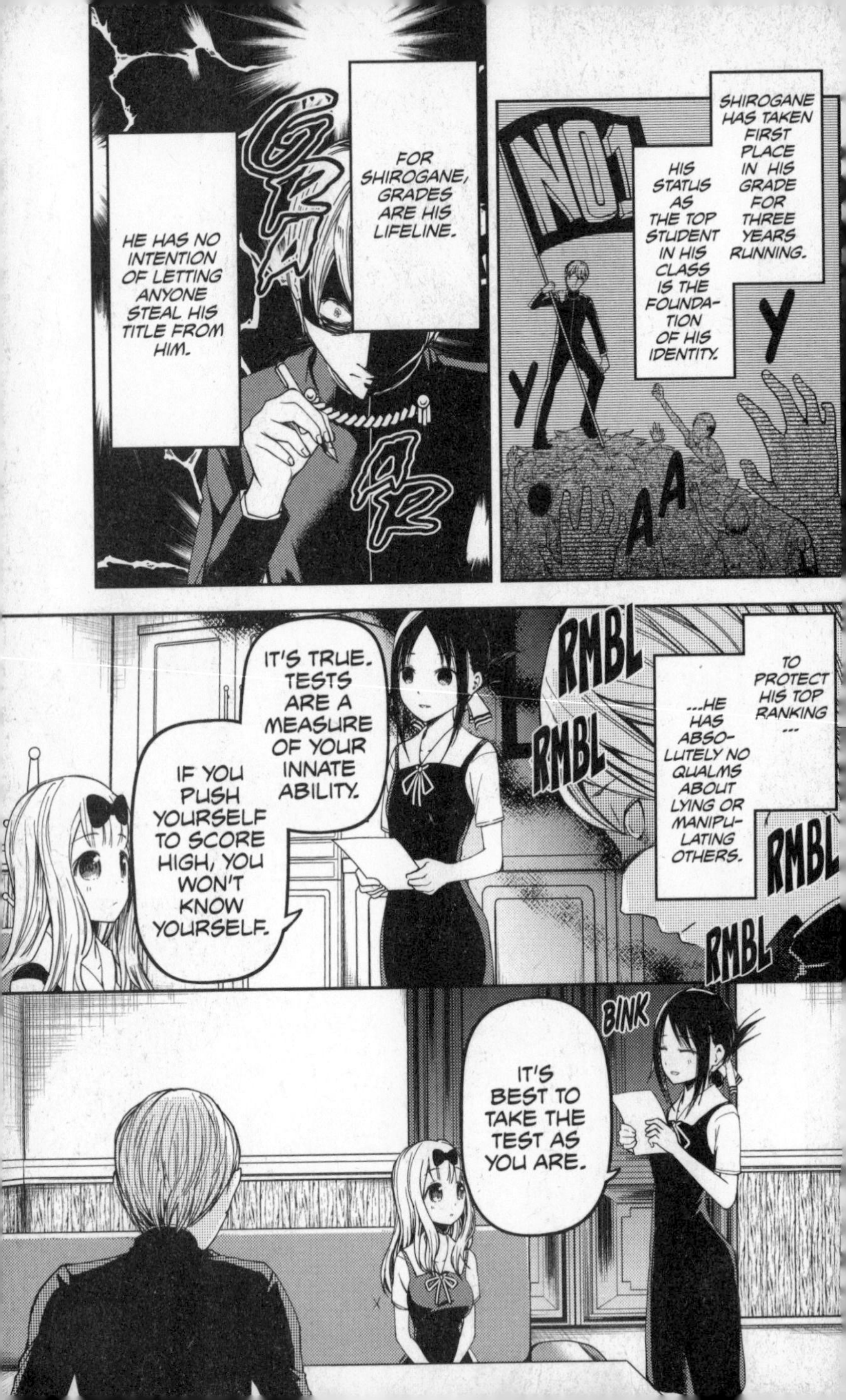
SHIROGANE HAS TAKEN FIRST PLACE IN HIS GRADE FOR THREE YEARS RUNNING.
HIS STATUS AS THE TOP STUDENT IN HIS CLASS IS THE FOUNDATION OF HIS IDENTITY.
NO.1
Y
Y
A
A
FOR SHIROGANE, GRADES ARE HIS LIFELINE.
HE HAS NO INTENTION OF LETTING ANYONE STEAL HIS TITLE FROM HIM.
TO PROTECT HIS TOP RANKING...
...HE HAS ABSOLUTELY NO QUALMS ABOUT LYING OR MANIPULATING OTHERS.
RMBL
RMBL
RMBL
RMBL
IT'S TRUE. TESTS ARE A MEASURE OF YOUR INNATE ABILITY.
IF YOU PUSH YOURSELF TO SCORE HIGH, YOU WON'T KNOW YOURSELF.
BINK
IT'S BEST TO TAKE THE TEST AS YOU ARE.

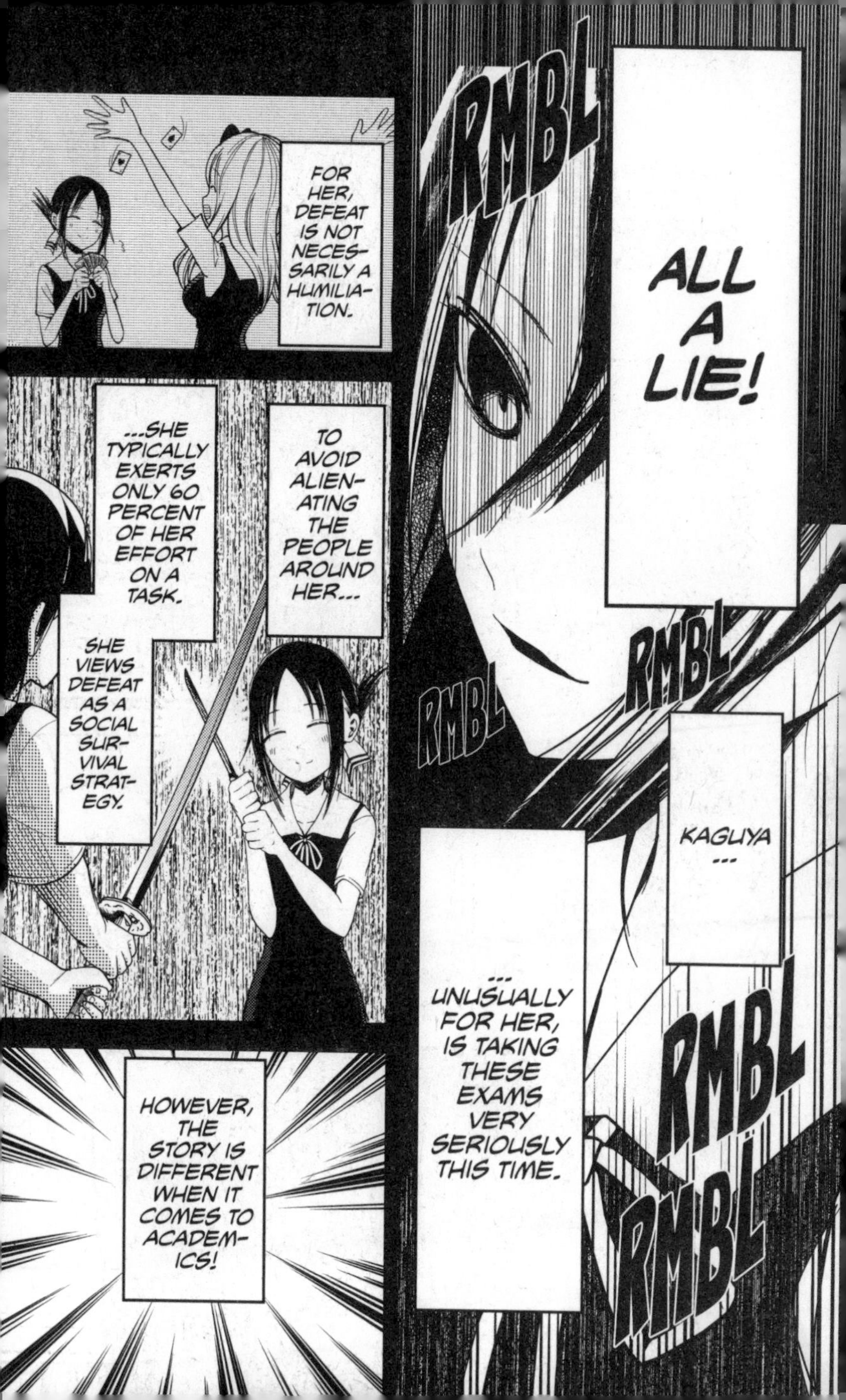
RMBL
ALL A LIE!
RMBL
RMBL
KAGUYA ...
... UNUSUALLY FOR HER, IS TAKING THESE EXAMS VERY SERIOUSLY THIS TIME.
RMBL
RMBL
FOR HER, DEFEAT IS NOT NECES-SARILY A HUMILIA-TION.
TO AVOID ALIEN-ATING THE PEOPLE AROUND HER...
...SHE TYPICALLY EXERTS ONLY 60 PERCENT OF HER EFFORT ON A TASK.
SHE VIEWS DEFEAT AS A SOCIAL SUR-VIVAL STRAT-EGY.
HOWEVER, THE STORY IS DIFFERENT WHEN IT COMES TO ACADEM-ICS!

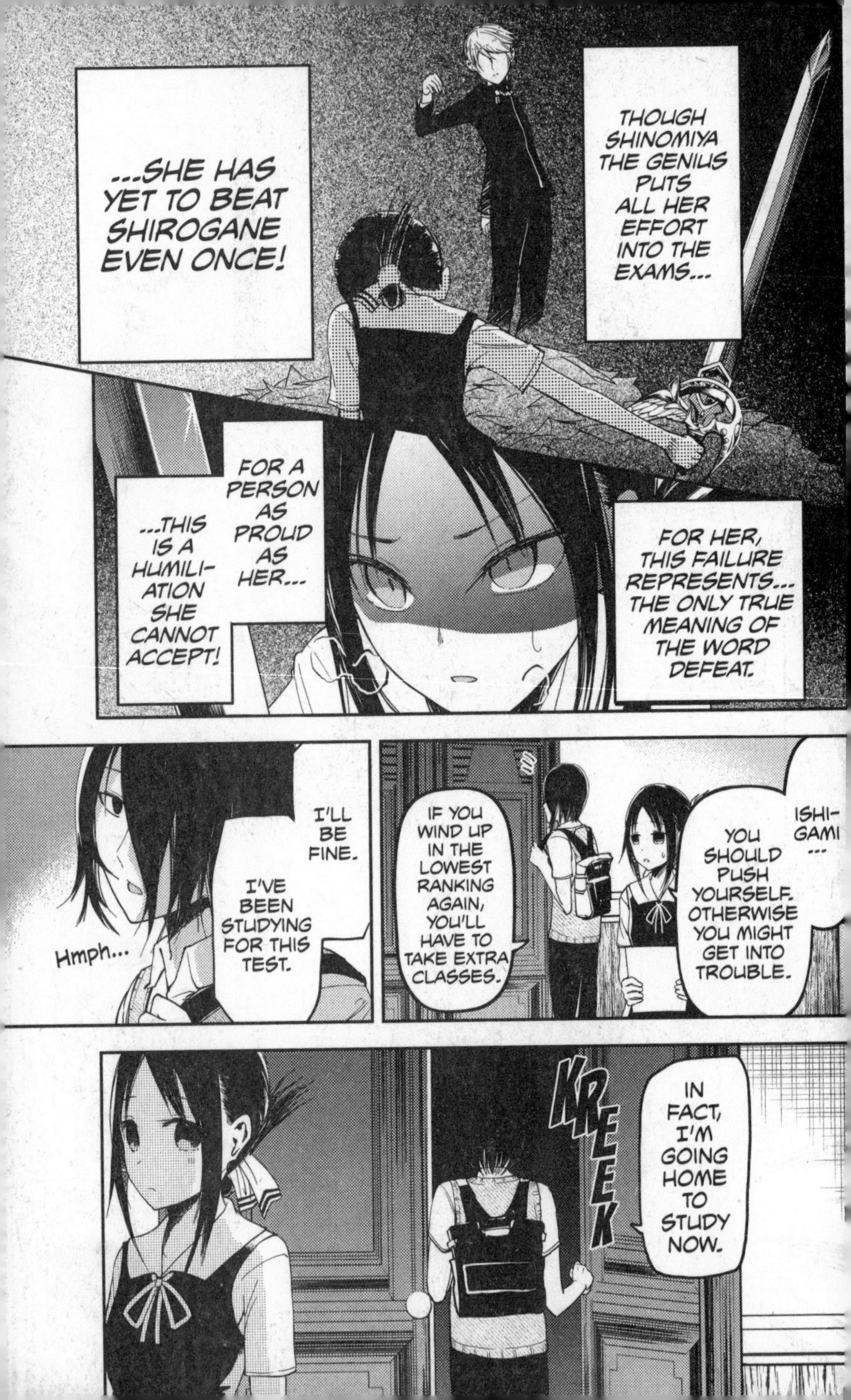
THOUGH SHINOMIYA THE GENIUS PUTS ALL HER EFFORT INTO THE EXAMS...
...SHE HAS YET TO BEAT SHIROGANE EVEN ONCE!
FOR HER, THIS FAILURE REPRESENTS... THE ONLY TRUE MEANING OF THE WORD DEFEAT.
FOR A PERSON AS PROUD AS HER...
...THIS IS A HUMILIATION SHE CANNOT ACCEPT!
ISHIGAMI...
YOU SHOULD PUSH YOURSELF. OTHERWISE YOU MIGHT GET INTO TROUBLE.
IF YOU WIND UP IN THE LOWEST RANKING AGAIN, YOU'LL HAVE TO TAKE EXTRA CLASSES.
I'LL BE FINE.
I'VE BEEN STUDYING FOR THIS TEST.
Hmph...
IN FACT, I'M GOING HOME TO STUDY NOW.
KREEK

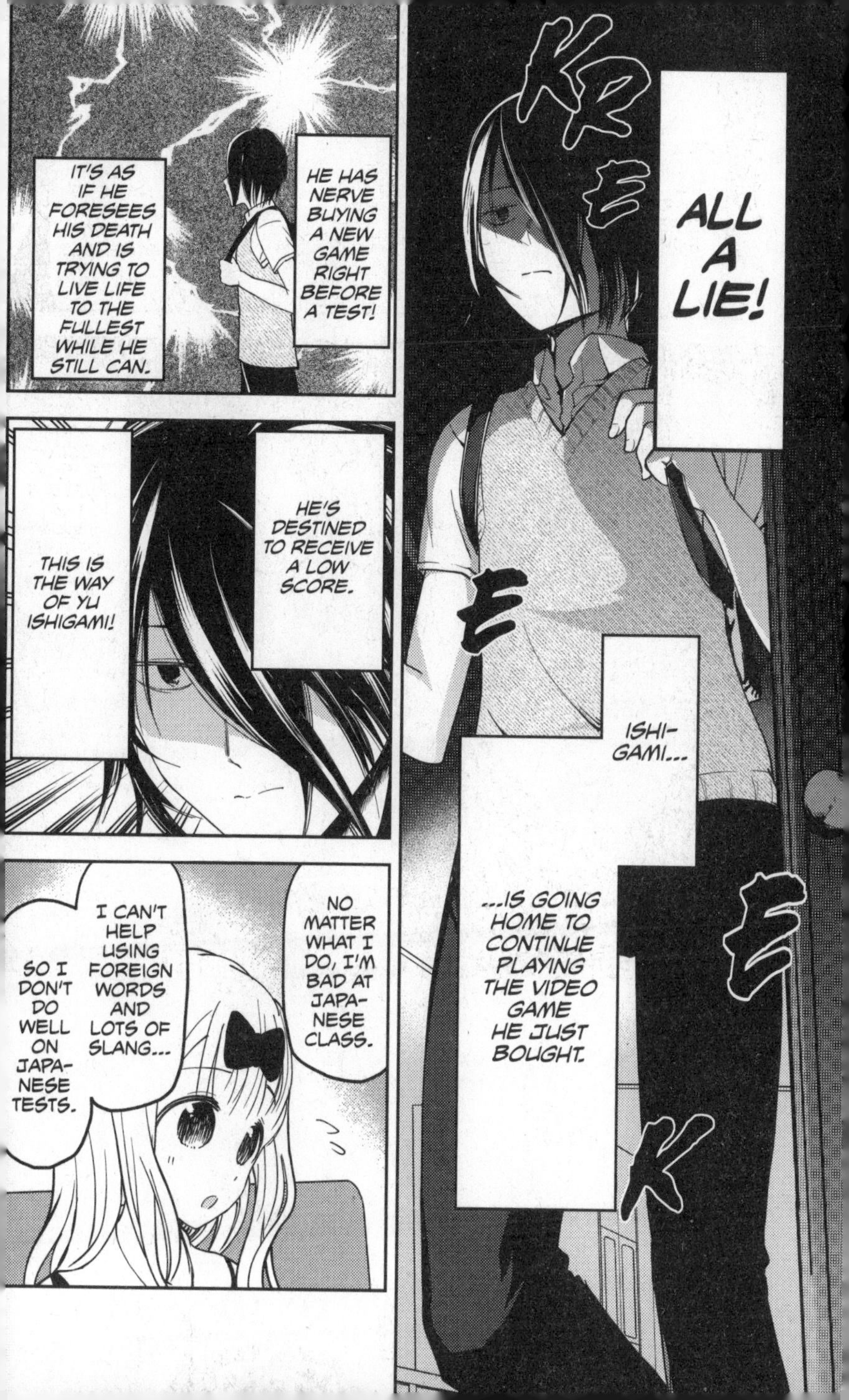
KREEEK
ALL A LIE!
ISHI-GAMI...
...IS GOING HOME TO CONTINUE PLAYING THE VIDEO GAME HE JUST BOUGHT.
HE HAS NERVE BUYING A NEW GAME RIGHT BEFORE A TEST!
IT'S AS IF HE FORESEES HIS DEATH AND IS TRYING TO LIVE LIFE TO THE FULLEST WHILE HE STILL CAN.
HE'S DESTINED TO RECEIVE A LOW SCORE.
THIS IS THE WAY OF YU ISHIGAMI!
NO MATTER WHAT I DO, I'M BAD AT JAPANESE CLASS.
I CAN'T HELP USING FOREIGN WORDS AND LOTS OF SLANG...
SO I DON'T DO WELL ON JAPANESE TESTS.

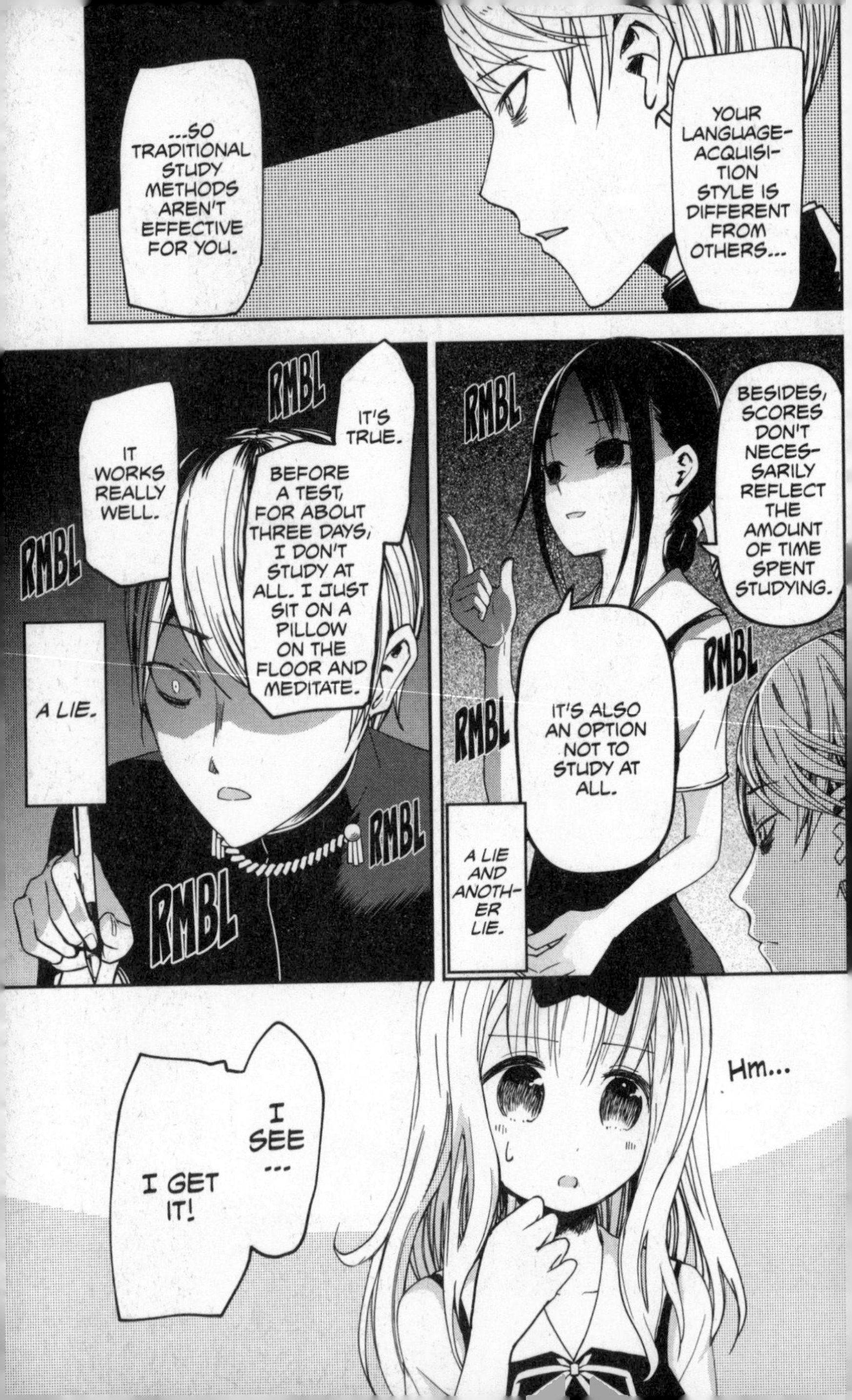
YOUR LANGUAGE-ACQUISITION STYLE IS DIFFERENT FROM OTHERS...
...SO TRADITIONAL STUDY METHODS AREN'T EFFECTIVE FOR YOU.
RMBL
BESIDES, SCORES DON'T NECESSARILY REFLECT THE AMOUNT OF TIME SPENT STUDYING.
RMBL
RMBL
IT'S ALSO AN OPTION NOT TO STUDY AT ALL.
A LIE AND ANOTHER LIE.
RMBL
IT'S TRUE.
BEFORE A TEST, FOR ABOUT THREE DAYS, I DON'T STUDY AT ALL. I JUST SIT ON A PILLOW ON THE FLOOR AND MEDITATE.
IT WORKS REALLY WELL.
RMBL
A LIE.
RMBL
RMBL
Hm...
I SEE...
I GET IT!

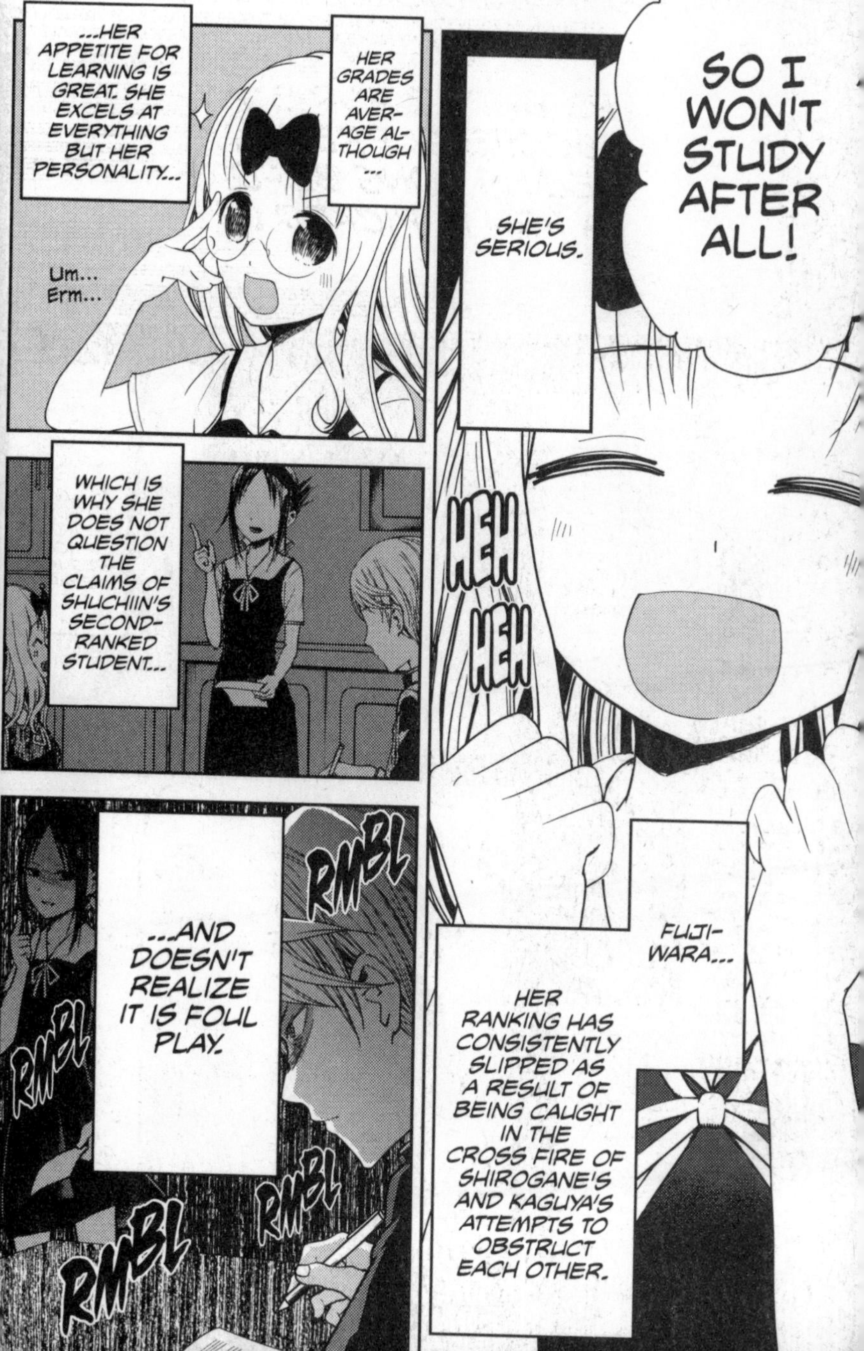
SO I WON'T STUDY AFTER ALL!
SHE'S SERIOUS.
HEH HEH
FUJI-WARA...
HER RANKING HAS CONSISTENTLY SLIPPED AS A RESULT OF BEING CAUGHT IN THE CROSS FIRE OF SHIROGANE'S AND KAGUYA'S ATTEMPTS TO OBSTRUCT EACH OTHER.
HER GRADES ARE AVER-AGE AL-THOUGH...
...HER APPETITE FOR LEARNING IS GREAT. SHE EXCELS AT EVERYTHING BUT HER PERSONALITY...
Um... Erm...
WHICH IS WHY SHE DOES NOT QUESTION THE CLAIMS OF SHUCHIIN'S SECOND-RANKED STUDENT...
RMBL
...AND DOESN'T REALIZE IT IS FOUL PLAY.
RMBL
RMBL
RMBL
RMBL

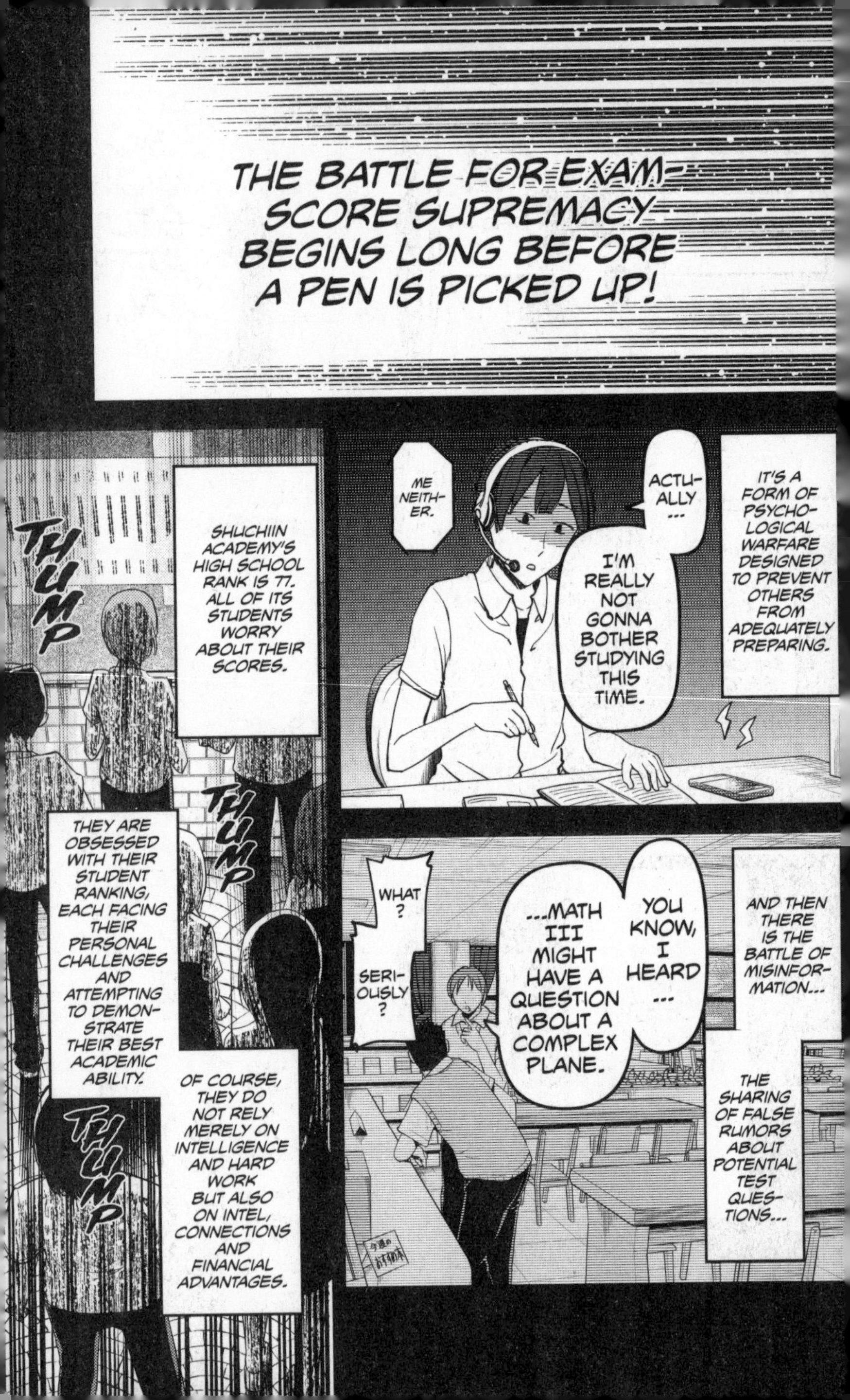
THE BATTLE FOR EXAM-SCORE SUPREMACY BEGINS LONG BEFORE A PEN IS PICKED UP!
IT'S A FORM OF PSYCHOLOGICAL WARFARE DESIGNED TO PREVENT OTHERS FROM ADEQUATELY PREPARING.
ACTUALLY...
I'M REALLY NOT GONNA BOTHER STUDYING THIS TIME.
ME NEITHER.
AND THEN THERE IS THE BATTLE OF MISINFORMATION...
THE SHARING OF FALSE RUMORS ABOUT POTENTIAL TEST QUESTIONS...
YOU KNOW, I HEARD...
...MATH III MIGHT HAVE A QUESTION ABOUT A COMPLEX PLANE.
WHAT?
SERIOUSLY?
SHUCHIIN ACADEMY'S HIGH SCHOOL RANK IS 77. ALL OF ITS STUDENTS WORRY ABOUT THEIR SCORES.
THUMP
THUMP
THEY ARE OBSESSED WITH THEIR STUDENT RANKING, EACH FACING THEIR PERSONAL CHALLENGES AND ATTEMPTING TO DEMONSTRATE THEIR BEST ACADEMIC ABILITY.
OF COURSE, THEY DO NOT RELY MERELY ON INTELLIGENCE AND HARD WORK BUT ALSO ON INTEL, CONNECTIONS AND FINANCIAL ADVANTAGES.
THUMP

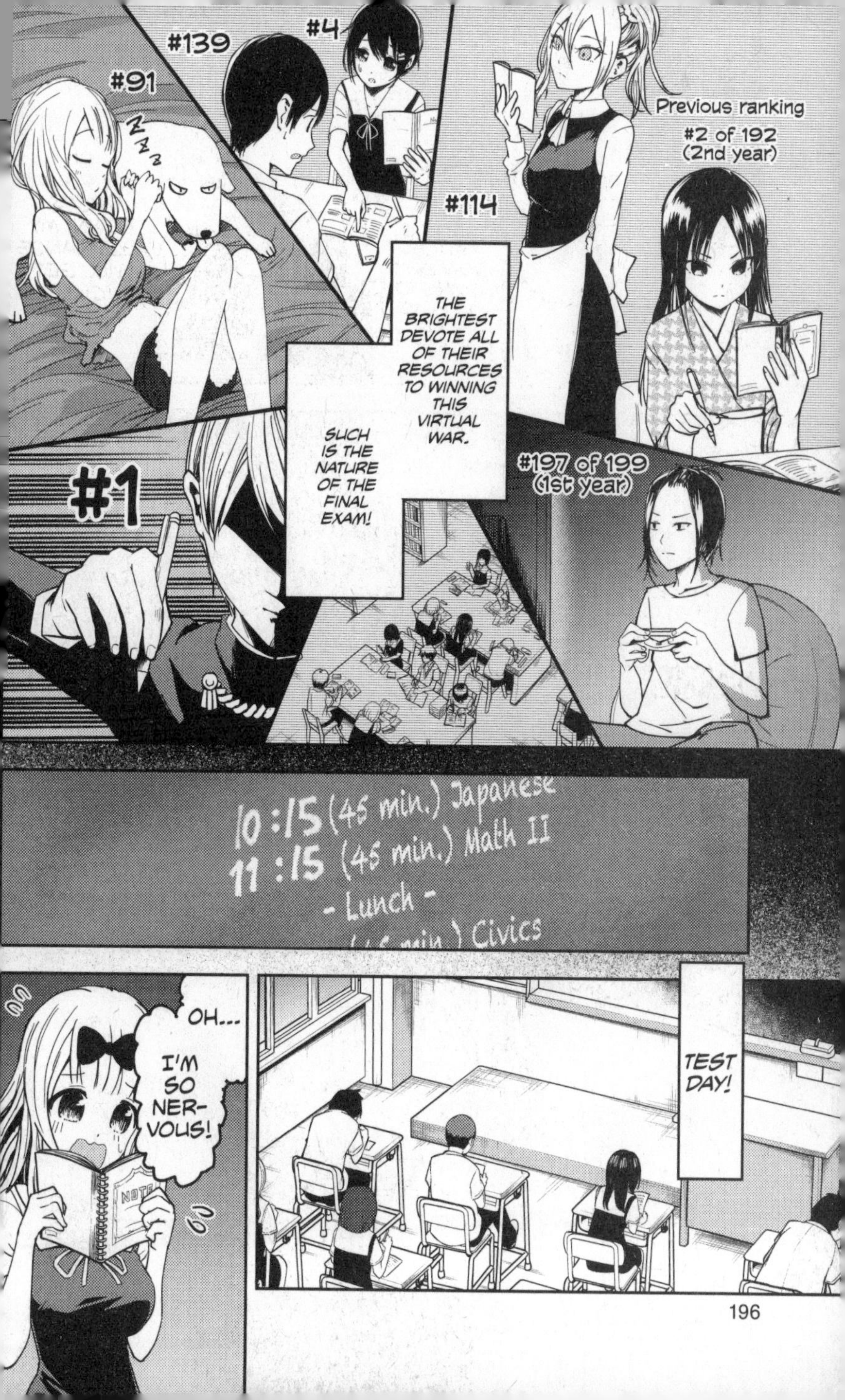
Previous ranking
#2 of 192
(2nd year)
#114
#4
#139
#91
THE BRIGHTEST DEVOTE ALL OF THEIR RESOURCES TO WINNING THIS VIRTUAL WAR.
SUCH IS THE NATURE OF THE FINAL EXAM!
#197 of 199
(1st year)
#1
10:15 (45 min.) Japanese
11:15 (45 min.) Math II
- Lunch -
Civics
TEST DAY!
OH...
I'M SO NERVOUS!

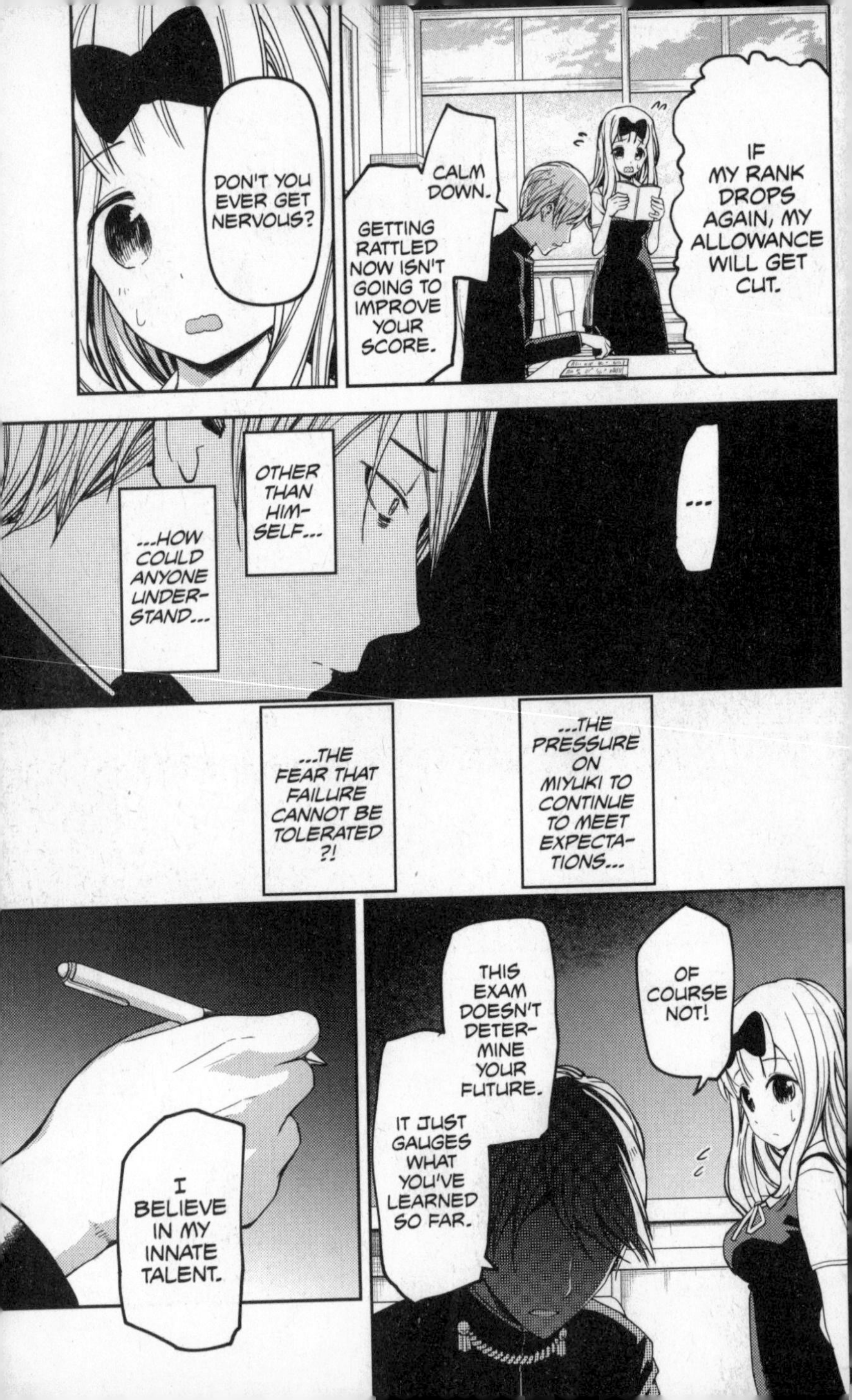
IF MY RANK DROPS AGAIN, MY ALLOWANCE WILL GET CUT.
CALM DOWN.
GETTING RATTLED NOW ISN'T GOING TO IMPROVE YOUR SCORE.
DON'T YOU EVER GET NERVOUS?
...
OTHER THAN HIM-SELF...
...HOW COULD ANYONE UNDER-STAND...
...THE PRESSURE ON MIYUKI TO CONTINUE TO MEET EXPECTA-TIONS...
...THE FEAR THAT FAILURE CANNOT BE TOLERATED ?!
OF COURSE NOT!
THIS EXAM DOESN'T DETER-MINE YOUR FUTURE.
IT JUST GAUGES WHAT YOU'VE LEARNED SO FAR.
I BELIEVE IN MY INNATE TALENT.

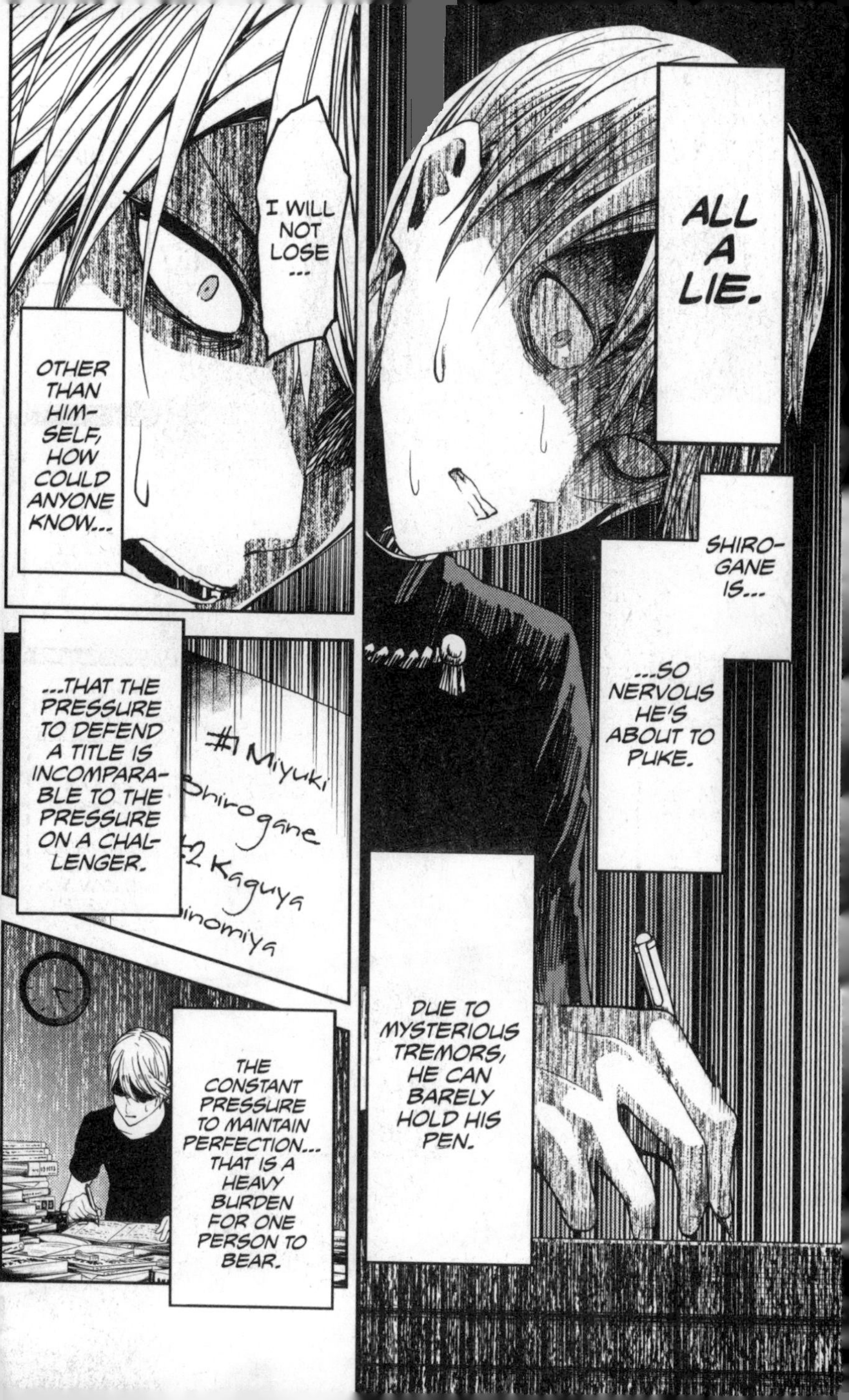
ALL A LIE.
SHIRO-GANE IS...
...SO NERVOUS HE'S ABOUT TO PUKE.
DUE TO MYSTERIOUS TREMORS, HE CAN BARELY HOLD HIS PEN.
I WILL NOT LOSE...
OTHER THAN HIM-SELF, HOW COULD ANYONE KNOW...
...THAT THE PRESSURE TO DEFEND A TITLE IS INCOMPARA-BLE TO THE PRESSURE ON A CHAL-LENGER.
#1 Miyuki Shirogane
#2 Kaguya
THE CONSTANT PRESSURE TO MAINTAIN PERFECTION... THAT IS A HEAVY BURDEN FOR ONE PERSON TO BEAR.

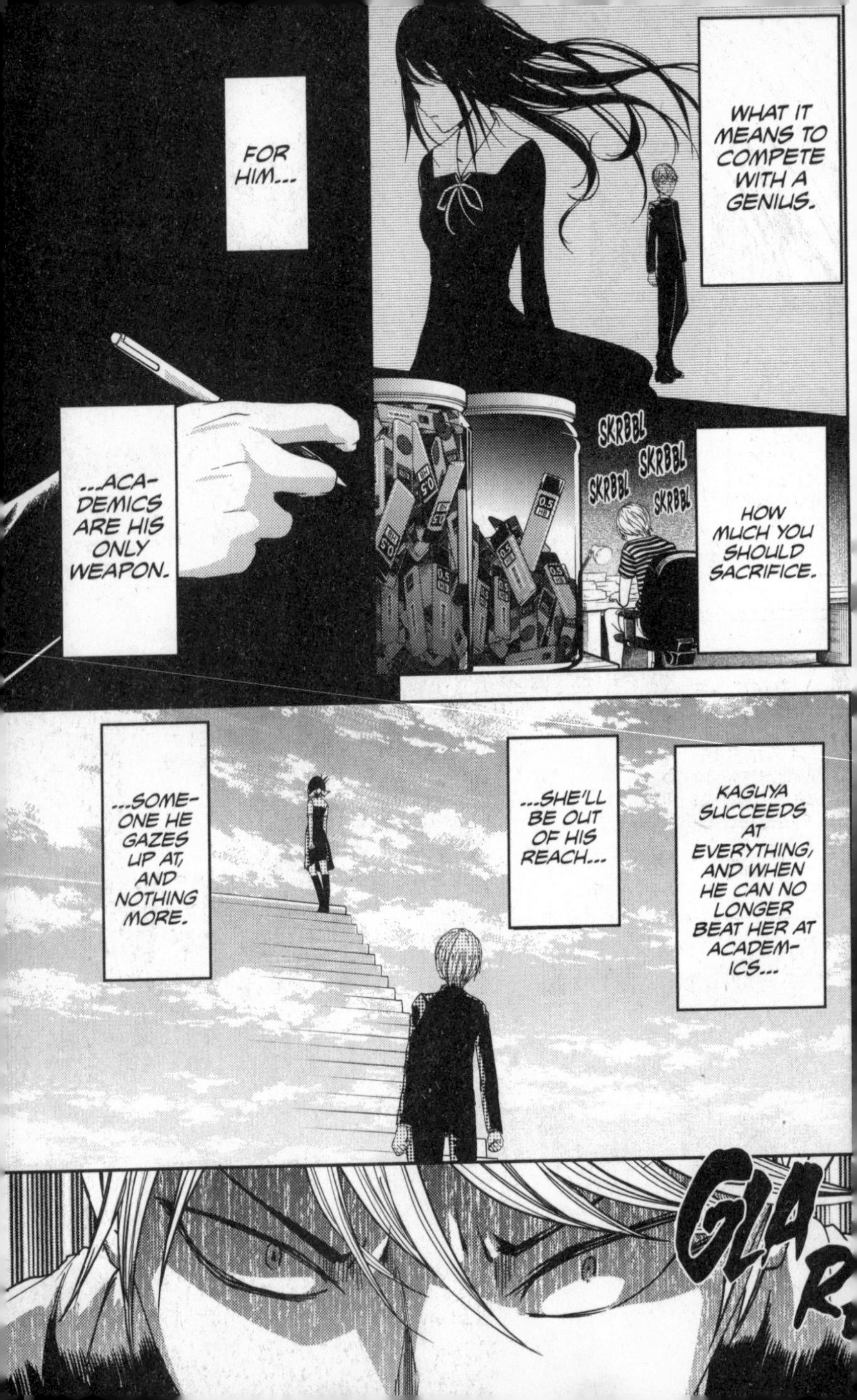
WHAT IT MEANS TO COMPETE WITH A GENIUS.
SKRBBL
SKRBBL
SKRBBL
SKRBBL
HOW MUCH YOU SHOULD SACRIFICE.
FOR HIM...
...ACADEMICS ARE HIS ONLY WEAPON.
KAGUYA SUCCEEDS AT EVERYTHING, AND WHEN HE CAN NO LONGER BEAT HER AT ACADEMICS...
...SHE'LL BE OUT OF HIS REACH...
...SOMEONE HE GAZES UP AT, AND NOTHING MORE.
GLA

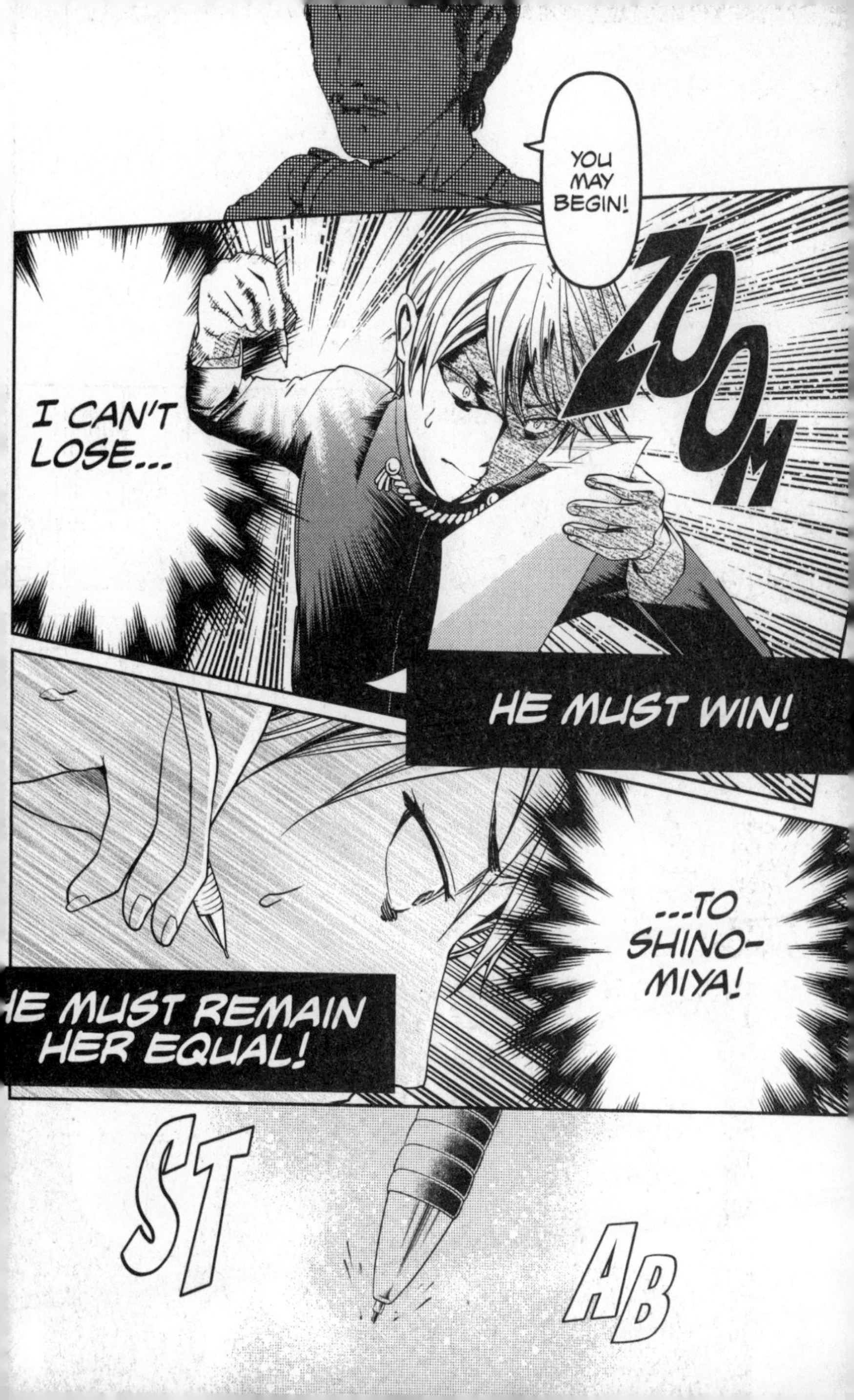
YOU MAY BEGIN!
ZOOM
I CAN'T LOSE...
HE MUST WIN!
HE MUST REMAIN HER EQUAL!
...TO SHINO-MIYA!
ST
AB

#1	Miyuki Shirogane	492
#2	Kaguya Shinomiya	487
#3	Maki Shijo	486
#4	Kazuo Abe	478
#5	Taiga Arikawa	475
#6	Saburo Toyosaki	474
#7	Nagisa Kashiwagi	471
#7	Koichi Sumitomo	471
#8	Ryu Saito	469

First Semester Final Exam Results

Listed here are the names of the 50 highest-ranking students. We hope these individuals continue their pursuit of excellence and serve as an example to others.

Sincerely,
Your teachers

YADDA YADDA

YADDA

AS EXPECTED, SHIROGANE.

YADDA

YADDA

YADDA

IT'S NOT JUST LUCK.

NO, I KNOW HOW MUCH EFFORT YOU PUT IN.

OF COURSE, LUCK PLAYS A ROLE. WHO KNOWS WHAT WILL HAPPEN NEXT TIME AROUND.

YOU TOO, SHINOMIYA.

I FULLY ACCEPT MY LOSS.

SPIN

I STILL HAVE A WAYS TO GO.

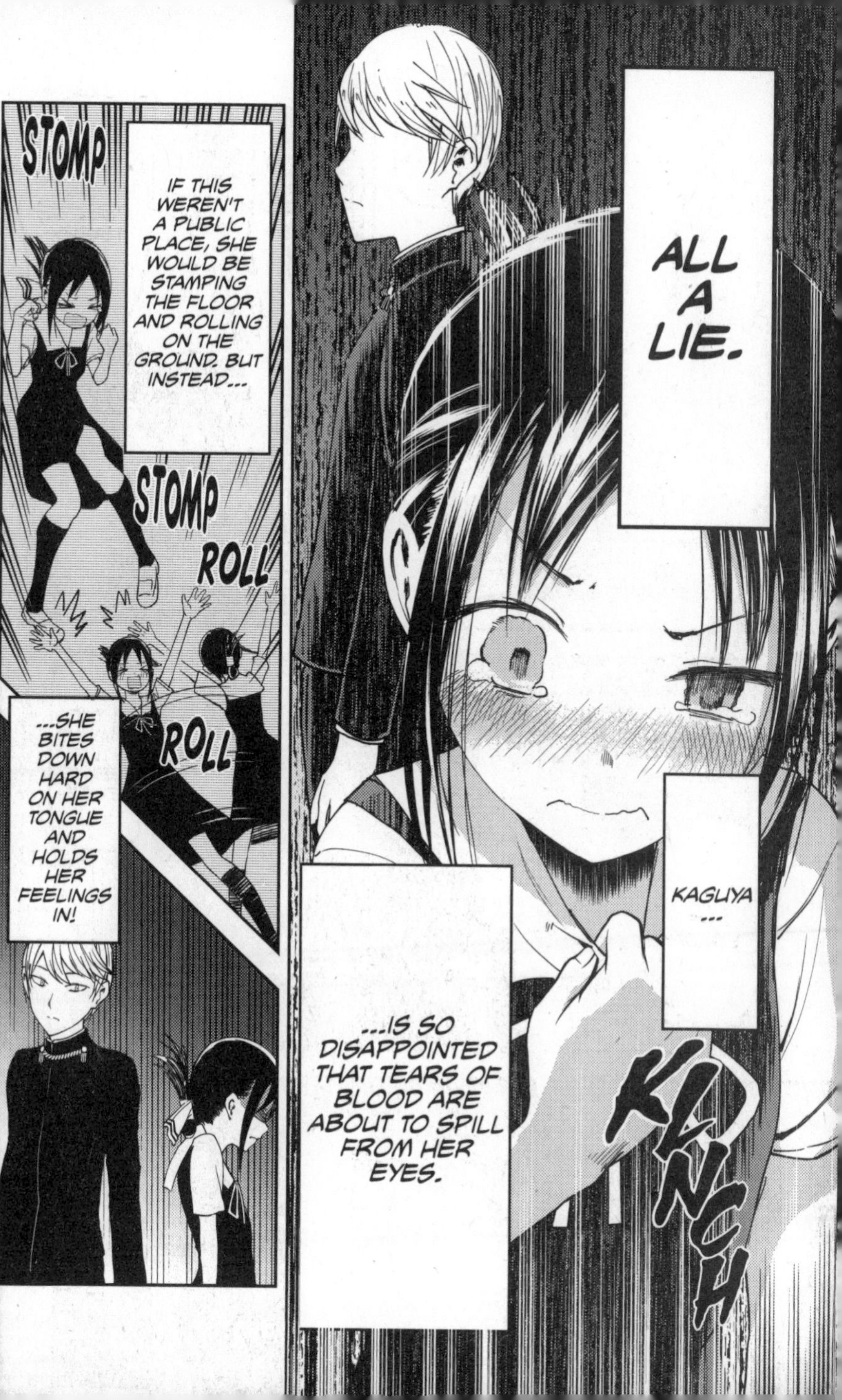
ALL A LIE.
KAGUYA...
...IS SO DISAPPOINTED THAT TEARS OF BLOOD ARE ABOUT TO SPILL FROM HER EYES.
KLNCH
STOMP
IF THIS WEREN'T A PUBLIC PLACE, SHE WOULD BE STAMPING THE FLOOR AND ROLLING ON THE GROUND. BUT INSTEAD...
STOMP
ROLL
ROLL
...SHE BITES DOWN HARD ON HER TONGUE AND HOLDS HER FEELINGS IN!

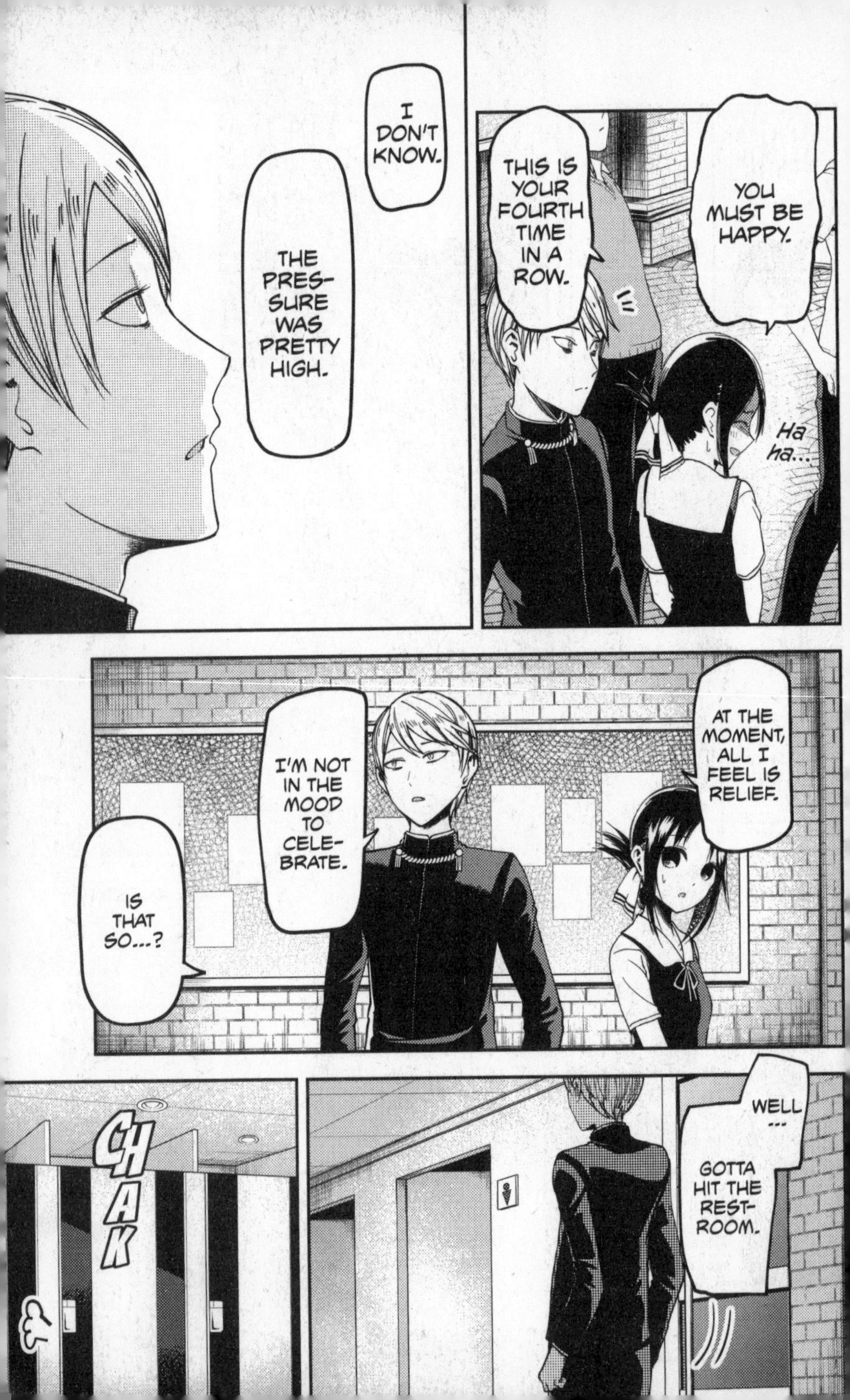
YOU MUST BE HAPPY.
THIS IS YOUR FOURTH TIME IN A ROW.
Ha ha...
I DON'T KNOW.
THE PRESSURE WAS PRETTY HIGH.
AT THE MOMENT, ALL I FEEL IS RELIEF.
I'M NOT IN THE MOOD TO CELEBRATE.
IS THAT SO...?
WELL...
GOTTA HIT THE RESTROOM.
CHAK

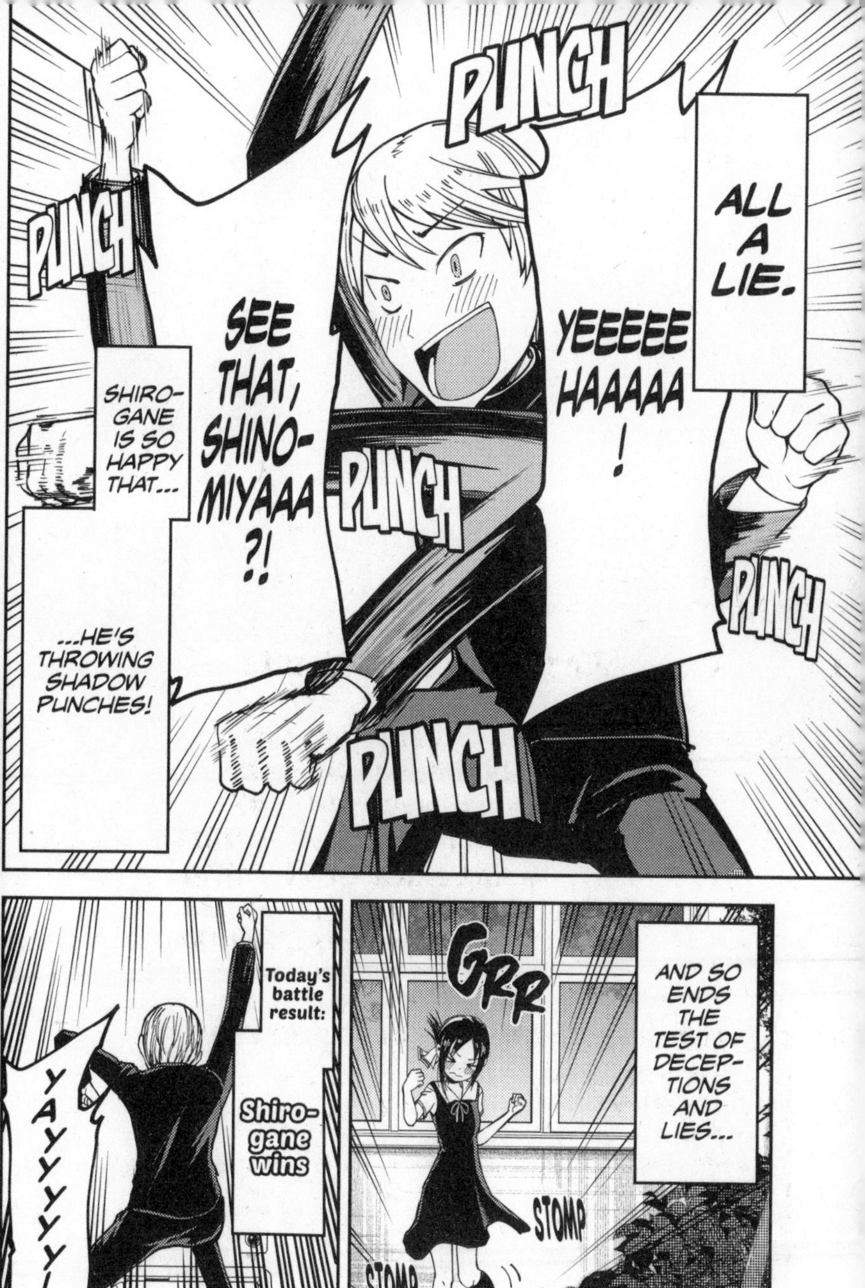
ALL A LIE.
YEEEEEE HAAAAA!
PUNCH
PUNCH
PUNCH
SEE THAT, SHINOMIYAAA?!
PUNCH
PUNCH
PUNCH
SHIROGANE IS SO HAPPY THAT...
...HE'S THROWING SHADOW PUNCHES!
AND SO ENDS THE TEST OF DECEPTIONS AND LIES...
GRR
STOMP
STOMP
Today's battle result:
Shirogane wins
YAYYYYY!

To be continued...

First Semester Results

Miyuki Shirogane #1 → #1
Kaguya Shinomiya #2 → #2
Nagisa Kashiwagi #4 → #7
Chika Fujiwara #91 → #101
Ai Hayasaka #114 → #114
Kashiwagi's Boyfriend #139 → #89
Yu Ishigami #197 → #177

#1	Miyuki Shirogane	492
#2	Kaguya Shinomiya	487
#3	Maki Shijo	486
#4	Kazuo Abe	478
#5	Taiga Arikawa	475
#6	Saburo Toyosaki	474
#7	Nagisa Kashiwagi	471
#7	Koichi Sumitomo	471
#8	Ryu Saito	469

First Semester
Final Exam Results

Listed here are
the names of the
50 highest-ranking
students. We hope
these individuals
continue their pursuit
of excellence and serve
as an example to
others.

Sincerely,
Your teachers

A WISE MAN TOOK TEN YEARS TO KNOW TRUTH, WHILE A FOOL TOOK 100 YEARS. THE WISE MAN TOOK 100 YEARS TO KNOW LOVE, BUT THE FOOL ALREADY KNEW IT.

AKA AKASAKA

Aka Akasaka got his start as an assistant to Jinsei Kataoka and Kazuma Kondou, the creators of *Deadman Wonderland*. His first serialized manga was an adaptation of the light novel series *Sayonara Piano Sonata*, published by Kadokawa in 2011. *Kaguya-sama: Love Is War* began serialization in *Miracle Jump* in 2015 but was later moved to *Weekly Young Jump* in 2016 due to its popularity.

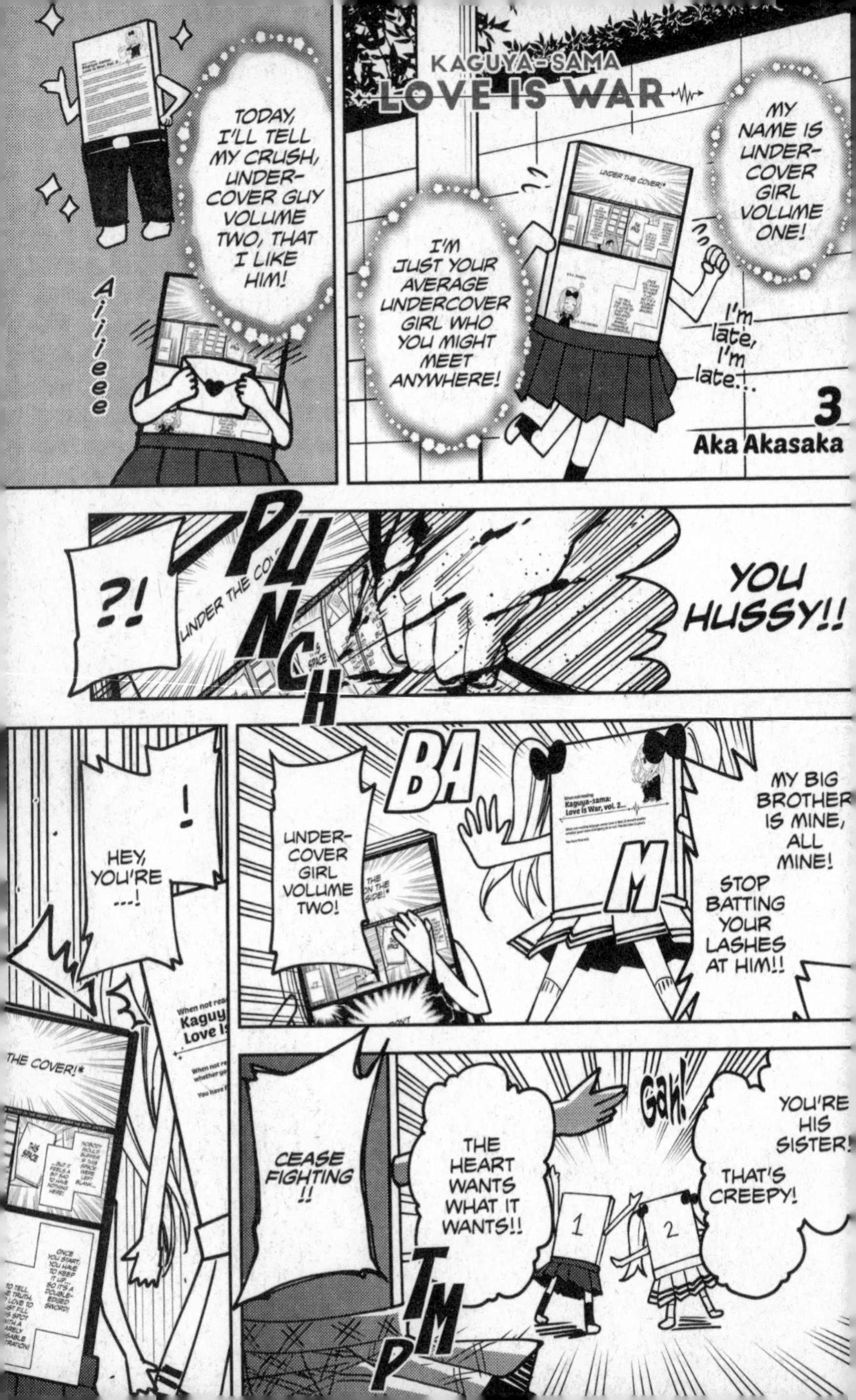
KAGUYA-SAMA
LOVE IS WAR
MY NAME IS UNDERCOVER GIRL VOLUME ONE!
I'M JUST YOUR AVERAGE UNDERCOVER GIRL WHO YOU MIGHT MEET ANYWHERE!
I'm late, I'm late...
3
Aka Akasaka
TODAY, I'LL TELL MY CRUSH, UNDERCOVER GUY VOLUME TWO, THAT I LIKE HIM!
Aiiieee
YOU HUSSY!!
PUNCH
?!
MY BIG BROTHER IS MINE, ALL MINE!
STOP BATTING YOUR LASHES AT HIM!!
BAM
UNDERCOVER GIRL VOLUME TWO!
YOU'RE HIS SISTER!
THAT'S CREEPY!
Gah!
THE HEART WANTS WHAT IT WANTS!!
CEASE FIGHTING!!
TMP
!
HEY, YOU'RE ---!

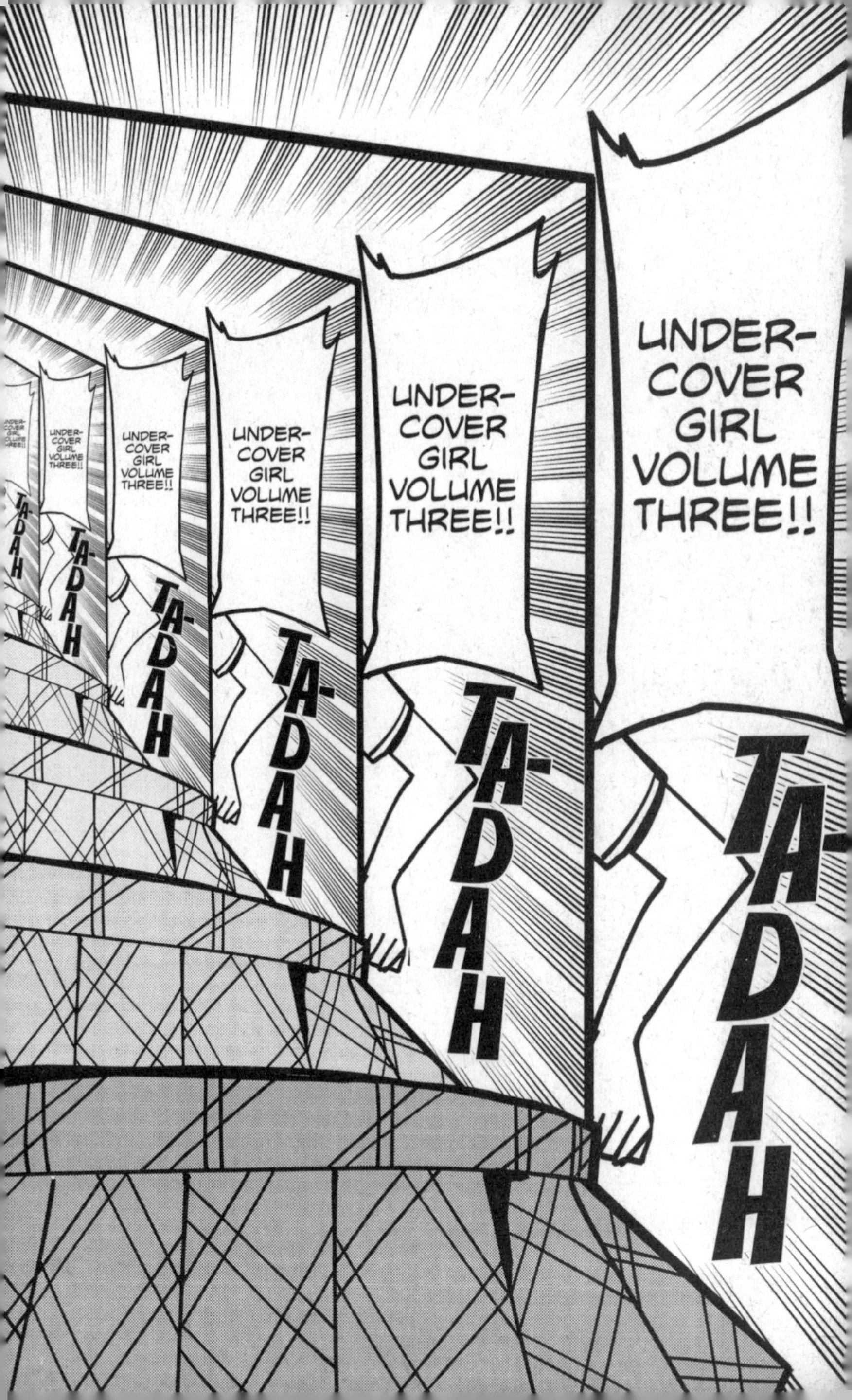
UNDER-COVER GIRL VOLUME THREE!!
TA-DAH
UNDER-COVER GIRL VOLUME THREE!!
TA-DAH
UNDER-COVER GIRL VOLUME THREE!!
TA-DAH
UNDER-COVER GIRL VOLUME THREE!!
TA-DAH
UNDER-COVER GIRL VOLUME THREE!!
TA-DAH
TA-DAH

KAGUYA-SAMA
LOVE IS WAR

SHONEN JUMP MANGA EDITION

3

STORY AND ART BY
AKA AKASAKA

Translation/Emi Louie-Nishikawa
English Adaptation/Annette Roman
Touch-Up Art & Lettering/Stephen Dutro
Cover & Interior Design/Izumi Evers
Editor/Annette Roman

KAGUYA-SAMA WA KOKURASETAI~TENSAITACHI NO REN'AI ZUNO SEN~
© 2015 by Aka Akasaka
All rights reserved.
First published in Japan in 2015 by SHUEISHA Inc., Tokyo.
English translation rights arranged by SHUEISHA Inc.

The stories, characters and incidents mentioned in this publication are entirely fictional.

Printed in Canada

Published by VIZ Media, LLC
P.O. Box 77010
San Francisco, CA 94107

10 9 8 7 6 5 4 3 2 1
First printing, July 2018

viz.com

shonenjump.com

COMING NEXT VOLUME

KAGUYA-SAMA
LOVE IS WAR

STORY & ART BY
AKA AKASAKA

Will Kaguya and Miyuki outsmart a psychological test designed to reveal their true feelings? Is spoon-feeding each other cake the way to each other's hearts? Also, Miyuki visits Kaguya's home for the first time, but she is too sick to enjoy it. Kaguya tries to befriend Miyuki's little sister, but Chika has beaten her to the punch. Then summer vacation arrives, but the student council still hasn't agreed on a destination.

Fireworks are supposed to be romantic.

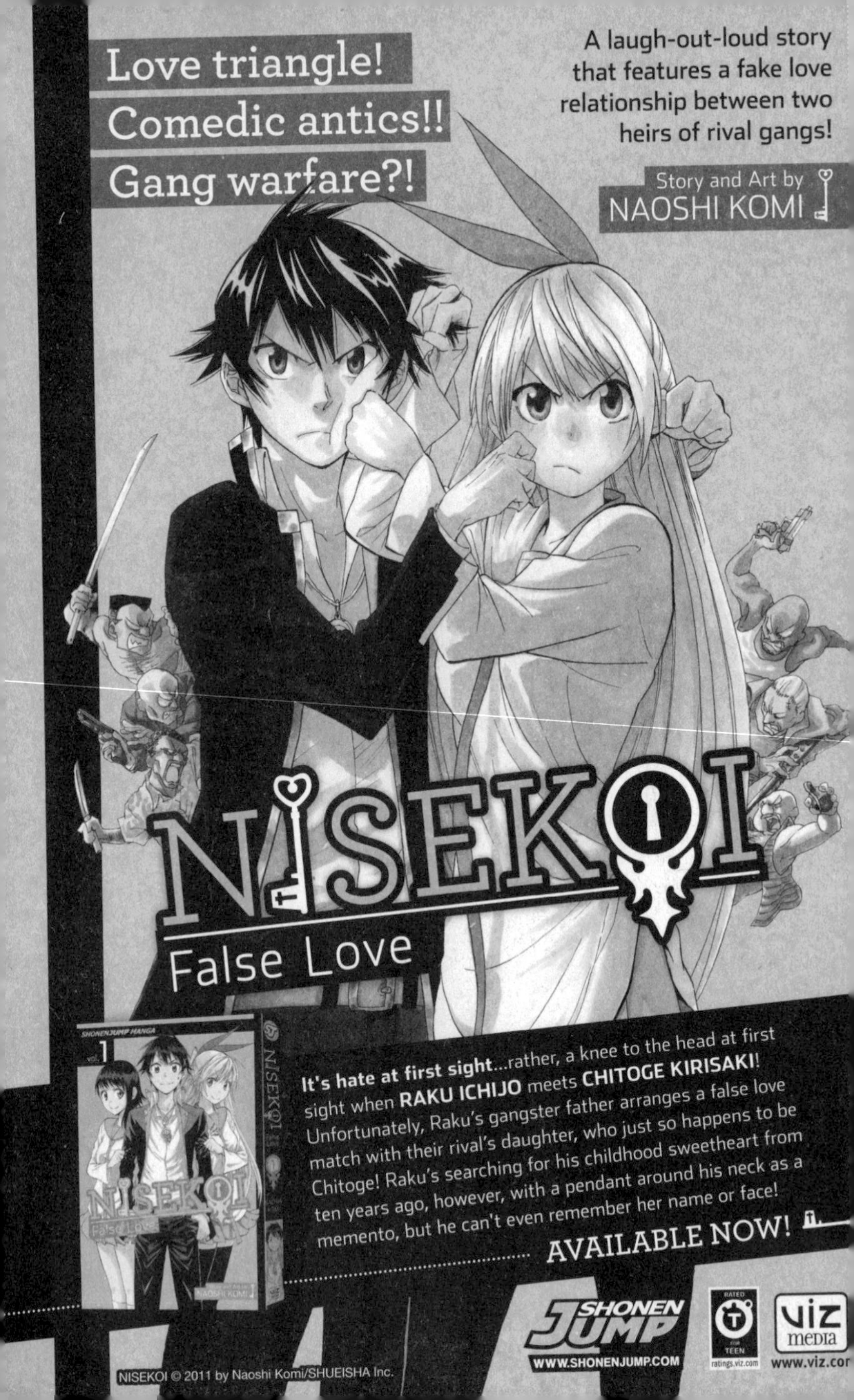
Love triangle!
Comedic antics!!
Gang warfare?!
A laugh-out-loud story that features a fake love relationship between two heirs of rival gangs!
Story and Art by NAOSHI KOMI
NISEKOI
False Love
It's hate at first sight...rather, a knee to the head at first sight when RAKU ICHIJO meets CHITOGE KIRISAKI! Unfortunately, Raku's gangster father arranges a false love match with their rival's daughter, who just so happens to be Chitoge! Raku's searching for his childhood sweetheart from ten years ago, however, with a pendant around his neck as a memento, but he can't even remember her name or face!
AVAILABLE NOW!
SHONEN JUMP MANGA
vol. 1
NISEKOI
False Love
NAOSHI KOMI
SHONEN JUMP
WWW.SHONENJUMP.COM
RATED T FOR TEEN
ratings.viz.com
viz media
www.viz.com
NISEKOI © 2011 by Naoshi Komi/SHUEISHA Inc.

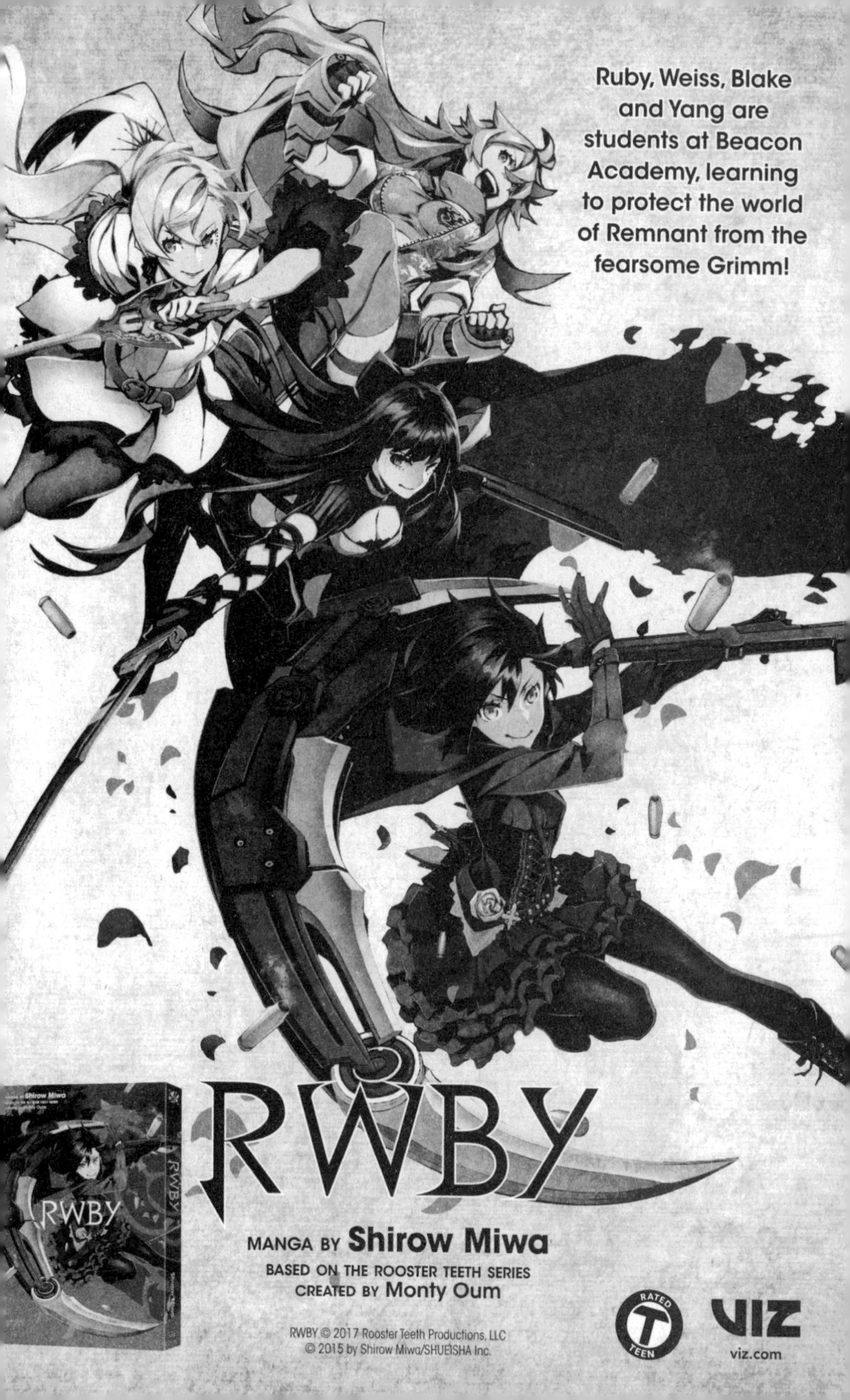
Ruby, Weiss, Blake and Yang are students at Beacon Academy, learning to protect the world of Remnant from the fearsome Grimm!
RWBY
RWBY
MANGA BY Shirow Miwa
BASED ON THE ROOSTER TEETH SERIES
CREATED BY Monty Oum
RATED T TEEN
VIZ
viz.com
RWBY © 2017 Rooster Teeth Productions, LLC
© 2015 by Shirow Miwa/SHUEISHA Inc.

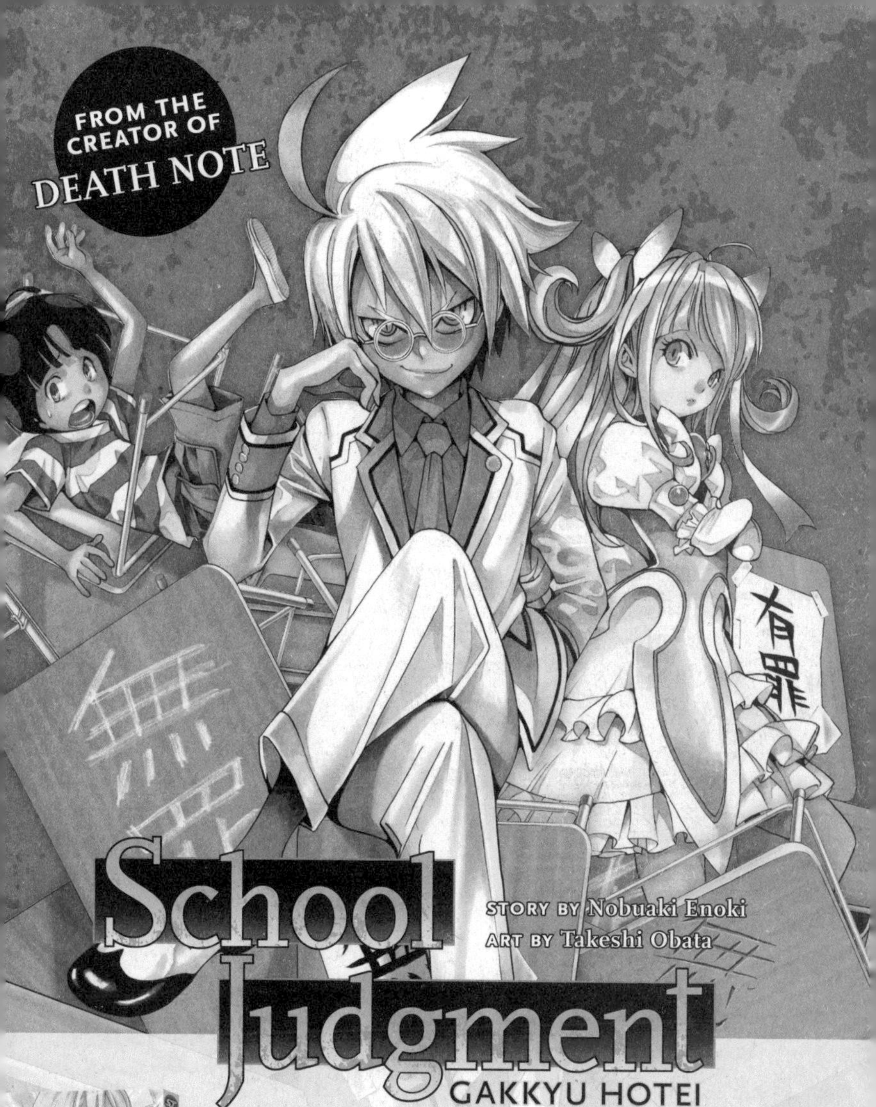
FROM THE CREATOR OF DEATH NOTE
School Judgment
STORY BY Nobuaki Enoki
ART BY Takeshi Obata

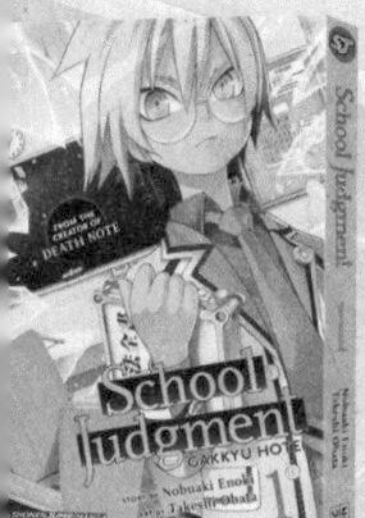
School Judgment
GAKKYU HOTEI
1

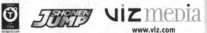

YOU'RE READING WR... WA...

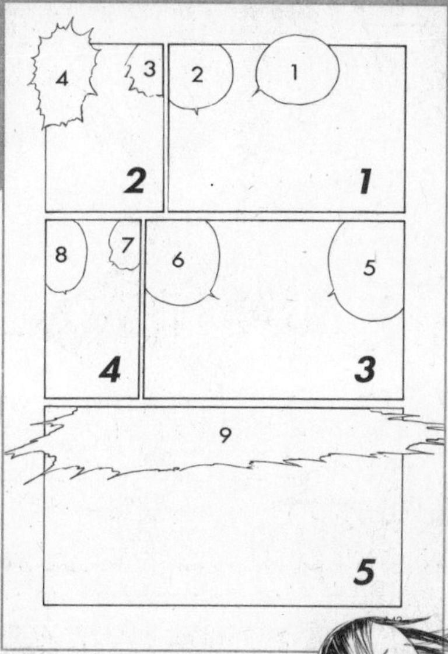
1
2
1
3
4
2
5
6
3
7
8
4
9
5

KAGUYA-SAMA: LOVE IS WAR reads from right to left, starting in the upper-right corner. Japanese is read from right to left, meaning that action, sound effects and word-balloon order are completely reversed from English order.

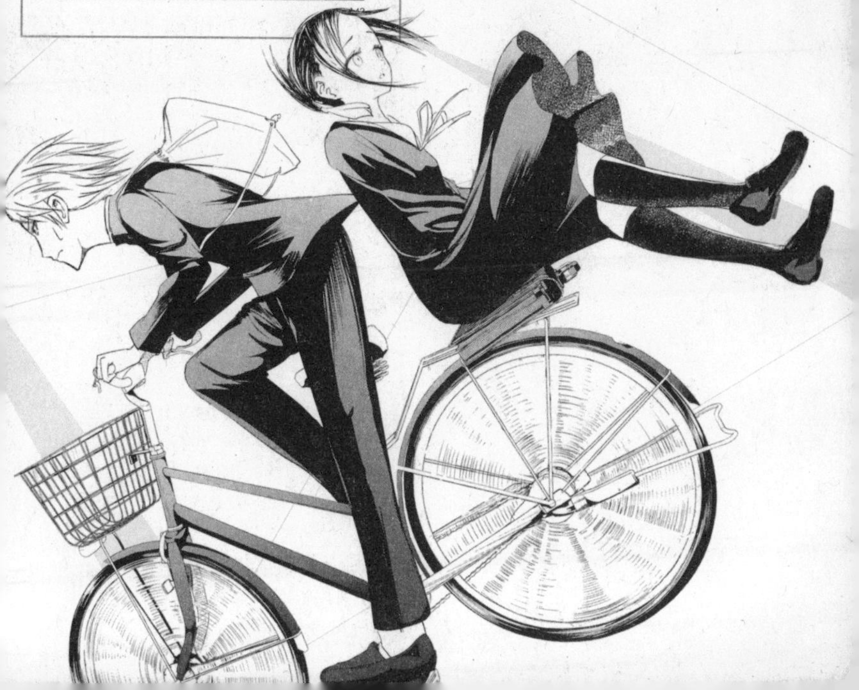